DELIGHTS, DILEMMAS AND DECISIONS

The Gift of Living Lightly

MARGARET MCAULIFFE BEDROSIAN

KNOWLEDGE, IDEAS & TRENDS, INC.
THE POSITIVE PUBLISHER

MANCHESTER, CONNECTICUT

Illustration:
    Elizabeth McAuliffe Gollen
    Sam Horn

Cover design and cover art:
    Gilbert Fahey

Page design:
    Cindy Parker

Library of Congress Cataloging Data
    Delights, dilemmas & decisions: the gift of living lightly / by Margaret McAuliffe Bedrosian.
    ISBN 1-879198-05-3
    1. Conduct of life - Anecdotes. 2. Bedrosian, Margaret McAuliffe - Anecdotes. I. Title. II. Title: Delights, dilemmas and decisions.
    BF637.C5B43 1992
    158. 1 - dc20

First published in 1992.
KIT
Knowledge, Ideas & Trends, Inc.
The Positive Publisher
1131-0 Tolland Turnpike, Suite 175
Manchester, Connecticut 06040

Printed in the United States of America

10 9 8 7 6 5 4 3 2 1

DEDICATION

To Marty and Chuck
My balance, bounty, and blessings

CHAPTER ONE

Sidelifes — The Parallel Universe

Things I Find on the Way to Somewhere Else

Look at yourself.

When was the last time you felt fully balanced, vital, relaxed, alert, and rested? Do you remember what it is like to be brimming with energy at the start of a day? Remember the satisfaction as you complete a project and feel proud of your work? Remember a moment when you feel part of the human family, kin to all around you? Remember a small quiet joy when sunset surprises you as you step outside one evening?

Most of us have these experiences.

And you may be like me and let them get smothered in the daily drain. The obligations, the appointments, the errands, the schedule, the budget, the bills, the calls to return, the meetings, the assignments, the current crisis, the competition, the priorities, the kids, the folks, the holidays. Life becomes my to-do list. I am trapped by the success I sought.

And then there are my SideLifes—things I notice on the way to somewhere else—the small treasures and underappreciated joys of every day. It's as if every moment of my hurried schedule has a parallel universe, right next door, waiting for me. It's as if there is usually some glimpse of comfort, richness, happiness, or love that is nearby, hovering, waiting for me to notice. But I keep focusing on my next task. I've gotten out of the habit of simply seeing.

And, as I forget to see the gentle blessings, they disappear from my life. I focus on the clamor; it costs me the quiet.

I want balance.

To savor the joys of each day while I am in it.
To keep perspective as the thousand tiny abrasions of life wear
me down.
To brim with the possibilities before me.
To shape my future without losing my present.
To feel fresh, strong, and energetic.
To revel in prosperity and abundance.
To give up being fearful, angry, tired.
To nourish my body and my brain with wholesome choices.
To feel peace of mind about my family.
To share health, wealth, and happiness with others.

I want richness of spirit.
I want challenge and adventure.
I want resilience and buoyancy.

I want back the gifts of every day. I want a romance with
reality. Not the fantasy of champagne, fame, and luxury. I
want a romance with silverware and seatbelts, with family loss
and love, with broken pipes and pancakes, with recession and
rainbows.

I want to notice when a butterfly lands on my briefcase. The
butterfly will soon be gone. But his bright legacy can color my
whole day. And when I pick up that briefcase full of reports,
proposals, and paperwork, it will be lighter.

OVERWHELMED OR UNDERAPPRECIATING?

So many people today are using the word "overwhelmed," to describe their experience of being alive. This frightens me. I am so easily lured into this feeling. And, when I believe myself overwhelmed, I am tempted to give up, to stop trying.

There are times when I am truly overwhelmed. One of us is sick, we are doing repairs, projects are overdue, money is dangerously low, mom's nursing home fees are going up. There are rare times when I am truly overwhelmed.

But, most of the time, I am making it up. I get into the habit of feeling overwhelmed or of overwhelming myself. I say "yes," to things I should turn down. I set ambitious goals for a vacation or holiday. I keep waiting for a return to the boom economy of the 1980's without accepting that those days are gone forever. I overschedule. I overcommit. I create my own overwhelm.

Once I tell myself I am overwhelmed, I feel less able to tap my own vitality, creativity, focus, and skills. I start to fold in on myself. Every telephone ring prompts a mental curse. I am pulled apart by conflicting priorities, and I don't have my "best," available to give to any of them. I'm a mess.

I have a choice.

I can revisit my values, remember why I am doing all this, appreciate the air that is nourishing my body at this moment and making it possible for me even to operate. I can notice the small things, praise the ordinary.

I can remember Aristotle's simple definition of happiness: "The exercise of vital abilities, along lines of excellence, in a life that affords them scope."

And I can remember what Armen said at one of our family gatherings. "Every time I get to play golf, I look down at the grass, and I'm glad I'm on this side of it."

For me, the opposite of feeling overwhelmed is to feel appreciating. To notice what I have control over, what I have choices about, what contributes to my vitality and balance, what gives me energy and focus.

Glimpses and Reflections —
As the World Churns

This is an odd book. It is only about 12% a how-to book. It is mostly a book of glimpses and reflections.

What does it look like, feel like, taste like, sound like, and smell like when I am feeling balanced and vital? How is it when I hold these feelings for a while, and how is it when they whirl away?

What do I look like in the many mirrors of my world? How do they show me myself in an unguarded moment?

How do past, present, and future blend into each other in every moment? Is all of time magically present right now? Am I my parents, my ancestors, my children? Who receives my legacy?

How are comedy and drama played out in today's episode of "As The World Churns?" Where do humor and hope fit in, and how do I get more of both?

I began to write this book as a how-to book, compilations of strategies and insights from experience and research that might offer guidance to readers. I was writing in my teacher voice.

Shortly, I noticed a change. I began to write more personally, more reflectively, more uncomfortably, more dangerously. I was surprised by some of what I was saying. I was writing in my learner voice.

When I am "teacher," I seem to have mastered some of the challenges of a tricky slope.

When I am "learner," I inspire reflection. I seem to be wrestling with the same issues you confront.

In the end, as always, it is up to you.

A BRIEF DETOUR INTO LOGIC

You probably already know more than you need to know about how to put more balance in your life. You know about exercise, diet, spiritual values, family communication, time and stress management. Knowing isn't doing.

In fact, the surplus of information you already have may contribute to your feeling of being overwhelmed.

This brief exercise is designed to help you take a logical and objective look at your life as it is today and as you would like it to be. The purpose of this look is to strip away distractions.

The LIFE BALANCE INVENTORY, a 42 item questionnaire, invites you to define your current and desired future levels of balance in each of the seven major areas of your life—health, family, spirit, community, career, finance, self.

There are no right or wrong answers on this inventory. Just tell yourself the simple truth. On each of the items, you will mark where you are today and where you would like to be. The most powerful feedback from this inventory is to look at the gap between those two.

Once you complete the inventory and determine your personal Balance Satisfaction Gap, you will have clues as to where to start focusing resources in your life. Which area is giving you the most nourishment right now? How will you keep that area replenished? What hurts the most? How might you begin to heal that area?

First, though, look at where you are right now.

LIFE BALANCE INVENTORY

This brief exercise is a glimpse at balance in the seven zones of your life. On each of the following items, circle the number that reflects where you are today. Star the number that reflects where you would like to be. 1 = absolute no; 10 = absolute yes.

1. I sleep easily and awake refreshed.

    1   2   3   4   5   6   7   8   9   10

2. I eat the variety and amount of food that helps me feel nourished and alert.

    1   2   3   4   5   6   7   8   9   10

3. I am pleased with my overall appearance.

    1   2   3   4   5   6   7   8   9   10

4. I have enough energy to meet my goals.

    1   2   3   4   5   6   7   8   9   10

5. I exercise regularly and enjoyably.

    1   2   3   4   5   6   7   8   9   10

6. I avoid excesses of salt, sugar, tobacco, alcohol, and caffeine.

    1   2   3   4   5   6   7   8   9   10

7. I spend as much time as I want with my spouse/partner.

    1   2   3   4   5   6   7   8   9   10

8. I spend as much time as I want with other family members.

    1   2   3   4   5   6   7   8   9   10

9. The time I spend with family refreshes and restores me.

    1   2   3   4   5   6   7   8   9   10

10. Family communication is satisfying.

    1   2   3   4   5   6   7   8   9   10

11. Family members share past memories, present challenges, and future visions.

    1   2   3   4   5   6   7   8   9   10

12. Belonging to this family is of great value to me.

    1   2   3   4   5   6   7   8   9   10

13. I am comfortable with my views on what happens after death.

    1   2   3   4   5   6   7   8   9   10

14. I believe my life has meaning — I make a contribution.

    1   2   3   4   5   6   7   8   9   10

15. I operate consistently with my personal sense of honesty and ethics.

    1   2   3   4   5   6   7   8   9   10

16. I have a clear sense of the role God plays in my life.

    1   2   3   4   5   6   7   8   9   10

17. Shared spiritual values strengthen my relationships.

    1   2   3   4   5   6   7   8   9   10

18. I dedicate time regularly to my spiritual needs.

       1   2   3   4   5 6   7 8   9   10

19. I am a contributor to my community, nation, world.

       1   2   3   4   5 6   7 8   9   10

20. I participate in professional, church, school, and/or community groups.

       1   2   3   4   5 6   7 8   9   10

21. I donate time/money to issues I believe in.

       1   2   3   4   5 6   7 8   9   10

22. I participate in the political process.

       1   2   3   4   5 6   7 8   9   10

23. I stay informed on global issues.

       1   2   3   4   5 6   7 8   9   10

24. I am proud of my participation in my community/world.

       1   2   3   4   5 6   7 8   9   10

25. My career is challenging.

       1   2   3   4   5 6   7 8   9   10

26. I am recognized and rewarded for my work.

       1   2   3   4   5 6   7 8   9   10

27. What I do is important.

       1   2   3   4   5 6   7 8   9   10

28. I have the mental, physical, and financial resources to accomplish my objectives.

       1   2   3   4   5 6   7 8   9   10

29. What I do makes a difference.

       1   2   3   4   5 6   7 8   9   10

30. Work gives me a strong feeling of accomplishment.

       1   2   3   4   5 6   7 8   9   10

31. My financial affairs, retirement, and estate planning are in order.

       1   2   3   4   5 6   7 8   9   10

32. I have a will which reflects current realities and responsibilities.

       1   2   3   4   5 6   7 8   9   10

33. I have the money to do things that are important to me.

       1   2   3   4   5 6   7 8   9   10

34. I rarely worry about money.

       1   2   3   4   5 6   7 8   9   10

35. I am happy to give money, gifts, or donations when I want.

       1   2   3   4   5 6   7 8   9   10

36. I feel prosperous.

       1   2   3   4   5 6   7 8   9   10

37. I have time to myself regularly.

       1   2   3   4   5 6   7 8   9   10

38. I have time for things that are important to me.

       1   2   3   4   5 6   7 8   9   10

39. I have a keen sense of humor.

       1   2   3   4   5 6   7 8   9   10

40 I communicate effectively.

       1   2   3   4   5 6   7 8   9   10

41. I rarely feel guilty.
                 1   2   3   4   5   6   7   8   9   10

42. I am comfortable with who I am.
                 1   2   3   4   5   6   7   8   9   10

Total the numbers in circles. Total the numbers in stars. Subtract the stars from the circles. This equals your balance satisfaction gap.

0-50	*Exceptionally healthy balance*
51 - 100	*Unusually balanced*
101 - 150	*Average balance*
151 - 200	*Strained balance*
201 +	*Unhealthy balance*

SEVEN ZONES OF LIFE — Family, Career, Health, Finance, Spirit, Community, Self

BALANCE — the state of mind I create when I choose freely the level of harmonious equilibrium I want in all areas of my life while appreciating my resources, relationships, and results.

ACTION STEPS I WILL TAKE —

Information, Vision and Action

An ounce of action is worth a pound of information. The goal of the book is to move you to action. To think. To respect. To choose. To reflect. To rejoice. Action rarely comes from information.

Action comes from an informing vision. *This book helps you shape your own vision by visiting images.* These images are the operational glimpses of balance (or the lack of it) at work in the real world. Some glimpses are like caricatures, a few are like old, faded, yellowed photographs, many are like current photos, and some special few are like X-rays, focusing on the secrets inside.

These images are bound by gender, time, and culture. They were assembled by a woman, born in the USA in the 1940's. White, middle class, Irish, from a large family, bred in the middle west, living now in a metropolitan suburb. All of these tags frame the images. But some of the images transcend the tags. Some are universal, and some are highly personal. Some are both, simultaneously.

They are all designed to help you answer for yourself the only two questions there are. Who am I? Why am I here? Balance is a bonus that sometimes comes from being at peace with your answers to those questions.

That peace is momentary, dynamic rather than static. And that brief moment refreshes and renews you for the next challenge in a churning world.

The images are grouped into chapters named after the seven areas of life. Each chapter starts with a logical and abstract description of one of the seven areas. This abstract definition is expanded with eight to eleven images of that area operating in real life today.

Not every image relates directly to the theme of the chapter. Some of the relationships are oblique, some are obvious. Like the images we get in life.

At the end of each chapter are some questions or activities you may want to experiment with for further insight into your choices in that zone.

Chapter Two

Health

DELIGHTS, DILEMMAS & DECISIONS

HEALTH

People with balance in health have vitality, stamina, strength. They take care of their body and recognize that the body doesn't lie. They pay attention to nutrition, exercise, and relaxation.

They don't always follow all the rules but tend to make healthy choices most of the time.
They learn to like more and more things that are good for them.

When they elect to go overboard, eat one or two desserts, they enjoy it enough to make up for the consequences.

They go in for regular check-ups and dental visits.

They stay aware of family health history but don't become obsessed by it.

They avoid hostility and worry, two of the faces of fear.

They know that science and medicine do wonders today, and they may even slow some of the aging process right about the time they need it most. They sometimes think even Ponce de Leon was a pessimist.

Health matters interest them, and they read about studies and research. They are also open to ancient medical practices like accupuncture.

Paying attention to what gives them vitality, stamina, and strength, they notice that humor is a wonderful medicine with no harmful side affects.

Sleep also is a great restorer.

They find things in their everyday lives to help them relax.

INTERIOR DECORATING

My doctor has a real secret for interior decorating. His waiting room is comfortable and reassuring without making me wonder how much of my fee is budgeted for keeping him in antiques. The treatment room is impersonal and competent—everything pristine and orderly. His office is paneled in luxurious dark wood and lined with the obligatory bookcases full of scholarly reference material. (Does he ever really read any of that stuff?) Several impressive diplomas hang on the wall by the door. His desk is an acre of authority.

Behind the desk, centered on the wall, the focal point of the room is a dark reflective screen. It seems an odd visual vacuum in such a carefully orchestrated room. He greets me, slips large sheets of grey-black onto the dark screen, and turns on the light behind. And there I am. My X-rays. The center of his office for this consultation. He has my attention. He turns around and talks to me. Occasionally he points to something on the X-ray. "Nothing to worry about," he reassures me.

I tune him out and stare at the pictures of my insides. How could I forget day-to-day what a system I am. What a typical part of nature. How branched like a leaf. How symmetrical like a shell. How bony like a fish. How could I ever neglect or fail to take care of that fragile fretwork I see before me?

For the truth is that I know things I don't tell the doctor. That I am not taking care of myself like I should. That I am wreaking damage that just doesn't show up yet. That not all of the damage I do can be detected by his technology.

I make some promises to myself and to the God who made those bones I see up there. I am now keeping those promises.

WEIGHTY MATTERS

What a red-letter day! I've reached my goal of losing 26 pounds.

It's taken three years.

Veteran of dozens of diet attempts, I have tried everything in the past. For me the secret this time was to get committed to glowing health and vitality. As long as I was trying to lose weight for the "swim suit season" or to rid myself of "those unsightly bulges," I continued to fail.

 If I was doing this to please other people, I'd somehow sabotage my own efforts. Maybe I wanted to make them prove they would love me exactly as I was. Or something like that.

Once glowing health and vitality became a priority, a lot of choices were much easier. I became willing to invest time and money and patience. My fitness and health needs were important in the family budgeting process. Investing in fitness today might save time and money for medical attention down the road. I am doing this to increase my energy, my stamina, my brain power. And I'll probably look sexier.

Some people have noticed my progress and said they'd like to do the same. My process might not work for them. But this is what it took for me to keep some promises I had made to myself. I intend to live in this body for another 50-70 years. I spend time and money maintaining my car and my house. Why not my body?

•I start my program with five days at a spa where a counselor helps me set goals for weight and percentage of bodyfat. At that time, the program seemed expensive. But that's the difference between having an intention and being committed. If this is my commitment, I find the resources. I also did not think it would take me three years to reach this point.

•After my spa visit, I spend about four months fighting the wisdom they gave me. My sabotage instinct dies hard. I start being more regular in exercise. I start eating fruit and drinking water every day. I don't change much else.

•I finally let more of the wisdom in. I start enjoying my exercise more. I eat better. I give up alcohol. I feel better.

•I lose 16 pounds the first year. That's hardly more than a pound a month. These aren't miraculous results. But they are consistent and relatively painless. I reassure myself. It took me ten years or so to add all that weight and get so logy. Why not allow myself a similar long time to feel streamlined again? After the first year, I'm losing only a pound every three months. This feels discouraging.

•After twenty pounds, people notice and offer compliments. That is an unnecessary, but welcome bonus. I keep feeling better. I remember a doctor telling me years ago that even a pound a year makes a big difference after ten or twenty years. He's right.

•What's important to me is to keep moving in the right direction. I gain a little weight on holidays or vacations, but not much. And I come back down again gradually because this is the way I like to live now. I indulge in buttered pancakes about once a week and enjoy wallowing in weakness occasionally. But I keep sight of that commitment. Glowing health and vitality is a priority for me.

I see a cycle. Commitment yields priority which commands resources which produces results which fulfill the commitment. At times in the past, I hadn't bothered to commit. Or I hadn't focused the commitment into a priority. Or I had been unwilling to invest the resources. Now the whole system is in place. It works for me.

HIDE AND SEEK

Mom.
86.
Alzheimer's.
Wheel chair.
Nursing home.

That sounds like a bleak portrait. Yet it isn't. She's in San Diego where my brother and sister go to see her twice a week. On my last visit from Washington, D. C., my brother Conn and I went to see her. We usually spot her chair in the hallway. She's rarely in her small room, still preferring to be "out and about," following sound or action, feeding her continuing curiosity. The home is well-designed for those in wheelchairs, providing a hand railing at chair height so stronger residents can pull themselves along the railing.

Once we see her, we begin the dance of not-quite recognition. She sees us approach, our faces are smiling, she beams back a big grin and opens her arms wide. She may not know us by name, but she knows we belong to her. We swoop down for a feeble hug, and the visit begins.

Only this time I make a mistake. I start to swoop down first. She gently brushes me by and goes for Conn. She still knows she'd rather hug a man than a woman. Alzheimer's and 86 don't change my mom. The coquette won't be quenched.

We wheel her into the sunny courtyard with year-round fresh flowers and sit in the comfortable shade. We talk to her with lots of eye contact. Topics are arbitrary. I tell her about a friend's daughter's first communion at St. Patrick's last Saturday. Conn asks if she's harvested the potatoes. She nods and smiles for answers and occasionally pats my hand. Sometimes she speaks a phrase or sentence. She seems so content and comfortable. We all laugh together—half resigned, half sincere.

I know again that her disease is a sad loss for us but less tragic for her. She has been spared so many painful things in the last few years—the death of her youngest sister, the death of her oldest son, and then her youngest son. She has food, safety, sleep. Her children visit often, do her laundry, and provide her with regular treats. She has the best wardrobe in the place with coordinated slippers, robe, knee warmers, and hats in five or six colors.

Conn says she sometimes thinks he is daddy and sometimes knows he is one of her sons. He knows immediately who she thinks he is by her reactions. When she thinks he is daddy, she is focused and upright, wondering if they have tended to this or that detail, and reminding him of tasks to take care of. When she thinks he is one of her boys, she is playful and flirtatious.

Remember the old folk tales of three wishes? It seems like the receiver of the wishes always makes the first two foolishly and has to use the third wish to repair the situation. I sometimes think that mom got most of her wishes about growing old. She wanted to be safe, secure, comfortable, and have her children take care of her as she had taken care of them for so long. She just forgot to wish she would know it was all happening.

Since Mom likes the "greeting" part of each visit so much, we finally get to enjoy the only benefit of Alzheimer's. We sometimes leave her alone in the courtyard for a few moments and enter again as if it were a whole new visit. It's like a dark/light version of adult peek-a-boo.

The brief visit is over. We wheel her back inside, sad to resign her to the institution, pleased to have found such a good one for her to be in (after three difficult tries).

The smells remind me. I used to be full of guilt, anger, and fear when I came here. Guilt that I wasn't personally taking care of her. Anger that we'd lost so much of her and left so much unsaid. Fear for my own health and mortality. (Notice how we tend to identify with the health of our same-gender parent and track our life milestones with theirs?)

It is finally settling on me that guilt, anger, fear do nothing for me or for her. Once I can let go of them, I can appreciate all we've had and all I still learn from her...her cheerfulness, her coquettery, her appreciation of small comforts, her unyielding curiosity, and her unquenchable independence.

For, as we turn to leave, hoping she doesn't cling and awaken the pain, we see her touch the rail along the wall and pull herself away from us...and toward her next curious encounter.

Mom.
86.
Alzheimer's.
Mom.

One of Life's Greatest Luxuries

Washing dishes by hand is one of life's great luxuries to me.

It's almost ceremonial as I watch the hot tap water plunge into the liquid ooze of soap and manufacture bubbles by the hundreds. The scent of this month's soap-on-sale selection hovers for a moment as I soak the flatware while arranging everything else on the counter. I wash each fork, spoon, knife, sometimes remembering the occasion when that item joined our polyglot collection. I rinse the silver in the left sink. The blue towel stands ready to absorb the water droplets and start the drying process.

Glasses are almost sacred. I like stemware and delicate glasses even for juice. The sponge, the soap, and I surround the full globes of the glasses and trace their long, lean stems.

Plates are more pedestrian. So here I look out the window, feel the fresh air, notice the day. This is a quiet moment. I try to still my thoughts and just stay right with the dishes.

Pots require a moment of discipline, scrubbing.

If the silver is a lilting soprano, glasses a burnished alto, plates a textured tenor, then pots are the fundamental bass.

I rinse my hands again in the still-silky-slick water, marveling at what a sensory treat this process is.

When I have the time/take the time to wash dishes by hand, it means several things.

1. I'll have clean nails yet another day.
2. We've probably saved some water for the planet as opposed to running the dishwasher.

I send a quiet thanks to my mom. We kids always had the job of clearing the table, but she reserved the dishwashing to herself. Perhaps this conferred on dishwashing an aura of adult privilege. Probably she wanted the peace and quiet of a cup of tea with daddy after dinner and knew that she was better off letting her impatient helpers escape. In any case, I am the beneficiary .

It also means I am treating my time as a luxury. I don't have to do everything in a rush. I can pause in the flurry and enjoy the soapy water. I can be here for the daily routine processes of living. I can delight in them.

Mutiny of the Boundaries

I didn't notice it till I started doing the Christmas cards that year. It was difficult to write, and my scrawlings were almost unreadable. My hand was in mutiny. It wasn't obeying the captain in my mind. It was a drunk and disorderly deckhand who wouldn't cooperate with the rest of the crew.

Looking back, I realized I'd been doing my lists on ever-larger pieces of paper for several months. But I kept excusing my unreadable scrawl saying I was in too much of a hurry to write neatly.

Now I had to face the fact. I was physically incapable of writing legibly. Even with great concentration, I could barely create a readable line. Suddenly I needed writing for everything. I attended a training session and wore out my hand, arm, and mind taking sketchy notes I could barely decipher later. I could hardly enter phone numbers in my calendar.

This mutiny. A part of my body that was fully functioning last time I was aware of it. Now closed away. Now unavailable. Is this what men feel when they have bouts of impotence? "Hey, this thing worked last time I checked, what's wrong with it now?"

Why didn't I notice it when it was working? Why didn't I celebrate it then? Why is my body escaping from my control? Why is the mutiny starting in my extremities? Does this mean my feet could go next? And what do I do now?

MEDITATION ON A MEAL

Everything on the table once had a life of its own. The sweet corn grew in tall, green, geometric rows in a sun-soaked field in Indiana. The brown rice developed on slender stalks in wet paddies. The lean beef came from living cows like the ones I like to watch in fields. Tomatoes from a neighbor's garden grew up just one street over. Even the coffee beans knew the kiss of breezes and the coat of soft rain.

And many people helped to bring this food to me today. The farmers, the pickers, the truckers, the grocers. Ingredients for the fragrant bread were blended by human hands and baked with an attentive eye.

And I prepare this food casually. Hardly conscious of the blessings here. Sometimes I eat it while watching television. The food fills my stomach while the news drains my soul. And so, today, may I stay aware.

May I be worthy of the food I eat.

THE PARADOX OF POWERLESSNESS

A friend describes the beginning of her recovery.

Step one in Alcoholics' Anonymous - admitted we were powerless over alcohol. I was a functioning alcoholic holding up a fragile bubble of fear and facade. Pretending everything was normal while committing slow suicide. Who knows where or why it started? After a while it took over. Thinking about drinking. Then a long time of thinking about not drinking. Physical symptoms, mental symptoms, social symptoms, career symptoms...until the symptoms took over and became the reason for drinking.

Addiction. To substances, to work, to sex. It's a retreat from life. A blunting of the burden of existence. A swaddling of the harshness of reality. A softening of the sharp edges.

So this is the shape life is in when I admit powerlessness. Get this amazing thing. Up until admitting powerlessness, I am "totally in control." All I have to do is pretend every minute to be normal. Pretend every minute not to be paralyzed by fear. Pretend every minute that all this pretending isn't killing me.

So I admit I'm powerless. Am I flooded with terrible feelings about giving up the heaviest deception I've ever imagined? No, I'm relieved of the guilt and drain that holding up the facade cost me on a daily, hourly, instantaneous basis.

The paradox. Admitting I am powerless over alcohol gives me a higher power.

Another person describes the process of becoming addicted.

I guess it was when I started school. I'm starting out in unknown territory, swimming in uncharted waters. I am almost too buoyant. I don't seem to have the steadiness and ballast that others seem to have. I discover somehow that I could put a pebble in my pocket to feel a little more steady, another pebble to feel more sure of myself. Then I find myself paying less attention to the water and more attention to the pebbles.

At some point, the pursuit of pebbles takes over. Now I'm lost and afraid. The pebbles meld into a large rock. I know the rock is dragging me down, drowning me, but it's the only security I know. So I keep trying to stay afloat while holding onto the rock for dear life.

A power tries to come into my life. This power says, 'Let go of the guilt, let go of the fear, let go of living the lie...and you'll float.'
But I can't let go of the rock.
'Let go of the rock.'
But I can't let go of the rock.
'Let go of the rock.'
Well, maybe I can get one hand free and swim harder.
'Let go of the rock.'
If I paddle like crazy, maybe I'll reach shore and the

rock won't matter.
'Let go of the rock.'
And this dialogue continues as long as I let it.

One day, not too different from others, I let go of the
rock. I float. I see the sky, feel the breeze, come back to
life, head for shore. I glance back at the rock. There are
moments when I'll miss it. I'm alive.

Few things in my life will ever be as beautiful as my first
sober Springtime. Every daffodil, every gleaming dog-
wood blossom, every crisply green new blade of grass
reflects my awe at the wonder of being alive. I let go of
the rock. I float.

AA a place where people grow up, feel and express
complex emotions, tell their truth, laugh, find differ-
ences, find commonalities, enjoy humor. Mostly a
place of sharing experience, strength, and hope. A
place to savor the experience of being a human being.

Few people recognize the most pivotal sentence in this story.
"I don't seem to have the steadiness and ballast that others
seem to have." It's the trap of comparing my own insides with
other's outsides. The trap of thinking that I am the only
person who has conflicting emotions. The trap of believing
the facade of other people.

Comparing my insides to someone else's outsides.

DELIGHTS, DILEMMAS & DECISIONS

What it Takes to Have a Good Day

When I started having to go for a medical treatment on a regular basis, I unconsciously selected someone with excellent credentials whose office was miles away.

There are two routes to her office. I can go on the beltway and route 50—that route takes about 65 minutes. Or I can go the back roads—more direct but slower. That route takes about 75 minutes. On the country road, I usually see animals in fields, strolling through sunlight. The extra ten minutes of traveling turns the driving time into part of the healing time.

I wasn't aware at first, but now I realize that any day I see livestock is a better day than one on which I don't. I start thinking about what it takes for me to have a good day. The list expands slowly over time. These are the things I've identified lately:

I usually have a good day when...
> I wake up without a buzzing alarm in my ear
> I wake up
> Livestock graze in a field as I go by
> The sun is not yet up, and I can be aware of sunrise
> Work feels easy and productive
> There's time for exercise before I enter into the to-do
>   list part of the day
> I smell hot oatmeal spreading contentment through the
>   kitchen
> A client says thank you
> I have a hot, vigorous shower
> The car starts
> I have plenty of gas

The sun shines
I hear my brother's voice light up when I answer my
    phone
I feel healthy
It's cloudy or rainy
I taste fresh, tangy grapefruit
I see people
Beauty abounds in everything I see around me at a
    single moment
I help a client
I spend time alone
I listen to music that shapes my mood
A butterfly lands on the table outside my window
I pray
People I call are there and available
I hit a work hurdle and meet the challenge
I think of my family
I am lost from all I know in creative absorption
A client pays a bill
I bemoan the fact that my bathroom is broken while
    blessing the fact that it's my second bathroom
I am grateful for breathing.

The list lengthens daily. Items seem contradictory. How can a
rainy day be as good as a sunny one? If I spend all my time
thinking about these things, I'll never get anything done. I'll
just spend my whole life being thankful for everything I have
and am and do.

Yep. And amazingly, I still get things done. I get to do them
with the fleet mind of joy.

A Mantra For Elevators

It starts the minute I punch the button and see a reassuring light behind the selected arrow. My elevator is now summoned. It will soon arrive to do my bidding.

A community near us has declared itself a nuclear-free zone. Hundreds of restaurants, buildings, and areas have declared themselves smoke-free zones. I am training myself to see elevators as stress-free zones. I'm turning my daily or weekly elevator rides into pockets of felicity.

I hear the tone, see the light announcing the imminent arrival of my car. The doors slide smoothly open and invite me in. I unhook myself from the busyness of the business day. I remember that I've promised myself a stress-free ride.

When alone, I revel in the privacy, the gliding quiet. When joined by traveling companions, I notice their sights and sounds, occasionally appreciating the smell of coffee someone carries back to the office.

We stop today on 4, 7, 8, and get to 11. I exit. The world floods back quickly enough. But I've just taken a four-minute holiday. It's a little easier now.

Your Annual Report

Dr. Peter Miller of the Hilton Head Health Institute asks a good question: If your body issued an annual report, what would your bottom line look like right now?

Let's adapt the question.

Suppose you were preparing such a report and wanted to chart the origin and development of your business (YOU) from birth to today. The point of this exercise is to focus on milestone events that have influenced you as you locate each event on a timeline (if you think in a linear style) or a mural (if you prefer a symbolic style). Different people doing this exercise have charted from ten to forty or more major events. These include:

Birth
Siblings
School
Religion
Jobs
Career
Relationships
Marriage
Military
Children
Friendships
Accomplishments
Losses
Gains
Other highlights/milestones

An alternative focus is to chart your whole life—birth to your 100th birthday or beyond.

Prepare your own using as many milestones as you think important. Give yourself plenty of time to reflect on your milestones. Give yourself plenty of space also. Tape several pieces of paper together if necessary.

Your milestones needn't all be the same "size". The death of a parent isn't the same as getting a good review at work.

Consider everything you might include, and select the events of most impact. If it shaped your life, include it.

Don't worry if yours is not neatly divided into identical increments. Some decades may take an inch, some may take a foot. Some items on your mural will let you know how big they are in your life by how big they become on your page.

Look back over your creation. Are there any milestones you left out?

If you want to consider further, code your milestones in the following categories. Items in parenthesis are answers some people have given in each category. "Spouse," for example, has been given in each of the four categories by different respondents.

A- This is something I choose consciously and freely (spouse/house/fitness?)

B - This was a compromise between what I wanted and what was practical or available at the time (job/career/where I live?)

C - This I just let happen (weight/health/children?)

D - This was entirely out of my control (parents, intelligence, war?)

What picture are you getting of your life?
See any patterns emerging?
Are there things you want to do differently in the future?
Are there things in the past that still burden you and affect your ability to move fully into your present and future?

PERSONAL REFLECTIONS

Something in my health that concerns me is...

Something I am satisfied by...

When I think about the health histories in my family...

My weight and appearance...

My energy and stamina...

My tendency toward or away from addiction...

Something I do to relax...

CHAPTER THREE

Family

FAMILY

People with balance in their family zone have history, security, and love. They have a spouse, children, parents, brothers, and sisters or others who assume some of those roles for them.

Someone remembers and reminds them what they were like 10, 20, 30 years ago. Someone shares their view of where they came from and where they are going. Someone cares enough to challenge and confront them.

Someone helps them fight their battles, fuels their determination, and applauds their successes.

These are real relationships. Not all made of greeting card sweetness and television-commercial sunshine. They suffer bruises and keep on holding on.

Whether the ties are blood or choice, the relationships are profoundly involving, deeply satisfying or disturbing, and capable of bringing both enormous joy and enormous pain, sometimes in the same moment.

Communication is at the core of family. And it is rarely straightforward, verbal exchange. It lives in the subtleties. It sometimes asks that we listen fluently in several languages.

PERMANENT PARTNERS

Tides.

The sand I am walking on was ocean a few hours ago. Supporting the waves. Giving them a reason to curl and ebb.

Now it is land. A tentative territory belonging to the dry world. A place for dogs to romp, leaving paw-print-shaped tide pools to catch the sky's reflection. A place for me to walk and feel the moist sand, smell the abundant air of morning, hear the shush and thunder of the waves, see the day present itself in dim layers of distant hillsides backed by clouds.

How old yet how enduring this co-existence of ocean and beach. Each entity is immutably separate. Yet they are joined in the daily dance of yielding and taking endlessly.

Shifting boundaries. Which is which? Like marriage, like parenthood, like life and death, like itself, the ocean moves. Perpetually changing yet permanently stable. Somehow soothing and stimulating at the same time.

DON'T GET TOO ATTACHED

Aargh. I have just finished reading a mystery book and am jarred by the ending. The author has followed most of the hallowed conventions of writing a mystery except one. He killed off the female main character on the next-to-the-last page. As I pass the book along to my younger sister to read, I toss in one casual comment. "Don't get too attached to the girl."

Of course, my sister reads the book warily. She discounts everything appealing about the female character. When Bridget finishes reading, she too is disappointed in the book. "It wasn't so good. I never really got involved in it."

In my zeal to protect the vulnerable sensibilities of my sister, I have robbed her of having any genuine experience as a reader.

This is a joke between us now, of course. The loss of one reading experience isn't such a big deal. But how many other times have I overprotected those I love? Why hadn't I trusted her to have her own reaction? Why do I seem to believe that I am the best filter for reality, that I should judge what my family/friends/colleagues/boss/clients should experience? Have I ever asked them if they want this protection?

And what am I not experiencing myself because I am electing myself "buffer zone" for all of them? Is there not something else I should be learning, some other way I might be growing, if I were not always on guard? Do I somehow think I'm finished and right?

THE SONG OF THE SEATBELT

He's heading off for work on the first day of his first professional job. Twenty-three, a newly degreed engineer. New shoes, a new haircut, a new business suit in charcoal grey, a tie, heading off to Vanguard Research. He's been living with us since graduation three months ago; he has no money for rent yet.

His dad and I are both on hand to see him launched. Oddly, it's like watching him leave on that first day of elementary school. Then he had a bandaid on his knee and a red plastic lunchbox to show he belonged. Today it's the tie. We walk him out to the driveway, superficially casual about this milestone. We share a hurried hug and wish him luck. He settles into the driver's seat. Just as we step backwards out of the way, I hear the click of the seatbelt.

The click brings it all home. We are stepping back. He is going out on his own. He knows how to take care of himself. He has accepted most of what we ever considered really important. He will protect a life we hold so dear. He may be zipping off, independent in a shiny red car, but he's taking us along too.

Yes, he tosses off the phrase "love ya," every once in a while. But when I hear that click, I hear, "I love you." I hear, "Thank you." I'm realizing that one of my favorite declarations of love is for someone to say by action, "This life we share is important to me; I'll help us have as much of it as possible."

Chuck's click says, "I love you." My husband's sweat on our walks says, "I love you." My sister's nutrition says, "I love you." My brother's laughter says, "I love you."

Do they know or care what self-indulgent pleasure I am taking in all their secret messages?
Does it matter?

Prisoners — Sibling Rivalry

I grew up Irish in Terre Haute, Indiana.

I'm the 7th of 8 children of immigrant parents, Cornelius Jeremiah and Margaret Hart McAuliffe.

We didn't have money, but what we had in abundance were good saints names...Francis Malachi, Cornelius Patrick, Mary Theresa, Martin Joseph, Kathleen Patricia, Bridget Veronica (Del), and Margaret Ann.

Lots of saints names. And, of course, each of us in the family had a special role designator. The other kids were so much older that I don't remember theirs. But I remember my sister's and mine. Bridget was Popular and I was Smart.

So Bridget became the tomboy, played with all the rowdies in the neighborhood, was good in sports, often got into trouble, and lived a colorful life.

And I stayed indoors, read, drew, held adventures in my imagination, and learned to be a good little girl...and lonely. It sometimes seemed as if words and books were my only companions.

And I looked at her—sweaty, laughing, full of fun, and I longed, of course, to be popular.

And she looked at me—praised, rewarded, holder of golden ribbons from school and she longed, of course, to be smart.

We so often saw only the bright side of the other's gifts and the dark side of our own.

And so we were. Prisoners of our own visions of the other's bright success and prisoners, worse, of our own sense of lacking what the other excelled in. We carved out our territories in life so as not to have to compete against each others strengths.

Prisoners Two — Sibling Rivalry

Many years later, my sister and I both live in the Washington, D. C. area. Still surprisingly competitive though all the earlier prizes have vanished. Maybe it's instinct.

One tough winter, she urged me to take her twice-a-week aerobics class. For only $54 dollars I could watch her lead us in exercise. Though we live in the same area, geography, rush hour, and schedules conspire to keep us separate. So I signed up for the class.

She's a great teacher. Focuses on the music and on the class members. She never chats while she is teaching. One night, she said, "This song reminds me of my sister." I was so surprised that she spoke, I didn't notice the song.

The next week, I listened to the cycle of songs. I decided that the one she had dedicated to me must have been "It's hip to be square." A cute song, not especially noteworthy, a teasing jab. I asked her about it later. "No," she said, "it's the next one." I had to wait another week to hear the cycle again.

Tonight as we jump and stretch and sweat and dance through a vasty cold giant gym room, we are across the gym from each other. I listen and hear the words. "Years may come and go...there's one thing I know...all my life...you're a friend of mine."

Tears spring into my eyes. As I glance up and see her, our lifetime connection washes over me like a saturating wave. The dancers in the room are unwittingly weaving invisible silken strings of love and grief between my sister and me.

Across the cold gym floor. Touching even themselves. Our oldest brother, mentor, hero died this winter. We are learning how to be a family again.

Her gift is dance, music, teaching, leading. My gift is words and the courage to tell some truths. Prisoners released, finally, we get to revel in each others gifts.

THIS HUSBAND IS A PERFECT DOLL

Imagine a husband who's nearly perfect:
> He's a great dancer and dances whenever I want to.
> He absorbs everything I tell him and never interrupts.
> He doesn't interfere with my schedule, budget, social plans, decorating, family plans, friendships, or career.
> He goes with me, uncomplaining, to any event I wish to take him to.
> He is meticulous in never making any mess or creating disorder around the house.
> He is always ready to go to bed when I want to, and he never crunches peanuts or watches television when I want to sleep.
> He never drives too fast or complains about my cooking or my failing to cook.

Who is this paragon? Well, he's a perfect doll. He is a full-size soft sculpture done by an artist. He's a clone. He looks exactly like my husband, but he's not graying.

It's interesting to have a "perfect" version of my husband. Often, I catch myself mentally complaining about some comment or action by my "real" husband. When this happens, I ask myself if the clone would have done this better. Would I prefer a lifeless decoration who never does anything wrong, with no mind, body, or needs of his own to the abundantly human husband I have?

The husband who's less perfect:
>
> Touches me warmly when I'm discouraged or lonely.
>
> Gets moist eyes while we see plays or shows about immigrants like our parents.
>
> Hands me a towel by the side of the pool as I come shivering out of the water.
>
> Yearns for more time to relax, to play, to exercise, to share together.
>
> Surprises me sometimes when he hears exactly what I mean.

I remember reading letters to advice columnists in which people complain about one or another annoying habit practiced by their spouse/parents/kids. The columnist says a few reassuring words and then reminds the writer "...a day will come when you'd give anything to hear that snore again."

I enjoy the perfect doll of a husband. I love the other one.

SUNDAY

This is a perfect morning. Slightly cool. Invigorating.

I want to write about my family today. Short pieces. Funny, warm, poignant, or pointed. The kinds of scenes that make you feel closer to your own family as you read. Make you want to "hug a kid" today.

But I don't get to write.

They are all around me.

"Mag, can I make you an omelet?"

"Can you help me with my resume?"

"Where's the sports section?"

"What's this check notation for $60 to Maureen. Who the hell is Maureen?"

I love my family. I like to reflect on how wonderful they are. But sometimes the magic of them comes more easily from reflecting on them rather than from actually living with them.

I can hardly believe I am once again catching myself living my life second-hand. Giving up the tug-of-life called NOW for some burnished and edited nugget from the past.

Think I'll stop writing and join them for watermelon. Maybe we'll spit some seeds together.

TALENT TREE

At Diamond Lake in Oregon one summer, there are thirty or so of the family gathered though it isn't an official reunion. McAuliffes are everywhere. Even now, fourteen of the kids and grandkids are playing frisbee in the parking lot. Mom and I are walking over to the lodge for our mid- afternoon cup of tea and piece of hot cherry pie ala mode. In the middle of the parking lot, she stops and gets an odd expression on her face.

"What is it, Mom?"

Her eyes mist. "Just to think, Daddy and I made all this..." She looks around softly at the sweat-soaked competitors. We stay for a moment, watching. Then we go in for our pie.

She starts me thinking about family lines. Mom and dad. Eight children. Twenty some grandchildren. More great-grandchildren arriving daily. A lot of family from one couple.

Martha and Conn did some family genealogy. They have done an impressively thorough job of tracing the family back just three generations in good detail. As I look at these names I wonder how this gene pool plays out in my own generation and the two I know as nieces, nephews and great nieces and nephews.

I have a picture in my mind of another kind of genealogy. After completing the family tree of blood lines, you do a talent tree of gifts practiced by each person and passed on or skipped in the next generation.

Where did Luke, Liz, and Kathleen's art talent come from? And Barbara's acting, and Meg's gift for nursing and nurturing, and Mary's for lighting up a room by her presence, and Mark's for carpentry and the practical arts? And Kevin's gift for sales, Sean's for science, Maura's for animals and motherhood, Nick's for music history, Brian's for loyalty, Chuck's for engineering and on through Matt, Dan, Frank, Carol, Mary T, Mickey, Carrie, Brendan, Mike, Scott, and Doug.

Sure it is easy to see some of the gifts handed down through the generations, but I think it is often more complex.

It is even possible that these kids display gifts brought in from the individuals who married into our family. What a strain of family ego to admit that. Especially the Italian, German, Scottish, and Armenian contributions.

AFTER 20 YEARS

"Can I write one?"

My entrepreneur-engineer-type husband volunteers to commit words, thoughts, feelings to paper? I am awestruck. In the twenty years I have known him, I've only seen ten or twelve samples of his writing. And most of those were letters he sent when I had to take a month away to take care of my dad the year after we were married.

He's read about nine of my personal glimpses for the new book. Some he likes. Some he doesn't "get." Now he wants to write one. And he hates writing.

It's nearly midnight. We have to get up at 5:30 for an early run to BWI airport as I leave for a week. We're just in from a town meeting and a long walk home.

"Sure. I'll get you some paper."

"Not now, just sometime."

"Do yourself a favor. Capture the first seven words on the paper right now, and they'll help you remember what you wanted to say."

"OK"

He bends intently over the paper. I can almost see the tongue sticking out of the corner of his mouth—the habit kids have when they are concentrating hard on forming letters.

I walk away, thinking he may be seduced by the writing. I get ready for bed.

He comes in twenty minutes later. Aglow. "I can see why you love this. It feels wonderful to get this down."

"Would you like me to read it?" I ask.

He offers it shyly, like a fresh-picked daisy.

It's a 300-word sketch of the scene of his mother's 1922 rescue from the Aegean Sea by a brave Greek fisherman during the Armenian massacres. It is beautiful. I tell him so.

We turn out the light. Say a special and close goodnight. Lay quiet in the dark. Struggling for sleep with overstimulated brains.

"How do you spell gnarled?" he breaks the quiet.

"G-N-A-R.."

"I knew it wasn't K. I'm such a jerk."

We're talking into the dark like two bad kids who won't go to sleep after their lights are turned out. A conspiracy of discovery.

We can scarcely go to sleep. Such a surprise after 20 years. I'm up at 4:11 a.m. writing this down before I fly away. Just couldn't take a chance of forgetting...

WAKING UP IN THE SAME ZIP CODE

I am often invited to travel on business. I prefer to think of it that way, rather than to say I HAVE to travel on business. (Though I do if I want to work).

It's hard to leave my husband, and he misses me too. One of the benefits, though, is that we now have a language to express our sense of incompleteness.

We miss each other most when we are separated by several time zones. I usually call between six and seven every night—nine and ten his time. He is settled, relaxed, fed, closing down for the day. I'm often calling from a pay phone in a hotel lobby just outside a meeting room or from a phone in the restaurant where I'm about to have dinner. We share an update on the highlights of the day, and may have a cozy thought or two. But our minds are in the different time zones, too. He goes from the call back to quiet, and I go back to commotion.

Sometimes I'm only one hour away, and we can match much better in the evening call. We can even talk together in the morning if we want to. This is nicer.

And sometimes we are in the same time zone. This call often feels like he's just across town. I'm not sure why we are sleeping in separate quarters, but it feels comfortable.

The day comes when we're in the same zip code, maybe the same house, often the same room, finally the same bed. I'm home.

PERSONAL REFLECTIONS

The time I feel most a part of my family...

The family roles I fill are...

The thing in my family that gives me the most joy/pain...

When I see couples who have been married 50 years, I think...

One memory that is very strong for me is...

My favorite family holiday is...

I want a break from my family when...

The thought of a family reunion...

My family at work...

Chapter Four

Career

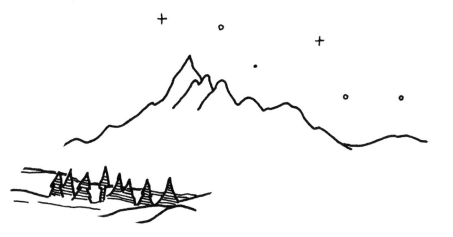

CAREER

People with balance in their career feel challenged, significant, productive. They feel that they are expected to perform at their best, using all the resources at their command.

It makes a difference whether they show up every day. What they are doing is important, and they were selected for this job because they are good at it.

They have a strong sense of the role their own activities play in the overall product or service their organization offers. From the geriatric surgeon to the Navy fighter pilot to the guest-services manager at a metropolitan hotel, they are aware of their place in the scheme of things.

They see the span of their career as a long and potentially satisfying element of their lives. They look beyond just the next promotion or the next job and have a view of the 20, 40, 60 year flow of their working lives.

They relish learning. They recognize that this helps them adapt and compete in the ever-changing world around them. Everything they learn today can yield satisfying benefits for the entire length of their lives.

They balance risk and opportunity. They know the seduction of staying too comfortable and the exhilaration of stepping out beyond the comfortable. They have faced moments of tremendous discouragement and stood their ground. They have delighted in some of the accidents of good fortune.

They recognize that they always have choices if they are willing to accept the consequences. They continue asking questions, listening to the answers, growing.

JOGGING TO CATALINA

She jogs to Catalina once a week. Maybe not literally to the island, but she does her 26 miles by jogging five days a week and taking two long walks.

She's Sue Grafton, creator of Kinsey Millhone and the Alphabet murder series—A IS FOR ALIBI, B IS FOR BURGLAR... Sue tells an interesting story of her road to the best-seller list. And the most provocative line in her story is: "If someone told you at age 25 that you could have anything you wanted, but it would take 25 years, would you be happy to hear that?"

Grafton's path included writing many unpublished novels, and having a novel published, optioned as a film, and working on the screenplay of that book, THE LOLLY MADONNA WAR. She later worked on television scripts and finally created her niche with the alphabet books.

She writes one book a year, published on May 2 annually. She's only up to the letter "I", so she has 17 more books in the alphabet series—a commitment of another 17 years. Already one older fan is urging her to hurry because the fan wants to read the complete series before she dies.

Sue tells of someone attending her writing session at Antioch. Grafton candidly tells the audience that it will take them five years to write decently and even longer to get published and even longer to get any recognition. One woman complains, "I didn't pay good money to come here and be discouraged like this." "But the five years are going to go by anyway," Sue responds. "Wouldn't you rather have developed a talent in that time?"

"I plan to write till I'm 110 so that gives me time to finish this series and to do two additional series of 20 books each." She is not a health nut—and she plans to live a long time.

She shares with the audience a letter she wrote to her father when she was 25. She talks of the pain and frustration of not succeeding. "I am full of yes, and the world is saying no." She goes on in wrenching detail about the experience of being rejected time after time after time. And continuing.

She asks us..."What if you could have anything you want, but it takes you 25 years?"

Unpublished Poem

This is a poem by a friend who taught high-school English. Kids in high school, as you may remember, are prisoners of hormones and peer acceptance. Mostly they don't connect with what the curriculum is supposed to cover. But sometimes, some rare wonderful times, they do. This poem was never published in the journal of the National Council of Teachers of English.

Sometimes
I feel like
Shit.

But

Sometimes
I feel
like
Manure

Energy Management 101

I need something beyond time management. I need to find balance and vitality in an overwhelming world. I need help with energy and focus.

Why doesn't "time management" work for me. I know all the principles. I have the necessary skills. But I don't apply them.

If my office were sealed from the outside world right this minute, it would take me about six hours to get everything organized. But every time I invest one of those hours, more stuff comes in the door, more opportunities come over the phone, more challenges spurt out of the fax.

Only 20% of my time management problems respond to the traditional solutions. My biggest problem in time management is not that I am burdened with too many things I don't want to do or don't know how to do. It is that I'm blessed with too many things I do want to do. Too many appealing alternatives for each moment of my attention.

I'm emerging some basic principles of energy and focus management. They are:

The Hemphill Principle-CUT CLUTTER
"Clutter is postponed decisions." I heard this sentence during a training session one day and felt it plunge immediately to my core of indecision. I went home that very day and attacked a stack of clothing waiting to be mended. I fixed two items and boxed the rest for charity. I had been waiting long enough to change sizes or styles. Within a week, I had also cut through some of the clutter in my office.

Barbara Hemphill, author of *Taming the Paper Tiger*, gave the perfect message at the perfect time to get me to take action.

The Wilson Principle-REVEAL DAVID

Picture Michaelangelo's David. The simplicity and beauty of that sculpture was created by chipping away everything that was not David. Larry Wilson, author of many books on operating at your full potential, used this metaphor in a speech I heard recently and reminded me that I often think of creating my life's masterpiece by adding a few more dabs of this and that.

Wilson wakes me up. Focus on what is already there and eliminate the unnecessary.

The Covey Principle-IMPORTANT, NOT URGENT

How often do I invest attention on things that are important, but not the current crisis? Stephen Covey, in his book THE SEVEN BASIC HABITS OF HIGHLY-EFFECTIVE PEOPLE, distinguishes between four quadrants of time management.

The one with the most potential to improve my life is Q2-those things which are important, not urgent. This includes looking at patterns. Where do things get snagged in the current process? How can I improve my system? Such improvements cut down on the emergencies that otherwise drain my time and energy.

A lot of this kind of work takes place away from my desk. When I am walking or exercising. Clearing out the cobwebs so the clarity can shine through.

The Bedrosian Principle-COMMIT HIGHER
I wake up and feel especially lazy. My self-starter won't start. Or I get cold feet before making phone calls to ask for support. I'm afraid what I'm offering isn't good enough.

Then I remember that a part of the money from this project is committed to Alzheimer's research, part to scholarships for kids with cerebral palsy. Can I get started for them, if not for myself?

Sometimes the answer is no. I need the time to rest, to laze. And sometimes the answer is yes. I am not just clearing my to-do list here. I am not operating out of one more guilt-laden obligation. I am making my freely-chosen, specific, unique contribution.

Do these ideas work all the time? Of course not. But they give me reminders of how I like to think. How I prefer to view my choices. How I can focus my energy when I choose to.

DELIGHTS, DILEMMAS & DECISIONS

DISTANCE (OR) FOR PEOPLE WHO QUOTE TOO MUCH

"Distance," she says, and for me the half-filled restaurant instantly stills. No longer do I hear the silverware, the chatter, the piped-in music. I hear the echo of her word in my heart and mind. She has pinpointed my problem with laserlike precision.

Leslie is helping me put together an important speech. This afternoon, she listened as I read the outline and some of the material I thought I would use.

"You are doing a good job of structuring information, but I don't see or hear you personally in this talk. Where is your own viewpoint, your own special slant? Where is your unique perspective? Why are you denying your own authority?"

Suddenly it all makes sense. This is why I'm having trouble preparing this speech. I keep thinking that one more piece of research, one more quote, one more powerful example will work magic with the audience. I have a tremendous sense of incompleteness. A sense that I'll never make it good enough or strong enough. That I'll never really move someone in the audience to grow, to learn, to connect.

So I withhold the only thing that is truly mine to share. My own voice, my own experience, my individual view of the world.

I will always be the seventh of eight children, eater of the wings of the chicken. Afraid to ask for my place at the big table. Not often daring to hope for new clothes for the first day of school. Finding comfort, solace, escape, even friend-ship in the reading I love. Believing that others possess cre-dentials I am too humble to claim as my own. Waiting to be noticed. Fearful of failing to please.

All this hit within seconds of the moment in Tampa when Leslie said the word, "distance." My eyes filled. I thanked her. And backed safely away from getting too quickly too close to this truth. I'm still exploring the gift of that word.

May I now be fearful of the distance. May I tell my own truth so that those who want to hear it are nourished in the listen-ing as I am nourished in the telling. May those who don't wish to hear have other songs in their heads. May I finish waiting. May I count the day rich in the number of opportu-nities I do not pass by in the name of humility. May life be my credential now. All I want. All I need. Enough.

ZERO QUESTIONS

It's a lively discussion among colleagues. The session leader introduces a new topic. Know your purpose for writing. Yawn. Conversation goes flat as people glance around the group as if to say, "What a zero question. Everybody knows why you write a book."

Linda starts. "I don't know about the rest of you, but I'd like to get all my thoughts down on paper just to circulate among the people I know who are interested in these same areas and applications. It would be kind of an underground networking book."

One of those who already had one book out and was working on two more commented, "I use my book as an expensive business card. When I meet someone I may want to work with some day, I give him or her an autographed copy. Most people don't throw it away. My name is there on their shelf if they need somebody in my specialty."

"I use them to define the niche in which I am an expert. I'm careful that all my books are related to my central specialty and build my overall credibility." Neil contributes. "And besides, they allow me to raise my fees."

"No doubt, I think they help attract business." Mike stays rooted in the positive and practical.

"I just think the job of managing and supervising is so tough. When I write my book, it will be to help them do their jobs more easily and more effectively." Mike says.

Another quiet lull.

Mary's voice is almost wistful. "I hadn't thought about it until we started this discussion, but my father wrote a book. And the whole family was very proud of that. I feel good about publishing a book. It's almost as if I am honoring my father in some way. And I like the fact that my children might feel that way about me."

Carlene now. "And then there's the issue of having something to say. Wanting to, needing to share a vision."

"I remember a professor I had once." offers Linda. "She wrote her first book to quell her anger. Or maybe to integrate her experiences and make some sense of the pain of them. I often wondered if she ever wrote a second book. And, with the anger quenched, would it be as good?"

"And let's don't kid anybody. There are certain ego needs that publishing a book helps fill. This is my best shot at being interviewed for morning TV."

"On the practical side, the book is a convenient way to give people a collection of my insights without having to write them anew every time anybody asks or every time I have to talk to the new hires. It's like having a permanent handout available—at least it has a longer shelf-life than most of the things I produce."

"I want to give my readers a springboard to seeing themselves differently. I think they do such important work, and they aren't recognized for it even by themselves. If I can help them see that..."

"It seems to me that writing provides a context for learning, formulating research and thoughts in a disciplined way so it can reveal some general patterns or systems. I know I spend a tremendous amount of time thinking before I can write anything."

"I'm doing something similar on the personal level. I'm writing on balance because I've been forced to learn so much about it. And if I establish my expertise in this area, I have to hold myself accountable to live that way. So writing is shaping a context for living."

It had been a zero question. Not worth asking. Until we started to play with it. Then we found the themes:

- sharing with others, serving others, empowering others
- shaping decisions, policies, lives
- continuing or establishing family traditions
- providing a context for learning or living
- having impact
- requiring a high level of accountability
- building credibility, reputation, income

How many other zero questions are we not asking because we think the answers are obvious and would be the same for each of us? What if you were to interrupt the usual talk over lunch or dinner today and ask, "Why do we work..." or, "What difference do we make in the world?"

THE HIERARCHY OF INSECURITIES

I never thought there'd be any insecurities left by the time I got to this age. When I was a kid, I thought those eighth graders had it all figured out. In my teens, I was sure that once a person got married, everything became instantly clear. In each job, I imagined that those one or two levels above me had it made.

As I reached each of these peaks in my own life, I found that certainty and security receded like the horizon. Even so, a part of me persisted in imagining that a moment would come, a crystalline moment of completion, after which everything made sense and became easier.
A part of me still believes this may be true.

If there has been progress, it is in thinking that some of the things I worry about now are "better" to worry about.

Maslow formulated a theory of human needs.
He thought that people operated first at the level of survival. "Do I have something to eat?" Next, at the level of security. "Will I have a roof over my head next month?"
Next, at the level of connection. "Are there people in my life I can share love with?"
Next, at the level of recognition. "Do others know I make a difference in this world?"
Finally, at the level of self-actualization. "Am I so much a part of humankind that I am more myself?"

Maslow also suggested that people ascend this hierarchy step by step in an evolutionary progression. It takes a long time to get to the top. And, once there, it is easy at any given moment to move back down on the scale. Example: The person who has just discovered the cure for cancer leaves the lab and senses a stranger lurking in the parking lot. This scientist goes from making a global lifesaving contribution to primitive survival instinct (kill or be killed) in a heartbeat.

Is there, perhaps, a lighthearted parallel in things I have been insecure about? These don't fit as neatly into categories. For me, the concept of pleasing others leaks over into all the categories a little. It is painful to admit this. Maybe I'll be a grown up when this no longer bothers me at all. Or maybe I'll be dead.

Pleasing others. "Will they let me play? Why don't they like me?"

Pleasing myself. "Does my hair look good this way? I wonder what I should wear?"

Earning my place. "What right do I have to tell them what to do? Can I challenge someone from the Harvard Business School?"

Making a contribution. "What is the highest and best use of all of my resources in support of something that matters? What is the next right thing for me to do today?"

The more I keep my questions at that fourth level, the better time I have answering them. And the less time I have for any of the other questions. This doesn't yield a joyless life of dogged and earnest endeavor. Quite the contrary. Often the next right thing is to indulge myself or my family to replenish my resources for accomplishing "important work." I have fun with the process.

And I never forget that, when the call comes saying I'm about to go on a national TV show, the first questions that pop into my mind are..."What should I wear? Will they like me? Does my hair look OK?"

Two Roads

It sings to me one morning from the business section of the Washington Post. They have taken everything I have ever done or wanted to do at work and written a job description, put it in a 3 by 4 inch display ad, and wrapped it in a stately border.

Associate Vice President for External Relations of a prestigious university. I haven't applied for a job in ten years. I haven't wanted another job for ten years. But I want this one. The speed and intensity of my decision amaze me. I was just sitting here having tea, and suddenly I am willing to change my life. "I can weigh all the issues later," I reason. "Let's see if I even have a chance."

I finish my tea. Go directly to my computer and fling myself wholeheartedly into crafting a resume. Crafting is right. I hone each word deliberately to fit snugly around the job description. I spend two days working on a top-quality packet and send it off certified mail.

A week later I get a call while I'm at a conference in Dallas. "We've had 532 applications so far, and there are still two weeks to go before the deadline," he says. I realize I am holding my breath, waiting for what I hope will come next. "But you're the first person I am calling. I like your resume. Let me fill you in on the position."

I take notes on everything I am hearing, knowing my heart and mind are racing in a field of delight and possibility. "We'll be interviewing the second week in September, making a selection by October 1," he concluded. "Just wanted you to know the process."

Now I weigh all the factors. Some are surprisingly easy. My husband is fully prepared to give up his business, relocate, and go back to school for a couple of years. The small university town affords relatively comfortable living on the salary offered. My mother and stepson are both settled away from us now anyway. The timing is perfect.

I wonder if I can be an employee again. Then I think of some advantages. In these years on my own in business, I've been learning about organizations from the outside in. This role would give me a grounding from the inside out. As a business owner, I always had to fund my own learning and research. Now I'd have some resources of a reputable university to work with. People are sometimes more inclined to listen to a representative of a major institution than to listen to one more consultant whispering in the wind.

August speeds by as I wait for the call to schedule an interview. It never comes. I finally call the vice president. "We just sent you the letter today," he says. "We're only interviewing 5 candidates, and you were number 6."

Simultaneous reactions:
> Rejection - They don't want me.
> Surprise - I can't believe I didn't even make the interviews.
> Cockiness - They have no idea what they're passing up.
> Rationalization - Who really wants to supervise all those people anyway?
> Consolation - At least I was 6th among hundreds.

This isn't a daunting blow. Just a disappointing setback. I have put our lives in a twirl for four months juggling attractive options, and now the choice is out of my hands. So once again I trust life's wisdom. I believe it's been worth it, and the outcome is for the best.

This happened two years ago.
It's one of the few times in my life I can look back on and say that if I had taken that road I'd be a slightly different person today.

Yes, I can see that choice so clearly. I can see the university with its ivy, intellect, and politics. I can see the small town with its sense of community and its rivalry between town and gown. I can see my husband blossoming in a learning environment. I can see a house near a lake with geese flying over in November. I can see my office, a center of influence and contemplation. I would have learned different things and different people in that life. And that would have changed me somewhat.

And I would have missed most of what has come into my life these past two years. I look back, totally without regret. But once in a while, curious.

SHAPING TOMORROW; SAVORING TODAY

"The year is 2022. It's a Saturday afternoon in October in suburban Washington, D. C., and a crowd is gathered. On this crisply golden afternoon, we are celebrating my 80th birthday and my final retirement. Family, friends, and colleagues are here, and I'm pleased to see my young grandchildren, just starting out on their own careers. The brief speeches 'roast' me playfully, and the day is full of merriment. Several themes come through it all, though, and I am gently reminded of what I have been able to contribute over my 58-year career..."

This is one person's vision of what it will be like to look back over a long and satisfying life. This particular vision reflects a life in which career was very important. Mine may be similar or it may be very different.

What is important is to look at how I want my life to unfold and what steps I can take to create the richest and fullest life possible. What is important is to look at preparing for the future without losing the adventure that is the present. What is important is shaping tomorrow while savoring today.

What might I want to learn today that could make all those years more satisfying, more rewarding, more productive, and more profitable? How do I want to be remembered? What legacy do I want to leave behind?

What are the highlights of my life, looking back from 80?

PERSONAL REFLECTIONS

Something I would like to learn...

When I was a kid, I thought I'd grow up to be...

Someone I admire...

The work I would love to do...

If I didn't need to work for the money, I would...

The most discouraged I've been in my career...

If a favorite niece or nephew asked advice on going into a career similar to mine, I'd tell them...

Someone whose work gives them an interesting life is...

My colleagues...

CHAPTER FIVE

Spirit

SPIRIT

People with balance in their spirit zone have comfort, connection, and a sense of meaning in their lives. Whatever their beliefs as to the purpose of life and the promise of an afterlife, they are at peace with their convictions.

They derive their code of conduct and their sense of direction and ethics from the strength of their beliefs. This certainty is private and personal, yet they share their views freely when sincerely questioned or called on for help or guidance.

They realize that others may believe differently, and they respect each person's right to make a personal choice.

They avoid judging others, knowing that their responsibility is to focus on themselves.

They model their beliefs. They live their own lives so that anyone looking at them closely will see the daily definition of the ideas they hold most dear. This is their way of inviting others to join them in their faith.

They join others in spirit and in song. They know the family of fellowship and the strength and direction it can offer. Whether this family is in a church or wherever they gather with others, they know their kindred souls.

They know temptation. They know the darkness that comes from an occasional lapse. And they know the uncomplicated joy of staying true, holding fast.

They know reflection. They recognize that in today's complicated world there are many grey areas. They seek the counsel of their conscience and keep a loving heart.

They know thanksgiving for the bounty and the beauty of the life they have and the world around them.

They know comfort and joy in being connected to something greater than they are.

They pray.

GOD'S JOKE

There's a Robert Frost poem that goes:
    Forgive, oh Lord, my little jokes on thee
    And I'll forgive thy great big one on me.

I'm never quite sure what God's big joke is, but I seem to catch glimpses of it all the time.

Like the way I thought as a kid. Watching adults lumber their way through a spring day and sometimes even take a nap on purpose, I swore that I'd NEVER sleep in the daytime when I was a grown up.

And as an adolescent. I vividly remember the raging-of-hormones stage when I KNEW with the certainty of youth that, once I was safely married, I'd have sex all the time.

And, as a young professional, I was sure that retirement programs and security were just not important. A career that promised a 20-year retirement seemed like a life sentence—I'd be stuck there till at least my 40's.

I was so certain about many things in those days:
    That my college fiancee would make a perfect lifetime
        mate in spite of family objections
    That I'd always be totally opposed to capital punish
        ment
    That I'd become a mini-celebrity in some field
    That life would always treat me reasonably well
    That I'd always scorn those who gave up the poetry of
        existence to become embroiled in business
    That ambition, intelligence, energy, and luck were my
        tools for the future.

It wasn't the details of my beliefs that were part of God's joke. It was the certainty with which I held them. The joke with my beliefs is that every one of the things I was most certain of has reversed or double-reversed itself in my life.

And I've been the richer for it.

To me, the most amazing part of the joke is that I'm now laughing, too. All the things I was certain about, the things I knew I would always or never do are keys to some of my greatest delights today...
> A well-deserved, luxurious nap
> A rewarding second marriage
> Enough difficulties in life to make me grateful for this conscious daily treasure.

It hasn't been a joke ON me, it's been a joke FOR me.

And then there is paradox - all the seeming contradictions that actually make the most harmonious and often humorous sense.

> When I was a kid, I looked forward to staying up late and watching all the TV I wanted. Today, it's a joy to read and fall asleep early.

> In those days, I thought I'd have parties all the time when I had "my own place." Today, I resist having company.

When I was young and thin, I couldn't afford nice clothes. Today, I could maybe afford them and no longer feel driven to decorate my body.

Back then, I thought I'd spend all my money on travel and adventure because a house was just a shell for sleeping in. Today, I'm so fond of my home I sometimes even enjoy oiling the woodwork.

Maybe another part of the joke is that I so often want balance NOW. I'm impatiently seeking serenity. Do these seem like odd juxtapositions of words? Why a word like "balance" which suggests a soft harmonious flow and words like "NOW" and "impatiently," which suggest aggressively insistent demand?

I don't quite get the joke. But I still enjoy the glimpses.

(I just stood up from the computer, stepped out a door of my office into a Spring evening with Dogwoods delicately blooming and birds chirping. The smells, the soft air after four days of rain. I'm aware of traffic sounds not far away, but they don't break the sunset spell of April. The earth is soft.

Where are you? What is nearby? What are the sights, tastes, smells? Are you here? Are you now?)

I'm usually pleased when I remember I'm living inside the joke.

Sharing a Grapefruit

It's 6:05 a.m. in the normal coastal cloud of early morning in California. I head out to the small commuter plane and glance back, surprised to see a best-selling author walking behind me. We've just come from a writer's conference. He was a speaker; I, a listener.

The flight to L. A. is short, and we sit across from each other in the narrow plane. He's heading to a family reunion in North Carolina. He talks about getting to study art in China.

I peel the grapefruit I've brought along. My nostrils prickle at the familiar tart scent. I pull the sections apart gently, watching juice well up as the membranes tear. I place several sections on a napkin and offer it to him. He declines gently. I offer again, without insisting.

How can I communicate more clearly that I hope he will accept? That I would like the joy of sharing one of nature's treasures with a fellow human being on a small plane hurtling through the early morning sky?

He declines again. I eat and enjoy the whole grapefruit.

We talk some more, land in L. A., and head for our connections. Later, I think about that grapefruit. It's not a big deal, but why did he turn it down? Doesn't he like grapefruit? Too early in the morning to eat? There are several good reasons for his response.

But I keep thinking he did it out of politeness. As if he didn't want to intrude on my limited food supply. As if the early morning unavailability of food in traveling made it impolite to accept. As if I might have felt obligated to offer, my generosity might have been forced.

It's probably not fair, but I remember a story from Robert Fulghum's first book, *Everything I Ever Needed to Know, I Learned in Kindergarten*. It was the haunting story of a man who withheld from his family the knowledge that he was terminally ill. Out of concern for their feelings, he kept his secret till it was too late. He thought he was doing them a kindness by protecting them from the harsh and tragic reality. They were angry at his lack of trust of them. They were sad they didn't get to help make the end easier.

That's a long way from refusing grapefruit. But it made me think of the things I do or don't do out of politeness, out of turning down offers of help, support or even grapefruit. Out of misreading that true charity often comes in the form of receiving gracefully.

I hope I remember to say yes the next time someone offers to share a slice of life or nature with me. No promises, of course.

POCKETS OF FELICITY

A pocket - a part of a garment. Usually small. Usually made of the same fabric or hidden within a seam. Designed to hold things conveniently, securely, close to the body.

A pocket of felicity. A part of my day, usually small, usually made of the same fabric as the rest of the day. But I shift some small unit of my attention. I notice or collect a single part of the texture of the landscape of the day. And this shift gives me a moment of felicity—a sense of well being.

A slice of startlingly blue sky between tunnels of tall buildings as I hurry to my next appointment.

A moment of comfort when the mail arrives and there are no new bills.

A glimpse of a father and child hugging hello in an airport.

My husband's earthy grumble as he gets up at 5 a.m. to launch me on an early day.

An isolated moment of morning beauty as I pause beside a fish pond.

The feel of my pillow and sheets welcoming me at the end of a full day.

Time to notice twilight.

The anticipatory aromas before that first, inviting bite of hot pasta.

These pockets are a part of my everyday fabric if I take a moment to notice them. When I give mself that moment of pause, I remember that life is rich, mostly good, mostly sane.

If I notice and keep them close to me for a while, my day is richer, mostly good, mostly sane.

I like to pocket some small felicity, convenient, secure, close to me all day.

Life Isn't Fair

Some days I look at the newspaper and realize the number of headlines I've never been featured in:

INDIANA GIRL STRUCK BY HIT-AND-RUN DRIVER

PEACE CORPS VOLUNTEER SUCCUMBS TO DENGUE FEVER IN THE PHILLIPINES

WEDDING SCENE OF TRAGIC SHOOTING

HOUSE BURNS IN ROCKVILLE: FAMILY RESCUED

LIGHTENING DESTROYS COMPUTER AS AUTHOR'S BOOK NEARS COMPLETION

FREAK ACCIDENT COSTS SPEAKER HER VOICE

BANK FORECLOSES ON LOCAL FAMILY

DREAM VACATION TURNS INTO A NIGHTMARE

You get the idea.

It seems like a lot of people talk about whether or not life is fair. It's not and I'm glad. How could I, or most of us, ever deserve to live so richly? How could I deserve to be alive when opportunities abound in so many different areas? How could I have been so lucky as to have the advantages that science and technology have brought?

How do I even deserve to be alive?

So sometimes, when I am tempted to huff in righteous indignation that I haven't yet won my "rightful" lottery or huge contract, I think about those headlines. I'm grateful life isn't fair.

THE CHOREOGRAPHED COMMUNION

It's a springtime Saturday morning, and the parking lot starts attracting the cars from the street. One, two, six, ten, forty, ninety, one hundred thirty and now people are parking near yellow curbs and along fire lanes. It's first communion at Saint Patrick's--the initiation of first grade children into perhaps the most holy sacrament of the Catholic church.

I go into the crowded church. Here, too, people are parked illegally, standing in aisles of the packed building.

The children are carefully clustered in the front rows, each dressed in white, most of the girls wearing veils on their heads. The ceremony begins. Everything is elaborately rehearsed and scheduled. In humbler times, in smaller parishes, first communion was a significant yet modest event. Today, with crowds and video intrusion, the service becomes a ceremony if not a production.

The children's choir lends tremulous music. The priest stages a moving story about how the very land on which this church was built was a gift from farmer Pat who used to live "just over there on the hillside." The son of farmer Pat came back one day and gave communion to his father in this new church— the first communion dispensed by this newly ordained priest. So today's first communion was both new and old, following the tradition of centuries.

Of course, I notice the Priest's occasional stage directions to the official video camera operator for the day. And I notice the proud parents occasionally popping out of their seats to snap their flash cameras. The children advance one by one to the altar. I notice the teacher prompting each row to stay in line, don't fidget, don't chew the host. I notice that the distractions are losing their ability to distract me.

I'm back at Saint Ann's. I'm one of the children. I'm one of the choir. I'm one of the watchers. I'm part of innocence, part of regret, part of the bittersweet pull of ties that have loosened.

I'm here to see the daughter of friends take her first communion. Meredith advances in the line. She turns to face the congregation, and her eyes fall again to her hands folded in formal devotion. She returns to her row.

Now it's time for the adults to take communion. The line is long and advances swiftly. Her family comes past Meredith, seated on the end of her row. Her mother and father smile at her as they go by. Her grandmother maintains her own pious quiet as she goes past. And her grandfather, not often expressive, caresses the top of her head briefly, then takes his seat.

By such small sweetness does a ceremony become again a sacred service, stitching together families across time. By such does all the crafted choreography fall away before the simple majesty of those ties.

I stray from my roots—but not far.

SHE SINGS

She asks us to be kettledrums. 1255 people sit in front of her
— in clothes ranging from sweats to sequins. It's 8:15 a.m. —
the morning general session at a national convention. She
will sing a parody of the song "Shall We Dance?" from the
KING AND I, and we will come in using "yes, yes, yes," as the
kettledrum chorus...

"Shall I speak?"

"Yes, yes, yes."

"Using laughs, words, and music shall I speak?"

"Yes, yes, yes."

It works. 1255 people really do sound like booming kettledrums in response to her voice.

She toys with us. We laugh together. She highlights several
messages about play, about music, about mental health, about
diversity, about the fullness of living .

She tells the stories of the gifts different audiences have given
her. Gifts of awareness, gifts of appreciation. Some of the gifts
are painful.

There was the woman once who felt Rosita was making fun of
people with accents. Rosita learned from the pain they both
felt. There was the man who waited in line to talk with her,
and, when he got there, the words wouldn't come. They

hugged, and learned. There was a woman once who feared she might be going crazy several years after she survived the accident that had killed her three children. Rosita held the woman and held her pain.

I began to see again this singer of life. To see that in all her joy and music is the fullness of life that also embraces pain and sorrow. I see the image of a pin-cushion. A heart-shaped pain-cushion which others pierce easily with their needs. I used to see sacrifice as dripping with blood and thorns. Rosita shows it flowing with music and flowers. Sacrifice for her is an offering.

While laughter and music are her gifts, she uses them so generously to heal the pain she sees. She left the field of mental health years ago to go onto the speaking platform. She didn't go far.

CEREMONIES

His face is puzzled as he observes me humming "Taps" while lowering a favorite pair of sweat socks into the trash can.

"Mag, why are you doing that?"

"These socks are shot. They are finally beyond repair."

"Not the socks, the music part."

I smile as I think back to a spectacular vacation some years ago. We had dreamed for a long time of going to Hawaii. Finally, we decided to go there with friends.

Maui is perfect.

Up the first morning at 3 a.m. to make the long drive for sunrise at the crater at Haleakula. We arrive, shivering at the pre-dawn chill. One of life's pristine moments. Clouds below us in the canyon floor, stars above, fading goodby, as the sun breaks the surface tension and brims majestically over the jagged crater rim. We are at the brink of life, nature's beginning, the moment of creation. Awe.

A few days later, John accidentally goes into the Pacific for a swim wearing an expensive and delicate watch he treasures. Awful.

Alice gives him a choice. "The watch," she says, "is history. You can spend the rest of our whole vacation grieving for the watch, or you can release yourself from the watch and continue having a good time with the rest of us."

Her process for "releasing yourself from the watch" includes:
- •a reasonably short time to grieve that he lost some thing he loves
- •finding the most beautiful spot on the beach to bury the watch
- •conducting a small ceremony to say goodby
- •appreciating that a small part of him will always be on that beach in Maui
- •whenever in the future he has a pang of yearning for the watch,visualizing the joys of that trip to balance out the loss.

I still don't like to let go of favorite things. I develop an enormous loyalty to socks that are really comfortable. When they are finally worn out, I thank them for the way they have cradled my feet, absorbed my sweat, helped my health and stamina, kept my toes happy. And I hum to them.

It's easier that way.

THE BOUNTY BOMBARDMENT

It's an amazing week. Monday morning, I leave at ten of six to go talk to 400 Navy secretaries and salute their contribution. It's a little over an hour on the metro, so I have some time to reflect on when I first came to Washington as a secretary. I was 17, straight out of high school. I worked for the government then. Part of me today has stayed that fresh small-town girl, awed at being able to work in the big city.

I talk for 40 minutes. We laugh, we look at life and work and today's dilemmas. We celebrate survival. And I meet an admiral who knew my oldest brother, Frank, years ago at Port Hueneume. By 9 a.m., I'm finished for the day. Not really, because I've scheduled two appointments. But I FEEL finished once I've done something so intense first thing in the week. I like the feeling that the rest of the day/week is coasting.

Tuesday, a friend recommends a book—a mystery by Scott Peck titled *A Bed by the Window.* Amazingly, I see that very book on a sidewalk sale later in the day. I have to buy it. The cover describes it as "a novel of mystery and redemption." I read the first two pages, meet a character with Alzheimer's, think of my mom and decide, "I can't read this." By page three, I'm thinking, "I have to read this."

In the story, characters in a nursing home have a variety of physical afflictions. They also have a variety of spiritual afflictions and some moments of blessings. The murder plot allows for skillful exploration of the interplay of hope and healing with occasional touches of humor. Some souls are smothering while others are lilting. And the sound-of-body are in as much need of healing as their patients. It's a powerful book for me.

Wednesday, I work, keep reading, and notice nothing particularly significant.

Thursday after work, I take a long walk through hilly parkland. It's one of those evenings where some breezes hide in the hollows and stir up around my ankles and calves as I walk by. I'm loving the sensation. Shifting from warm to cool on my legs as my stride strengthens. My mind is buoyant, floating comfortably among the sights, smells, and sounds of the walk. Unbidden, a freight-train of a thought slams through me. It hits me fully formed, whole sentenced, and with welcome force. "Margaret Ann, you have always been abundantly loved."

It is so clear and powerful a message that I nearly look around to see who is speaking.

It is like the difference between doubting, believing, and knowing. In this moment, I no longer doubt or just believe. I know.

Such a feeling passes, but it never goes away. For a moment, I know. Having known, I can never be entirely innocent of abundant, unconditional love again.

Friday, heading into the J. W. Marriott flagship hotel near the White House, I face an exciting and challenging day. I'm program co-chair and panelist at an inaugural event helping my industry strengthen its partnership with our clients. We'll make a touch of history here today. I am nervous.

Heading for the revolving doors, I notice a tall man with a name badge. The badge shows the name "Frank McAuliffe." I stop for a moment and introduce myself. "That's my oldest brother's name," I tell the stranger. He responds that he is here from England, enjoying his visit, and appreciating such a bright morning greeting. And, of course, the rest of the day unfolds splendidly.

After the conference, I have a stimulating computer lesson from Dick and finish this week at a lecture by Master Jhoon Rhee. Korean-born Rhee, master of the martial arts, ties spiritual, mental, and physical health together. He speaks strongly of the difference between believing and knowing.

It's been five years since my brother died. Why, in one week, would I have two chance encounters with his name? Why would I have two experiences with believing and knowing? Why would so many elements fall so magically into place for me? It feels like a year's worth of blessings just showered down into one week. Is there any way I can invite that to happen again? Does this happen other times when I am to busy or too blind to notice? How can I live inside these experiences?

Saturday is entirely normal.

A Borrowed Garden

I leave my hotel room a little early this August Friday morning. On my way to work in downtown Philadelphia, I steal a few moments in a borrowed garden.

A melodious bell a few blocks away tolls 8 a.m. Traffic rushes briskly by only 50 yards from me on Chestnut Street. But here a bird sings. And I listen.

These formal gardens, a part of Independence Park are open to the public as a pass-through. Or, as in my case today, a sit-a-while.

The garden is small, formal. Outlined in brick, boxed into forms. The glory and abundance of nature offset any stiffness. The formality of topiary trees and low boxwood are punctuated by the breezy brightness of yellow daisies and other flowers I can't identify. Today, their names are small-purple-star-flowers and pink-orange-flame-flowers.

Above it all, an ancient ginko tree loosens a leaf. Harbinger of the coming autumn.

I sit here only ten minutes on a summer morning. My luggage at my side. I take the train home after work today. Enough.

PLUGGING INTO PURPOSE

There are three questions you might want to ask yourself to help connect to your purpose in life.

1. ASK THE CHILD WITHIN

It's called the Walt Disney question. "Would the child you once were be proud of the adult you are now?" If the six year old version of you were standing at the far side of a grassy field, and you were standing at the other, would your child spot you, know you, and come running wildly across the gap, arms and legs flying to leap into your arms and hug you tight? Or would your child be shy. Hang back. Twist a toe in the grass and wonder who that person is over there.

There's no right answer to that question. My guess is that there are a huge range of possible answers, each subject to several interpretations. The power is in asking the question. Your answer will offer you one clue about your purpose.

Often that child wanted you to be an adventuring explorer, a famous star, a noble doctor, a daring pirate, or at least a firefighter, nurse, police officer or teacher. What your child might have a hard time recognizing is that your life is so complex now. It's hard to say in a word or two what you contribute to the world. It's hard to remember how you got from that young, naive dream to your work today which may not even have existed when you were a kid.

Suppose you took that kid for an ice cream soda and talked about what you do. What would you tell him? What would you tell her? How do you contribute? How do you matter in the world?

What are some of the things you would tell that child?

2. KNOW YOUR SOURCE OF POWER

Suppose you are the most modern and sophisticated television set in existence. You have the very best in technology, the most advanced sound quality, picture, programmability, and every feature imaginable. Sometimes your plug slips out of the socket. And you even have photovoltaic cells that allow you to pull power right out of the ambient light. This power is sufficient for most functioning. But if you are left on too long, or if you're surrounded by a prolonged dark spell, you start to dim. Then, you are plugged back into the system. You have access to abundant and dependable power. Literally, you get the picture.

We are like that super TV. We are plugged into some source of power in order to operate. For most people, that power is positive as in the power of God or a universal life force. Some few people get their sense of connection from anger or negative power. Here's one person's report:

> When I was younger, I was plugged into positive power. I guess I got too busy to stay connected. I took it so much for granted. Somehow, I slipped out of the socket. Chronic stress was like that period of being left on too long. Personal troubles were like the period of

prolonged darkness. It probably would have been easier for me if all I had to do was to plug into the socket again, but I had forgotten the socket was even there. I had a long time of feeling dimmed.

Are you plugged into your power? What is the source of power for your sense of purpose?

3. DEFINE YOUR MISSION

Why do you exist? Why are you on earth? Is it possible that you have a role to play in the unfolding of eternity? If so, what would it be?

A friend once told me jokingly that she was greatly distressed. She thought she had figured out what God had in mind for her. He wanted her to be ordinary.

Maybe there's a lot to be said for the ordinary life. Ordinary people love their families, paint their houses, go through loss and pain, make a contribution to their world, go on vacation, send birthday cards, get laid off, and eat popcorn. With all the mixture and texture, the interplay of joy and pain, that's not such a bad life.

We could easily make ourselves crazy if we became obsessed each and every day with questions about our purpose and mission. "Let's see, would the universal life force want me to take out the garbage tonight or can I wait till the morning?" It's good that we can take the big questions for granted most of the time or we'd never make it to lunch.

But we go overboard. Eventually, life becomes our to-do list, or our daytimer, or our quarterly report, or our portfolio. We forget that there are bigger questions. We forget to focus on our mission.

Corporations have mission statements. They use them to guide policy and define the corporate culture. What does your mission statement say? Here are a few samples .

I was born to be happy and to make others happy. My goal in life is to help everyone I reach know just how to be happy here and now—no waiting till they lose 20 pounds, till they make their first million, till the kids finish college. Right here, right now, just exactly the way things are.

I'm not sure what my mission is, but I'm sure it includes some adventure, lots of learning, a love of human honesty, and a desire to profit while helping people communicate.

I'm here to pack it all in. Life is short, and I want to try everything.

My talent is to start a business, get it through its first stages, and get out of it before it gets too complex. Maybe my mission is to be an initiator, not a maintainer.

For now my mission is to listen and learn and then to figure out what my mission is.

I want to rekindle in people a sense of curiosity and wonder about the miracle of being alive so they can go joyfully through their day instead of plodding along in shadows.

Notice that these statements vary from the lyrical to the practical. Your own statement will reflect your style and tone. Some of these focus exclusively on career, some include all of life. Some might serve for a long-term statement, some reflect the here-and-now. All the statements are short—under 100 words or so. If you had to write your mission statement on a matchbook cover....

Rather than follow some prescriptive formula for writing the perfect mission statement, why not tell the truth? If you were to record the purpose/mission of your life as you see it today, what would it say? Don't go for graceful prose or profound thoughts. Don't try to please the phantom judges in your head. Tell yourself the truth.

PERSONAL REFLECTIONS

The faith of my childhood...

My religious education as a kid...

Something in my beliefs that has changed since then...

Something that stays the same...

Someone whose spiritual life I have admired...

One temptation I feel...

The most difficult spiritual struggle in my life...

My personal connection to a supreme being...

Something that stirs my soul is...

After death...

A time my beliefs have brought me comfort...

When tempted to judge others, I...

Something that confuses me...

Prayer...

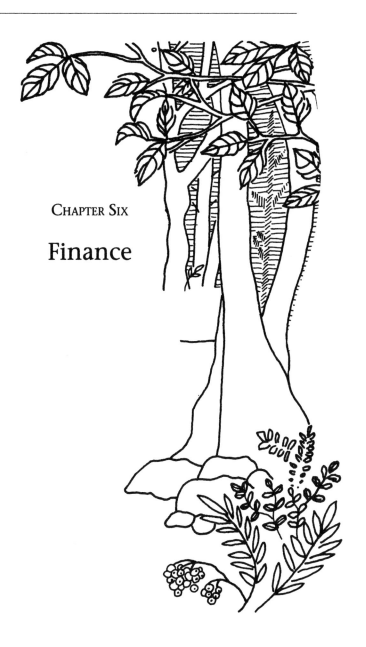

CHAPTER SIX

Finance

FINANCE

People with balance in this zone feel abundance, choices, and prosperity.

They have asked themselves, "How much is enough?" Whatever their income, they recognize that "enough" is just slightly less than what they have. Thus, they always have more than enough.

Rather than have an arbitrary dollar figure as a net-worth goal, they set a life-style goal. They want enough money to have choices about where they live, what they drive, what charities they contribute to, where their children go to school, and whether they vacation.

They cover the necessities first and consider everything else a luxury. They savor and appreciate each luxury.

They plan for occasional financial emergencies. They are never just one paycheck from disaster.

They have a current will. They have designated guardians for their children in case of their untimely deaths. They have a personal and family financial plan.

They allow themselves an occasional financial fling just for the fun of it. They may take a spontaneous holiday (camping or Cancun). They may give somebody a surprise $100, send flowers to a friend, buy a penny stock, indulge themselves in a new briefcase, donate generously to a cause they care about.

They recognize that they have invested a lot of time to earn this money, so they elect to spend some time making informed choices about how much to save, whether it is smarter to rent or buy, the benefits and risks of tax deferred annuities, treasury bills vs. municipals vs. mutual funds. They are cautious about where they place their trust.

They know that most people make financial mistakes. From buying a lot in Florida at a slick sales presentation during a free lunch at a hotel, to buying a car that never works well. Once they have made a mistake, they take the learning from it that they need. They then move past it and refuse to let it darken their lives.

They also refuse to be owned by their possessions. House, car, furniture, even golf clubs are all things. They could be replaced by money. They might become fond of these specific things, and they can replace them anyway if they are gone.

Some very few things are beyond price. They guard them intelligently.

CLIMBING THE RAINBOW

"The juicy part of being an entrepreneur is not the pot of gold at the end of the rainbow. It's climbing the rainbow itself." It's our Saturday morning walk, and my husband is talking about a business opportunity and how he will evaluate whether or not to get involved.

The image intrigues me. Climbing the rainbow. It's not like climbing the corporate ladder where you have a reasonably clear sense of where the effort will take you. It's more transitory and evanescent than that. Nor is it like skipping along the rainbow with nary a care in the world. It's more focused and demanding than that.

It takes me back over some things I needed to learn in my years as employee and my years as entrepreneur.

As an employee, I saw my limitations and failures as out of my control. Sometimes, I wasn't given the resources to do the best job possible. I could fight for more resources, seek creative alternatives, and, finally, blame the rest of the gap on "them." What do they expect anyway? They keep giving me too many top priorities.

As an entrepreneur, I see that I have full and total responsibility. Yes, I may elect to overload my own resources, and I will pay some price for that. I may ignore certain opportunities, and I will pay some price for that. I may misjudge my market, and I will pay some price for that. But there's no one to blame for these prices I pay. I am fully responsible.

The field may not be level for all players, but it's equally unlevel for most. Genes and fate have dealt me certain skills and talents. My set is different from every other set in the world. My job is to find out how to match my set to the needs of the marketplace. I then attract money effortlessly doing exactly what I do well, love doing, that somebody needs, wants, and is willing to pay for. I don't need to attract obscene levels of money. Enough for some comforts, some security, and an occasional luxury.

I don't need more because I'm living in the richness of that rainbow.

The other giant learning is that I always used to think that the right choice of product or service made the difference. My daydreams drifted toward discovering a product like oxygen—something people need, want, and use up quickly so they come back for more.

Maybe I could dream up the perfect product for home offices now that more people are telelcommuting. Or start up a compelling catalog to a small, select market niche. Or write the next megabook that will produce instant fame and riches. Or devise the fad of the decade.

I thought the secret rested in selecting the perfect item of such premier quality to offer the public. I asked myself, "What could I do or make of such sterling quality that the marketplace would beat that pathway to my door to get it?"

That would be fair. Virtue and effort would be rewarded. After all, it's tremendously difficult to invent a product or write a book, pour my heart, soul, sweat, and hours into a task for a year or more with no reasonable guarantee of a yield at the end of such a project.
(I didn't know I believed these things, and they sound hopelessly naive as I see them here. But some of my disappointments over the years have let me see that I did believe the world should work this way.)

And, smilingly, out in the entrepreneurial world for ten years, I notice it doesn't happen like that. The questions I now ask myself in evaluating a project: Who needs it? How, when, and why do they need it? What are they willing to invest to get it? Can I produce it? How will they find out about it? How can I get it to them? Will they benefit? Will I? Will I enjoy the process?

I used to see just the idea and prototype as the whole picture. Now I know there's manufacturing, marketing, and distribution as well. The scale matters whether you are talking single items of designer jewelry or thousands of copies of a book or millions of units of a gadget. But the basics remain the same.

It's been a tough education at times. It's full of logic, analysis, and rationality that my youthful poetic soul would have scorned. Business itself is full of dancing complexities and intricate interrelationships. It may be a coldly calculating ticket to the rainbow. But oh, the light, the music, the color.

DELIGHTS, DILEMMAS & DECISIONS

12 Ways to Get More Time in My Life

1. Slow down - Take the extra time to do things right, and save the time I'd have to spend to do them over.

2. Say NO - Just because someone has requested that their issues or concerns become important to me, doesn't mean I have to agree. My needs weigh at least equally with theirs.

3. Define my mission - Think of all the clarity that comes from knowing where I am going and why I am on a certain path. From that clarity comes vigor. From vigor, the energy to accomplish what I want. Know where I am going.

4. Delegate - The trick about delegating is that I have to be ready to accept that things will be done a little differently than I might have done them. Once I delegate, I have to be willing to let them bring their own vision, process, and reasonable autonomy into the project. If I turn something over to a committee, I know it will bear their fingerprints as well as mine. But it has a chance of getting done within the best window of opportunity. If I keep it to myself, it may sit here forever waiting for my window of attention.

5. Eliminate - I remember the year I was president of a local professional group. I got about 20 invitations to holiday parties. I had about five minutes of feeling suddenly popular, and then I felt besieged. I came up with a system that worked. My earlier habit had been to put each invitation aside to think about and decide later "as my schedule firmed up." Finally, I started turning them down the minute they came in the door. For the one or two I could finally attend, I called the hosts a

day ahead and checked to see if there would be room. There was. Several of the hosts later thanked me for my prompt response. "You wouldn't believe how many people never bother to call or say 'yes' and don't show up," they complained.

6. Simplify - I notice I am more likely to exercise in the morning if I don't have to get up and figure out what clothes to exercise in. That sounds odd to me, but reflects just how complex my day feels. Therefore, I keep a stack of doesn't-matter-if-they-mix-and-match exercise "uniforms" on the shelf closest to the bed. If I get up in time for exercise, the tough choice about what to wear is already made for me.

7. Buy time services - I cut my own hair, but I don't mow my own lawn. We all make our budget choices, and, at some point a couple of years ago, I decided it was worth money to me not to spend the fleeting summer hours sweating with machinery and swatting bugs. I treasure the two hours that I keep for myself each week by paying for those services. I use them to keep up my mental and physical health. What I spend on the lawn today, I may save at the doctor's tomorrow.

8. Exercise/energize - One of life's big surprises. It wasn't till my 40's that I became a convert to the benefits of moving voluntarily. I've been amazed, though, to discover the following:
> •Exercise gives me energy, vitality, alertness, and stamina
> •It gently reduces my appetite and burns calories to maintain weight

•It gives me peaceful sleep
•It helps me feel I've earned my shower
•And it's fun!

9. Relax/savor - I can take a five-minute mini-vacation in my brain whenever I remember to. I can close my eyes, breathe deeply, drift away, and think soothing thoughts. Or I can notice the world around me and experience it more alertly and intensely by just making an inventory of what I am seeing, hearing, feeling, smelling, tasting. These choices are available to me in the middle of an intense board meeting or as I ride on an elevator. I like to remember to use them.

10. Learn/renew - I feel so awkward trying to learn a new skill, going back to the state of not-knowing. I feel this way approaching new software, a new client, a new project, a new challenge. The very awkwardness is part of the youthful feeling that comes from learning. I get to be a kid again with all the stumbling that suggests. It feels good.

11. Be aware - I can hardly imagine living an entire day with full sensory awareness. A full day to suck the juices of the day I have. A day to stay aware of light, air, breathing, the taste of a single slice of orange, the feel of silky fabric on my skin, the smell of baking bread. A day of the unheralded joy of the ordinary. It might almost be too rich for a day; perhaps I can give myself this gift for a few moments along the way of every day.

12. Design perfect version - How would I really like to be spending my time? I draw a circle representing a 24-hour clock and chart the way I am spending my time now. Then, I draw a second circle representing a preferred future distribution. If I don't know how I'd like to spend my hours, days, years, how will I know when I've done it? This gives me some clarity about things I can say "no" to and what I might want to learn.

BONUS - the best thing I can do is to remember to apply these as often as possible.

Experience Annuity

Annuity. I love the word. I'm not sure of the dictionary meaning, but I associate it with one of my financial plans for the future. When I left my last career, I withdrew all the money I had in the employee pension plan and bought a single-payment annuity. The annuity kicks in when I'm 60 or so and provides a monthly payment for as long as I live. Since I come from long-lived genes, that is important to me.

I'm trying to do the same thing in my career. I invest time today in doing things that yield dividends over twenty or thirty years. The individual dividends may be small, sometimes invisible. But I see and feel them accumulating. The three primary areas I invest time in are learning, credibility, and reputation.

Learning. If I plan to work for the next 30 years or so, look at the yield I can get from something I learn today. When I get discouraged at my progress with computers and technology, I try to remind myself of this. I remember the hundreds of hours I'll save over several years to come by investing each day in developing my knowledge and skills.

Writer Ray Bradbury reports that he reads every day. At least one poem, one essay, and one short story, "feeding the language mind," he calls it. I also nourish my learning mind richly and regularly.

Credibility. Being seen as an expert. If my learning is focused, I develop mastery and expertise. I become an authority. I realize that a lot of what I need to learn, a lot of what the world might need to know from me, is not taught in a PhD program.

Life is my credential. Experience is my teacher. But not just the raw "stuff" of minutes passing by. It takes a lot of concentration, structure, and discipline to process what I learn and transform it into something of value to the marketplace.

The most difficult person to convince of my expertise is—me. I suffer from a fear of faking. I know that "faking it" takes more energy than I want to sustain. Once I earn the credential in my own eyes, it is possible to take it into the world.

Reputation. Taking my credibility into the world builds my reputation. Sharing my insights and expertise as generously as possible helps others know what I can contribute. Every time I speak to a group, write an article, coach someone, teach a rookie, I am serving my industry or my purpose. I am also building the visibility and reputation that attracts people to me with questions or needs in that area.

Patiently, over time, I am a recognized authority in my field. If a group wants me to address their conference and I'm not available on the date they ask for, they change the date of the conference. No substitute is considered suitable. In this particular pond, whether large or small, I am a "name". There are a lot of ponds out there. I used to try too hard to make a splash in all of them. Now I'd like to make a ripple in a very few.

When I have a reputation at this level, people call me 5, 10, and 20 years later to come back and address their new group of executive interns or the banquet honoring the 25th anniversary of the founding of their company. Sure, I'm known as the "venerable old perennial who always has something provocative to say." I like that. They're still listening.

It's a satisfying cycle. Every minute I am learning, I am growing credibility and building reputation. So a walk in the woods is part of my job. Noticing what it feels like to spend an hour in the grocery store is part of my learning. Remembering to laugh at myself is vital to living out my credibility as an authority on balance.

My experience annuity. Making the investments today that yield dividends the rest of my life. Cherishing the freedom to make those investments.

WHICH COMES FIRST?

Seventy-eight year old Sammy Cahn is up on stage in front of 400 of us doing a command performance at the request of a good friend. Most of us recognize the songs he wrote the lyrics to..."Call Me Irresponsible..." "High Hopes..." At least, we come to recognize them once he starts to sing them.

"Which comes first, the melody or the lyrics?" he asks. "Raise your hand if you think the melody comes first." A smattering of hands inch up. "Raise your hands if you think the lyrics come first." The audience wants to please him. They know he is a lyricist. They think they have given the right answer. Hands shoot up this time. "You're all wrong," he barks. "The phone call comes first."

The phone call comes first? What is this man saying? That music is subject to the vagueries of the marketplace? That one commits the sacred act of writing in response to a commercial need? That art responds to commerce?

Yep. That's what it sounded like to me.

Sammy Cahn may not be Beethoven, and his voice and work may not survive through the centuries, but he sure seemed to have led a charmed and stimulating life. Can I possibly be getting to a time in life where the accolades of "artist" and "genius" and "timeless treasure" seem to cost too much next to the opportunity to live a simple, free life that makes a contribution?

Yep. That's what it sounds like to me.

High Finance

I love to go out for breakfast. It's the one meal I feel most free to indulge in wherever I am. I like the choices on the breakfast menu. And I like the idea that it is almost always affordable.

When we were going cross-country in 1971 for five weeks, camping nightly in a canvas tent, we would often stop for a luxurious breakfast at places with china cups and linen napkins to treat ourselves. That fond recollection lingers.

I can have breakfast almost anywhere I want.

So why should I get so caught on unit-price analysis?

One of the places I go for breakfast regularly, serves great pancakes. A shortstack of two pancakes costs $1.75. A regular order with three pancakes costs $2.95. Here's where logic lets me down. I would like to eat three pancakes. Logic tells me that pancakes one and two in the shortstack cost 87 1/2 cents each, and pancake three costs $1.20. Logic won't let me order the third pancake.

Logic also argues that the law of diminishing returns tells me that I get my primary pleasure from the first two pancakes and that the third, most expensive pancake, actually yields the least pleasure. I order the shortstack.

My friend, Dick, says I'm addicted to efficiency. I guess I'd rather see myself as a sucker for logic.

WRESTLING WITH THE ANGEL

We sit across from each other at a luxurious treat—a date for Saturday morning breakfast. The clicking of the spoons stirring coffee is the only sound for several minutes. Luxury turning slightly tense.

This is one of those times when my husband and I are having a small disagreement. The topic—how to spend the next 10 years of our lives.

The disagreement is "small" because we are doing ok day-to-day. We are enjoying our life as we live it. We just don't feel in harmony about where we are going.

In our years together, we have tried to trade off having a regular job. First, I was the stable income while he was a free-lance electronics designer. Then, he went full-time and we realized how tough it was to keep a household together with two regular jobs. So I became the free-lancer.

The "regular job" person has four major responsibilities:
- operate in the 50 to 60-hour a week working world
- keep us in health insurance
- bring home a regular paycheck
- expend the vital and non-recoverable essence of each day in the service of the organization ("spending the best years of my life in this place...").

The "free lance" person has five minor responsibilities:
- produce some income every year
- stay home and available for every repair or delivery person necessary to the household

- do all errands that can only be done during regular business hours
- handle all family, business, and social responsibilities (cards, gifts, scheduling)
- listen to the "regular job" partner complain about "spending the best years of my life...".

It's time for us to switch. I should go full-time, and he should go free-lance. We "sort-of" agreed to this system 10 years ago.

I have a better idea. My business evolves slowly into promise. The income is still erratic and uncertain, but I can show progress. Why can't we both be free-lance now? But he's become more security conscious in the last 10 years. "What if we can't make the mortgage payment? What if we can't pay our bills? What if we can't live here anymore?"

We talk about it. I ask, "What if we had a six-month cushion in savings and knew we could go that long before you had to earn anything? What if we move to a less expensive part of the country? What if we think of twenty choices so you don't feel so trapped?"

"No, I'd be worried the whole time about what happens next."

"You know, if I did take a full-time job, we'd hardly ever spend any waking hours together and, when we did, I'd be a zombie like you are now."

"I know...and yet..."

And so it goes...the interplay of freedom and responsibility. The wrestling of loving cooperation. The struggle of two adults to spend their energy and essence in a life that has a meaning beyond the steady paycheck. The shifting demographics of our national future being individually negotiated over one more specific breakfast table on one more Saturday morning.

RECESSION STATISTICS, CALAMITIES, AND FAMILIES

"It's a boy!" My sister just called from San Diego to tell us that my niece, Carol, had her baby. 9 pounds 15-and-three quarter ounces. Full head of black hair. Almost as if he knew the video camera would roll soon, and he wanted to look the best—a genetic trait he gets from our side of the family.

Burley, the proud father, wants to call him Moose. Moose Mullins. I doubt that Carol will agree. But that's his name for today. Kim and Megan, the baby's older sisters, are "over the moon about him."

One year ago, Carol and Burley lived in Willowick, Ohio, just east of Cleveland. They had a lovely home on three acres. Their girls were thriving on life in the countryside. Kim, 10, has cerebral palsy. She moves more actively and more easily in the wide open spaces. Megan, 2, brims with mischievous energy and rambunctiousness. Burley worked as a manager-in-training, and Carol had a responsible position with a national firm. Carol was the primary breadwinner because she had been at her job for 7 years, promoted frequently.

The family was pleased when they realized a new baby was on the way. Just after Christmas, Carol took a few days off work. While she was at home, she got word that she was being laid off. No more job, no more benefits, no paid maternity leave.

They were a recession calamity just waiting to happen.

Carol is half Irish, half Italian. She can tend to fluctuate between joyful and morose in the best of times—a heritage from both her lines. I avoided calling her when I first heard the news because I didn't know if I was strong enough to lend much support if she was deeply down.

I finally called, and she sounded chipper. "We have our house on the market. I got a call 10 minutes ago from somebody who is coming over to look at my car. We're selling everything. We're packing up and heading west. We can stay with mom and Bob for a while and get on our feet again."

"Carol, I'm amazed. You sound so great. I know you love that house, and the girls seem so happy and settled. How are you keeping your spirits up?"

"I think about it like this, Aunt Margie. Both sets of my grandparents immigrated to this country. My new step-father is an immigrant. All these people left everything to venture into a new country where they hoped to survive and maybe prosper."

"But still, I'm so impressed with your spirit and determination. Where are you getting this vision?"

"Everybody in the family said they would make room for us. Brian said we could come there, Frank and Jody invited us to Atlanta, Mary T offered to come out and help us. I figured with all the support from our families, I'd be a wimp to stay depressed. And besides, Aunt Margie, I think about what you've done in the last few years. You've accomplished a lot."

The rest of the call blurs in my mind. I keep forgetting that I've scaled some mountains recently. Once I'm past one, I keep focusing on where I'm going and forget to look back.

I am moved to find that someone I love has been looking on, cheering for me, and taking heart where she needed it.

It is now six months later. Carol, Burley, and family live with the Kennedys in San Diego. They are scheduled to open a small business there this week. And Carol just had a baby boy.

Welcome to the world, Moose Mullins. You are part of a family.

A Penny For Your Habits

I want to change a habit. I know the resources I need:
A goal
10 pennies
2 pockets
a calendar
21 days

Five simple resources can make a change in my life. It's not
entirely accurate that I want to change a habit. I would rather
my husband and stepson change. And it's nearly a metaphysi-
cal certitude that they are not going to do that.

Living with them, I have developed a spicy vocabulary. I catch
myself thinking and sometimes saying language that may
distress my clients or others around me. I don't necessarily
consider this "bad language." It's just that I probably don't
need to use it to get my point across. And it may tend to
distract listeners from my ideas.

So who is in charge of the words in my brain and my mouth?
I'm so fond of language and listening that I tend to pick up
the accents and words of those around me. I'd love to blame
this recent shift on my men and their lockerroom vocabulary.
Instead, I gather my resources and tackle the job myself.

My goal - to eliminate the impulse to use language that may
distress or distract listeners.

The rest of the resources work like this. I mark the 21 days on
my calendar because that is the usually accepted length of
time it takes to break the hold of a habit.

On day one, I start out with the ten pennies in pocket one. Every time I say something I wish I hadn't, I move one penny to the second pocket. If I have to move all ten pennies, I make a tally mark on that date in my calendar. At the end of each day, I count the tally marks and the pennies in pocket two and record my number. I am building awareness.

On day eight, I start out again with the ten pennies in pocket one. Each time I say something I regret, I move one penny. Each time I catch myself and substitute a more acceptable expression, I move a penny back to pocket one. My objective is to never make a tally mark in the calendar this week. I am building options.

On day fifteen, I start out with all the pennies in pocket two. At the end of each hour, I reflect back and decide if I have been comfortable with my language. If so, I move one penny to pocket one. My objective is to move all the pennies by the time I've been awake for ten hours. I mark in my calendar the number of hours I've been awake when I move the last penny. I am reinforcing better choices.

If the process hits a snag anywhere along the path, I change the rules. It's my game anyway. I'm the winner and/or the loser. It works with all sorts of issues from changing eating habits to changing thinking habits to changing driving habits to changing exercise habits.

Sounds like a perfect process. I start tomorrow!

PERSONAL REFLECTIONS

My financial situation now...

To me, money represents...

The most financially rich I have ever felt was...

My salary at my first job was...

The amount of money I think would be enough is...

Something I can learn or do to command more money in my career is...

The toughest time I have had with money is...

When I want to indulge myself, I...

My financial affairs (will, insurance, portfolio)...

If I die, my family...

Financial plans for my retirement...

Someone who does a good job with their financial resources is...

If I won the lottery...

CHAPTER SEVEN

Community

DELIGHTS, DILEMMAS & DECISIONS

COMMUNITY

People with balance in community feel involved, connected, contributing. They recognize that we prosper as families, groups, businesses, communities, states, nations, and as one world.

They are developing a greater sense of what Adlai Stevenson called "our spaceship earth." They understand that some resources are expendable, that economies are interdependent, and that hunger and disease threaten us all.

This understanding leads them to get involved and make a contribution. Sometimes they are overwhelmed at the number and urgency of issues that need their time, energy, or money. They resist the temptation to toss their hands up in despair at the complexity of the needs.

First, they study issues of particular importance to them. Then, they identify how they can have an impact. Next, they contribute in a way most appropriate to them.

Art Gunther, past chief executive officer of Pizza Hut, focused his concern on reading problems. This issue came to him as he struggled with his own son's reading difficulties. "What can I do to help him AND the kids coming after him?" Gunther asked. The end result was a reading incentive program offering pizza awards to kids whose teacher verified that they had reached their goals.

In the second year of the program, 288,000 classrooms participated, and 12 million kids ate 30 million dollars worth of free pizza. Art Gunther became one more person making his unique contribution toward shaping the future of his national community.

What's important in this story is not that Gunther used his resources to have a big impact. What's important is that he used his own uniquely-available resources creatively in service of a specific goal. He saw a need, and he did something.

People with balance in community don't necessarily try to fix the universe. They start with themselves, their family, their area. They use their own unique skills, talents, and resources to address a specific goal.

They don't worry about macro-mending the world; they are micro-mending their place in it.

INSTANT INTIMACY

Something amazing happens when I write or speak the way I have in this book. Whenever I tell what is most personal, most deeply secret to me, people come up afterwards and say "That's exactly how I feel. Thanks for saying it out loud." The words change. The details differ. But the melody lingers.

For a while, I treasured those assurances and the occasional confidences people shared with me. Then I realized something. When you tell me those responses, you and I feel good for a brief time, and then we don't cross paths again.

If anything you have read has opened any wellspring inside you, talk about your feelings with your spouse, children, a friend or colleague. Take whatever door has opened and share it with someone significant in your life who is available to you on a regular basis. That person may respond with her own thoughts or may just listen appreciatively to ideas you don't usually express.

What are you waiting for anyway? So often we weigh the risk of opening up to others. How often do we weigh the opposite risk. What happens if you don't tell your story, your feelings, your song?

You do not know how long you will have this person in your life. Tell him NOW what you are feeling.

I'm not shutting the door on talking to you myself, just hoping you go through your own door with the people important to you. Sometimes we lack the courage or the skills to start such a conversation. We have lost the art of probing conversation. We talk glibly about what we "do," where we've been, our health, what the family is up to. And we talk very little about who we are.

And sometimes such a conversation starts with a question. Try some of these:

- When are you most yourself?
- Describe a time when, with ease and joy, you had a sense of great accomplishment.
- What is there about you that makes you unique?
- What do you think about when you wake up at 4 a.m.?
- Who are your heroes?
- What do you want said about your life at your 100th birthday party?

Lifeguards — A Short Season

In June, they're fresh.
In July, they're frazzled.
In August, they're terminally bored.

That's a typical one-year career of a lifeguard at our community pool.

They start the season fresh and dewy. They have a job that puts them around sun, water, and other kids their age. And they make money.

Then reality nibbles away at them. They constantly need to yell at the kids to halt the running and pushing, they clean up after water fights in the dressing room, they rescue a toddler's popsicle from falling into the baby pool, they watch one of the adults swim until closing time and head belatedly for the shower room. They wipe off and arrange the furniture every day, and they clean the bathrooms every night. They help at swim meets and diving lessons. The freshness fades. The frazzle chips away.

By August, they are calling across to each other, "Are you gonna stick it out till Labor Day?"

"No, I'm going to Ocean City and get some sun."

Yet, always, a small few keep their spark. They smile, greet the regulars, chat. They seem to look forward to getting back to school, yet they enjoy today, too.

I empathize with those who fade. They have so much to put up with. But I treasure those who keep their shine. They find so much to respond to.

I guess I'm a lifeguard, too. With my own life and lives to guard. With my own lifelong season for making that same choice.

ASKING THE RIGHT QUESTIONS

Out on my morning walk. I spot a familiar face coming down the path from the other direction. A woman I know casually.

We stop for a rare chat, and she looks down fondly at her puppy on the leash. The german shepherd stands by obediently as we talk. I remember seeing them so often taking this same walk through the neighborhood. The fit woman with her long, healthy stride; the maturing puppy, vigilantly alert. This is one of the few dogs in the area who is always on a leash. Now it makes sense.

"He's in training as a seeing-eye dog. I keep him about 14 months, taking him into shopping malls, grocery stores, along city streets and wooded paths. I get him used to being a part of everyday life. I hate taking him into malls. He wants to react to everything." She glances at him indulgently as if he were a mischievous child.

"I get him ready for two review processes. After he passes the second screening, he and his blind partner are matched for personality—you'd almost think it was a dating service! They go through residential training together at a converted motel up in Pennsylvania . I get to be there for their graduation. It's a great feeling, watching them walk down that aisle together. It does feel almost like watching one of my kids graduating."

"How did you get involved in doing this?" I ask.

"I put a dog through quarantine on my first trip over from England when my husband was posted to Washington. I swore I'd never do that again. But I'd be in the US about 18 months at a time, and I missed having my dog. At that time, I thought my only choices were to go without a dog or to take a risk of having to abandon one every time I moved to or from England.

"A friend suggested there might be a simple solution. Seeing-eye dogs need loving and disciplined training lasting about as long as my typical assignment in the area. I started working with this group, and this is the sixth dog I've trained."

After a few more exchanges we go our separate ways into our separate days.

I think about her a lot today. How often do I see only one or two alternatives in a difficult situation. Why do I assume there are only a few ways a dilemma can be addressed? How often does my lack of seeing a "simple solution," keep me from finding one? How can I start to "see" more widely, more wisely?

I remember one of the standard questions from creative problem solving. "If there were an ideal solution to this problem, what would it look like, feel like, taste like, smell like, sound like?" The best way to start toward an ideal solution is to see that one is possible or to imagine in vivid detail what it would be like if it were possible. Then make it so. Discover or invent pathways to possibility. Cindy has done exactly that.

Behind Every "Yes" There's a "No" or Two

I like to say "yes".

"Can I come by for some help on this speech?"   Yes

"Want to come over and join us for some carry-in dinner?"
   Yes

"Will you arrange the speaker for March 17th?"   Yes

I like to say "yes", and I try to realize that every time I do, I'm saying no to something else. I'm saying "no" to getting the laundry done and making the week go more smoothly. I'm saying "no" to some exercise which could boost my energy. I'm saying "no" to private time with my family. I'm saying "no" to a quiet walk at sunset through my favorite woods.

I have three stages of "yes"—relished, reserved, and reluctant.

1. The relished "yes" is for things I don't even need to weigh or evaluate. An option appears, my atoms and fibers sing YES. This type of "yes" brims out of me, makes any effort easy, and nearly always produces good results. I respond this way to questions like:
    "Do you want some raspberries?"
    "Would you like to sign the contract now?"
    "How about a walk?"

2. The reserved "yes" is for something I need to consider and weigh before deciding. I evaluate whether the benefits will be

worth the investment. I like to be sure the yield will be high. This type of "yes" takes a few minutes to consider. I sometimes feel ambiguous even as I am doing what I agreed to do. It usually produces acceptable results. Questions may include:

"Can you FAX us a proposal today?"

"Will you bring some potato salad?"

"How about taking the truck through inspection tomorrow?"

3. The reluctant "yes" is for those things I know I am supposed to do even though I may fight them. This "yes" feels like it is stealing my time for no reward other than the avoidance of guilt. This "yes" costs me a lot. I sabotage my own performance of the promise. The outcome rarely satisfies anyone.

"Will you be block captain for the heart association this year?"

"Will you show up at 7:30 to show support for the new officers?"

"Can you drive me out to the airport right after work today?"

In categories one and two, I go gleefully or discover satisfaction along the way. It is easy to do the task. It is easy to do a good job. In category three, I go grudgingly and please no one.

The year I did agree to be block captain for a fund drive, I waited till the very last day of the drive. I went to every house praying that nobody would answer my knock. I left the reply envelopes and hoped people might contribute. I don't think I contributed well to my community. I don't think the drive benefitted from my compromised, reluctant efforts.

I learned from that experience. I now volunteer my services where I can say "yes" with relish. I joined the resource pool of the United Way/United Black Fund. When they call on me for video coaching, I give gladly.

And, when I say "no" to the next fund drive, I am saying "yes" to my family, my exercise, my work. I am even saying "yes" to the drive which is now free to find someone who will live up to their commitment more generously than I was able to do.

Simple words "yes" and "no". Why does it take me so long to keep them clear?

GHOSTS

Cleaning out my closet for the Goodwill the other day, it hit me. Everything in this closet I wanted once. I thought about most of these acquisitions, I shopped for them, I wore them rarely or often. I tired of them, or they went out of style, or my size changed, or my work patterns changed. They hang here.

Unused, unappreciated, weighing down the bar that sags in its journey from wall to wall. I don't bother to clear them away. I don't bother to reclaim the room they are stealing from me. I don't bother to deselect them from my life. I push them from one side to the other to find my still-current favorites obscured by these ghosts of past preferences.

I clear them out. Goodwill welcomes the donation, mends what was broken. They recycle my things to a new life of serving someone else who wants them. I feel refreshed, stripped of surplus, cleaner, leaner.

Can the same be true of all the other material things I "own?" Do I still want or need those fondue forks? Are there any things to eliminate from my house?

And what about the people I have collected? Now I'm in a danger zone. How could I consider deselecting people? Is there anyone to eliminate from my life?

At the center of it all are my thoughts. Are they still serving me? Are my beliefs supporting what I want to accomplish in my life? Are there any thoughts to eliminate from my mind? Is there any Goodwill to send thoughts to for mending?

WINTER HAYRIDE

I head up to the parking lot at 7:20. It's dark, starry, and so cold my nostrils prickle inside. The tractor and hay wagon await. Cars converge. We spill from the cars decked in our warm winter woolies and hats. Heartier souls climb aboard the hay wagon. Fragile folk follow in cars.

Some kind person has organized the list and notified the homeowners so we know what houses we will visit tonight. She has also provided songsheets, though it is usually too dark to read them. It wouldn't matter. We never seem to agree on the correct wording for the verse of "We Wish You A Merry Christmas."

We carol the first house. A couple who moved in only a month ago. They hear our songs, accept our small welcome gift, and join us for the rest of the caroling.

At the next house, the pajama-clad children join their parents at the doorway. The kids cling to their parents in the glow from inside the house as they gaze in wonder at eighteen strangers singing "Frosty" on their front lawn. The family invites us in for fragrant mulled cider and cookies. We welcome them to their first Christmas in the neighborhood.

At the next house, the owners enjoy the songs and invite us in to tour the room they are adding to their new home. And so it goes. Four more houses. Four more families new to the area being greeted for the holidays.

Do I participate for the fun of the hayride, the caroling itself, or for the gracious social afterwards at Molly's house? Do we do it out of holiday spirit or because we are eager to see what the newcomers are doing to their homes? Do we adapt to different traditions or beliefs as the area grows more culturally rich and diverse? Yes and no.

For me, it's a Norman Rockwell night. An old-fashioned no-hassle evening of song, stars, and frosty breath. A crisp, uncomplicated slice of the real holiday season.

Encounter With a Hero

This is one of the highlights of my year. I heard Charles Schultz, creator of Snoopy and the Peanuts cartoon strip, speak to our conference night before last. Schultz told a wonderful story about how he got his first book published. The point of his story was that you have no way of knowing which of your loves will lead you to what you want in life.

It seems Schultz is a devoted admirer of Beethoven. Out of that love, Schultz created the character Schroeder who debuted in the cartoon strip playing on a miniature piano. Without even thinking about it, Schultz used the actual opening notes of Beethoven's 29th Symphony in the cartoon panel.

Another Beethoven admirer, who happened to be in publishing in New York, noticed that this crazy cartoonist way out in California actually seemed to know classical music. He observed the strip for a month, delighting in the character of Schroeder. He contacted Schultz and offered him a contract for his first book.

The story entertained and inspired me. I wanted to tell Schultz that, but there were so many admirers I let the moment go.

This morning, I spot a distinguished older man walking all alone across the hotel grounds as I start my walk and swim. We share a cordial "Good morning." After he passes, I kick myself. "That was Charles Schultz, all alone. You could have thanked him for his inspiration." I chide myself. I spend the first part of my walk thinking of all the things I might have said to him and reviewing how much I'd gotten from his talk.

In one of those amazing gifts some days bring, he comes back alone as I relish my cool morning swim. He pauses poolside. "Been at this since I saw you?" he begins.

We talk for several minutes. I do thank him. We laugh comfortably and casually. We talk about family origins. I tell him that I got married to get to the front of the alphabet. I liked being an "M" as a schoolkid, and it's fun to be a "B" as a grown up. I slide back into the water as he leaves.

I lay back and churn my feet to create a fountain of spray. I'm a little kid having just met a living breathing hero. He's totally gentle and charming and helps me believe in being nice. I hope he might steal my line about marrying to get to the front of the alphabet. Isn't that the kind of thing Lucy might say as she dreams of being grown up and married?

I stay in a glow all day. Describing this encounter is the centerpiece of my call home that night.

Does it really matter that I find out the next morning that I have been mistaken? That it isn't Schultz I have talked to, but one of the professors connected to the conference who is also a delightful person? So now I've had the fun of an enjoyable encounter, a rich day of reveling in a special event, and a laugh at myself for a harmless, helpful mistake. Thanks again, Charles Schultz!

WALKING WITH FROST AND ESCHER

Walking down the unfamiliar streets of cities I travel to on business, I get a taste of the road not taken. Who would I be if I lived here?

What if I lived in this Ann Hathaway cottage near the ocean in Santa Barbara? Who am I, living in this house with the "fixer" car out front in Indianapolis, Indiana? Who am I, living in the penthouse condo stacked in this luxurious filing cabinet of a high-rise building in Marco Island, Florida? Who am I in this whitewashed enclave in Costa Rica?

Is that me heading through the doorway of the Tudor house with today's mail in my hand, or is this me watching as I walk by wondering which life I'm in.

A harmless distraction, as long as I can smile at the end of it and be just as pleased to be heading home to my modest comfort in Maryland.

Just The Way My Mind Works

Quiet and unassuming, he sits across the table at the hotel restaurant. We've been here 35 minutes and haven't been waited on. He is easy to ignore.

And he is brilliant.

Singlehandedly, in the 70's, he designed a major telecommunications system that dwarfed a parallel system the engineers at a giant international firm had been working on for years. Equipment built from his design handles most of the long-distance calls made today, so you, also, are the unaware beneficiary of his brainpower. The company he worked for at the time started modestly as an R and D firm. They went through a clouded and inauspicious public stock offering in 1980, and, today, they do over 800 million dollars a year in business. His design is still their central product.

The point is, the man is brilliant.

And, as we sit at breakfast talking over a business deal, he interrupts to ask a question. "How does your mind work?" Without expecting an answer, he goes on to explain that he has a lot of trouble writing. "I'm a pretty good writer if I have plenty of time. I get some thoughts down, work them over several times till they make sense, and finally polish them. It takes forever. I guess it's just that I don't think in words at all. I never think in sentences. I think in abstract images, and they are so hard to translate into words. It feels like there's something wrong with the way I think. I guess it's just the way my mind works."

AARGH. Here is a person who works in conceptual shorthand at multiple levels in total mathmatical abstraction. He sees the end and the totality all at the same time in constant three-dimensional streams of millions of interrelated units of information. And he's apologizing for the way his mind works.

When do we get it through our heads that each of us has different gifts? If we could only unlock the secret of how to discover and harness each separate one of those gifts and blend them finally in unison, we might begin a true civilization.

I don't know, it's just the way my mind works.

WHERE DID I LEARN THAT?

I can't swim. I can move through the water without drowning and stay in there a long time if I want to, but my form is terrible. I never seem to trust that I'll be able to get the next breath. When I try to swim correctly, there's always hair or wavelets or something else making me feel blinded, choking, helpless. So I chop through the refreshing water with my neck half stiff so I can stay in control of that next breath. I move from one end of the pool to the other, half suspecting that the callow young lifeguard is smiling inwardly at my ineptitude.

As I turn at the other end of the pool, I transform myself into a relaxed floater, moving swiftly or serenely, as I choose, back to my starting point. Then, I flip over and churn my way back, earning my right to float again. I do this for half an hour or so, getting entirely lost in thoughts and sensations in the process. I'm not sure why I impose this pattern on my play. Why do I mix the "discipline" and the relaxation? All I know is that it usually works. It gives me back to the moment and back to myself.

Of course, the fact that I can't be in the sun and usually wait till 6 or 7 p.m. to swim helps because the pool is usually nearly empty by then.

So where did I learn this skill of floating? Where did this lifelong gift of replenishment come from? I think back to Martha Shriner at South Lake in Indiana. I must have been about 10, my younger sister, about 8. Over the years, we had been to the lake a few times and had seen the bigger kids swimming. We still managed to have fun playing and fighting in the water, a break from doing those same activities back on 14th Street.

Martha is dating our big brother, Conn. They are in college. We are in awe of their sophistication.

"Come on, Margaret Ann, this one is called the 'dead man's' float. You just lean over, face down into the water and hold your breath. You won't sink, I promise. Here, I'll put my hand under your stomach."

I try it. It works! I am in control of myself in the water—and I'm not touching the ground!
Of course, I won't use this particular technique for long because I like breathing.

"Now try the same thing on your back. Lie back, I'll put my hand under your back . Relax your neck. Feel the muscles going slack. Relax. Trust the water to hold you up. That's it. Keep on floating. Now, open your eyes and see the sky."

It works again. Another world opens up.

Funny. Of all the learning I've done in a full and busy life, I don't always remember who helped me learn the important things. It pleases me to think of Martha today.

Thirty some years later, I thank her again in my mind as I float, as I smell the honeysuckle down toward the end of the pool, as the azure blue sky opens in front of my eyes. As I relax my neck, as I feel the muscles going slack, as I trust the water, as it holds me.

FINE TUNING THE DESTINATION

My friend swears this is a true story. She gets on a
plane in Los Angeles, and a young man sits down next to her.
He immediately falls asleep and stays asleep for two hours. As
he wakes, he stretches, rubs his eyes, and yawns. "Gosh, it
seems like I've been asleep for a long time. How much longer
till we get to Oakland?"

"Oakland?" she responds, "This plane is headed for
Auckland!"

What a small nuance, what a colossal consequence. But how
often do I do the same thing? My colleague says, "We need to
build the business." I hear modest growth, he means massive
campaign. Oakland/Auckland. My husband says, "Why don't
we try to plan a vacation?" I hear a quiet retreat, he means Las
Vegas. Oakland/Auckland. A friend says, "Why don't we do
something special for Jan's birthday?" I hear a massage, Alice
means find her an antique. Oakland/Auckland.

This isn't always cured by being sure I heard the words correctly. Sometimes I have to ask my communication partner
what those words mean.

It's so nice when we both land on the continent we were
heading for.

Personal Reflections

The issue facing the world that most disturbs me is...

The kinds of projects I have been involved in in the past are...

The kind of contribution I most like to make is...

When I hear myself described as a "global citizen," I feel...

Issues like conservation and environment...

If I were awarding a prize for community contribution, it would go to...

The issues I think will be most important 5 years from now are...

I think more money should be spent on...

Something I don't hesitate to contribute to...

A time when I have benefitted from the concern of my community was...

The kind of environment or setting where I'd like to spend my retirement...

CHAPTER EIGHT

Self

SELF

People with balance in self feel accepting, respecting, and reflecting. They can say to themselves honestly, "I am who I am and I do what I can."

They accept their strengths and their snags. Though they focus on improvement, they appreciate who they are now and how they got that way. They give themselves credit for their accomplishments and forgive themselves for their failures and lapses.

They resist smug self-satisfaction. Instead they take risks, challenge themselves, and move forward.

They spend time alone. Not hiding behind a book or television to avoid thinking. They reflect on their lives, their convictions, their philosophy, their direction. They may take walks alone, exercise alone, or travel alone occasionally.

Or they can follow William Stafford's advice in the poem "Freedom."

> "Freedom is not following a river, or following
> a river if you want to. It's deciding now by what
> happens now."

He goes on to advise that not everyone feels free, but you can usually feel free if you get up at four in the morning when nobody else is around. This can be a time to reflect. This can be freedom.

They keep the past and the future in their hearts, and live vividly in the present. They have boundaries and boundlessness in different areas of their thoughts. They hold abundance in their minds. They believe in brimming over with life. They protect this belief by monitoring the amount of bad news they elect to let into their system each day.

They laugh at themselves. They try to reduce the time between when they do something ridiculous and the time they can laugh about it. Why wait five years to let an embarrassing story become funny?

They sometimes catch themselves singing, humming, whistling spontaneously. Unconscious music flows from them in the car, in the shower.

They feel moved by life. They sometimes have that lurch in the stomach that signifies both their separateness and their connectedness.

They have a vision of the future, and they take positive steps to create the reality, while enjoying the effort and the rewards of every day.

I Am Grateful For a Stepson

Was it the year Del was 6 and I was 8? What I remember is that my sister and I got tiny baby chicks for Easter. They were so small that their sounds were almost bigger than their bodies. They were soft.

They were like reverse dandelions. Dandelions start a hearty yellow and soften into wafting filaments of white, borne on the breeze. The chicks started pale, soft, and white and moved toward yellow each day.

Bigger pets in our household always seemed to belong to the bigger kids in the family. Del and I were delighted to have babies of our own to tend. We even got to keep them in our room.

Del was always the one to take care of any creatures who were wounded or seemed to need attention. We always knew that she was a natural nurturer, a natural mom. I kept my distance. Maybe I knew that mom wanted me to consider nursing as a career, and I was rebelling even then. Del was the primary guardian of the chicks, and I, the older, was her assistant.

The chicks would chirp at night, waking us up. Del and I would slip out of our twin beds and go over to their box. In the morning, we would wake up on the linoleum floor. About the third night we thought of a better idea. We could bring them into bed with us, keep ourselves and them warmer, and take better care of them.

We moved the beds together, lay down on opposite sides like parentheses facing each other, the chicks in the enclosure between us. We stayed awake and played with them for a long time. Finally, we slept.

We woke to find the chicks smothered by our small child bodies. We weren't big or powerful, but we could kill something smaller than a fist. We had protected and loved them to death.

Prayers didn't help, tears didn't help. Even mom and dad didn't help. I don't remember whether they made us go to school that day. I don't remember whether we buried the chicks. I don't remember any other Easter pets. What I do know is that my stomach is tight writing this.

And I haven't had children.

ALIEN MIRRORS

The mirror in my bathroom at home is my friend. Over the years, we have taught each other light and angles that allow us to coexist peaceably. I don't get angry with my home mirror.

One of the biggest risks of travel is alien mirrors. Mirrors in unexpected places, in unflattering or merely unfamiliar light . Mirrors positioned so as to reflect parts of my body I don't usually study. Mirrors that give perfectly objective feedback.

Woody Allen says that we're the only ones who don't know what the backs of our ears look like. Strangers on elevators and buses see the backs of our ears. I live in comfortable distance from that reality.

Video is a variation on the alien mirror. When I see myself on tape, I am surprised. I am older, heavier, more gawky on video. My voice is higher, less authoritative.

Usually, my picture of what I look like is based on that rested face I see in my familiar morning mirror. Or the business portrait in my press kit. Those faces aren't grimacing or moving as much as the one in the alien mirror.

Occasionally, there is a grace-note in such unfamiliar self-sightings. Sometimes the sight of myself hurrying through a day reminds me to slow down and enjoy this slice of eternity. Sometimes the sighting gives me a gentle grooming hint.

And sometimes I am struck and stopped. To seem to be a picture, signed in the corner by my father.

COBWEBS

I open the oven door today and see the round pizza pan, covered neatly with aluminum foil. The part of the image that distresses me is the three grizzled pieces of pizza it still holds. We heated them up for a hurried dinner five nights ago and forgot them.

Two of the items I encounter in the refrigerator today in recycled food containers are UFOs—Unidentifiable Foodlike Objects. These are bad enough that I pitch even the containers.

Trying to make very simple chocolate icing for brownies, I break an almost indestructible pyrex bowl. The shattered glass makes a pretty pattern on the floor. I sit out on the front porch for five minutes looking at clouds and eating ice cream before I can make myself clean it up.

Last week, during exercise, I watched the first three hours of a miniseries we had taped from television. Part of me is embarrassed to even admit this. My husband accidentally taped over the rest of the show. The part of me that loves TV trash is really mad at the part of him that didn't check the tape. And the other part of me is mad at myself that I care.

Neglect seems to ooze from everything I touch today. All these problems seem petty—almost funny. I'm good at real challenges. I handle disasters skillfully. It's the little things that make me leak. My vitality and resilience are on hold.

I think I need more balance.

Toys for the Mind

Words are my friends. I've been in love with words, language, reading, writing since I can remember. This is a hobby that takes very little equipment, doesn't require teammates, schedules, registration fees, championships, or uniforms. It is independent of weather, location, time of day, and rules.

So I've made up a few rules of my own.

Only 12 favorite words at a time. These are usually words I like because of the melody of their pronunciation or because of the light in them, the spirit they call forth from me. Or for reasons I don't need to understand. My current list of words and one impressionistic facet of why I like each one includes:

Hyacinth	the early fragrance of spring
Core	getting to essence
Perpendicular	an absolute, no-nonsense, definable reality
Translucent	the interplay of seeing and hiding and sensing; light/shade
Leprechaun	the kiss of whimsey
Tintinabulation	the sound of bells
Flame	so much power in such a small word
Quicken	energy, yeastiness, growth, birth
Yearning	to reach, to harness desire to move beyond limits
Gamatz, gamatz	an Armenian term, slowly, slowly
(And others)	

Once a word becomes an OD (Overused darling), I cut it from my list.

Prudent was a word I was warming up to until it became a buzz word for government policy and a favorite joke of Bush imitators.

I like having to choose. I like going back to revisit old favorites. Words are toys for my mind. Toys that can be held, shaken, sung, yelled, whispered, written.

I treasure the humor in words.
If I can regret something, do I get to gret it first?
Like comic Wright, could I put a humidifier and a dehumidifier in the same room and watch them fight it out?

Barnaby Conrad opens the Santa Barbara Writer's Conference each year with a challenge to those attending to come up with the worst opening sentence. "Write a sentence that will be guaranteed to stop a reader in his tracks, put your book down, and never read another word," he challenges on opening night.

Offerings include:

"His tongue tentatively explored each syllable, using it as an experimental drawbridge into the word beyond."

"Seeing him cradle the infant you wouldn't guess he'd been captive and dirty, don't-brush-your-teeth-dirty, for 43 days."

"Here, then, is the detailed saga and thumbnail sketches on each member of the wide and varied Smythe (with a Y) clan ranging all the way from baby Snookums Smythe to Lady Millicent Smythe-Cavarocchi to our illustrious Senator Sam (Sultan of Succotash) Smythe."

Conrad may have a fiendish strategy here. By toying around with what makes a truly dreadful opening, we almost invariably stumble across some powerful secrets for writing a good one.

BOUNDARIES

I read once that you can't go to the doctor for your kids. Even if you'd rather have the appendectomy for them, it won't work.

When I love someone, I lose track of where they stop and I begin. The boundaries fade.

Sometimes, I think I am in charge of the universe. Amazing. I can't get upstairs to organize my attic, and I think I am the mainstay of civilization.

A friend told me once of a note that had been placed anonymously on her desk. It read.

> Dear Beverly,
>
> I think I can get along
>
> without your help
>
> for the next 24 hours—
>
> and maybe longer.
>
> Give yourself a well-deserved break.
>
> Signed,
>
> *God*

DELIGHTS, DILEMMAS & DECISIONS

Life Teaches Me Something Every Day if I Listen

"The pipe's busted and she's inside the cement slab. Gonna have to bring in the jackhammers..."

The plumber's eyes gleam with expectation as mine dull with dread. On two accounts. Four adults will now share the one remaining bathroom. And I can imagine the bill for all this.

We noticed the leaking sound about five days ago. The first plumber came out, looked around, and confessed he couldn't find it. Did we want to start tearing out the walls and floor, track down the source, and call him back to do the actual plumbing?

We agree reluctantly, spend six hours on Sunday demolishing small sections of the bathroom. My husband actually admits that he took out the floor under the vanity first, not because he thought the leak could be there, but because that area would be easier to repair if the leak had been there. That's a logic I can live with.

For five days, we have kept the water to the whole house shut off except for "urgent needs." It is like being in California during the drought when polite signs even in luxury hotel bathrooms remind me to "use water" only when necessary. About twice a day, we turn the water on, take quick showers, wash dishes, flush toilets, and fill the jugs to get us through the next twelve hours.

We adopt the philosophy that we are camping in a great national park, in a luxurious tent with all the amenities except water. It's playful for a while.

And, now that we have found the leak, the plumber is saying: "It may be two weeks before we can get to your job...and I guess it'd take about two weeks to finish it."

I roll my eyes to the ceiling. Why did we buy an older house subject to such breakdowns? Why had we encouraged Chuck to move back home for a while?

We call another plumber. He's coming tomorrow. Enough of summer camp before a tough day at work! We're under attack by the earwigs, inch-long black squirming bugs coming up out of the hole we made in the floor. Chuck found one in his toothbrush this morning. Ugh.

And it turns out that our homeowner's insurance does not cover plumbing repairs. They will, however, cover "damage to the house which is necessary for the plumber to make necessary repairs." That's going to be a significant portion of the total since we have to tear out the floor and the bottom of the ceramic shower. The financial part of the debacle is somewhat softened.

I look around me at some of the learnings of this situation.

1. I HATE inconvenience. I hate not having water. I hate "giving up" a Sunday to demolish the bathroom. I hate having a vanity and sink in my bedroom to stub my toe on as I head blindly and automatically for the bathroom which is not even functional. I hate making the phone calls to plumbers. I hate slashing my schedule to be here for the estimators and then the repair guys to show up or not. I hate making the

decisions about whether we should go through the walls, through the ceiling, through the floor. I hate juggling the billing and paperwork between us, the plumbers, the tile people, the insurance company.

Why should I hate these things so much? Do I have some belief that I'm too special or important to engage in the minor skirmishes of life? Is my humor reserve so low that I can't stay afloat with some laughter?

2. I HATE spending all this money on something practical, giving up the other options that money could have provided. And when it's all over, if we're lucky, we'll have the bathroom back the same way it was before the leak. It won't be bigger, brighter, or better. If we're lucky, it will be as good as it was. They don't even throw in a skylight for all that money. I don't like to ever be aware of the infrastructure of my house or of my life. I don't like to have to invest in maintaining or repairing anything that doesn't even show.

What do I think the money is for if not to ensure continuing ease and comfort? Isn't it good we can get the money for this? Are there any other parts of the infrastructure of my house or life that I'm now more aware of, feeling more vulnerable about, feeling more appreciative of?

3. I LOVE unusual events on occasion. One of my goals in life is to build memories—individual memories and family memories. Are we likely to remember these few weeks more vividly than we'll remember some others from this year? Will

we tease each other years from now about our reactions to the "attack of the earwigs."

There's the concept of paradox again. I like a comfortably predictable life most of the time, and I still enjoy some unexpected spice now and again. This spice is probably not so damaging in the long run. I'm just glad earwigs don't bite.

VEG-A-MATIC EYES

Clothes have never been especially important to me. That's not true. I longed for pretty clothes as a kid. At the time, I thought that if I just dressed more like the other girls they would accept me, invite me into the inner circles, help me get over being so shy.

The first new matching designer shorts and top I ever owned were a gift from a neighbor lady who lived on the alley near us. It was a Ship and Shore set of matching bermuda shorts and crop-top blouse. White with sea-green rick-rack trim and a couple of sea horses on the left side of both blouse and shorts as a design. I wore them to death, feeling very sophisticated all the while.

Today, I prefer either very casual clothes or very dressy clothes. It's that in-between stage, conservative business clothes, that I often find oppressive. I'll take sweats or sequins, and you can keep your suits.

All this gets me to a pang I had the other day at a nearby health club. I'm coming into the dressing area from a vigorous, sweaty walk. My arms are swinging along in fortitude and freedom as my baggy t-shirt ripples with my stride. I encounter three of the tennis players in their beautifully coordinated outfits and enviable grooming. Their conversation stopped, and they gave me such a look. Their bodies sent out a chorus of "What's someone dressed like that doing here?" Their eyes sliced and diced me like the famous veg-a-matic from late-night commercials.

They gave me the looks, but I gave myself the pang. I sometimes don't like to admit that I put myself back in emotional elementary school in wanting to be accepted by strangers. They bring out the veg-a-matic, but I give them the juice to plug it in!

I got past the pang very quickly. An exercise high does that for me. And I wished them well. Wished them the same vigor and buoyancy I felt from my own exercise. But those old traces are still there.

One of Those Days

I drag myself through today kicking and screaming minute to minute. "This is not the way it's supposed to be. This isn't what I had in mind."

The externals are picture perfect. A summer Sunday. Husband fixed breakfast. A walk and a swim. Visit with my sister. An easy chicken dinner baking in the oven. No special obligations or responsibilities. No special fears or anxieties.

Just this rebellious feeling all day long that no matter what I am doing in that moment, I am out of sync. And, of course, I'm part brat to feel irritated and rebellious when everything is fine. Our family is in good health. We have jobs. We are comfortable. And still it feels like nothing is right today.

Where does this come from?

Yes, there's a nagging concern about my other sister's health, a feeling of being fragmented in my current work project, a sense that I'm doing a lot of accommodating for the people around me.

Naw. I think I'm mad at myself for some work I am letting slip. When I'm mad at myself, I don't feel like I fit in my own life. Yet I smell that chicken baking in the oven and know I live here.

Maybe it's just some down time I need occasionally and often pretend not to. It happens sometimes. Now that I think about it, the best thing I can do is finish my day, go to sleep, and wake tomorrow to a fresh new beginning. Each day an opportunity to begin again. What a wonder.

CONTROL AND INDEPENDENCE

Control and independence dance through a lot of relation-ships—male and female, wife and husband, parent and child, teacher and student.

Control is the taller partner—often the male or the older one of the pair. Independence is the unquenchable partner—often the female or the younger one of the pair.

Control usually wants things to stay the way they are/the way they used to be/the way they should be. Independence wants things to move toward the way they will be/the way they can become. Control yearns for the past. Independence insists on the future.

They can both win.

Georgia O'Keefe was a struggling young artist when she met older, established, and powerful Alfred Stieglitz. Their May-December marriage of two strong-willed artists quickly em-braced the struggle between control and independence. Stieglitz insisted that they spend every summer at Lake George in an extended family setting full of life, noise, activity, and people. O'Keefe needed privacy to work. Her friend invited her to spend time in New Mexico.

Stieglitz complained bitterly. He became so upset his heart protested. "How good of life to give us a warning before exacting its final toll." He pleaded, cajoled, ordered. She packed. He resigned himself to her "desertion," and had an affair for comfort.

She returned. He appreciated the genius and the volume of work she produced in her spartan New Mexican landscape. But he hoped she would never leave him again. She determined to go again the next summer.

Finally, in gracious despair, he penned a document and asked for her signature.

"We promise to love each other forever and to always reside on the planet earth together."

Control and independence, power and latitude, the lion and the lamb, lie down together.

The Carnivore at the Vegetarian Picnic

"So, Aunt Margie, were you the black sheep?" my nephew Mark asks as we sit on his front porch watching his son Keegan keep testing gravity with a small ball.

"No," I protest too quickly. "That was Uncle Conn. He was the first to marry out of the church. The first to strike out west. He was the one who spit on your Aunt Kate's fan-club picture of Dick Contino. Conn was the official black sheep."

Later tonight, a train passing by in the early hours awoke me from a fitful sleep in an unfamiliar bed, I start to wonder. Am I the black sheep too?

The pattern emerges:
I left home the day after high school graduation to work in a strange big city.
I left the country the month after college graduation to serve two years in the Peace Corps.
I got married the first time half-way around the globe from home without a single member of my family present.
I was the first in the family to get a divorce.
I'm the only one of us who never bore children.
My second husband is from an ethnic background even more exotic than my own.
I quit a secure job at 38 to become an entrepreneur.

And in the business environment:
Hard-bitten bottom-line types see me as "human resource" focused.
Soft-bitten human resourcers see me as grindstone tough.

Fitness or spiritual specialists see me as abundantly human (flawed).

Average people see me as leaning toward wellness and spiritual values .

Those who focus on serving know I also attend to the bottom line.

Those who fix on profit see me practicing service .

I sometimes accidentally imitate the rough language of the two engineers I live with.

And I give others pause by the awe, wonder, and respect in my approach to daily marvels.

Part of me likes being the carnivore at the vegetarian picnic. Shocking people slightly. Being a softer version of the black sheep.

"Yes, Mark, I guess I am."

THE KINGDOM OF THE DARKENED KITCHEN

Daddy.

The gentle, distant giant of my childhood.

Any afternoon when I saw mom stop to apply fresh lipstick in front of the mirror between the double windows over the kitchen sink, I knew it was time for daddy to come home.

He walked half a block up 14th street from his ride with Mr. Deitz every day at 4:45. A tall man with a long stride in his grey prison uniform. He thought himself lucky to get a civil service job in the federal prison system in his early forties. He looked good to my little sister and me when we ran down the block to assault him for attention before he even got home.

Dinner is at 5 o-clock sharp. No phone calls. No visitors. Five of their eight kids are still at home.

"And what did you learn at school today, Kathleen?" Daddy asks my older sister.

"We didn't have school today, Daddy. It was a special holiday."

His face clouds, he strikes his fist on the table. "What am I paying all this good tuition for if you have so many days off school?" He pretends to thunder; we pretend to cower.

I don't remember much else about dinner conversation. We kids are always impatient to be away, squirming to get back outside. "Thank God, excuse me," we are required to say before leaving the table as polite imitation adults. Then, we have to wait for mom and dad to finish so we can clear the table and serve the tea before becoming kids again, wild, screaming, and sweating on Indiana nights as we play "all off" on Elm street.

The rule is we have to come inside "when the streetlights come on." So it 's dark as we straggle back in. The living room lamp is on. Mom is reading. The kitchen is dark. And I smell Daddy's King Edward cigar (6 cents each) and see it's red glow out in that dark kitchen. He sits there alone. In the quiet dark. He drinks a measured mug of beer from a quart bottle.

"Are you sure you washed behind your ears, Martin? Did you get the girls' elbows, Katie?" mom asks after we clean up and get into our pajamas.

I go back downstairs and say goodnight to daddy. "Goodnight, pet, don't forget to say your prayers."

Kneeling beside my narrow bed, I say my prayers. "Now I lay me down to sleep..."

Now again, years later, I think of daddy. Cigar. Small mug of beer. Alone in the quiet dark.

PERSONAL REFLECTIONS

The time I am most myself...

If I could have a board of six directors (from history, family, the arts, entertainment, fantasy, sports, living or dead) to advise me, I'd select...

The things in life I am grateful for...

Something I am working on...

The time I feel most alone...

Solitude...

My relationship with myself is...

If there were a few themes or patterns that seem to show up throughout my life, they would be...

What matters to me is...

The legacy I want to leave behind me is...

I dream of...

CHAPTER NINE

Afterglow

BALANCE AND THE THREE-LEGGED ELEPHANT

I usually have four of the seven zones in balance at any given moment. This gives me the luxury of taking them for granted and tampering with the other three. As long as the ratio stays four to three, I feel as if things are under control. The minute one of the four starts to wobble, though, I start feeling out of whack.

At this time in my life, the four that I can usually take for granted are health, spirit, community, and finance. This doesn't mean I don't recognize, respect, and appreciate their role in my life day to day. It's just that they tend to be relatively stable.

That gives me family, career, and self to play with, juggle, experiment with, and generally keep in motion. I get to wonder whether I want to take another class, to set up a weekend picnic, to invest in new software, to attend the consortium meeting. Most of my conscious time is spent in these areas.

It's like a hibiscus tree with three beautiful bright blossoms growing in a planter on the back of elephant who keeps lumbering along slowly with all four feet fairly close to the ground most of the time.

Invariably, something brings one of the stable zones up to the surface for a while, shifts a lot of my conscious thought to this area I prefer to take for granted.

Finance comes up when I encounter a large bathroom repair bill, an unexpected tuition deposit, or any other annoying and distracting expenditure.

Health comes up whenever I am anticipating a regular physical, when I notice anything unusual in my functioning, or sometimes even when I have a regular dental appointment.

Community comes up in response to global issues like the Persian Gulf war, a hurricane or earthquake affect ing many people, and even in response to a heated discussion about public vs. private road maintenance in our neighborhood.

Spirit comes to the foreground in response to the serious illness or death of someone close.

The elephant is trying to stand on three feet.

When one of these areas becomes especially critical, I tend to juggle four elements for a while. This exhausts me so much, I stuff something else down into the "take for granted" slot, just to regain stable footing.

Usually, the zone I stuff back away is the one called "self." I stop taking the time I need for renewal and renourishment. My resilience slowly leeches away. If I have to start neglecting a second area, my family goes next, career, next.

I don't know how I eventually regain balance. But it has always gradually returned in the past so I have great faith in the future. I think that faith helps.

It has been valuable for me to know this pattern. I can watch for warning signs. I can appreciate the general stability.

Do you have a pattern? How does it work for you?

LIFE AS A LANDSCAPE

What if I were challenged to come up with a picture of my life with balance in all seven zones? Visualizing a scenic, symbolic portrait of all the elements of my living, growing nature which determine my personal landscape. Here's how it might be:

First I see two mountains—one higher than the other. The tallest one is HEALTH because facing the challenge of getting and staying healthy is a worthwhile goal for me and will be there all my life.

The shorter mountain is CAREER because it is full of peaks to scale and generally continues on an upward trend for a long time. And yet, I also look forward to a time when I'm coming down that mountain—not really retired, but not always striving upwards.

A beautiful river flows right through the landscape, and that's my FAMILY—the place from which my blessings flow, the active, churning, dynamic force that surrounds and supports me. The essential water for survival. The sometimes turbulent, sometimes peaceful motion under me.

Family flows naturally right into a giant lake called COMMUNITY. Community is there. Reflecting the rest of the landscape. It's a beautiful, necessary, and logical part of the whole picture.

Next I see a rich green forest. That's FINANCE. It's a place whose shade can cool the summer heat and whose pine needles offer a fragrant sleep. It's a place whose moisture nourishes me.

Above all, there is a starry sky. That's SPIRIT. It is always there. Far away, sometimes hidden from view. Yet visible, close, real if only I remember to look.

These stars are full of secrets I don't yet understand. But I believe; I know they are there. It's often not at night when I lose my way, but in the bright pulsing demands of the day. So I remember the stars are there.

LIZ McAULIFFE GOLLEN 1991

And swooping gracefully through this whole landscape is the eagle—my SELF.

The one through whose eyes the landscape takes on meaning, the one who decides when and where to spend time and attention in all areas of this landscape—me.

How would I create my other pictures—times in my life when it doesn't feel this way? How would you create yours? Would it be more like a landscape with alpine meadows, turbulent oceans, scorching deserts? Or would it be like a sport or a movie or a play, or a food, or a city, or a tree?

AN ENDURING IMAGE

I heard the news over the radio that summer I was 18. Someone I admired greatly had died. He was the poet, e e cummings. I was young and romantic and hadn't much experience of death, but I felt an enormous loss.

That night, my sister and roommates wanted to go to the fireworks at the Iwo Jima memorial. I resisted. They talked me into going.

The evening eased me out of my ponderous thoughts. I began appreciating the dazzle of the displays overhead, the whistle of the launch, the boom burst sounds of the pyrotechnics, the respectful and appreciative "ahhh" of the crowd. And what I love most of all at fireworks is the percussive thump in my breastbone as my body echoes the biggest booms.

I can see myself, even now from this distant time. Face tilted up to the bright show. Fire trails reflected in my eyes. Finally a child again. Fully engaged in the moment. "How can anything be so wonderful?"

A momentary lull. Why are things so beautiful so quickly gone? My eyes glance down to the ground, then up again to the sky. I see the stars. Shining, shy, steadfast. They are bright enough and magical enough if only I am not distracted by the closer display of man-made fireworks.

I think again about my poet. His gift endures. Maybe life is more about the stars than about the fireworks. Maybe I need to look beyond the spark and flurry of each moment, each day, to what is faithful, fixed, steadfast. Maybe the sustained light is more important than the quick sparkle. There's a balance here somewhere.

Remember the first image in this book? Executive, briefcase in a deathgrip in one hand, ice cream cone melting down the other hand, hurrying down some steps to the next appointment.

I glance toward the fireworks today with my face firmly planted in the stars. And before each day melts away, I eat the ice cream.

A COMPANION TO THE THEATRE

Other books by the same author:

OPERAMANIA
THEATREMANIA
THE WIT OF THE THEATRE
WHO'S WHO IN SHAKESPEARE

A COMPANION TO THE THEATRE

The Anglo-American stage from 1920

by ROBIN MAY

HIPPOCRENE
BOOKS, INC.

HIPPOCRENE BOOKS, INC.
NEW YORK, N.Y.

First Published in Great Britain 1973
Lutterworth Press
Luke House, Farnham Road
Guildford, Surrey

First Published in the United States 1975
Library of Congress Catalog Card Number 74–16693
ISBN 0 88254–306–7

Printed in Great Britain by
Cox & Wyman Ltd.,
London, Fakenham and Reading

To
JOHN TREWIN

Acknowledgements

A British writer must be conscious that his knowledge of the American scene is inadequate and dangerously film-orientated. Books that have served to counter this, and which have been most helpful, are Brooks Atkinson's *Broadway*, Howard Taubman's *The Making of the American Theater*, and John Mason Brown's *Dramatis Personae*. Also very helpful has been regular reading of *Time*'s dramatic critic, now revealed to be T. E. Kalem, down the years.

Acknowledgements on this side of the Atlantic are especially due to half a dozen editions of *Who's Who in the Theatre*; the staff of *The Spotlight*; John Russell Taylor's Penguin *Dictionary of the Theatre*; for certain information, to the *Oxford Companion to the Theatre*; to the remarkable section in *Pears Cyclopaedia*, 'The Contemporary Theatre', written by Elizabeth Locke and annually brought up to date; to many books by J. C. Trewin, and to Frank Seton.

Finally, a word of thanks for the patience of the staff of the Reference Room at Wimbledon's Public Library, in particular Charles Toase and Patricia Harrison, who managed to smile even when the back numbers of *Who's Who in the Theatre* had to be got up from the vaults for the umpteenth time; and a word of thanks also to my wife, faced with a villainous manuscript to type.

R. M.

Illustrations

The author and publishers would like to thank the following for the photographs used between pages 144–145:

Angus McBean: Guthrie rehearsing *Othello*; Ivor Novello and Vanessa Lee in *King's Rhapsody*; Edith Evans and John Gielgud in *The Importance*; *The Lady's Not For Burning*; Joyce Redman as Juno; Joan Plowright as Sonya; Olivier as Othello.

Houston Rogers: Flora Robson in *Black Chiffon*; Peggy Ashcroft and Ralph Richardson in *The Heiress*; John Clements and Kay Hammond in *Man and Superman*.

Contents

Illustrations

Preface

THE AIM of this book is to provide a guide to the English-speaking theatre roughly from the end of the First World War to the present day, with occasional forays further back to include key figures like Harley Granville Barker and Miss Horniman. The balance of the book is weighted in favour of the last two decades, which means that a comparatively minor figure of today may have an entry as large as a star of the 20s. But there is plenty about the inter-war years, and hopefully, the balance is correct.

It should be stressed that, for reasons of space, the book is confined to the straight theatre with affectionate glances at musicals and revues. There is sadly no place for the glory of Fonteyn, the grandeur of Callas or the brazen splendour of Max Miller. And it is those who have done most *in the theatre* who have been included, not major film or TV talent unless their theatre work justifies it.

Again for reasons of space, all too many talented people have had to be left out—accidental omissions apart—which the present author, having once been an actor, has found most distressing. As to the structure of the book, it roughly follows the shape of the previous one in this series, Roy Pickard's *A Companion to the Movies*. Featured plays, productions, etc., are followed by *Who's Who* sections.

These featured shows are carefully chosen as representative of their genres. Some, like *Oklahoma!* and *Look Back in Anger*, made history; others, like *The Birthday Party*, were portents of major new talents. Still more, like *St. Joan, Juno and the Paycock, My Fair Lady* and *Long Day's Journey into Night*, are there in the way Everest is there.

The *Who's Who* sections are self-explanatory, but it should be pointed out—and there is some cross-referencing to assist the reader, as well as an index—that some actors and actresses appear in more than one chapter, the record number of chapter entries being held by Emlyn Williams.

It would be idle to pretend that this book is an impersonal record, but the only flagrant bias that may be detected is for musicals that are actually musical.

MODERN DRAMA

Some Notable Plays

SAINT JOAN   1923

This play, arguably Shaw's finest, and certainly his most lastingly popular work, opened in New York and London almost simultaneously. Powerful, moving, effective, witty and often downright funny, it has attracted a succession of fine actresses, though only the first British Joan, Sybil Thorndike, seems to have been equally and stunningly convincing as soldier, saint and peasant. The play is packed with good parts, and only the semi-flippant epilogue set in Charles VII's bedroom twenty-five years after Joan's death, with a top-hatted 20th century gentleman, as well as the Maid herself, putting in an appearance, has remained somewhat controversial.

First performed in New York at the Garrick by the Theater Guild, December 28, 1923, and in London at the New, March 26, 1924

Author	Bernard Shaw
Directors	Philip Moeller (New York)
	Bernard Shaw and Lewis Casson (London)
Designers	Raymond Dovey (New York)
	Charles Ricketts (London)

New York's Joan was Winifred Lenihan. Morris Carnovsky doubled La Hire and Brother Martin. Apart from Sybil Thorndike, the London cast included Ernest Thesiger as the Dauphin. Collectors' items: In New York Jo Mielziner was the Court Page, and in London Jack Hawkins was Dunois' Page and Sidney Bromley, Warwick's Page.

JUNO AND THE PAYCOCK   1924

Those who believe that tragic drama in English died in Jacobean times cannot know Sean O'Casey's two masterpieces, *The Plough and the Stars* (26) or the earlier, equally great, *Juno*. The latter is set in civil war Dublin in 1922, when Irishmen were busy butchering each other over a disputed treaty. Its near farcical comedy, allied to the grimmest tragedy, and its magnificent, albeit realistic, language, are in the Elizabethan tradition. Its main characters are Juno, the long-suffering compassionate, resilient wife of Jack Boyle, the strutting 'pay-cock' and snug bar wastrel. Of the other parts, the most notable is Boyle's quotation-spouting toady of a crony, Joxer.

Juno suffers a series of blows, but there is nothing to suggest that Fate has finished with her. Her lament near the end over her 'executed' son, which echoes her neighbour's on the same theme, is as shattering as anything in Greek or Elizabethan tragedy, and the ironic ending, with Boyle, fatuously befuddled, repeating his old refrain that the whole world's in a terrible state of 'chassis', is unsurpassed in modern drama. So is the play.

First produced at the Abbey Theatre, Dublin, March 1924

Author	Sean O'Casey
Director	Michael J. Dolan

Cast included Sara Allgood as Juno, Barry Fitzgerald as Boyle and Sydney Morgan as Joxer.

In 1925 the play opened at the Royalty in London, the main cast change being Arthur Sinclair in place of Barry Fitzgerald. Hailed as a masterpiece, it provoked James Agate's famous comment that the play 'is as much a tragedy as *Macbeth*, but it is a tragedy taking place in the porter's lodge'. A recent and memorable revival was at the National Theatre in 1966, with Joyce Redman, Colin Blakely and Frank Finlay, directed by Olivier. It was first performed in New York in 1926. Barry Fitzgerald and Sara Allgood appeared there in a revival in 1939.

PRIVATE LIVES   1930

Of all the Master's achievements, this high comedy, the finest written in English since *The Importance of Being Earnest*, seems destined to be regarded as his greatest. Even *Hay Fever*, its only rival, does not perhaps sustain quite such a high level of exhilarating wit and astonishingly brilliant dialogue.

The plot is minimal. Amanda and Elyot, once explosively married to each other, meet accidentally in a French hotel when each of them are on their second honeymoon. They decide they still adore each other and go off together, to be pursued by

Victor and Sybil, their abandoned partners, who confront them in Paris.

The author has criticized his 'dastardly and conscienceless behaviour' in making Victor and Sybil so wooden. Maybe. The play certainly needs acting. But even if there can never be another cast like the first one, revivals, even humble ones in Rep, only prove the play's greatness, as does a glance at nearly any page of the script.

First produced in London at the Phoenix, September 24, 1930

| Author and Director | Noël Coward |
| Designer | Gladys Calthrop |

The cast was Noël Coward as Elyot, Gertrude Lawrence as Amanda, Laurence Olivier as Victor, Adrienne Allen as Sybil, and Everley Gregg as Louise the maid.

The play transferred from London to New York in 1931. It has enjoyed successful revivals, including a very long one at the Apollo with John Clements and Kay Hammond, which opened in 1944. At the time of writing (72), it has been revived with Maggie Smith and Robert Stephens.

WAITING FOR LEFTY   1935

No play in modern times on either side of the Atlantic has had such an electric effect on its audiences as this one-acter by Clifford Odets, which opened at the battered Civic Repertory Theater on Fourteenth Street one February Sunday afternoon. It was a summons to arms; Elia Kazan's final strike call almost had the audience joining him. This 'whirling experience', as Brooks Atkinson called it, seems superficially dated today because of its Depression setting and extreme radical/communist message. But the fire, impact and humanity of at least half its scenes are dateless.

Based on a New York taxi drivers' strike, and with a basic thread of a workers' meeting, it consists of six scenes, most of them related to the meeting and the workers, including two pessimistic scenes of home life; a job interview between a lab assistant and a manufacturer of poison gas; a 'spy' being discovered at the workers' meeting; an actor trying for a job; and a scene between two doctors, one a Jew, which flays American medical practice and is not out-of-date today.

A theatrical tour-de-force—Lefty himself never comes, having been murdered—it is by no means the work of art that Odets's *Awake and Sing* of the same year turned out to be. But from it sprang American social conscience drama, and later disappointments of the author's career—too much being expected of him—cannot dim his achievement.

First produced by the Group Theater at the Civic Repertory Theater, in January, 1935.

Cast included Russell Collins as Fatt, Fayette and Reilly, Elia Kazan as Agate Keller, and Odets himself as Dr. Benjamin.

Several weeks later *Awake and Sing* opened at the Belasco; then, on March 26, 1935, *Waiting for Lefty* began a six month run at the Longacre after being played at Sunday Night Labour meetings. Collectors note: Lee J. Cobb played one of the voices.

A STREETCAR NAMED DESIRE   1947

Tennessee Williams's first success, *The Glass Menagerie* (45), made his reputation, but he came of age theatrically with *Streetcar* in which his authentic voice was heard. Its lyric quality, allied to its searing ferocity, made a tremendous impact on Broadway in Elia Kazan's production; even lesser productions elsewhere could not do more than slightly dilute its power.

The characters, Blanche, the nervous fading Southern Belle—school-teacher turned whore; Stanley, her brutish brother-in-law; her suitor who learns the facts about Blanche from him; Stanley's wife, physically enslaved by him, but happy enough, are memorably drawn and viewed with detachment.

Blanche's rape and last act removal to a madhouse have served as a green light to some directors to sensationalize the play and to some actresses to overact the part. This writer recalls a touring production where the Stanley, who was also the director, actually winked at the audience before carrying Blanche off. At the other end of the scale was the New York production which was a triumph for Kazan, his cast and his designer.

First produced in New York at the Ethel Barrymore Theater, December 3, 1947.

Author	Tennessee Williams
Director	Elia Kazan
Designer	Jo Mielziner

Cast included Jessica Tandy as Blanche, Marlon Brando as Stanley, Kim Hunter, Karl Malden and Gee Gee James.

The play ran for 855 performances. It opened in London at the Aldwych in 1949 with Vivien Leigh, Bonar Colleano, Renée Asherson and Bernard Braden, directed by Laurence Olivier. It was later filmed by Kazan with Vivien Leigh and Brando, who repeated his definitive performance.

DEATH OF A SALESMAN   1949

This is Arthur Miller's finest and most famous play. Its pitiful hero, Willy Loman, is a good man and a salesman, thrown aside in late middle age because of his failure to sell. Because of this failure he is going out of his mind. Finally, he kills himself. The other main characters are Willy's brave, long-suffering and understanding wife, Linda, to whom Willy is only unfaithful because of his loneliness on the road, and his sons, Happy, the womanizer, and Biff, a dreamer, backward and idealistic.

Willy is a little man sorry for himself, fooled by the slogans, betrayed by the system, so, it has been said, the play is not a true tragedy. But Miller's skill makes Willy's story tragic; the construction, including superb use of flashbacks, is masterly and lethal.

There are phrases in the play which have become almost classics, one being the chilling 'He's liked, but he's not—well liked.' And at Willy's 'Requiem', his friend Charley has a memorable speech about him, culminating in 'A salesman is got to dream, boy. It comes with the territory'. As for the wife's speech over Willy, it is worthy of the O'Casey of *Juno*. A great play.

First produced at the Morosco Theater, February 10, 1949

Author	Arthur Miller
Director	Elia Kazan
Designer	Jo Mielziner

Cast included Lee J. Cobb as Willy, Mildred Dunnock as Linda, Arthur Kennedy as Happy and Cameron Mitchell as Biff.

The play ran 683 performances in New York. It opened in London at the Phoenix on July 28, 1949, with Paul Muni, Katherine Alexander, Frank Maxwell and Kevin McCarthy as the family.

WAITING FOR GODOT   1953

This play, originally written by the Anglo-Irish playwright, Samuel Beckett, in French, is his masterpiece and one of the most influential works of the century. It is also a corner-stone of the Theatre of the Absurd (see p. 273). It is a tragi-farce about two clownish tramps who wait for the mysterious Mr. Godot. He will change things when he comes. A boy tells them it will be tomorrow, but Godot never does come. The other characters are a master, Pozzo, and his slave, Lucky, who is treated like an animal.

Thousands of words have been written trying to solve the play's meaning, trying to decide whether Godot is God, but ultimately, it can be safely said to be a comment on man today on his own in an apparently meaningless universe. Legend has it that the best reception the play ever had was from an audience of convicts in San Francisco jail.

First produced in London at the Arts Theatre, August 3, 1955

Author	Samuel Beckett
Director	Peter Hall
Designer	Peter Snow

Cast included Peter Woodthorpe as Estragon, Paul Daneman as Vladimir, Peter Bull as Pozzo (the play even survives his hilarious account of it in *I Know the Face But . . .*), Timothy Bateson as Lucky and Michael Walker as the boy.

This famous production later transferred to the Criterion. The play reached New York in 1956, where the tramps were played by Bert Lahr and E. G. Marshall, with Kurt Kasznar, Alvin Epstein and Luchino Solito de Solis completing the cast.

LOOK BACK IN ANGER   1956

It is just possible that this play will one day be a mere signpost in histories of the drama, like Robertson's *Caste*, possible but doubtful: there is too much passion in its hero, Jimmy Porter, too much humour and sheer rhetorical flair. Osborne's passion 'saved the English theatre from death through gentility' (Angus Wilson). It also inspired a generation of young writers to consider the theatre as a medium to be used.

Jimmy, the working-class sweet-stall keeper, educated not even at a Redbrick University but at a 'white tile' one, rages against society—'nobody thinks, nobody cares'—and especially against his wife Alison and her Anglo-Indian parents, particularly her unseen mother. Both of them have done their best to stop her marrying such an appalling young man. Finally, Alison's mask of self-control breaks. She flees from the bed-sitter, leaving Jimmy's most vocal critic, her actress friend, Helena, to take her place in bed and at the ironing board. The other lodger, Cliff, is solid, working-class, self-educated and sympathetic. Alison's father, in some of Jimmy's descriptions and when we meet him, is also sympathetic, the author's first exercise in nostalgia for a vanished Edwardian England, full of certainties, which haunts his work down to *West of Suez* (71).

Though far less the one-man-show its critics aver, it must be admitted that the play lives by Jimmy's abrasive, witty, brutal salvoes and barrages. It was almost as influential as *Tamburlaine*.

First produced in London at the Royal Court, May 8, 1956

Author	John Osborne
Director	Tony Richardson
Designer	Alan Tagg

Cast included Kenneth Haigh as Jimmy Porter, Mary Ure as Alison, Alan Bates as Cliff, Helena Hughes as Helena and John Welsh as Colonel Redfern.

The play reached New York the following year with the same principal players and was later filmed with Burton as Jimmy. Though the American theatre needed no land-mine set off beneath it, the play was most warmly welcomed and admired. For the record, the 'Angry Young Man' tag, a press officer's clever slogan which became attached to Jimmy and his creator, was foisted on a legion of writers, many of them totally calm, a phenomenon only a social historian could evaluate.

LONG DAY'S JOURNEY INTO NIGHT   1956

This 'play of old sorrow written in tears and blood' by Eugene O'Neill about the 'haunted' Tyrone family, a barely disguised pseudonym for his own, is now widely regarded as the greatest play written by an American. It is a very great play, period. What O'Neill had hinted at in earlier plays about his family, blazes out in this masterpiece, written in his lifetime, but not performed till after his death.

It is beside the point that, as some claimed, the portrait of the author's poor, Irish, penny-pinching father, who should have matched Booth but settled for an easy fortune in endless tours of a melodrama, is an unfair one. This is how O'Neill remembered him, and also his sweet, drug-addict mother. The others characters, a small role of a maid apart, are the elder brother, Jamie, and the younger brother Edmund. Jamie is a failed actor and wastrel and, though a 'pal' to Edmund (O'Neill himself), ferociously hates as well as loves him. As Helen Dawson wrote in *The Observer*, Jamie is the one O'Neill finds it hardest to forgive.

The play is tragedy in the Greek sense and is brutal and sublime, and shot through with moments of humour. It is Wagnerian in length. 'Beckmessers' flail O'Neill for his failure with words. Even an admirer like Brooks Atkinson can claim that he never wrote a quotable line. There is indeed none of O'Casey's poetic flair in the play, but there are lines of short Anglo-Saxon monosyllables which in context become stab wounds. Who having heard James Tyrone, in the supreme scene where he reveals himself to his son, deliver the line: 'It was in those days that I learnt to be a miser' will dare deny that O'Neill's language sometimes matches his vision and tragic sense? And there is the play's last line, the climax of a mad scene no less, spoken by the mother: 'I fell in love with James Tyrone and was so happy for a time.' The curtain falls on years of love and hate and blame and torment condensed into one terrible day and night.

First produced at the Helen Hayes, New York, November 7, 1956

Author	Eugene O'Neill
Director	José Quintero
Designer	Motley

Cast included Frederic Marsh as James Tyrone, Florence Eldridge as Mary Tyrone, Jason Robarts as Jamie and Bradford Dillman as Edmund.

The play with its much acclaimed cast ran 388 performances. It was first seen in Britain at the Edinburgh Festival (58), then London, with Anthony Quayle, Gwen Ffrangcon-Davies, Ian Bannen and Alan Bates, a fine cast, finely directed by Quintero. At the time of writing (72) it is being superlatively performed by the National with Olivier, Constance Cummings, Denis Quilley and Ronald Pickup, directed by Michael Blakemore.

THE BIRTHDAY PARTY   1958

This was the first Pinter play staged in London, where it did not even enjoy a scandal. It simply vanished after a week, praised by few, notably Harold Hobson. Even allowing for a production 'which did not please the author, its total rejection remains astounding, for it is one of his very finest works. Everything meant by the adjective Pinteresque is on display in this his third, and first full length, play: the pauses, the hidden menace, the unrevealed motives of key characters, the flair for dialogue, at once prosaic and electric.

The play is set in a seedy seaside boarding-house kept | by Meg, whose husband is a deckchair attendant, and who mothers Stanley, the lethargic lodger, apparently a failed musician. A girl called Lulu fails to rouse him. Into the house come Goldberg and McCann, a Jew and an Irishman, who lay on an alarming birthday party for Stanley which seems destined to end in his death. However, he becomes the aggressor, only to be taken upstairs by the two interlopers and removed the next morning bowler-hatted and gibbering. All explanations— Stanley as the artist who is forced to conform to the pressures of society, etc.—are guesswork and almost irrelevant. The inexplicable world of Harold Pinter has been presented memorably, funnily and alarmingly.

First produced in London at the Lyric, Hammersmith, May 19, 1958

Author	Harold Pinter
Director	Peter Wood
Designer	Hutchinson Scott

Cast included Willoughby Gray, Beatrix Lehmann, Richard Pearson, Wendy Hutchinson, John Slater and John Stratton.

The play's fortunes were retrieved by the Tavistock Theatre Company whose production (59) was boosted by the late-lamented *Encore* magazine. It was revived at the Aldwych (64) by the Royal Shakespeare Company with the author directing Newton Blick, Doris Hare, Bryan Pringle, Janet Suzman, Brewster Mason and Patrick Magee.

OH WHAT A LOVELY WAR! 1963

This was the finest and most famous of Joan Littlewood's productions for Theatre Workshop, a passionate, often hilarious, always tragic evocation of the horrors of the First World War, and a denunciation of all war which was worlds away from the callow effusions of the Theatre of Fact (sic), and the well-meaning but accidentally smug, 'actorish' rhetoric of *US*.

From the snappy pierrot opening through scene after scene (where Joan Littlewood showed she could do more with three men and a flag than most directors with a regiment) to the *Chanson de Craonne* at the end, with French soldiers bleating like sheep as they marched towards us to be slaughtered, the contents and direction were inspirational. The backbone of the whole was song, the soldiers' songs, cynical, marvellous and moving, the grisly patriotic songs of the Home Front. Yet for all the singing, this show would be totally out of place in the Musicals section of this book.

Some said the show was 'unfair' but satire is—legitimately so. If junior officers got less than their due (where would the compilers have been without the writings of some of them?) the heroism of the men was never denigrated. The selective sayings and writings of the generals, etc., may well have been 'unfair' but were genuine, as were the bitter statistics flashed on a moving screen. It is impossible to imagine anyone not being deeply stirred. Revolutionaries no doubt wished to rush to the barricades—for the show's message applies as much to today as to 1914–18—the rest, on all evidence, were emotionally garrotted. The theatre rarely changes the status quo. The première of Verdi's *The Battle of Legnano* is a rare example of a piece which stirred an audience to physical action. But in modern times, Joan Littlewood's masterpiece surely had an effect as great as its methods were grandly simple.

First produced at the Theatre Royal, Stratford, March 19, 1963

Director	Joan Littlewood
Authors	Charles Chilton and others
Designer	John Bury
Musical Director	Alfred Ralston

Cast: Ann Beach, Fanny Carby, Bettina Dickson, Myvanwy Jenkins, Barry Bethel, Brian Cronin, Larry Dann, Griffith Davies, John Gower, Colin Kemball, Murray Melvin, Brian Murphy, George Sewell, Victor Spinetti, Bob Stephenson.

The show transferred to Wyndham's and was later seen in New York and in many parts of the world, including Italy, where, to the annoyance of the Italians, it was discovered that they had been left out of the War. It was later brilliantly re-created on film by Richard Attenborough.

THE CHANGING ROOM   1971

No-one would claim that David Storey is the most 'significant' playwright to emerge in the late 60s, but he is arguably the best to do so, and the most wide-ranging. This play, following *Home* and his latest at the time of writing, is about a Rugby League team before and after and during the interval of one Saturday's game. It would be foolish to minimize the extraordinary contribution of Storey's regular director, Lindsay Anderson, to the success of the production: ensemble takes on a new, intense meaning under his guidance. But the play, a play with a minimal plot in the usual sense, is the thing.

The suspense before the match, the feeling of communal activity, the humour, the humanity, are all present in a documentary way, and, such is the effect of the concentration of effort, in a poetical way as well. Storey, without pressing his points, usually provides a deeper meaning. For Michael Billington, the Rugby League World symbolized a mechanized industrial society in which 'prodigious effort is expended for the profit of the few'. For Harold Hobson there was the Wordsworthian Spirit, 'the still, sad music of humanity'. Benedict Nightingale was inspired by a 'celebration both of individual energy and of the spirit of co-operation'.

Some who have not seen the play have felt that such realism is best left to films. But no film can stay in one small room, in this case, a small, scruffy changing room, and triumphantly survive: this is the theatre's realism. Every member of its audience, so it would seem, is as deeply involved in the action as the masseur who dresses an injured player, the Russophobe cleaner who never watches a match but whose life is bound up with the game, and as the trainer who urges his battered team in the interval to start putting the pressure on.

First produced at the Royal Court, November 9, 1971

Author	David Storey
Director	Lindsay Anderson
Designer	Jocelyn Herbert

Cast: Alun Armstrong, John Barrett, Peter Childs, Warren Clarke, David Daker, Paul Dawkins, Michael Elphick, Brian Glover, Matthew Guinness, David Hill, Geoffrey Hinsliff, Edward Judd, Barry Keegan, Brian Lawson, Mark McManus, Don McKillop, Frank Mills, Jim Norton, Edward Peel, John Price, John Rae, Peter Schofield.

A WHO'S WHO OF MODERN DRAMA

ABBOTT, GEORGE (1887–). American dramatist, director and actor, renowned for his work in musicals (see p. 204). Like Kaufman, he helped shape the fast-moving side of the theatre scene in America between the wars. His plays include *Broadway* (26) with Philip Dunning, *Coquette* (27) with Ann Bridgers, which made Helen Hayes a star, and *Three Men on a Horse* (35) with John Cecil Holm. A very skilful play doctor.

ACLAND, RODNEY (1908–). British dramatist and actor. Mainly known as a fine adaptor: *The Old Ladies* (35), *Crime and Punishment* (45), *The Diary of a Scoundrel* (49) and *Before the Party* (49) from Maugham's story. His plays includes *A Dead Secret* (57), inspired by the Seddon case, an excellent psychological study which in London starred Paul Scofield.

ADAM, RONALD (1896–). British actor who managed the Embassy from 1932–39, many of his productions—*Ten Minute Alibi, Close Quarters, Judgement Day*, etc.—transferring to the West End.

ALBEE, EDWARD (1928–). American dramatist who first came to notice with *The Zoo Story* (58), a tense, lurid one-acter. An eclectic satirist, after *The Death of Bessie Smith* (59) and *The American Dream* (61), he moved from Off-Broadway to Broadway with his triumphant *Who's Afraid of Virginia Woolf?* (62), a passionate, intense study of near-lethal domestic conflict as ferocious as Strindberg. Brooks Atkinson called it a contemptuous cartoon of marriage. Other plays have included *The Ballad of the Sad Café* from a story by Carson McCullers (63), *Tiny Alice* (64), *A Delicate Balance* (66) and *All Over* (71). Has also produced a number of plays.

ANDERSON, LINDSAY (1923–). British director most notably of the plays of David Storey (see p. 64) having previously directed a screen adaptation of his novel, *This Sporting Life*. Associated with the English Stage Company since 1957. Productions include *The Long and the Short and the Tall, Progress to the Park* and *Sergeant Musgrave's Dance* (59), *Billy Liar* (60), *The Diary of a Madman* (63), *Andorra* for the National Theatre (63) and *The Cherry Orchard* at Chichester (66). A distinguished film director.

ANDERSON, MAXWELL (1888–1959). American dramatist who ranged from comedy and social criticism to historical and verse dramas. With Laurence Stallings, he wrote *the* American First World War play, *What Price Glory?* (24). His historical plays include *Mary of Scotland* (33) and *Valley Forge* (34). *Winterset* (35) is a poetic drama inspired by the Sacco-Vanzetti case, and other plays of the 30s include *High Tor* (36), *Knickerbocker Holiday* (38) and *Key Largo* (39). A skilled man of the theatre, in these and later plays, which included *The Bad Seed* (54). He wrote at length about the need that great drama has for great poetry. How much of his distinguished output will survive seems uncertain.

ANDERSON, ROBERT (1917–). American dramatist, whose most successful play as yet has been *Tea and Sympathy* (53). In this, a college boy is wrongly suspected of being a homosexual, and is comforted by a mother-mistress figure. Characterized by John Russell Taylor as a 'smooth matinée study', strong casts on both sides of the Atlantic helped make it effective. Later plays include *I Never Sang for my Father* (68).

ANTROBUS, JOHN British actor and dramatist whose plays include *The Bed Sitting Room* (63), co-author with Spike Milligan, and the hilarious *Crete and Sergeant Pepper* (72). Parts have included Glendenning in *The Contractor* (69).

ARDEN, JOHN (1930–). British dramatist whose exciting, uneven output includes *Sergeant Musgrave's Dance* (59), arguably the finest post-1956 play. An 'historical parable' to allow the author to draw modern comparisons (an event in Cyprus), it has a convincing Victorian atmosphere. It is set in a mining town *c.* 1880, to which Musgrave and three comrades come, officially as a recruiting party, actually as deserters. Musgrave, horrified by a reprisal he has perpetrated, is determined to ram home his exposé of war's horrors by an atrocity of his own. He and the other characters typify Arden's passionate concern and understanding, and his near-Shakespearean refusal to load the dice too strongly on one side, despite his clear hatred of violence. He created an almost Breughel-like world of believable people in believable surroundings, using Brechtian means, including song and dance. But unlike Brecht and too many of his committed followers, he recognizes the complexity of man and his environment.

Other plays include *Live Like Pigs* (58) set on a housing estate, *The Happy Haven* (60), his 'vulgar melodrama', *The Workhouse Donkey* (63) about corruption and the power struggle in a Northern town, and *Armstrong's Goodnight* (64), part-

Border Ballad, part political play, a perhaps too ambitious piece, made more complicated by Arden's invented dialect. *Left-handed Liberty* (65) is about Magna Carta and later plays include one about Nelson, written with Arden's wife, Margaretta d'Arcy, *The Hero Rises Up* (68). Their *The Island of the Mighty* (72) was staged by the Royal Shakespeare Co., whose production they disowned.

ARDREY, ROBERT (1908–). American dramatist. *Thunder Rock* (39), Shadow of Heroes (58), etc.

ARONSON, BORIS (1900–). American designer. Worked with the Group Theater, including settings for *Awake and Sing* (35). Among his other designs have been those for *The Country Girl* (50), *The Rose Tattoo* (51), *The Crucible* (53), *A View from the Bridge* and *The Diary of Ann Frank* (55), *Orpheus Descending* (57), *J. B.* (58), *Fiddler on the Roof* (64) and *Follies* (71). At the time of writing (72), Londoners have been able to see his striking geometric steel set for *Company*.

AUDEN, W. H. (1907–). British-born poet and dramatist, now an American. In the 30s, wrote verse plays with Christopher Isherwood, including *The Dog beneath the Skin* (35), *The Ascent of F6* (36) and *On the Frontier* (38); also the libretto for *The Rake's Progress* (51). The plays have modern themes and the verse is used for specially significant moments.

AXELROD, GEORGE (1922–). American dramatist and author of *The Seven Year Itch* (53), *Will Success spoil Rock Hunter?* (55) and *Goodbye Charlie* (59).

AYCKBOURN, ALAN (1939–). British dramatist, director and actor. Author of *Relatively Speaking* (67) and *How the Other Half Loves* (70), both highly successful West End comedies, the first of which has been performed in innumerable countries west and east of Suez. Another hit with *Time and Time Again* (72).

BAGNOLD, ENID (1889–). British dramatist and novelist, author of *National Velvet*. Plays include *Lottie Dundass* (43), a romantic drama, the acid, witty, high comedy, *The Chalk Garden* (55) and another, almost as scintillating, *The Chinese Prime Minister* (63).

BANBURY, FRITH (1912–). British director, actor and manager. Has directed many new commercial plays, including *The Holly and the Ivy* (50), *Waters of the Moon* (51), *The Deep Blue Sea* (52), *The Diary of Ann Frank* (56), *Flowering Cherry* in New York (59), *The Tiger and the Horse* (60), *The Right Honourable Gentleman* in New York (65), *Howard's End* (67), *Reunion in Vienna* at Chichester (71), etc.

BARNES, PETER (1931–). British dramatist. Author of *The Ruling Class* (68). Adapted *Lulu* (70).

BARRIE, J. M. (1860–1937). British dramatist and novelist. The significant career of this famous Scot lies before the time-span of this book, unless one includes *Mary Rose* (20) and the clever one-act unfinished whodunit, *Shall We Join the Ladies?* (22). *The Boy David* (36), written for Elizabeth Bergner, was cursed with ill-luck but it has its admirers. Meanwhile *Peter Pan* lives! And so do *The Admirable Crichton* and one or two other Edwardian pieces.

BARRY, PHILIP (1896–1949). American dramatist very popular in his day, his *Paris Bound* and *Holiday* being two of the most enjoyed comedies of the 20s. The very symbolic fantasy *Here Come the Clowns* (38) was much admired, but more likely to last is his utterly delightful comedy, *The Philadelphia Story* (39), later filmed, and still later re-filmed as the musical *High Society*.

BECKETT, SAMUEL (1906–). Irish dramatist and novelist, whose *Waiting for Godot* (53), one of the most influential plays of the century, is discussed above. No major playwright can have existed in a more narrow (yet universal?) world than Beckett's. Although highly poetic, few dramatists can have gained such a deserved following with such theatrically static pieces. His nihilism repels the sanguine, who nevertheless admit his influence. A founding father of the Theatre of the Absurd (see p. 273), though Taubman, amongst others, has pointed out the mischievousness of such a useful blanket label.

Beckett settled in France (37) and his most famous works were originally written in French, including *Godot* (53), his first play. *Endgame* (57) concerns a pitiful group of people living in dustbins in a tower cut off from a dead world (a summary that invites parodies from anti-Beckettians). *Krapp's Last Tape* (58) has a single character listening to a 30-year old tape recording of his life. In *Happy Days* (62) we have a chattering woman buried in a heap of earth. In *Play* (63), a one-acter like *Happy Days* there are three characters in urns, talking when the light is on them. The play is acted twice in succession. Audience alienation has grown with the years. The listener must hope to glean something in the way he does when listening to the music of Stockhausen and his successors.

BEHAN, BRENDAN (1925–64). Irish dramatist. His first play, *The Quare Fellow*, a powerful tragi-comedy set in a Northern Irish prison, was produced by Joan Littlewood at the Theatre Royal, Stratford East (56). *The Hostage*, a very inventive comedy set in a brothel-cum-I.R.A. post, was also produced at Stratford (58).

Tynan called this riotous, impudent piece *commedia dell'arte*.

BEHRMAN, S. N. (1893–). Highly successful American dramatist, whose hits include a number of adaptations: *The Pirate* (42) from a play by Ludwig Fulda and *Amphitryon '38* (38) after Giraudoux. His finest original plays are *The Second Man* (27) and *No Time for Comedy* (39). Considered the finest American playwright of the comedy of manners, he also wrote an autobiographical play of great charm, *The Cold Wind and the Warm* (58) about his unsophisticated youth.

BENNETT, ALAN (1934–). British satirist and dramatist. Author of *Forty Years On* (68), a sharp, but nostalgic and affectionate evocation of the century's social and literary life against a school setting, and *Getting On* (71), a witty comedy about a middle-aged, middle-class Labour M.P. The first supplied a major part for Gielgud, the second for Kenneth More.

BLAKEMORE, MICHAEL (1928–). British director, at the time of writing, an Associate Director of the National Theatre, for whom he staged the magnificent production of *Long Day's Journey into Night* (72). An Australian, he began as an actor. Co-Director of Glasgow Citizens's (66–8), where he directed *The Resistible Rise of Arturo Ui*, a production to convert non-Brechtians, with Leonard Rossiter giving a most memorable and technically brilliant performance as the Hitler-like lead (Glasgow, 68: London, 69). Blakemore is particularly associated with the work of Peter Nicols: *A Day in the Death of Joe Egg* (67), *The National Health* (69) and *Forget-me-not Lane* (71). At the time of writing (72) has brilliantly directed *The Front Page* for the National, also an excellent *Macbeth*.

BOLT, ROBERT (1924–). British dramatist, notably successful in popular, yet reputable, historical plays (a rarer art than some realize), especially his masterly *A Man for all Seasons* (60) about Sir Thomas More, also *Vivat! Vivat Regina!* (70). Without the depth of the former, this superbly fluent study of Elizabeth I and Mary Queen of Scots, ranging over a number of years, and brilliantly staged by Peter Dews (Chichester and London), had a huge and deserved success, as did the Elizabeth, Eileen Atkins.

Other plays include his first success, *A Flowering Cherry* (57), a study in failure, memorably played by Richardson, and *The Tiger and the Horse* (60) about detachment and idealism and their effects on a husband and wife, expressed in less realistic, larger-than-life style than he has used in his other plays. *The Thwarting of Baron Bolligrew* (66) is a good play for children (a rare commodity). His Barrie-ish *Gentle Jack* (68) some say lacks the theatrical life and characterization his admirers expect from him. Has also written distinguished film scripts. Unlike many modern dramatists, is a friend of the actress as well as the actor. Married to the actress, Sarah Miles.

BOND, EDWARD (1935–). British dramatist. His plays include *Saved* (65), *Early Morning* (68), *Narrow Road to the Deep North* (68), *Black Mass* (68), and *Lear* (71), a reworking of Shakespeare's play. More honoured (by performances) abroad than at home, he voices beliefs shared by many today about war, violence breeding violence, and the plight of modern industrial man, but his obsessive dogma that all auth-ority—State, Society and Church —is the ultimate evil seems to many to be anarchy carried to ridiculous lengths. His solution, as in *Narrow Road*, a play with a 17th-century Japanese setting, is man freed of authority and un-afraid, naked and reborn. As his concept of Man is at least partly violent, the outlook is bleak.

Bond's use of shock tactics, especially in *Lear*, is notorious but, as Benedict Nightingale pointed out after the play, it is an error to think that 'the multiplication of very literal horrors will do the job' of penetrating the defences we put up against today's horrors on TV, in the papers, etc. Bond's power was evident from the first, and it was soon realized that *Saved*, a play using the language of the inarticulate, and with the much-discussed baby murder scene in it, has true compassion. But many feel that his methods misfire, sometimes badly. J. W. Lambert wrote after *Lear* that Bond appears 'possessed to the point of frenzy by the very devils he wishes to exorcise'. Bond finds 'practically no critical understanding at all' of his work (*The Guardian*, 29.9.71, in an excellent interview with John Hall), but no one who knows it can doubt the value of arguing about it.

BOVASSO, JULIE (1930–). American actress, director and dramatist who introduced Genet, Ionesco, etc., to New York at her Tempo Playhouse. Her Claire in *The Maids* (55) was much admired. Wrote, directed and played Gloria B. Gilbert in *Gloria and Esperanza* (70) winning Obie awards for each facet.

BOWEN, JOHN (1924–). British novelist and dramatist. His plays include *I Love You, Mrs. Patterson* (65), *After the Rain* (67), a clever adaptation of his novel about survivors of a flood on a raft and how they re-enact history, *Fall and Redemption* (68) and a double bill, *Little Boxes* (68). The first play, *The Coffee Lace*, is about an ageing Variety troupe who have refused to go out for years since getting the bird, the second, *Trevor* features two Lesbians, one of whom, faced with a parental visit, hires an actor to impersonate a boy friend. *The Disorderly Women* (69) is Bowen's version of *The Bacchae*. Adapted Boucicault's *The Coriscan Brothers* for the Greenwich Theatre (70).

BRIDIE, JAMES (1888–1951). Pseudonym of a Scottish doctor playwright, O. H. Mavor, who also founded the Glasgow Citizens' Theatre (42). A prolific playwright (some think too prolific), his wit rarely failed him and his dialogue, which could rise to Shavian standards, never did, but his plots and construction were not consistent, for which he was regularly assailed by James Agate, amongst others. *The King of Nowhere* (Old Vic, 38) was one of several that trailed off badly after brilliant first acts. His range was extraordinary, embracing everything from broad to biblical comedy, and from plays of ideas to chillers. Generally speaking, the plays set in Scotland are his best.

His first major success was *The Anatomist* (30) about Dr. Knox of Burke and Hare ill-fame. Other plays include *Tobias and the Angel* (30), *A Sleeping Clergyman* (33) and *Mr. Bolfry* (43), an exhilaratingly witty piece set in a Scottish manse which gets a visit from one of the most splendid Devils in

literature. *Doctor Angelus* (47) is about murder in Glasgow, *Daphne Laureola* (49), gave Edith Evans a wonderful role, and *Mr. Gillie* (50), is about a village schoolmaster. Bridie is important enough for this selection of his plays to madden some by its omissions. Scotland's debt to him is immense and the British theatre as a whole benefited by his endless, intelligent vitality.

BRIGHOUSE, HAROLD (1883–1958). British dramatist, perhaps the best known today of Miss Horniman's Manchester School (see p. 259) because of his now classic comedy, *Hobson's Choice* (16). The best of his realistic North Country plays, it went into the National Theatre's repertoire (64).

BROOK, PETER. See p. 85.

BROWNE, E. MARTIN (1900–). British director who staged the first productions of T. S. Eliot's plays, also verse dramas of other playwrights, including Duncan's *This Way to the Tomb* (45) and Fry's *A Phoenix Too Frequent* (45), both in a season he ran at the Mercury Theatre. Directed the British Drama League (48–57).

BROWNE, WYNYARD (1911–64). British dramatist and novelist, best known for his very successful *The Holly and the Ivy* (50), about a clergyman and his grown-up family.

CANNAN,   DENIS   (1919–). British dramatist and actor. His *Max* was performed at the 1949 Malvern Festival, then *Captain Carvallo* (50), a thoughtful comedy, made his name. Three intelligent farces followed, also his adaptation (with Pierre Bost) of Graham Greene's *The Power and the Glory* (56). Wrote the original text of Peter Brook's *US*, and some would say a Cannan play on the subject would have been far more effective than the admittedly brilliant and sincere group effort by the Royal Shakespeare Co. His most recent play is *One at Night* (71).

CARROLL, PAUL VINCENT (1900–68). Irish dramatist, best known outside Ireland for his *Shadow and Substance* (34), which was acclaimed in New York in 1937. His second play, *Things that are Caesar's*, won an award at the Abbey Theatre, Dublin, where many of his plays have been produced.

CARROLL,   VINETTE   (1922–). American actress and director. Directed *Black Nativity* in New York (61), London and Spoleto (62). Artistic Director of the Urban Arts Corps.

CHAYEFSKY, PADDY (1923–). American dramatist. After his triumphant TV and film hit, *Marty*, wrote *Middle of the Night* (56), about a romance between a girl and an older man, notable for its dialogue and detailed observation of character. *The Tenth Man* (59) is a modern version of the old Jewish legend, *The Dybbuk*. *Gideon* (61) is a fanciful treatment of the Biblical character and *The Passion of Joseph D* (64) is about Stalin and Lenin. More notably, *The Latent Heterosexual* (68) is a serio-comic satire about a flamboyant poet, which begins as a spoof on drugs and homosexuality and ends more seriously as a comment on the effect Big Business has on people.

CHRISTIE, AGATHA. See p. 236.

CHRISTIE, CAMPBELL (1893–1963) and   DOROTHY   CHRISTIE (1896–). British dramatists and joint authors of successful thrillers and two exceptionally well-made plays in the best sense of the phrase, *His Excellency* (50) and *Carrington V.C.* (53). The former, about an ex-docker made governor of a Mediterranean island by a Labour Government, gave Eric Portman one of the best roles of his career; the latter is a court martial drama drawing on the author's professional knowledge of the Army.

CLURMAN, HAROLD (1901–). American director, manager and writer, and founder of the Group Theater (31). This exceptionally important venture is discussed on p. 244. Earlier, Clurman worked at the Greenwich Village Playhouse with, amongst others, O'Neill. After the Group broke up (40), he became a leading independent director, his productions including a famous one of Giraudoux's *Tiger at the Gates* in London and New York (55). Anouilh's *Waltz of the Toreadors* (57), Tennessee William's *Orpheus Descending* (57), *Incident at Vichy* (64), etc. Wrote *The Fervent Years—The Story of the Group Theater*.

COE, PETER (1929–). British director whose career has been notably international. Directed The Mermaid's opening production, *Lock up your Daughters* (59). *Twelfth Night* in Madras, *Oliver* in London, Australia and New York, *Pickwick* in London and New York, *The Rehearsal* and *Next Time I'll Sing to You* in New York, *Caligula* in London, also *Macbeth* at Stratford, Ontario (62) and *Tom Brown's Schooldays*, a musical (72). Productions at Chichester have included *The Skin of Our Teeth* (68) and *Peer Gynt* (69).

CONNELLY, MARC (1890–). American dramatist, who collaborated with George Kaufman on a number of plays, including *Merton of the Movies* (22) and *Beggar on Horseback* (24). With Frank Elser wrote *The Farmer takes a Wife* (34). His most famous work, *The Green Pastures* (30), Biblical scenes told in terms of Negro fantasy, would doubtless seem patronizing, self-consciously simple and, to some, downright offensive today, but in its period had an over-whelming effect, played by a Negro cast. Also an actor, director and producer. Has played the Stage Manager in *Our Town* in New York (44) and London (46).

COOPER, GILES (1918–66). British dramatist best known for his radio plays. His two plays, *Everything in the Garden* (62) and *Happy Family* (66), both sharply satirical comedies with ominous overtones, suggested a major playwright in the making.

COTES, PETER (1912–). British actor, manager and director. Highlights of his career have been his management of the New Lindsey (46–8) where his productions included *Pick-up Girl*, *The Master Builder* and *Miss Julie*, and his control of the New Boltons (50) where he staged *The Children's Hour*, *Candida*, *A Pin to See the Peepshow* (about the Thompson Bywaters murder), etc., the last being presented in New York (53). In TV for many years. Wrote the splendidly controversial book *No Star Nonsense* (49) and a biography of George Robey (72). Married to the striking Canadian actress, Joan Miller (see p. 177).

COWARD, NOËL (1899–1973). British dramatist, composer, lyric writer, novelist, wit and entertainer, who appears in many parts of this book. Apart from his supreme achievement, *Private Lives* (30), featured above, his two finest plays are *Hay Fever* (25), the first of the Master's plays to be in the repertoire of the National, and *Present Laughter* (43). *The Vortex* (24) made his name and gave him a notoriety not unlike Osborne's after *Look Back in Anger*. His *Cavalcade* (31) was a hugely successful and very skilful patriotic saga. *Design for Living* (32) is an underrated piece. Some of his one-acters are sheer joy, and many consider *Blithe Spirit* (41) to be as good as his three masterpieces. If none of his post-war plays quite match the earlier ones, several, including *South Sea Bubble* (56) have been very popular. At the time of writing, *Private Lives* is once more in the West End (72), having again been a Broadway hit in 1969. The Master lives!—for his command of English, his wit, craftsmanship and, more often than is supposed, for his humanity.

COX, CONSTANCE (1912–). British dramatist who has adapted many classics for the stage and TV.

CRAWFORD, CHERYL (1902–). Influential American producer and director. A founder of the Group Theater (31) directing *The House of Connelly*, etc. After independent productions, founded The American Repertory Theater (46) with Eva Le Gallienne and Margaret Webster, both featured in Chapter 2. Joint General Director

of the A.N.T.A. play series (50–). A founder of the Actors' Studio, etc.

CROSS, BEVERLEY (1931–). British dramatist. Author of *One More River* (59). Adapted *Boeing-Boeing* from the French (62). The book of *Half a Sixpence* (63). Librettist of operas, including *The Mines of Sulphur* (65).

CROTHERS, RACHEL (1878–1958). American dramatist and director. Her plays, beginning with *Nora* (03), spanned four decades and often dealt with women's rights, lightheartedly sometimes after they had been won (?). *Susan and God* (37), about the Oxford Movement, gave Gertrude Lawrence a fine part. A champion of the rights of theatre workers.

DANE, CLEMENCE (1888–1965). British dramatist and novelist whose plays included her first great success, *A Bill of Divorcement* (21), and *Granite* (26) with a marvellous part for Sybil Thorndike. Author of the famous theatrical novel, *Broome Stages*.

DEAN, BASIL (1888–). British director, manager, actor and head of Forces' entertainments for two years of the First World War and the whole of the Second World War. After directing at Liverpool (11), and a spell as assistant director to Tree (13), his reign as one of the first—and toughest—of the new profession of producer (director) began in the 20s. Only *Who's Who in the Theatre* (14th Edition) can do justice to his huge number of productions, which included *A Bill of Divorcement* (21), Hassan (23), *The Constant Nymph* (26), *Johnson over Jordan* (39), a famous production of a neglected Priestley play, and, Priestley's *An Inspector Calls* (46) for the Old Vic at the New.

DELANEY, SHELAGH (1939–). British dramatist who, having seen a Rattigan play, decided she could do better and wrote *A Taste of Honey* when she was seventeen. Revised and directed by Joan Littlewood at the Theatre Workshop, Stratford East (58), this story of a young girl neglected by her mother and befriended by a kindly homosexual youth while she waits for her black baby, suited the theatrical climate of the time, and remains interesting. Less successful is *The Lion in Love* (60).

DELDERFIELD, R. F. (1912–72). British dramatist, novelist, historian and Napoleon buff. His best and most successful play is *Worm's Eye View* (45), a very funny, pleasant, realistic romp set in an R.A.F. billet in Blackpool early in World War Two.

DENNIS, NIGEL (1912–). British dramatist, novelist and critic. A satirist, two of whose main targets are religion and psycho-analysis. His first play, adapted from his novel, was *Cards of Identity* (56) about the latter. *The Making of Moo* (57) concerns a colonial civil servant who invents a new religion, and *August for the People* (61) is a less effective study of publicity and power against the background of a Stately Home. A witty writer in the Shavian and Voltairean traditions.

DEWS, PETER (1929–). British director, Birmingham Rep (66–72). At Chichester (69) directed *Antony and Cleopatra* and *Vivat! Vivat Regina!* His *Hadrian VII* (Birmingham and the Mermaid, 68; New York, 69) won him a 'Tony' award.

DIGHTON, JOHN (1909–). British dramatist. Author of the very funny *The Happiest Days of Your Life* (48), *Who Goes There?* (51), etc.

DRINKWATER, JOHN (1882–1937). British dramatist, actor and director, and collaborator of Sir Barry Jackson at the Birmingham Rep. The finest of his several worthy verse and chronicle plays is *Abraham Lincoln* (19). More successful than most in trying to re-establish verse drama in the British Theatre.

DONLEAVY, J. P. (1926–). American dramatist and novelist whose plays include *The Ginger Man* (59) and *Fairy Tales of New York* (60).

DUNCAN, RONALD (1914–). British verse dramatist and author, whose best known play is *This Way to the Tomb* (45), a religious masque. Wrote the libretto for Britten's *The Rape of Lucretia* (46). Adapted *The Eagle has Two Heads* from the French (46).

DUNSANY, LORD (1878–1957). Anglo-Irish dramatist who wrote many plays for the Abbey Theatre, including *The Glittering Gods* (09) and *The Laughter of the Gods* (19).

DYER, CHARLES (1928–). British dramatist and actor. After his successful *Rattle of a Simple Man* (63) about a shy football fan's encounter with a prostitute, he wrote *Staircase* (66), a frank comedy about a homosexual couple, one cruel and sarcastic, the other gentle, which was staged by the Royal Shakespeare Co. with Paul Scofield and Patrick Magee. *Mother Adam* (70).

EDWARDS, HILTON (1903–). British actor and director who, since founding the Gate Theatre, Dublin (28), with Mícheál MacLiammóir has been a key figure in the Irish theatre. Has directed over 300 plays there and at the Gaiety and played many classical and modern leading parts.

ELIOT, T. S. (1888–1965). American-born British poet and dramatist. His attempts to revive religious and poetic drama were distinguished and in their day often successful, if not very theatrical. Curiously, in his later plays it is hard to detect that verse is being used.

Eliot's first important play, possibly the one most likely to live theatrically, was *Murder in the Cathedral* (35), a fine religious drama about Becket, particularly suited to church performances. Revived by the Royal Shakespeare Co. (72). *The Family Reunion* (39) has a modern setting but draws inspiration from classical Greek drama, with one character pursued by the Eumenides. Some prefer this obviously poetic play to his later works. These were *The Cocktail Party* (49), his greatest success, *The Confidential Clerk* (53) and *The Elder Statesman* (58), all of which were first performed at Edinburgh Festivals and all, like the earlier plays, directed by E. Martin Browne (see above).

The religious and classical influence can be detected in the background of these three plays —in order of production, drawing-room comedy, farcical comedy and drama. For all their lack of true theatrical power and characterization, together with Fry's, they helped bring quality to the theatre in the 40s and early 50s at a time when it was sadly lacking. But it is for his poetry, not his plays that Eliot will live.

ERVINE, ST. JOHN (1883–1971).

Anglo-Irish dramatist and critic. Some of his early works were staged at the Abbey Theatre, Dublin, which he managed for a time. His best known plays are *Jane Clegg* (13), which gave Sybil Thorndike a fine role with Miss Horniman's company at the Gaiety, Manchester, and *Robert's Wife* (37), a West End success with Edith Evans and Owen Nares. Was dramatic critic of *The Observer* for most of the inter-war years.

EYRE, RONALD (1929–). British director and author of TV plays. Directed John McGrath's *Events while Guarding the Bofors Gun* (66) and *Bakke's Night of Fame* (68), also Robin Maugham's *Enemy* (69), and Donald Howarth's *Three Months Gone* (70). His delightful, inventive and affectionate production of Boucicault's *London Assurance* was a popular hit for the Royal Shakespeare Co. (70: New, 72). Directed a convincing *Mrs. Warren's Profession* (71) at the National Theatre.

FEIFFER, JULES (1929–). American strip-cartoonist and dramatist. Author of *Little Murders* (67), a satire on man's fascination with war and violence, and *God Bless* (68), a play set in the 'the immediate future with America fighting on three continents'. *The White House Murder Case* (70).

FERBER, EDNA (1887–1968). Her novel *Showboat* (see p. 196) was turned into a brilliant musical (26). With George Kaufman, she wrote *The Royal Family* (27), a satire on the Barrymores, *Dinner at Eight* (32), *Stage Door* (38), *The Land is Bright* (41) and *Bravo* (48).

FERNALD, JOHN (1905–). British director who has staged a vast number of modern and classical plays since 1929, but whose greatest achievement was to transfigure *RADA* (55–65) in a most remarkable way. His wife is the actress Jenny Laird.

FIELDS, JOSEPH (1895–1966). American dramatist. Plays include *My Sister Eileen* (40) which ran 864 performances on Broadway, *Junior Miss* (41) both with JEROME CHODOROV, which ran almost as long, and *The Tunnel of Love* (57) with Peter de Vries. All three did well in the West End.

FRAYN, MICHAEL (1933–). British dramatist and humorist. Author of *The Two of Us* (70), four playlets for an actor and actress, at least one of which suggested that a farce-writer had been born; also *The Sandboy* (71).

FRISBY, TERENCE (1932–). British dramatist. Author of the huge success *There's a Girl in my Soup* (66).

FRY, CHRISTOPHER (1907–). British dramatist and poet, possibly overrated by those who, like this writer, came of age theatrically just after the war. His *The Lady's Not for Burning* (48), a spring-like play set in medieval times, must always spell enchantment for those who remember how it lighted up a bleak period, even though it has been since criticized for lack of dramatic impetus. A hit at Chichester (72), it was greeted with joy by Harold Hobson and John Barber and savagely abused by Irving Wardle.

His first major piece was the joyous one-acter, *A Phoenix Too Frequent* (46). With Eliot he brought back verse to drama, the difference being that the public recognized his as verse. Other plays include the Biblical drama *The Firstborn* (48), *Thor with Angels* (48), the autumnal comedy *Venus Observed* (50), written for Olivier, a modern Mystery play *A Sleep of Prisoners* (51), *The Dark is Light Enough*, a 'winter piece' for Edith Evans, and *Curtmantle* (60) about Becket and Henry II, staged by the Royal Shakespeare Co.

Fry has also translated plays: *Ring Round the Moon* (50), *The Lark* (55), *Tiger at the Gates* (55), *Duel of Angels* (58) and *Judith* (60), all from the French, the first two by Anouilh, the rest by Giraudoux. Also *Peer Gynt* (70).

FUGARD, ATHOL (1932–). South African dramatist and director of a Theatre Group in Port Elizabeth. *The Blood Knot* (66), seen in London at the Hampstead Theatre Club, is a two-hander about Cape Coloured brothers one of whom tries to be white. This fine and powerful piece was followed by *People are Living Here* (70) set in a White Johannesburg kitchen, a grim, compassionate and comic glimpse of a small group of people.

GALSWORTHY, JOHN (1867–1933). British novelist and dramatist. His first play, *The Silver Box* (06), was produced at the Royal Court by the Barker–Vedrenne management. Many of his plays dealt with social problems, notably *Strife* (09) about a strike; *Justice* (10) about the law and prison. His later plays included *The Skin Game* (20), *Loyalties* (22), which touched on anti-Semitism, and *Escape* (26). His plays were well-made, forceful and honest, and important in their day: a scene in *Justice* showing the effects of solitary confinement had such an effect that it led to a change in the law.

GARLAND, PATRICK. British dramatist and director. After working in TV, mainly on Arts programmes, directed Alan Bennett's *Forty Years On* (68), and wrote and directed *Brief Lives* (68) with Roy Dotrice as Aubrey, which was later seen on Broadway. Directed *Cyrano* (70) at the National Theatre and Bennett's *Getting On* (71). Directed *Hair* in Israel (70) and *Hedda Gabler* in New York (71).

GASKILL, WILLIAM (1930–). British director mainly associated with the Royal Court and the National. First production at the former: *A Resounding Tinkle* (57). Directed *Epitaph for George Dillon* in London and New York (58), *Richard III* at Stratford (61). Associate Director of the National (63–5), where his productions included a brilliant *Recruiting Officer*, his Brechtian bias being confined to the programme notes. *Mother Courage* (65). Artistic director of the English Stage Co. (65–72), his productions including *Saved* (65, 69) and (Bond's) *Lear* (71). Directed *The Beaux, Stratagem* at the National (70). A notable teacher, encouraging actors to think deeply about their work.

GELBER, JACK (1932–). American dramatist. Author of *The Connection* (58), about drug addicts, and *The Apple* (61), a less successful experimental play about bigotry. Other plays include *Square in the Eye* (65) and *The Cuban Thing* (68).

GIBSON, WILLIAM (1914–). American dramatist, whose two-hander drama, *Two for the Seesaw* (58) was a great success, followed immediately after by *The Miracle Worker* (59) about the young Helen Keller. *John and Abigail* (69).

GOW, RONALD (1897–). British dramatist. Adapted *Love on the Dole* (35), *Ann Veronica* (49), *The Edwardians* (59), etc. Married to Wendy Hiller, see p. 167.

GRAY, SIMON (1936–). British dramatist and novelist. Plays include *Wise Child* (67), *Dutch Uncle* (68), *Spoiled* (71) and *Butley* (71), a brilliant and witty play which won the *Evening Standard* award for the Best Play of 1971.

GREEN, PAUL (1894–). American dramatist, author of regional dramas set in the South. His most notable play is *The House of Connelly* (31) produced by the Theater Guild, a neo-Chekhovian look at the Old South. *Johnny Johnson* (36) is an anti-war play, also staged by the Guild, with music by Kurt Weill. He later switched mainly to regional folk drama, notably the non-commercial North Carolina historical play *The Lost Colony* (37). *The Founders* (57) celebrated the first English colony at Jamestown.

GREENE, GRAHAM (1904–). British novelist and dramatist. His plays are *The Living Room* (53), a powerful drama of suicide and despair, *The Potting Shed* (57) about a return to belief, *The Complaisant Lover* (59), a serious comedy about adultery, and *Carving a Statue* (64), a tragi-farce. His books, *The Heart of the Matter* and *The Power and the Glory*, have both been dramatized, the former by himself and Basil Dean (50) and the latter by Pierre Bost and Dennis Cannan (56).

GREENWOOD, WALTER (1903–). British dramatist and novelist.

His adaptation (with Ronald Gow, see above) of his novel, *Love on the Dole* (35), a Depression drama set in his birthplace Salford, made his name. *The Cure for Love* (45) was a later success, as was *Saturday Night at the Crown* (54). *Hanky Panky* (71) was staged at the Mermaid.

GUARE, JOHN. American dramatist. Author of the grim farce *House of Blue Leaves* (71). 'Probably the most acerbic, ingenious comic playwright in America' (John Lahr).

HALL, PETER. See p. 104.

HALL, WILLIS (1929–). British dramatist, author of *The Long and the Short and the Tall* (58), a fine war play set in the Malayan jungle, about a patrol of N.C.O.s and privates and their attitude to a captured Japanese. Its quality was again realized in a revival (71). Has collaborated with KEITH WATERHOUSE (1929–), British dramatist and novelist, in several plays and screenplays, notably *Billy Liar* (60), from Waterhouse's novel. Best known for their film and TV work.

HALLIWELL, DAVID (1936–). British dramatist and director. Author of *Little Malcolm and his Struggle against the Eunuchs* (65), an entertaining satire on the 'angry young man' with underlying comment on violence and unrest, and of *K. D. Dufford* (69), a nobody who commits a child murder to become a somebody. Founder, with David Calderisi of the Quipu theatre group.

HAMBLETON, T. EDWARD. See p. 250.

HAMILTON, PATRICK. See p. 236.

HAMPTON, CHRISTOPHER (1946–). British dramatist. Resident dramatist at the Royal Court (68–70). His plays are *When Did You Last See My Mother* (67) about the problems of a young homosexual in a triangular relationship, *Total Eclipse* (68) about Verlaine and Rimbaud, and, most notably, *The Philanthropist* (70), an inventive, often startling comedy about a diffident, misunderstood and kindly philology don whose literal-mindedness adds to his troubles. There are several excellent parts in this often dazzling little piece, which is deliberately intended— though this need not concern the audience—as an ironic counterpart to Molière's *Le Misanthrope*. The role of the philologist gave Alec McCowen, and then George Cole, opportunities both took to give superb comedy performances. Translator of *Uncle Vanya*, *Hedda Gabler*, etc.

HANSBURY, LORRAINE (1930–65). American dramatist, whose hit comedy-drama, *Raisin in the Sun* (58) made an impact in its day because it was about a Black family. Just before she died she wrote *The Sign on Sidney Brustein's Window*, a more complex play which was greatly admired by many, despite a tepid reception.

HARE, DAVID (1947–). British dramatist who followed up his excellent *Slag* (71) with *The Great Exhibition* (72) a 'parody of all Court-type plays'.

HART, MOSS (1904–1961). American dramatist and writer of musicals (see p. 209). His first comedies were written with George Kaufman, including *You Can't Take It With You* (36), *I'd Rather Be Right* (37), *The Man Who Came to Dinner* and *George Washington Slept Here* (40). A later success was *Light Up the Sky* (48). Directed a number of plays of other authors including *Junior Miss* (41) and *Dear Ruth* (44). His autobiography *Act I* (59) is that rare thing, a theatre classic.

HASTINGS, MICHAEL (1938–). British dramatist and novelist, whose *Don't Destroy Me*, written when he was 17, is about a Jewish family in South London. It was produced at the New Lindsey Theatre Club (56). *The Silence of Lee Harvey Oswald* (66) is partly fact, partly an imaginative look at Oswald's life.

HECHT, BEN (1893–1964). American dramatist and novelist, whose best-known plays were written with Charles MacArthur. These include *The Front Page* (28), a racy newspaper story that even newspapermen admired, and the comedy *Twentieth Century* (32). The former is currently (73) a huge success at the National, its British première.

HELLMAN, LILLIAN (1905–). American dramatist, author of several scalding, well-constructed plays including *The Children's Hour* (34), which ran for 691 performances on Broadway. It was banned in Britain, its plot of the effects of gossip rumours of lesbianism on a school community being considered too much for sensitive playgoers. Other plays include the splendidly melodramatic *The Little Foxes* (39), later a Bette Davis film, *The Watch on the Rhine* (41), an anti-Nazi play set in America, *Another Part of the Forest* (46), the book for Bernstein's *Candide* (56) and *Toys in the Attic* (60), a torrid Southern drama.

HERBERT, JOCELYN (1917–). British designer especially noted for her work with the English Stage Co. where she is now a member of the Council and the Artistic Committee. Designed all Devine's Beckett and Ionesco productions, also the Wesker Trilogy (59–60). Other productions she has designed include *Sergeant Musgrave's Dance* (59), *The Changeling* (60), *The Kitchen* and *Luther* (61), *Inadmissible Evidence* (London,

64; New York, 65), *A Patriot for Me* (65), *Home* (London and New York 70), *The Changing Room* (71). Elsewhere has designed *Richard III* at Stratford (61) and the Olivier *Othello* (64), *Mother Courage* (65), *A Woman Killed with Kindness* and *Tyger* (71) for the National. Not a 'star' designer, simply one of the best in the world.

HOME, WILLIAM DOUGLAS (1912–). British dramatist who, after a prison drama, *Now Barabbas* (47), turned to comedy with huge success. His biggest hits have been *The Chiltern Hundreds* (47), *The Reluctant Debutante* (55), a classic of its kind, *The Secretary Bird* (69) and *The Jockey Club Stakes* (70). Has written a worthy autobiographical play, *The Bad Soldier Smith* (60) and has entertainingly attacked the critics. Currently (73) has another hit, *Lloyd George Knew my Father*.

HOOPER, EWAN (1935–). British actor, director and playwright, founder of Greenwich Theatre (opened 69).

HORNE, KENNETH (1900–). British dramatist whose pleasant comedies include *Love in a Mist* (41) and *Fools Rush In* (46).

HOWARD, SIDNEY (1891–1939). American dramatist, only one of whose plays, *They Knew What They Wanted* (24), would seem to have lasting appeal. This sentimental, gusto-laden comedy-drama about a mail order bride (played originally by Pauline Lord) has been filmed and also turned into the musical *The Most Happy Fella*. Other plays included *Yellow Jack* (34), a fine though unsuccessful piece about Yellow Fever and its conquest, and *Alien Corn* (33) with Katharine Cornell. Also adapted several plays.

HOWARTH, DONALD (1931–). British dramatist, actor and director, whose plays include *A Lily in Little India* (65) and *Three Months Gone* (70), linked by the same characters.

HOUSEMAN, LAURENCE (1865–1959). British dramatist and novelist, best remembered for his *Victoria Regina* (35) which—incredibly—ran into censorship trouble in Britain before becoming a popular hit (37), and doing Victoria's image much good in those Lytton Stracheyish days. Pamela Stanley played V.R. On Broadway, the play was a great success with Helen Hayes.

HUNTER, N. C. (1908–71). British dramatist, whose neo-Chekhovian plays were an easy target for the critics, but whose flair for writing good acting parts attracted star casts. His plays include *Waters of the Moon* (51) with Evans, Thorndike and Wendy Hiller, *A Day by the Sea* (53) with Gielgud and Richardson, Irene Worth and Megs

Jenkins, and *A Touch of the Sun* (58), with Redgrave, Wynyard and Ronald Squire; also *The Tulip Tree* (63) with Celia Johnson and John Clements. Significantly, these minor but atmospheric pieces held their audiences outside London and without stars.

INGE, WILLIAM (1913–). American dramatist, whose atmospheric, brooding, small-town dramas have been successful on stage and screen. His plays include *Come Back, Little Sheba* (50), *Picnic* (53), *Bus Stop* (55) and *The Dark at the Top of the Stairs* (57). *Bus Stop* is considered by many his finest work. Few romances in modern drama are so pleasing as this funny and moving love story of the gauche cowboy and the talentless nightclub 'chanteuse'.

JAMES, HENRY (1843–1916). Anglophile American novelist who only achieved the fame he sought in the theatre in other men's adaptations of his books long after his death. The best of these have been *The Heiress* (47) by Ruth and Augustus Goetz, from *Washington Square*, *The Innocents* (50) from *The Turn of the Screw*, adapted by William Archibald, and *The Aspern Papers* (59), adapted by Michael Redgrave. *The Turn of the Screw* was turned into a masterly opera by Benjamin Britten (54).

JEANS, RONALD (1887–). British dramatist. Wrote revues for Cochran and Charlot between the wars. Plays include the very successful *Young Wives' Tale* (49).

JELLICOE, ANN (1927–). British dramatist and director, and translator of Ibsen and Chekhov. Her first play, *The Sport of My Mad Mother* (56) is a violent, emotional, ritualistic and symbolic view of a gang of Teddy Boys and their not very understandable leader, Greta. *The Knack* (61)—the knack of getting the girl—is an amusing look at three flatmates and a girl. *Shelley* (65) is a biographical study of the poet. *The Giveaway* (69) is a satire on TV and other giveaway competitions. Her first two plays are theatrically her most exciting and successful.

JOHNSTON, DENIS (1901–). Irish dramatist, whose satiric *The Lady Says No!* (29) was followed by the famous, *The Moon on the Yellow River* (31), about an idealistic revolutionary who opposes the building of a power plant. His only other play which is sometimes revived is *The Dreaming Dust* (40) about Swift.

JONES, DAVID (1934–). British director, with the Royal Shakespeare Co. since 1962. His productions have included Mercer's *Belcher's Luck* (66) and *After Haggerty* (70) and two very fine Gorky revivals, *Enemies* (71) and *The Lower Depths* (72). His wife is SHEILA ALLEN, an Old Vic and

R.S.C. Portia, etc., and the creator of Helen Rawston in *Belcher's Luck*.

JOYCE, JAMES (1882–1941). Irish writer. His great *Ulysses* was dramatized as *Ulysses in Nighttown* (59) by Marjorie Barkentin, and *Bloomsday* by Allen McClelland (58), but not until 1970 was his only play, *Exiles*, triumphantly performed in London in a production by Harold Pinter, first at the Mermaid, then at the Aldwych (71). What has been dismissed in the past as inferior Ibsen, turned out to be a topical examination of a small group of people discarding conventional morality and attempting personal freedom.

KANIN, GARSON (1912–). American dramatist and director of plays and films, husband of Ruth Gordon (see Chapters 2 and 3). His best known play is *Born Yesterday* (46) which made a star of Judy Holliday, who played an ultimate dumb blonde with a moral streak. Among the many plays that he has directed, a particularly fine production was *The Diary of Anne Frank* (55).

KAUFMAN, GEORGE S. (1889–1961). American dramatist and director. Most of his long line of successes were written in collaboration with others, notably *Dulcy* (21) with Marc Connelly, which made a star of Lynn Fontanne, also *Merton of the Movies* (22) and *Beggar on Horseback*, their finest joint effort (24). Other successes included *The Royal Family* (27), inspired by the Barrymores, *Dinner at Eight* (32) and *Stage Door* (36), all with Edna Ferber; also *You Can't Take It With You* (36), a Pulitzer prize-winner, and *The Man Who Came to Dinner* (39), two splendid comedies, with Moss Hart. A post-war hit was *The Solid Gold Cadillac* (53), with Howard Teichmann. Also wrote musicals (see p. 210).

'The Great Collaborator' was also a great man of the theatre and a first-rate director of his own and other people's shows. This brilliant satirist was originally a humorous writer on the *New York Times*. He was one of the greatest of all Broadway figures. For a portrait of him, see *Act One* by Moss Hart.

KAZAN, ELIA (1909–). Turkish-born American director. An actor with Group Theater (32–9). Since 1940 has directed some of the most important plays of the modern American stage as well as some magnificent films. A brilliantly creative director, his productions include *The Skin of Our Teeth* (42), *All My Sons* and *A Streetcar Named Desire* (47), *Death of a Salesman* (49), *Cat on a Hot Tin Roof* (55), *J.B.* (58) and *Sweet Bird of Youth* (59). Co-director of the Lincoln Center (62–4). Has done more than any other American to bring about the modern Director's Theatre.

KENNY, SEAN (1932–). Irish designer, formerly an architect trained by Frank Lloyd Wright. Though the theatre has seen too little of him recently, from *The Shadow of a Gunman* (57) at the Lyric, Hammersmith, until the mid-60's his non-stop work included *The Hostage* (58) for Theatre Workshop, *Lock Up Your Daughters* (59), the opening production at the Mermaid, also *Oliver* (60), *The Devils*, *The Miracle Worker* and *Altona* (61), *Blitz* and *King Priam* (62), *Oliver* in New York (63), the National Theatre's opening production of *Hamlet* (63), *Pickwick* (65) and the much-booed, much applauded *Flying Dutchman* at Covent Garden (66). *Peer Gynt* (Chichester, 70).

A master of stage mechanics, including automation, most strikingly demonstrated in his collaboration with Lionel Bart. *Oliver* was automatically controlled by a stage crew of one.

KIMMINS, ANTHONY (1901–63). British dramatist. Author of the once notorious *While Parents Sleep* (32), *The Amorous Prawn* (59), etc. Wrote and directed many films.

KINGSLEY, SIDNEY (1906–). American dramatist and director whose first play, *Men in White*, won a Pulitzer prize (36). Other plays include his finest, *Dead End* (35), a Depression drama set

in New York's slums, *The Patriots* (43), and *Detective Story* (49), later made into a fine film. Brooks Atkinson describes *Dead End* as a raucous tone poem of the modern city. *Darkness at Noon* (51), from Koestler's novel, etc.

KOPIT, ARTHUR (1938–). American dramatist. His *Oh Dad, Poor Dad* (61), to use its shortened title, is a tragi-farce about the horrors of the American 'Mom'. *Indians* (68), as directed for the Royal Shakespeare Co. (its première) by Jack Gelber, and overloaded with an endless, irrelevant Dodge City scene by the author, failed to exploit the brilliant idea of getting across the White Man's treatment of the Indian in terms of Buffalo Bill's Wild West Show. American productions seem to have righted the matter.

KOPS, BERNARD (1920–). British dramatist, whose *The Hamlet of Stepney Green* (56) is an East End Jewish comic fantasy. Other plays include *Enter Solly Gold* (62). The author adds dance, song and verse, as well as local colour and sheer charm, to studies of family relationships and his social criticisms.

LANGLEY, NOEL (1911–). South African dramatist. Author of *Cage Me a Peacock* (46) and, with Robert Morley, *Edward, My Son* (47), etc., also the filmscript of *The Wizard of Oz*.

LAURENTS, ARTHUR (1920–). American dramatist. His *Home of the Brave* (45) about war-wounded veterans, dealt with anti-Semitism, which was switched to colour prejudice in the more famous film. *The Time of the Cuckoo* (52) about a spinster's fling in Venice, gave Shirley Booth (and later, in the film *Summer Madness*, Katherine Hepburn) a fine role. For his work in musicals see p. 212.

LAWLER, RAY (1922–). Australian dramatist, whose *Summer of the Seventeenth Doll* (55) about an ageing sugar-cane cutter is realistically tough and written with considerable understanding. His other plays have not matched this achievement.

LAWRENCE, D. H. (1885–1930). British novelist, poet and dramatist. Though his plays were written earlier than the span of this book, they were only discovered in the 1960s thanks to the English Stage Co. Admirers of the author will feel completely at home in the Nottinghamshire mining community depicted in *A Collier's Friday Night*, *The Daughter-in-Law* and *The Widowing of Mrs. Holroyd*. The director, PETER GILL (1939–), was mainly responsible for these re-discoveries.

LAWSON, JOHN HOWARD (1895 –). American dramatist. A Marxist and Expressionist, his first professionally produced play was *Roger Bloomer* (23). Author of many film scripts until blacklisted in 1948. His finest play is *Processional* (25) which he called a 'jazz symphony of American life'. The ordinary citizen is seen as the victim of capitalism and hostile organizations.

LEONARD, HUGH (1926–). Irish dramatist. Plays include *Stephen D* (Dublin, 62; London, 63). Also a well-known TV writer.

LEVY, BEN (1900–). British dramatist, married to the fine American actress, Constance Cummings (see p. 93). His plays include *Clutterbuck* (46), *Return to Tyassi* (50) and *The Rape of the Belt* (57).

LINDSAY, HOWARD (1889–1968) and RUSSEL CROUSE (1893–1966). American dramatists whose family comedy *Life with Father* (39) ran for 3,213 performances in New York and over 400 in London. A later success was *State of the Union* (45), a political comedy that gained a Pulitzer Prize.

LINKLATER, ERIC (1899–). British dramatist, novelist and historian, whose comedies include *Love in Albania* (49) and *The Atom Doctor* (50), set in his native Scotland. Has also written the historical play, *Breakspeare in Gascony* (59).

LITTLEWOOD, JOAN. See THEATRE WORKSHOP, p. 254.

LIVINGS, HENRY (1929–). British dramatist and actor, author of several hilarious, realistic and at times fantastical comedies and farces, mainly about disaster-prone little men who challenge and bring down Authority. The background is usually Northern and working class. Plays include *Stop it, Whoever You Are* (60) whose hero is a lavatory attendant called Perkin Warbeck (see p. 226), *Big Soft Nellie* (61) about a mother's boy, *Nil Carborundum* (62), set in an R.A.F. kitchen, *Eh?* (64) about the wrecking of a factory by an underdog of a boilerman, and *Honour and Offer* (69). His first *Pongo Plays* (71) are short Lancashire folk comedies set in the late 19th century, and not unlike *Commedia dell'arte* plays.

LOGAN, JOSHUA (1908–). American dramatist, director and author of the South Pacific war comedy *Mister Roberts* (48). For his notable work in musicals see p. 213. His straight productions include *Picnic* (53), *Middle of the Night* (56) and *The World of Susy Wong* (58).

LONSDALE, FREDERICK (1881–1954). British dramatist. Author of popular Society comedies of manners of considerable craftsmanship, most notably *Aren't We All?* (23), *The Last of Mrs. Cheyney* (25) and *On Approval* (27), none of which look like being forgotten.

LOOS, ANITA (1893–). American

CTT–D

dramatist and author. Plays include *Gentlemen Prefer Blondes* (26) with John Emerson, and *Gigi* (51).

LOWELL, ROBERT (1917–). American poet and dramatist. Author of *The Old Glory*, three verse plays from stories by Melville and Hawthorne. The third of them, *Benito Cereno*, set on a slave ship in 1800, but with many contemporary implications, made a considerable impression at the Mermaid in Jonathan Miller's production (67).

LUKE, PETER (1919–). British dramatist whose adaptation of Corvo's (alias Rolfe's) novel, *Hadrian the Seventh*, where the author imagines himself Pope by wish-fulfilment, was a great success in London with Alec McCowen in the lead (67).

MacARTHUR, CHARLES (1896–1956). American dramatist. Author, with Ben Hecht (see above) of the fine newspaper play, *Front Page* (28), a splendidly racy and popular melodrama, now a hit at the National (72), and the satirical society comedy, *Twentieth Century* (32). The husband of Helen Hayes (see p. 167) and father of the actor JAMES MacARTHUR (1937–), he also wrote many screenplays, mostly with Hecht.

MCCLINTIC, GUTHRIE (1893–1961). American director, manager and actor. Husband of

Katherine Cornell (see p. 156). Together with her and in plays without her, he played a key role in helping raise standards on Broadway, especially from the 30s onwards when his work included *The Barretts of Wimpole Street* (31), a very fine *Romeo and Juliet* (34), and three successful plays of Maxwell Anderson, *Winterset* (35), *High Tor* (36) and *Key Largo* (39). Later productions included Anouilh's version of *Antigone* (46) and Fry's *The Dark is Light Enough* (54).

MCCRACKEN, ESTHER (1902–71). British dramatist and author of two huge successes, *Quiet Wedding* (38) and *Quiet Weekend* (41).

MCCULLERS, CARSON (1917–67). American dramatist and novelist, whose biggest success, adapted from her novel, has been *The Member of the Wedding* (50). *The Square Root of Wonderful* (58) was an original play, while her dark, unromantic, love story, *The Ballad of the Sad Café* (63), was successfuly adapted by Edward Albee for the stage.

MACDONALD, MURRAY (1899–). British director, manager and former actor. Productions include *The Road to Rome*, *Judgement Day* and *Robert's Wife* (37), *Romeo and Juliet* (38) at the Vic, *The Eagle has Two Heads* (47). Since then has directed many commercial plays, including *The Jockey Club Stakes* (70).

MACDOUGALL, ROGER (1910–). British dramatist, author of several well-written comedies including *To Dorothy, a Son* (50) and *Escapade* (52).

MCGRATH, JOHN (1935–). British dramatist. Author of two striking plays, the finer being *Events while Guarding the Bofors Gun* (66), later filmed, and *Bakke's Night of Fame* (68) about a condemned American murderer successfully provoking everyone involved with him in the Death Cell. *Plugged in*, three short plays (72).

MACLEISH, ARCHIBALD (1892–). American poet and dramatist. His *J.B.* (58), very successful in America, is a modern Job drama set in a circus tent. With Kazan's direction and a star cast it did not convince everyone that it was a major poetic drama, but received great acclaim and a Pulitzer Prize.

MACLIAMMÓIR, MICHÉAL (1899–). Irish actor and dramatist, see p. 118.

MacOWAN, MICHAEL (1906–). British director and, from 1954–66, Principal of the London Academy of Music and Dramatic Art. His most important prewar post was as Director of the Westminster Theatre (36–9), where he directed a remarkable range of plays, including *A Month in the Country*, *The Wild Duck*, *Waste*, *Heartbreak House*, *Anna Christie*, *Hamlet*, *Volpone*,

Marco Millions, Miss Julie, Candida and other important revivals. Later productions included *The Linden Tree* (47), *Rosmersholm* (50), *A Sleep of Prisoners* (London and New York, 51) and other Fry plays, *The River Line* (52), *The Burning Glass* (54), both by Morgan, *The Seagull* (56) and *The Potting Shed* (58). Rapidly transformed LAMDA into a major drama school and is still associated with it, also with the National Theatre School of Canada in Quebec.

MACRAE, ARTHUR (1908–1962). British actor and dramatist. His plays include two big successes, *Under the Counter* (45) and *Traveller's Joy* (48). Also contributed to some very famous revues, including *The Globe Revue* (52) and *Airs on a Shoestring* (53). Translations from the French include Roussin's *Figure of Fun* (51).

MCWHINNIE, DONALD (1920–). British director of *The Caretaker* (London, 60; New York, 61), *Everything in the Garden* (62), *There'll Be Some Changes Made* (69), *The Apple Cart* (70), etc., and many TV and radio plays.

MAMOULIAN, ROUBEN (1898–). Russian-born American director of plays, films, operas and musicals (also see p. 213). For the Theater Guild (27–31) his productions included *Marco Millions, R.U.R.* and *A Month in the Country*.

MANKOWITZ, WOLF (1924–). British novelist and dramatist, author of *The Bespoke Overcoat* (55) and several musicals, see p. 214. Has presented plays including *A Taste of Honey* (58).

MARCUS, FRANK (1928–). British dramatist and critic (of the *Sunday Telegraph*). Plays include the very successful *The Killing of Sister George* (65) and *Mrs. Mouse, are you Within* (68), both amusing, tolerant views of relationships, also *Notes on a Love Affair* (72), like the others centred around women, a rare characteristic in modern drama, as every actress knows.

MAROWITZ, CHARLES (1934–). American dramatist, director, critic and one-man ginger group resident in Britain, founder of the Open Space (68), London's leading experimental theatre. Assisted Brook in the LAMDA Theatre of Cruelty season (64); associated with *Encore* magazine until its demise; brilliantly directed *Loot* (66), and has written three Shakespearean 'collages', one of which, *An Othello* (72), was surprisingly meaningful and worthwhile.

MARSHALL, NORMAN (1901–). British director of many modern and classical plays from the late 20s onwards. In the 30s, ran the Cambridge Festival Theatre and, later, the Gate Theatre. A busy administrator and lecturer, apart from his directing commitments. The author of *The Other Theatre*

(47), a key book about the non West End theatre between the wars.

MAUGHAM, W. SOMERSET (1874–1965). British dramatist and novelist. Though none of his plays—he had four running in 1908—are likely to live as long as his best short stories and novels, his wit and sharp observation were evident from the first, reaching their height in the 20s. His plays from this period include *The Circle* (21), *The Constant Wife* (26), and, more seriously, *The Sacred Flame* (28), about a mercy killing, *The Letter* and *For Services Rendered* (32). Gave up the theatre after *Sheppey* (33), disappointed by its reception. His lively farce, *Home and Beauty* (19), was successfully staged at the National (68).

MERCER, DAVID (1928–). British dramatist. Author of *Ride a Cock Horse* (65), *Belcher's Luck* (66), *After Hagerty* (70) and *Flint* (70), and of TV plays and screenplays. A controversial playwright, who has veered from Marxism to concern for the individual, and who, from personal experience, is involved in the problems of the educated son of working-class parents. His most appealing play to date has been *Flint*, part melodrama, part farcical comedy, with a 70-year-old Kensington vicar, lecherous and agnostic, as its unlikely hero.

MESSEL, OLIVER (1905–). British designer. Has worked for Cochran in revue (26–31), in ballet and opera (most notably at Glyndebourne), musicals, the classics, films and modern plays. These last include *The Lady's Not for Burning* (49), *Ring Round the Moon* and *The Little Hut* (50), *Under the Sycamore Tree* (52), *The Dark is Light Enough* (London and New York, 54), *The House of Flowers* (54) and *Rashomon* (59) both in New York. Renowned for elegant, witty and romantically decaying settings, he also has a gift for mysterious enchantment, as in his *Dream* (38) and *Tempest* (40) His *Little Hut*—huge breadfruits and coconuts and lush plants—was a typical joy, as was his magical fairy tale contribution to *Ring Round the Moon*. Designed the interiors of New York's Billy Rose theatre, also the theatre at Whitehaven in Cumberland.

MIELZINER, JO (1901–). American designer, whose work has, since 1924, greatly enhanced well over a hundred plays and musicals (see p. 215). The plays range from Shakespeare, Chekhov, *The Barretts of Wimpole Street* and *Abe Lincoln in Illinois* before the war to *A Streetcar Named Desire, Death of a Salesman* and *Cat on a Hot Tin Roof* after it. With Eero Saarinen, designed the repertory theatre for the Lincoln Center.

MILLAR, RONALD (1919–). British dramatist and actor. His

plays include a good suspense drama, *Waiting for Gillian* (54), a hit comedy, *The Bride and the Bachelor* (56). Book and lyrics of *Robert and Elizabeth* (64). Recently enjoyed the biggest success of his career with *Abelard and Heloise* (70) which is also his finest play.

MILLER, ARTHUR (1915–). American dramatist. This major playwright, the finest, with Tennessee Williams, of the postwar years in America, was brought up in the Depression, and his work reflects a strong social conscience, deep interest in family and human relationships generally, and concern for the responsibilities of the individual. His admiration of Ibsen is admitted. The influence showed in his first great success, *All My Sons* (47), an exposé of war profiteering and individual guilt against a family setting.

There followed his finest and most famous play, *Death of a Salesman* (48), see p. 19. In the era of McCarthy, Miller first adapted *An Enemy of the People* (50) which (incredibly, from 3,000 miles away) flopped badly despite a magnificent cast, then wrote *The Crucible* (53) about the Salem witch hunts, but drawing an obvious parallel with the McCarthy smears. *A View from the Bridge* (55) was later seen in London in a longer version: in New York it was staged with *A Memory of Two Mondays. After the Fall* (64), taken by all to be an autobiographical play of

Miller's marriage to Marilyn Monroe, upset many, so its worth cannot yet be easily gauged. *Incident at Vichy* (68) is an examination of how the Nazi treatment of the Jews could come about, and a very powerful piece indeed. *The Price* (68), much more admired in London than in New York, is an intense realistic look at why two brothers have respectively succeeded and failed. *The Creation of the World and other Business* (72) disappointed his admirers.

The signs are that Miller, at the peak for many years now as a master craftsman, is less interested in the theatre than formerly. This must be a matter of deep regret to theatregoers.

MILLER, JASON. American dramatist whose *That Championship Season* (72) was voted the best of the season by New York's critics.

MILNE, A. A. (1882–1956). British novelist, the creator of Winnie the Pooh, and author of light, whimsical comedies, notably *Mr. Pim Passes By* (19) and *The Dover Road* (23). Now best remembered for his adaptation of *The Wind in the Willows, Toad of Toad Hall* (29).

MORGAN, CHARLES (1894–1958). British novelist, critic and dramatist, whose plays are serious and worthy. They were topical and written in what John Russell Taylor has called 'self-consciously beautiful mandarin prose'. They are *The Flashing*

Stream (38), *The River Line* (52) and *The Burning Glass* (54). Dramatic critic of *The Times* (26–39).

MORTIMER, JOHN (1923–   ). British dramatist with a flair for dialogue and characterisation, especially in his one-acters, *The Dock Breif* (57) and *Lunch Hour* (60). His autobiographical *A Journey Round my Father* (70) is perhaps his best play, *Collobo-ration* (73) his funniest.

NASH, N. RICHARD (1916–). American dramatist best known for an enchanting piece of Americana, *The Rainmaker* (54).

NAUGHTON, BILL (1910–). British dramatist, whose most successful comedies are *Alfie* (63) and *Spring and Port Wine* (64).

NICHOLS, MIKE (1931–). American director and enter-tainer. Productions include *Bare-foot in the Park* (63), *The Odd Couple* (65), and *The Prisoner of Second Avenue* (71). A very professional director who became widely known in *An Evening of Elaine May and Mike Nichols* (60).

NICHOLS, PETER (1927–). British dramatist, whose first play, *A Day in the Life of Joe Egg* (67), was a sensitive yet comic handling of the strains of life on a marriage when the only child is spatic. *The National Health* (69), is a tragi-comic look at a hospital ward. *Forget-me-not Lane* (71) is a brilliant,

semi-autobiographical piece based on the author's child-hood during the war.

NOVELLO, IVOR (1893–1951). British composer, dramatist and actor. This first of a number of appearances in the book is to note him as a straight play-wright, especially with the melo-drama *The Rat* (24) collaborating with Constance Collier, and the comedy *We Proudly Present* (47).

O'CASEY, SEAN (1884–1964). Irish dramatist. His *The Shadow of a Gunman* (23), followed by *Juno and the Paycock* (24), see p. 15, and *The Plough and the Stars* (26) revealed a great playwright. Not since Jacobean times had a writer in English achieved tragedies, interspersed with comedy and near farce, written in language that was at once realistic, poetic and always memorable.

With these produced at the Abbey Theatre, he ceased writ-ing about the Dublin of the Troubles (16–22) which had in-spired all of them. He settled in England where he wrote a magnificent anti-war play, *The Silver Tassie* (28), 'to go into the heart of war' in a symbolic second act. This was rejected by the Abbey, but produced in London by Cochran. For many years he refused to allow his plays to be performed at the Abbey.

The finest of his later plays are

possibly the comedy, *Purple Dust* (40) and *Red Roses for Me* (43), a symbolic drama about Ireland. His final works blaze with vitality, but are less convincing. An immortal.

ODETS, CLIFFORD (1906–63). American dramatist whose first great success, *Waiting for Lefty* (35), is featured on p. 17. Next came his portrait of a working class Jewish family, *Awake and Sing* (35) and its 'struggle for life among petty conditions'. Its now evident sentimentality has not affected its impassioned truthfulness. His biggest commercial success, produced like the earlier plays by the Group Theater, was *Golden Boy* (37), about a young violinist ruined by being forced to become a successful boxer. Not until *The Big Knife* (49) and *The Country Girl* (50), renamed *Winter Journey* in Britain, did he achieve another major play. The first was an attack on the Hollywood where he worked, the second a magnificently theatrical show business story. Both were later filmed. Too much was expected of Odets after his first successes, but, as it stands, his career was a notable one by any reckoning.

O'NEILL, EUGENE (1888–1953). American dramatist. His autobiographical *Long Day's Journey into Night* (56), see p. 22, is now generally regarded as the greatest play written by an American, and his position as America's leading and most influential playwright seems finally established.

The son of the star actor, James O'Neill (James Tyrone in *Long Day's Journey*), his first success came with *Beyond the Horizon* (20). There followed fourteen very productive years, the plays including *The Emperor Jones* (20), about a Negro ruler, *Anna Christie* (21), fallen woman redeemed by love, *All God's Chillun Got Wings* (24) and *Desire Under the Elms* (24), a tortured emotional drama set on a New England farm of the 1850s. Then came his finest play so far, *The Great God Brown* (26), followed by *Marco's Millions* (28), an unusually serene comedy satire, and the huge, very powerful and emotional *Strange Interlude* (28). *Mourning Becomes Electra* (31), again very long, is the Oresteia set in post-Civil War New England, and *Ah, Wilderness* (33) is a warmly personal and nostalgic comedy.

O'Neill returned to the theatre with *The Iceman Cometh* (46, written earlier), a Gorky-like, pessimistic piece set among life's derelicts. Its revival in the 50s marked the beginning of the playwright's reappraisal and rise to his present fame. His last play was the unsuccessful *A Moon for the Misbegotten* (43, produced 47), then after his death came *Long Day's Journey into Night* and final recognition of his greatness, warts and all.

The chief 'wart' according to some, is his poverty of language.

Tynan, reviewing *Iceman*, admitted that O'Neill wrote clumsily and top-heavily, but spoke of his autobiographical intensity and of being in the presence of someone whose 'vision of life is as profoundly dark as any since Aeschylus'. So great was O'Neill's involvement with his characters that structural deficiencies, the sometimes poor, cliché-ridden dialogue—which always acts better than it reads—count as nothing. The present author, with lines from *Long Day's Journey* still ringing in his ears, is not prepared to agree that O'Neill's language is so impoverished.

ORTON, JOE (1933–67). British dramatist and author of black comedies and farces, whose brilliant dialogue and grisly, inventive plots make up for lack of characterization. His first success, *Entertaining Mr. Sloane* (64) won a critics' award and was followed by his best play, *Loot* (see p. 227). Other plays followed, his last, *What the Butler Saw*, being produced posthumously (69).

OSBORNE, JOHN (1929–). British dramatist whose *Look Back in Anger* brought about a major revival in British drama (see p. 20). An earlier play, *Epitaph for George Dillon* (Cambridge 56: London 58), written with Anthony Creighton, followed. It is regarded by many as a better constructed, though less crucial play. *The Entertainer*

(57), a splendidly theatrical piece, has proved an easy target for critics, who cite its failure to integrate the Brechtian music hall scenes with the realistic rest, and the central theme of England in decay, yet it works wonderfully with a fine actor in the central role of Archie Rice, the third-rate music-hall comic.

Osborne's most acclaimed plays have been *Luther* (61) with the historical rebel as its hero, *Inadmissible Evidence* (64) a study of a solicitor in disintegration, and *A Patriot for Me* (65), arguably his finest play the story of an historical Austro-Hungarian officer, blackmailed for his homosexuality into becoming a spy. This theme is set against a brilliant panoramic view of a period and contains a famous 'Drag' ball scene.

His later plays, *Time Present* (68), *The Hotel in Amsterdam* (68) and *West of Suez* (71) have found the playwright increasingly under attack from critics of every generation, some of the younger ones apparently resent his growing objectivity and the disappearance of Porter-like rebels from the scene. Yet many find the mood he evokes enthralling, notably in *Hotel in Amsterdam* and, especially, *West of Suez*, a moving, amusing and evocative piece, set in an ex-colony, whose underlying theme is, some feel, the power and glory of the English language and the communication it brings about, together with a lament that it is being assaulted by barbarians. It should be noted that even Osborne's detractors allow him extraordinary eloquence, theatrical flair and the ability to write juicy parts for actors and, increasingly, actresses. At the time of writing (72) his *A Sense of Detachment*, a Pirandello-like look at contemporary problems, has had his detractors howling.

OWEN, ALUN (1926–). British dramatist of stage and, especially, TV plays. His first theatre piece was *Progress in the Park* (59), a love story set in Liverpool against a background of parental opposition and religious and racial tension. *The Rough and Ready Lot* (59) is an historical drama of religious and revolutionary strife in the South America of the 1860s, the protagonists being mercenaries. *There'll Be Some Changes Made* (69) has a Negress encouraging a White to revenge herself on men.

PAGE, ANTHONY (1935–). British director, particularly noted for his productions of Osborne's play, including *Inadmissible Evidence* (64), *A Patriot for Me* (65), *Time Present* (68), *The Hotel in Amsterdam* (68) and *West of Suez* (71). Began his association with the English Stage Company in 1958, becoming artistic director (65) for a season and again in 1971. His productions for the Company, Osborne apart, have included *A Cuckoo in the Nest* and *Waiting for Godot*. Other productions have included Livings's *Nil Carborundum* at the Arts (62), *Hamlet* at Nottingham (71), and *The Rules of the Game* for the *National Theatre* (71). Has also directed several important TV productions.

PATRICK, JOHN (1902–). American dramatist. Plays include *The Hasty Heart* (45), set in a jungle hospital in World War Two and later filmed, and *The Teahouse of the August Moon* (53)—from Vern Sneider's novel —a huge and well-deserved hit on both sides of the Atlantic, set in American-held Okinawa after the war. This very funny play about the effects of local customs on the Americans is part broad comedy, part fairy tale and sheer delight. The stellar film, though good enough, tried too hard and missed the bliss.

PENN, ARTHUR (1922–). American director, who before becoming a major film director was responsible for a number of Broadway productions, including *Two for the Seesaw* (New York and London, 58), *The Miracle Worker* (59), *Toys in the Attic* (60) and *All the Way Home* (60). Later stagings included *Golden Boy* (64) and *Wait until Dark* (66).

PINTER, HAROLD (1930–). British dramatist, director and actor and the most internationally acclaimed British playwright for several decades. The master of the pause, to the extent that a

'Pinter pause' is now theatre English, as is 'Pinteresque'. Also renowed for the hidden menace, for showing the jockeying for position in relationships, and for what Ronald Hayman calls 'the irrationality of dialogue', a rare thing in drama where dialogue tends to be far sleeker than in reality. His hold over his audience is often total, in striking contrast to other members of the Theatre of the Absurd into which he has been conveniently slotted.

Pinter does not claim to know everything about his characters —only what happens to them on stage—unlike most novelists and dramatists. His early plays are mainly concerned with the working-class, his later ones are more sophisticated, more sexual, a different form of jockeying for power. But all his plays are in different degrees ambiguous, simple, complex, dreamlike, disturbing and often riveting. They are also often very funny.

The plays include *The Room* (57, produced 60), the even more menacing *The Dumb Waiter* (57, produced 60), *The Birthday Party* (58), now widely regarded as one of his finest plays (see p. 23), and *The Caretaker* (60) his most famous play, with two particularly memorable characters, Ashton, who has had shock treatment, and Davies, the tramp whose papers are at Sidcup.

There followed *A Slight Ache* (61), *A Night Out* (61), more realistic than most, *The Collec-*

tion (62), a comedy of manners, *The Lovers* (63), a masterly piece, and *The Homecoming* (65), Pinter's biggest Broadway success, but too detached for many of his admirers. Next came *Landscape* and *Silence* (69), the former a short and 'easy' piece with a husband and wife reminiscing, but not at each other, and with one of the most moving last lines in drama, and the second with a motionless, Beckett-like trio in a void. *The Tea Party* and *The Basement* (70) were successful transfers from television, in which medium Pinter has had many successes, as he has in radio, and in writing screenplays. He has recently become a director of plays other than his own, including Simon Gray's *Butley* (71) and James Joyce's *Exiles* (71).

PLATER, ALAN (1935–). British dramatist. Author of *Close the Coalhouse Door* (68), etc., and many TV plays.

PRIESTLEY, J. B. (1894–). British dramatist and novelist, whose theatre career began with his adaptation, with Edward Knoblock, of his novel, *The Good Companions* (31). Next came his three plays about Time, *Dangerous Corner* (32), *Time and the Conways* (37) and *I Have Been Here Before* (37), also the pleasant comedy, *Laburnum Grove* (33), *Eden End* (34) and the farcical comedy *When We Are Married* (38). Two experimental plays were *Music at*

Night (38) and the much under-rated *Johnson over Jordan*, and later plays have included *An Inspector Calls* (46) and *The Linden Tree* (47). Apart from his adaptation of Iris Murdoch's *A Severed Head* (54), he would seem to have given up the theatre, much to the theatre's loss. His widely differing plays have rarely been less than theatrically effective, his social comment has often got across, and, as generations of playgoers know, he is a true man of the theatre who knows how to write for both actors and audiences.

QUINTERO, JOSÉ (1924–). American director and founder of the Off-Broadway Circle-in-the-Square. Director of two famous productions of O'Neill's works which finally established the playwright's supreme place in American drama, the revival of *The Iceman Cometh* (56) and, on Broadway, the first production of the posthumous *Long Day's Journey into Night* (56), see p. 22. Other productions have included *Strange Interlude* (63), *More Stately Mansions* (67) and *Gandhi* (70).

RATTIGAN, TERENCE (1911–). British dramatist whose immense popularity has been earned by a series of very well-made comedies and dramas, several of which were perfect examples of their kind. These are *French Without Tears* (36), his first big comedy success, *The Winslow Boy* (46), a drama

based on the Archer-Shee case, *The Browning Version* (48), a one act tragedy about a failed school-master, and his most famous play, *The Deep Blue Sea* (52). In this 'searing study of the destructive zeal of love' (Tynan), he wrote one of the finest parts for an actress in modern times, originally played by Peggy Ashcroft. Kenneth More was her ex-R.A.F. lover who could not meet up with her demands. The play's only weakness—the film had many—was, arguably, a tidy, instead of tragic, ending.

Other successes have included *While the Sun Shines* (43), *Separate Tables* (54) and *Ross* (60), about Lawrence of Arabia. His latest play (70), *Bequest to the Nation*, a study of Nelson and Lady Hamilton, was less successful. Few playwrights have given more widespread pleasure than Rattigan, who has also worked extensively in films. Knighted (71).

RICE, ELMER (1892–1967). American dramatist. After an early success with *On Trial* (14), his first major play, usually considered his finest, was the expressionist *The Adding Machine* (23), which attacked regimented, materialistic society. *Street Scene* (29) was realistic social comment with sentimentality and violence combined, and won a Pulitzer Prize. Other plays are *Councellor-at-Law* (31), *Dream Girl* (45) a sentimental fantasy, and two anti-Nazi pieces, the powerful *Judgement Day* (34) and the less effective *Flight to the West* (40). Rice was one of the founder members of the Playwrights' Producing Company. Author of two revealing books, *The Living Theatre* (64) and his autobiography, *Minority Report* (64).

RICHARDSON, TONY (1928–). British director. Became Associate Director of the English Stage Company (55) (see p. 242), for whom he staged John Osborne's *Look Back in Anger*, *The Entertainer* and *Luther*. Other notable productions of modern drama have included Ionesco's *The Chairs* and *The Lesson* (57), Faulkner's *Requiem for a Nun* (London, 57; New York, 59), Tennessee Williams's *Orpheus Descending* (59). His Stratford production of *Pericles* (58) and *Othello* (59) were respectively forgiveably and entertainingly wilful, and, in the latter, lacking in good casting and impact. The verse-speaking in his *Dream* (62) at the Royal Court was happily unique. Also a television and notable film director.

RIGGS, LYNN (1900–54). American dramatist whose folk play, *Green Grow the Lilacs* (31) presented by the Theater Guild, was later faithfully transformed by Oscar Hammerstein for the Guild into *Oklahoma!* Also wrote other regional dramas.

ROBINSON, LENNOX (1886–1958). Irish dramatist, director, manager and critic associated for many years with the Abbey Theatre. Plays included political and patriotic tragedies, also comedies. His greatest success was *The White-Headed Boy* (16). An imaginative and sympathetic craftsman, of immense influence in the Irish theatre.

ROOSE-EVANS, JAMES (1927–). British director and founder and artistic director of the very successful Hampstead Theatre Club (59–70). Directed many plays there himself, including West End transfers: *Spitting Image* (68), *The Happy Apple* (70), etc. Directed *The Dumb Waiter* at the Royal Court (60). Author of *Directing a Play* and *Experimental Theatre*.

ROSS, GEORGE (1907–) and CAMPBELL SINGER (1909–). South African-born co-authors of plays with a business background, including the long-running *Guilty Party* (61). The latter is the well-known actor.

SAROYAN, WILLIAM (1908–). American dramatist whose friendly one-acter, *My Heart's in the Highlands* (39) was followed by his best and best-known play, *The Time of Your Life* (39), set in Nick's, a San Francisco honky-tonk. His vein of breezy and genial romantic realism has been tapped in a number of plays since, including *The Cave Dwellers* (57) set in an abandoned theatre.

SAUNDERS, JAMES (1925–). British dramatist whose early plays show Ionesco's influence, notably *Alas, Poor Fred. Next Time I'll Sing To You* (63) is a study of the hermit of Great Canfield and *A Scent of Flowers* (64) is a moving tragi-comedy. Co-dramatist (with Iris Murdoch) of *The Italian Girl* (68). *The Travails of Sancho Panza* at the National (69). *Games after Liverpool* (72).

SAVORY, GERALD (1909–). British dramatist and actor, whose *George and Margaret* (37), a very funny domestic comedy, ran for 799 performances. Later plays include *A Likely Tale* (56) and *Come Rain, Come Shine* (58). Head of Plays, BBC TV (65–).

SCHARY DORÉ (1905–). American dramatist, director and producer, whose plays include *Sunrise at Campobello* (58). New York's first Commissioner of Cultural Affairs (70).

SCHNEIDER, ALAN (1917–). Russian born American director, whose many important productions in New York, Washington D.C. and elsewhere have included *Who's Afraid of Virginia Woolf!* (New York, 63; London, 64). Has also directed Pinter, Beckett, etc., including *Godot* (71).

SHAFFER, PETER (1926–). British dramatist who made his name with *Five Finger Exercise*

(58), a strong, realistic portrait of family tension. A delightful double bill, *The Private Ear* and *The Public Eye* (62) was followed by a fine and boldly epic treatment of the Spanish conquest of Peru, *The Royal Hunt of the Sun* (64), overwhelmingly performed at the National Theatre. *Black Comedy* (65) is a short joy. *The White Liars* (67). *The Battle of Shrivings* (70) is a brave effort to make a major philosopher the central figure of a play. For his brother, Anthony Shaffer, see p. 235.

SHAW, GEORGE BERNARD (1856–1950). Anglo-Irish dramatist and critic and the most influential British playwright since Shakespeare. Now a classic, most of his colossal career lies outside the span of this book, the major works which lie within it being *Heartbreak House* (20), *Back to Methusalah* (22) and *St. Joan* (23), see p. 15. Perhaps his political comedy, *The Apple Cart* (29), is almost in the same league as these masterpieces, though parts of the mighty *Methusalah* are second-rate Shaw, notably *The Tragedy of an Elderly Gentleman*. Of the later works, only *The Millionairess* (36) and, perhaps, *In Good King Charles's Golden Days* (39) have survival value.

Yet, as most regular, Shaw-hunting theatregoers know, even the least of his later works have much to offer, and not just a command of language which remained until the end. *Too True to be Good* (32) has been successfully revived in the 60s, many other late plays not unsuccessfully. Accusations of weak characterization and construction often crumble when even the slightest of the plays is actually staged. The Shavian ideas, expressed with lucidity and steady wit, survive after the follies they expose have been reformed, except when the ideas are sub-standard and quirky as in *Geneva* (38). Obituaries have been written over his work since his death with fatuous regularity, the pigmy writers being unaware that a mountain cannot be felled by mice.

SHAW, IRWIN (1913–). American dramatist whose first two plays, the anti-war *Bury the Dead* (36) and *Siege* (37) about the Spanish Civil War, were notably fiery. In *The Gentle People* (39) described by the author as a fairy tale, a racketeer is overthrown by two old men.

SHERRIFF, R. C. (1896–). British dramatist and screen writer, and author of the classic First World War play, *Journey's End* (28), a realistic, very well-written and effective drama set in a dug-out in the trenches just before the German offensive in 1918. In its time the play was a significant landmark, killing the myth that audiences would not accept plays about the Great War, and presenting a glimpse of that war which deeply affected survivors, pacifists and neutral observers

alike, as it has at all later revivals. His other plays include *Badgers Green* (30), *St. Helena* (Old Vic, 36) and a good thriller, *Home at Seven* (50). At the time of writing (72), *Journey's End* is once again in London in Theatre 69's fine production, and has attracted reviews from young critics which must have left their elders astonished and delighted at their enthusiasm.

SHERWOOD, ROBERT (1896–1955). American dramatist of considerable range. His first play, *The Road to Rome* (27) treated Hannibal's march—and war—in a satirically comic way. *Waterloo Bridge*, a melodrama better known as a film, followed (30), then the high comedy, *Reunion in Vienna* (31). Later plays included the gangster drama, *The Petrified Forest* (35), *Idiot's Delight* (36), a prophetic, ironic look at a second world war, very effective in its day, and a fine chronicle play, *Abe Lincoln in Illinois* (38). His *There Shall Be No Night* (41), originally played by the Lunts, was set in the invaded Finland of 1940 and created a deep impression. A man of liberal conscience as well as a man of the theatre, he was one of the major playwrights of his day.

SIMON, NEIL (1927–). American dramatist. His many popular situation comedies include *Come Blow Your Horn* (61), *Barefoot in the Park* (63), *Plaza Suite* (66), and his two best plays, *The*

Odd Couple (65) and *The Prisoner of Second Avenue* (71), an 'urban gallows humour' look at what T. E. Kalem of *Time* called 'an everyday urban purgatory of copelessness'. *The Gingerbread Lady* (70) is a rare sombre work about an alcoholic singer. Currently (72), has another hit, *The Sunshine Boys*, about an ex-vaudeville duo.

SIMPSON, N. F. (1919–). British dramatist of successful plays of the Absurd (see p. 273). *A Resounding Tinkle* (57) was followed by his finest play, *One Way Pendulum* (59), a suburban fantasy in which, amongst other things, one of its characters is teaching weighing machines to sing the Hallelujah Chorus. There is also a do-it-yourself Old Bailey in the living room. The tyranny of things is the mainspring of the piece. *The Cresta Run* (65) pokes fun at counter espionage.

SMITH, DODIE (1895–). British dramatist and novelist. Beginning with *Autumn Crocus* (31), her pleasant comedies include *Call It a Day* (35) and *Dear Octopus* (38), whose stellar cast included Gielgud, Marie Tempest, Angela Baddeley and Leon Quartermaine.

SPEWACK, SAMUEL (1899–1971) and BELLA SPEWACK (1899–). American dramatists. This husband and wife team's most famous show is *Kiss Me Kate* (see p. 200). They collaborated on *My Three Angels* (53) from the French of Albert Husson, and other plays, and Samuel Spewack wrote *Under the Sycamore Tree* (52). Also collaborated on a number of films.

STEINBECK, JOHN (1902–68). Major American novelist and also dramatist, notably *Of Mice and Men* (37), his finest play, from his novel, *The Moon is Down* (42) and *Burning Bright* (50).

STOPPARD, TOM (1937–). British dramatist, whose *Rosencrantz and Guilderstern are Dead* (66) is an entertaining, Godot-like look at *Hamlet* with Shakespeare's two nebulous friends of the Prince as the heroes of the play, and with Hamlet's scenes with them incorporated into the action. The Players have a major and very theatrical part in the play, contrasting with the bewildering inaction of the two protagonists. A great success at the National Theatre. *Enter a Free Man* (63) is a comedy about a would-be gadget inventor. *The Real Inspector Hound* (68) is a burlesque incorporating a play within a play, with two critics watching a thriller and joining in the action. *Jumpers* (National Theatre, 72), is a 'stark raving sane' play (John Barber) set in a lunatic future and starring an ageing philosophy don and his (ex-musical comedy star) wife. This 'comedy with brains' (Michael Billington) is an uproarious but serious tribute, perhaps, to the joy of an irrational, daft world rather than one with too much order and sanity.

STOREY, DAVID (1933–). British dramatist and novelist, arguably the most hopeful talent to emerge in the 60s. His five plays are *The Restoration of Arnold Middleton* (67), *In Celebration* (69), *The Contractor* (69), *Home* (70) and *The Changing Room* (71) (see p. 25). Associated with the director, Lindsay Anderson, who directed the magnificent film of his novel, *This Sporting Life*.

The playwright dramatizes work with extraordinary skill in *The Contractor*. The erecting and dismantling of a wedding reception tent is the all-important central fact of the play, though we get to know the workmen and the family. Storey apparently sometimes sees the play as showing the decline of capitalist society, or as a metaphor for artistic creation, but it is important to stress that we can simply see the play as a story of some men who put up a tent and take it down again.

Another side of the work of this notably wide-ranging writer is his keen interest in the problem of the educated children of a working-class family. This is the theme of *In Celebration*, where a miner, his wife and their three sons celebrate the parents' 40th wedding anniversary, and where one of the sons is hell-bent on destroying the family's relationships by exhuming the past. Mental trouble is another theme of Storey's work, in *Arnold Middleton*, a very funny play about a clowning young schoolmaster who is going mad, and, even more convincingly in *Home*. This is set in a mental home, as we gradually realize. It has been said by some that its dialogue and plot are a little monotonous, but it has been widely and rightly acclaimed. Set in a garden and with only five characters, the play is very moving and, incidentally, gave Gielgud and Richardson two of the finest roles of their careers. Does the play reflect the decline of Britain (hinted at in the old gentlemen's dialogue) or the decline of life and hope? It is up to the individual, for Storey's remarkable plays do not flaunt their themes. As he says 'all the options are open'. A rare talent.

STRASBERG, LEE (1901–). Very influential American director and teacher. Co-founder of the Group Theater (31), see p. 244, for whom he directed many plays, and founder of the Actor's Studio (48), see p. 239. The chief exponent of the 'Method' acting, see p. 278. Has lectured widely in America and Europe.

TAGG, ALAN (1928–). British designer of plays, operas, exhibitions, including the Shakespeare Exhibition at Stratford (64), the Victoria and Albert's Berlioz (69) and Covent Garden (71) exhibitions. Designs include those for Osborne's *Look Back in Anger* and *The Entertainer* at the Royal Court, Mercer's *Belcher's Luck* and *After Haggerty* for the Royal Shakespeare Co., also *London Assurance* for the company (70). His *Black Comedy* setting for the National won a 'Tony' award in New York (67).

TAYLOR, SAMUEL (1912–). American dramatist. Author of *Sabrina Fair* (53) and co-author (with Cornelia Otis Skinner) of *The Pleasure of his Company* (58).

TERSON, PETER (1932–). British dramatist, notably prolific and with a flair for dialogue and creating personalities. His early plays were written for Peter Cheesman of the Stoke-on-Trent Theatre. Most of his later ones, including *Zigger-Zagger* (67), set against a background of a football crowd, and *The Apprentices* (68), set in a factory yard, have been for Michael Croft of the National Youth Theatre. His most recent plays at the time of writing are *The Samaritan* and *Good Lads at Heart* (71). The early plays, unlike these later pieces, are partly concerned with the power of nature and have a slightly sinister quality. Several are set in the Vale of Evesham, where Terson was once a games master. Few modern dramatists have written more convincingly, exuberantly and sympathetically about young people.

CTT–E

TRAVERS, BEN. British dramatist and master of farce. See p. 229.

TURNER, DAVID (1927–). British dramatist whose plays include *Semi-Detached* (62).

USTINOV, PETER (1921–). British dramatist, actor, entertainer and talker. So much is expected of this imposingly versatile and witty entertainer, that only two of his plays have received universal praise. *The Love of Four Colonels* (London, 51: New York York, 53) and *Romanoff and Juliet* (London, 56; New York, 57). The first, a realistic play turned fantasy, contains pastiches of Shakespearean comedy, Molière, Chekhov and primordial American local drama, which at their best rise to inspired heights of comedy; and the second, a Russo-American love story set in a comic opera mini-state, is a sensible, sentimental delight. Other plays include *The Empty Chair* (56), *Photo Finish* (63) and *Halfway Up The Tree* (67). *The Unknown Soldier and his Wife* (Chichester, 68). At the time of writing (73), this last, very amusing play is enjoying a London run.

VAN DRUTEN, JOHN (1901–57). Prolific Anglo-American dramatist, notorious in the 20s for his school story, *Young Woodley* (28) with a boy falling for his housemaster's wife. His other plays include *The Voice of the Turtle* (43), *Bell, Book and*

Candle (50), a strangely under-rated modern witchcraft comedy, and *I Am a Camera* (51), from Christopher Isherwood's *Goodbye to Berlin*.

VIDAL, GORE (1925–). American novelist and dramatist. Author of *Visit to a Small Planet* (57) and *The Best Man* (60), a comedy about a Presidential election. *An Evening with Richard Nixon and* ... (72) backfired.

WESKER, ARNOLD (1922–). British dramatist and founder of Centre 42 (62) to bring art and drama—with Union backing—to ordinary people. Made his name with a trilogy of plays about a Jewish family from 1936–59, *Chicken Soup with Barley* (58), *Roots* (59), his most famous work in which, as it happens, the family does not appear on stage, and *I'm Talking About Jerusalem* (60). *The Kitchen* (59) is a brilliant and effective piece about a day in the kitchen of a restaurant, which in turn is a view of humanity and the world. *Chips with Everything* (62), set on an R.A.F. station, is the world in robot-like guise and is a strong and, at times, very funny play. *The Four Seasons* (65), a love story following the seasons of the year, was not a success, and his ambitious *Their Very Own and Golden City* (66) did not get into the West End. *The Friends* (70) is a disillusioned play. In his earlier, more famous plays, Wesker's involvement in his characters has been almost too intense, though they are never one-dimensional, their idealism never absurd. Not until the less realistic but very strong attack on the weakness of the ruled and the arrogance of the rulers in *Chips with Everything* did he gain detachment without loss of vigour and feeling. His latest play (72), *The Old Ones*, is a warm glimpse of a Jewish family. Max Wall was very fine in it as Manny at the Royal Court.

WHITEHEAD, E. A. (1933–). British dramatist. His *The Foursome* at the Royal Court Theatre Upstairs (71) won him the *Evening Standard*'s Most Promising Playwright award. He followed it with a searing two-handed look at marriage, *Alpha Beta* (72). Helen Dawson wrote that the author 'leaves Strindberg limping'.

WHITING, JOHN (1915–1963). British dramatist and actor. His early works include a delightful farcical fantasy, *A Penny for a Song* (51), about two Dorset eccentrics preparing to resist Napoleon. A balloon and a fire engine on stage are remembered joys. In the same year came *Saint's Day*, a play on which Whiting had worked for some time in the 40s. Its hero is an old, self-exiled revolutionary poet and it proved too difficult and obscurely symbolic for its audiences. Whiting explained much later that the theme was self-destruction, and the play became recognized as a pre-1956 landmark. *Marching Song* (54) is another essay on the same theme, the hero this time being a general who has previously lost a battle and is now faced with a trial or suicide. Opinions vary widely about its success and power, but its construction, clarity and topicality are not questioned.

The Devils (61) a version of Aldous Huxley's *The Devils of Loudon* about an actual case of the demonic possession of nuns in 17th century France, is his finest and most acclaimed play. Powerful, literate and poignant it is an examination of conscience and superstition, of the good and evil in a single person, the priest, Grandier, who is finally tortured, degraded and burnt alive. Whiting's early death just as he reached dramatic maturity was a cruel blow to the theatre.

WILDER, THORNTON (1897–1971). American dramatist and novelist who, after *The Trumpet Shall Sound* (26), which failed to reach Broadway, and adaptations of Obey and Ibsen, wrote *Our Town* (38). This was—and remains—a very successful evocation of small town life with a Stage Manager as our guide. Also that year came *The Merchant of Yonkers* from an old Austrian farce, a joyous play which became *The Matchmaker* (54) and, finally, the musical *Hello Dolly* (64). *The Skin of Your Teeth* (42), a 'history of the world in comic strip', proved marvellous theatre on both sides of the Atlantic—New York's heroine was Bankhead, London's was Vivien Leigh. It is a tribute to man's powers of survival; Wilder was an optimist. His version of the *Alcestis, Life in the Sun* (55) was produced at the Edinburgh Festival. *3 Plays for Bleeker Street* (62) are a group of one-acters. Both *Our Town* and *The Skin of Your Teeth* won Pulitzer Prizes.

WILLIAMS, EMLYN (1905–). British dramatist and actor (see Chapters 2, 3 and 6). This brilliant, Welsh-born theatrical all-rounder's finest plays are probably his thrillers (see p. 237). Amongst his others are *Spring 1600* (34), a spell-binding look at the flowering of our theatre, which apparently suffered because the ignorant thought it was a telephone number. It was later rewritten and revived (45). His *The Corn is Green* (38) is partly autobiographical. *The Wind of Heaven* (45) and *Trespass* (47) both tend to the supernatural. *The Late Christopher Bean* (33) was a very successful adaptation from the French. His readings from Dickens were theatrical highlights of the 50s, which also saw his *Dylan Thomas Grows Up* (55). Both *The Late Christopher Bean* and *The Corn is Green* had long Broadway runs, and the latter was filmed with Bette Davis.

WILLIAMS, HEATHCOTE. British

dramatist. Author of *AC/DC* (70), hailed by Charles Marowitz as the first play of the 21st century, and already revived three times at the Royal Court's Theatre Upstairs. This alarming look at the future with a group aspiring to 'brain to brain contact' and with language either alien or sick—'cancer is a kind of pearl'—is at the time of writing creating a growing following.

WILLIAMS,   HUGH   (1904–69). British dramatist and actor (see p. 192) and MARGARET WILLIAMS, British dramatist and actress (Margaret Vyner). Co-authors of several very successful West End comedies, in most of which the former starred, though only occasionally giving himself the best part. Two of the plays are first rate examples of their kind. These were their first play, *Plaintiff in a Pretty Hat* (56), a piece of great charm, and *The Grass is Greener* (59), a hugely successful play, later filmed. Later plays included *The Irregular Verb to Love* (61) and *The Flip Side* (67). The two also wrote the book of the musical *Charlie Girl* (65). The actor SIMON WILLIAMS is their son.

WILLIAMS, TENNESSEE (1914–). American dramatist. His first success was with his wistful, autobiographical 'memory' play, *The Glass Menagerie* (45). Next in order of production was his most famous play, *A Streetcar Named Desire* (47), see p. 18.

Summer and Smoke (48) once again had what Taubman calls 'the eternally baleful female' though its theme is loneliness.

There followed *The Rose Tattoo* (51), *Camino Real* (53) and *Cat on a Hot Tin Roof* (55), about non-communication in a Southern plantation family. This very rich period continued with *Orpheus Descending* (57), a revision of an earlier play, *Battle of Angels* in a lynch-happy Southern setting, *Suddenly Last Summer* (58), a broodingly powerful and horrifying piece, *Sweet Bird of Youth* (59), starring an ageing film star and a young gigolo with a climax of castration, *Period of Adjustment* (61), a domestic comedy, and *The Night of the Iguana* (62), a sultry, eerie play set among rejects in a Mexican coastal inn. Since this, Williams has written several plays, including *The Milk Train Doesn't Stop Here Any More* (63), none of which have reached his earlier work in which he ranks with Arthur Miller as the finest American playwright since O'Neill. However, with *Small Craft Warnings* (72, London, 73), the authentic Williams has returned.

His cast lists read like rolls of fame, so eager have famous players been to appear in his work. His finest parts are often reserved for the older woman and younger man. His work is lyrical, sensuous, often cruel, sometimes savage, his sense of theatre and atmosphere usually impeccable. His earlier pieces have Chekhovian and Puccinian moments, but he has created his own world which, even at its most extreme and repellent, has a cobra-like, hypnotic fascination.

WOOD, CHARLES (1932–). British dramatist, most of whose plays have had a military background and have expressed a love-hate relationship with the Army. The first of these was *Cockade* (63), though *Fill the Stage with Happy Hours* (67) is a play about theatre people. *Dingo* (67) is a violent attack on jingoism and the effects of war and fighting on individuals, culminating in the statement, which alienated many, that the Second World War was fought 'for all the usual reasons'. In five short words Mr. Wood detracted from the emotional impact of his play, though perhaps some unknowing young were able to swallow the provocative claim.

There followed the underpraised '*H*' at the National Theatre (69), about General Havelock's march on Cawnpore and Lucknow in the Indian Mutiny. A far better play because not grossly one-sided, it used Brechtian methods to considerable effect, though it suffered from a leading protagonist not quite strong enough in Wood's portrait to grip the audience. A playwright of great potential, whose latest play at the time of writing (72) is *Veterans*, an ironic look at filming on location inspired by the author's work on *The Charge of the Light Brigade*.

WOOD, PETER (1927–). British director. Arts Theatre (56–58) where his productions included Ionesco's *The Bald Prima Donna and The New Tenant* (56) and a superb production of *The Iceman Cometh* (58). Schiller's *Mary Stuart* at Edinburgh and the Old Vic (58), *As You Like It* at Stratford, Ontario (59), *The Winter's Tale* at Stratford (60). Since then his productions have included *The Devils* (61) for the Royal Shakespeare Co., Shaffer's *The Private Ear and the Public Eye* (New York, 62), also two major and classical productions for the National Theatre, *The Master Builder* (64) and *Love for Love* (65) and, boisterously and inventively, Stoppard's *Jumpers* (72).

YEATS, W. B. (1865–1938). Irish poet and dramatist whose part in founding the Irish dramatic movement lies before the time-span of this book, though not his role as a director of the Abbey from 1904 until he died. His post-1920 plays include his version of *Oedipus at Colonus* (26), used by Wolfit (53), *The Words on the Window Pane* (30), about Swift, and *Purgatory* (38). These are austere compared with his romantic 'Celtic Twilight' plays. His lyric poetry, however, remains his chief claim to immortality.

ZINDEL, PAUL (1936–). American dramatist whose first play, *The Effect of Gamma Rays on Man-in-the-Moon Marigolds* (70), a grim but compassionate study of family life, won him major awards, including a Pulitzer Prize. It was presented Off-Broadway. *And Miss Readon Drinks a Little* (71).

THE WORLD OF
SHAKESPEARE
AND THE CLASSICS

Some Notable Productions

HAMLET   1922

John Barrymore's Hamlet ranks with Forbes Robertson's and John Gielgud's as the most famous of the century. For Alexander Woollcott it was the 'realest Hamlet we have ever known'. Graceful, energetic, witheringly witty, poetic, well-spoken and fiery, it was by no means a bravura reading. One scene in particular made history, the confrontation with his mother, which was played as a love scene.

First produced at the Sam H. Harris Theatre, November 16, 1922

| Director | Arthur Hopkins |
| Designer | Robert Edmund Jones |

Cast included John Barrymore as Hamlet, Blanche Yurka as Gertrude, Tyrone Power Sr. as Claudius, Rosalinde Fuller as Ophelia, Sidney Mather as Laertes and Whitford Kane as First Gravedigger.

Barrymore came to London in 1925 with his Hamlet, which, if not so universally acclaimed as it had been in America, was widely admired and is still remembered fervently by many of those who saw it at the Haymarket. Fay Compton was his Ophelia, Constance Collier, Gertrude and Malcolm Keen, Claudius. Apparently there were several changes of cast necessary for Laertes, as Barrymore fought so realistically that blood was frequently drawn. This was almost the great actor's last appearance in the theatre. 'Ifs' are useless, but there can be no doubt that Barrymore's desertion of the classical stage, or, indeed, of the theatre, played a major part in virtually destroying the American Shakespearean tradition.

HAMLET   1930

Despite fashionable attractions like Barrymore's Hamlet,
Shakespeare was barely tolerated in the West End in the 1920s.
When Barry Jackson presented *Hamlet* (Colin Keith-Johnston)
at the Kingsway in 1925, he wisely put the cast in modern dress,
so over-sensitive were audiences (as opposed to theatrically
intelligent ones at the Old Vic) to the horrors of period or
'unreal' acting. The breakthrough was John Gielgud's first
Hamlet, transferred from the Old Vic to the Queen's. This was
the real thing, as were his later revivals, the nearest any Hamlet
has come—except, for those who favour him, Barrymore's—to
the matchless description of him by Ophelia, beginning 'O,
what a noble mind is here o'erthrown!' Yet even the most
du Maurier-trained addict could hardly claim it was too
'big', too 'theatrical'. It suited the times, and, as Harcourt
Williams said, '. . . there was an appeal in that youthful interpretation that broke the heart'. The doldrums of the twenties
were over.

    Director   Harcourt Williams
    Designer   Paul Smyth

First produced at the Old Vic, April 28, 1930. The play transferred to the Queen's, May 28, 1930.

Cast included John Gielgud as Hamlet, Martita Hunt as the
Queen, Donald Wolfit as Claudius—one of his most admired
performances—and Adele Dixon as Ophelia.

THE THREE SISTERS   1938

John Gielgud's famous season at the Queen's (37–8) is now
often regarded as the beginning of ensemble playing in Britain,
though veterans would probably go back to the early days of
the Old Vic Company, perhaps the Robert Atkins seasons in
the early twenties. The Gielgud ensemble was cast from experience, strength and young talent. Just to read the cast lists of
that season, which included *Richard II*, *The Merchant of Venice*
and *The School for Scandal*, is enough to ravage younger playgoers with the noblest sort of envy. The summit of the season
was, perhaps, *The Three Sisters*, directed by Michel St. Denis.
'We are not likely to see its equal again', wrote David Fair-
weather in *Theatre World*, and, though ensemble playing is

now an accepted, if not always achieved, fact, this production remains the most famous production of a Chekhov play ever staged in Britain, and the one which set the seal on the playwright's growing popularity with British audiences, not least because the play's humour was allowed to shine as Chekhov intended.

First produced at the Queen's, January 28, 1938.

Director	Michel Saint-Denis
Designer	Motley
Music	Herbert Menges
Translator	Constance Garnett

Cast included Gwen Ffrangcon-Davies, Carol Goodner and Peggy Ashcroft as Olga, Masha and Irina, Angela Baddeley as Natasha, John Gielgud as Vershinin, Leon Quartermaine as Kuligin, George Devine as Andrey, Glen Byam Shaw as Solyony, Michael Redgrave as Baron Tusenbach, Frederick Lloyd as Tchebutykin, also George Howe, Harry Andrews, Alec Guinness, Marie Wright and Barbara Dillon.

RICHARD III   1944

This was the third production of the now legendary Old Vic season at the New, which opened with the Guthrie-Richardson *Peer Gynt*. Great acting in the tradition of Kean and Irving had been at a discount for a generation. The idea of it had been kept alive by the inspiration of Barry Jackson, Lilian Baylis, Gielgud, Wolfit and a tiny handful of others. In 1944, it returned upon its hour to the very heart of London at the moment when Laurence Olivier made his first deadly-attractive spider of an entrance as Richard Plantagenet, Shakespeare's demon king. It was a great creative performance from that entrance to Olivier's trapped writhing, dance of death at the end, like some fearful, skewered animal.

This Richard was a sardonic, rampant Satan, a devil who made the most of having the best tunes, a misshapen monster who could yet charm a Lady Anne whose husband he had murdered, a viper often funny and always dangerous. Because of this performance, British heroic acting was publicly restored to favour to the extent that actors and audiences ever since have been able to think big. A good production and an excellent cast provided the framework for this jewel.

First produced in London at the New, September 13, 1944.

Director	John Burrell
Costumes	Doris Zinkeisen
Designer	Morris Kestelman

Cast included Nicholas Hannen as Buckingham, Sybil Thorndike as Margaret, Margaret Leighton as Queen Elizabeth, Joyce Redman as Lady Anne, Michael Warre as Hastings and Ralph Richardson as Richmond.

Collectors note: In the first-night programme the audience was informed that Richmond was afterwards King Edward VII. This production was revived with a weaker but adequate cast, which toured Australia and New Zealand (48) and appeared at the New (49). Olivier later filmed *Richard III* with a cast that included Gielgud as Clarence and Richardson as Buckingham.

TAMBURLAINE THE GREAT 1951

The tempestuous panoply of this production by Tyrone Guthrie at the height of his powers, allied to a towering performance of the title role by Donald Wolfit, which equalled his great Lear, made Old Vic and theatre history. It gave playgoers a rare chance to see this glorious, monstrous Everest of a play, performed like the ultimate epic that it is.

Cut to actable size by Guthrie and Wolfit, and with the actor (until late in the run when he fell back on actor-managerial scene-stealing tricks) working as leader of a strong ensemble, the result was revelation. Guthrie, the master of spectacle and movement, achieved the almost impossible feat of staging a huge tumult on the small Old Vic stage, aided by Leslie Hurry's eye-riveting designs. The audience trembled before tramping soldiers, infernal machines, torture cages and a cast of what seemed like thousands.

Wolfit, a Mongol horde in himself, and blessed with the experience and the vocal and physical stamina to stand the strain of a colossal 'unplayable' part, was lion and reptile demon and poet, a reveller in cruelty and beauty. After the final curtain, he is said to have raised his eyes to heaven and exulted: 'Kit, my boy, we've done it!' They had.

First produced at the Old Vic. September 24, 1951.

Director   Tyrone Guthrie
Designer   Leslie Hurry

Cast included Donald Wolfit as Tamberlaine, Margaret Rawlings as Zabina, Jill Balcon as Zenocrate, and Lee Montague,
Peter Coke, Richard Pasco, Colin Jeavons, Kenneth Griffith
and Ernest Hare.

TITUS ANDRONICUS   1955

Peter Brook has a way of dispelling heretical thoughts about the
Director's Theatre by regularly directing the best production of
its day. This was one of his very finest, to which he also contributed the setting and the *musique concrète*. Not since Wagner . . .

The play was a favourite Elizabethan horror comic and remains shot through with moments of glory. Brook presented a
'masterpiece of salvage and a display of extreme cunning in the
art of covering up' (Ivor Brown). He cut out oceans of gore
and horror, the 'children baked in a pie' line included. A
scarlet ribbon symbolized a wound. There were solemn pro-
cessions, and fine groupings and lighting in a vast landscape
setting. Everything conspired to turn rumbustious, near farcical
devilry into tragedy.

This could not have been achieved without a great performance by Olivier. Aaron was superbly played by Anthony Quayle
and Maxine Audley was a ferocious Queen of the Goths. Even
Vivien Leigh's Lavinia found champions to rebuff Tynan's
stinging acid. But it was Olivier, following his Macbeth, the
most acclaimed of modern times, whose performance was the
one that crowned the occasion. He began as a lined, bruised,
tired veteran, not as a Hero returning from the wars. He then
proceeded to portray a soul on the rack, and rising to the infin-
ite variety needed to make the endless chain of horror and
calamity truly overwhelming. The role has great lines—'For
now I stand as one upon a rock, Environ'd with a wilderness of
sea' and, later in the same scene a Homeric 'I am the sea . . .'
a speech Olivier cried so that, as Trewin wrote, 'its surge beat
on the world's far shore'. 'After this,' exulted Tynan, re-
joicing that Olivier had shown he could suffer as well as ex-
plode, 'all the great parts are open to him.'

First produced on August 16, 1955 at Stratford.

Director	Peter Brook
Designs and music	Peter Brook, with Michael Northern, Desmond Heeley and William Blezard

This Olympian production was later seen in Paris, Venice, Belgrade, Zagreb, Vienna, Warsaw and London (57).

THE WARS OF THE ROSES   1963–4

Stratford's celebration of Shakespeare's 400th birthday was also a most striking demonstration of the Royal Shakespeare Company's ensemble, led by Peter Hall in his fourth and fifth seasons at Stratford. The plays consisted of all three parts of *Henry VI* and *Richard III*, turned by John Barton into three plays, *Henry VI*, *Edward IV* and *Richard III*.

This grim realization of feudalism collapsing in a welter of blood, brought about by desperate ambition for power, was set by John Bury in a steel frame with props and furniture of iron to match the harsh story. Only Richard of Gloucester suffered by the treatment. Through no fault of Ian Holm's, Shakespeare's Demon King became a perverse power game figure on the make, though in the context of the production this was acceptable enough.

In this magnificent ensemble certain performances must be picked out, most of all Peggy Ashcroft's extraordinary and triumphant Margaret, which ranged from her teens to her old age, also David Warner's Henry, Donald Sinden's York, Brewster Mason's Warwick, Roy Dotrice's Edward IV and, despite reservations, Ian Holm's Richard. About the power and overall conception of Peter Hall, there could be no reservation at all.

First produced at Stratford: *Henry VI* and *Edward IV*, July 17, and *Richard III*, August 20, 1963.

Directors	Peter Hall and John Barton
Designer	John Bury
Music	Guy Woolfenden
Adaptation and editing of text	John Barton

The productions were later seen in London, sometimes all in one day, and were shown on BBC Television.

A MIDSUMMER NIGHT'S DREAM   1970

This is the most acclaimed staging of a Shakespearean comedy in memory, possibly the most admired of any Shakespearean production. Its critics, professional and amateur, seem few. Though its influence on lesser directors may produce disasters, Peter Brook's production is a triumph that deserves the over-used word 'historic'.

The setting is a white, squash-court of a room, equipped with trapezes, and off those walls the cast occasionally bounce like squash balls. Along the top is a much-used catwalk. The Fairies' magic is the magic of the circus. Oberon and Puck twirl saucers on wands; Bottom is translated by a clown's black nose; the trees are coils of wire held from above. The same actor plays Oberon and Theseus, the Hippolyta is Titania, Egeus is Quince, Philostrate is Puck.

And where is Shakespeare? Everywhere. The result of this treatment, which inevitably sounds gimmicky, is that the mind and the imagination are free to concentrate on verse and story as never before. The lovers, remarkably athletic in the wood, are triumphantly real, so are the mechanicals. Too much has been made of the cast coming through the audience at the end, though never have actors been more welcome. It has been called a radical reinterpretation, yet it is no more than a magnificent interpretation that only a genius like Brook, able to inspire a cast to excel itself, could achieve.

First produced at Stratford-upon-Avon, August 27, 1970.

Director	Peter Brook
Designer	Sally Jacobs
Music	Richard Peaslee with the actors and Felix Mendelssohn

Cast included Alan Howard as Theseus/Oberon, Sara Kestelman as Hipployta/Titania, John Kane as Puck/Philostrate, Philip Locke as Egeus/Quince, David Waller as Bottom, Mary Rutherford, Christopher Gable, Frances de la Tour and Ben Kingsley as the Lovers, and Glynne Lewis, Terrence Hardiman, Norman Rodway and Barry Stanton as the other Mechanicals.

The production has been seen at the Aldwych (71/2), in North America and in Europe.

A WHO'S WHO OF CLASSICAL DRAMA

ACKLAND, JOSS (1928–). British actor. Old Vic (58–61), where his parts included Sir Toby, Caliban, Falstaff in *The Merry Wives*, etc. Associate Director of the Mermaid (62–4). Parts included Galileo and Long John Silver. Gus in *The Hotel in Amsterdam* (68). Four parts in *Come As You Are* (70). Captain Brassbound (71). A fine, robust actor and TV star.

ADRIAN, MAX (1903–73). British actor. His enormous success in intimate revue just after the war in scenes of witty, devilish glee, followed and preceded many sharp classical performances, including Tattle in *Love for Love* (44), Pandarus (39, 60, 62) and a magnificently Websterian Cardinal in *The Duchess of Malfi* for the Royal Shakespeare Co. (60). The Inquisitor in *St. Joan* (Chichester and the National, 63). Polonius (63). From 1966, frequently gave his one-man-show, *An Evening with G.B.S.*

AINLEY, HENRY (1879–1945). British actor famous for his voice and looks. Best remembered for his Shakespearean and romantic performances before his career was shattered by what the great G. F. Cooke called 'my old complaint'. A magnificent Mal-

volio for Granville Barker (12). Another famous performance was his Hassan (23). In straighter parts, including Hamlet, he seems to have been less interesting. His son RICHARD AINLEY (1910–67) inherited his father's voice and presence and played at the Vic (29–31). Bassanio for Gielgud at the Queen's (37). Wounded in the war, he later became a magnificent teacher.

ALDRIDGE, MICHAEL (1920–). British actor. Since his King in *Love's Labour's Lost* (Old Vic at the New, 49), has played a wide range of leading parts and (since 66) has appeared at six Chichester Festivals: Banquo, Enobarbus, etc.

ANDERSON, JUDITH (1898–). Australian actress, most of whose career has been in the U.S.A., including her Medea (47), a 'raging inferno' (Taubman). Gertrude to Gielgud's Hamlet (New York, 36). Lady Macbeth, opposite Olivier at the Vic (37), which sharply divided opinion. An extraordinarily gifted actress at portraying evil, as her classical and modern performances, including Lavinia in *Mourning Becomes Electra* (32) and Mrs. Danvers in the film of *Rebecca*, have shown. D.B.E. (60).

ANDREWS, HARRY (1911–). British actor so renowned for his portrayals of Shakespeare's major supporting parts that Tynan felt moved to point out how other actors 'may be the heart, brain and fingertips of English Shakespearean acting' but that he is its 'indispensable backbone'. Was Gielgud's Tybalt (35) and Horatio (New York, 36). From then on, war service apart, has been mainly in the classics, including the Gielgud season at the Queen's (37–8) Old Vic (45–9), Stratford (49–53, 56, 59), also Old Vic (58). Played General Allenby in *Ross* (60). Since then, mainly in films, but played the lead in Edward Bond's *Lear* (71). A commanding figure with a rich voice and 'the capacity to humanize figures of authority' (Billington), amongst whose finest roles have been Bolingbroke, Buckingham in *Richard III*, Brutus and Kent, and Enobarbus for Olivier (51) and at Stratford (53).

ANNALS, MICHAEL (1938–). British designer, whose international work has included the magnificent sets and costumes for *The Royal Hunt for the Sun* (London, 64; New York, 65).

ARUNDELL, DENNIS (1898–). British actor, director, composer and author. Vic-Wells (33) where his parts included Trofimov and Lucio in *Measure for Measure*. Has played in Regent's Park, directed *Hamlet* in Helsinki (57),

composed the music for many plays, including his own Shakespearean productions, and, especially for Sadler's Wells, proved one of the best opera directors of the age. His best known commercial part was as Mr. Manningham in *Gaslight* (Richmond, 38; Apollo, 39). Has written the history of Sadler's Wells Theatre.

ASHCROFT, PEGGY (1907–). British actress whose triumphant career of more than 40 years began at Birmingham Rep (26). Early parts included Desdemona in London to Robeson's Othello (30) and Shaw's Cleopatra at the Vic (32). Her reputation was sealed after her Juliet (O.U.D.S., 32; London 35), as near perfection, some say, as any can ever have been. Nina for Komisarjevsky in *The Seagull* (26), then, in the now legendary Gielgud season at the Queen's (37–8), the Queen in *Richard II*, Lady Teazle, Irena in *The Three Sisters* and Portia.

Played Ophelia, Titania and the Duchess of Malfi in the famous Gielgud season at the Haymarket (44–5). Since the war, her parts have included Beatrice at Stratford (50), Cleopatra at Stratford (53)—'brilliantly miscast', Hedda (54) and Rebecca West (59). Her long association with the Royal Shakespeare Co. has been to the advantage of actors and audiences alike. Repeated her Duchess of Malfi and, amongst other parts, gave an extraordinary *tour-de-force* as Queen Margaret in *The Wars of the Roses* (63, 64), from her teens to old age.

For some of her many memorable commercial performances see p. 148. Her spellbinding portrayal of the murderess in Duras' *The Lovers of Viorne* (71) won her an *Evening Standard* award, as did her Margaret. The Ashcroft Theatre, Croydon, is named for her. D.B.E. (56).

ASHERSON, RENÉE. British actress. Classical parts have ranged from Kate Hardcastle for the Vic on tour (40) to Millimant at Bristol (67). Chichester Festival (69, 71). Katherine in Olivier's film of *Henry V*. Her non-classical parts have included Stella in *A Streetcar named Desire* (49). Was married to Robert Donat.

ATIENZA, EDWARD (1924–). British actor who, despite a debut in *Up in Mabel's Room* at Dartford, has played in the classics as often as not. Notable performances have included an hilarious Archbishop in *Romanoff and Juliet* (London, 56; New York, 57) and a memorable Fool in *Lear* (Stratford, Ontario, 72).

ATKINS, EILEEN (1934–). British actress. Jaquenetta in *Love's Labour's Lost* in Regent's Park (53). Stratford (57–9), where parts included Diana in *Pericles*. Old Vic (62), where she played Miranda, Lady Anne and, most notably, Viola. Eileen in *Semi-Detached* (62). Lady Brute in *The Provoked Wife* (Edinburgh at the Royal Court,

63). Juliette in *Exit the King* (64). Viola and Ophelia at the Ravinia Festival, Illinois (64). Her brilliant playing of Childie in *The Killing of Sister George* (London, 65; New York, 66) won her an *Evening Standard* award. Another memorable performance was her Celia in *The Cocktail Party* (Chichester and London, 68). Her Elizabeth in Bolt's *Vivat! Vivat Regina!* (London, 70: New York, 72) made her a major star after some years as a major actress. Currently (73) giving a tremendous performance in Duras' *Suzanna Andler*.

ATKINS, ROBERT (1886–1972). British actor, director and Rabelaisian wit. Began with Tree and also worked with Forbes-Robertson and Benson. Joined the infant Old Vic (15) as an actor, his parts ranging from Richard III and Iago to Sir Toby and Jacques. After war service toured with Ben Greet, then returned to the Vic as one of the finest directors in its history, getting by on next to no money, a belief in the principles of William Poel and sheer talent (20–5). His parts in this period included Lear and Sir Giles Overreach. Staged Britain's first *Peer Gynt*, with Russell Thorndike as Peer (22), a production which many consider first put the Vic on the theatrical map. Ran the annual seasons in the Open Air Theatre, Regent's Park (33–43, 46–60). Director at Stratford (44–5). To the younger generation, is best remembered as Bottom, Sir Toby, Dogberry, Caliban, etc.; to the theatrical profession as a glorious old pro, about whom stories, most of them true and earthy, clustered like ripe grapes.

ATKINSON, ROSALIND (1900–). New Zealand-born British actress. Many seasons with the Old Vic from 1941, parts including Volumnia (47) and the Nurse (61). Stratford's Countess in *All's Well* (55), a distinguished performance. Sister Godric in *Abelard and Heloise* (70).

AUDLEY, MAXINE (1923–). British actress who has given a number of striking classical performances, including Goneril at Stratford (50), Emilia in London (51) and Tamora in *Titus Andronicus* at Stratford (55) and in Europe and London (57). Since then parts have included Lady Macbeth, Constance and Helen in *Troilus*, and, in the commercial theatre Mrs. Hasseltine in Barry England's fine *Conduct Unbecoming* (69).

AYLMER, FELIX (1889–). British actor. Worked with Hicks, Terry, Tree and Granville Barker before the First World War, also at Birmingham, where he played many classical parts. A mainly commercial career between the wars and since, including many films, but was also a notable Shavian, including Warwick at the Vic (34), and the creator of Drinkwater's Robert E. Lee (23). Other parts have included the

Judge in *The Chalk Garden* (56). President of Equity (49–69). Knighted (65).

AYRTON, RANDLE (1869–1940). British actor whose preference for working out of London was London's loss. Between the wars at Stratford he gave some of the finest Shakespearean performances of the period, his Lear being possibly unequalled in this century until Wolfit's, who played Kent to him (36).

BADDELEY, ANGELA (1904–). British actress, wife of Glen Byam Shaw (see below). A fine actress whose Shakespearean parts have ranged from the little Duke of York (15) to her two splendid 1958 performances at Stratford, the Nurse in *Romeo* and the Bawd in *Pericles*. Lady Bracknell (63) and Mme. Ranevsky (65) at Nottingham. Her non-classical parts have been so numerous that one can only list her Olivia in *Night Must Fall* (35), Catrin in *The Light of Heart* (40) and Stella in *Eden End* (48). Sister of Hermione Baddeley (see p. 204).

BADEL, ALAN (1923–). British actor. Richard III at Birmingham (49). Stratford (50), where his parts included Lear's Fool. Old Vic (51–2) where his parts included Quince, Francois Villon in *The Other Heart*, and Romeo, a finely-spoken, passionately felt performance which, like nearly all Romeos, divided opinion. Eilbert Lovberg in *Hedda Gabler*

(54). At Stratford (56) played an almost frenzied Hamlet, which was both admired and criticized, Berowne, and a glitteringly sharp Lucio in *Measure for Measure*. Hero in *The Rehearsal* (London 61; New York 63), John Tanner in *Man and Superman* (65). At the time of writing, this exciting artist, who still divides opinion as to whether he is or is not a romantic actor—Tynan stated flatly after his Romeo that he was not—has recently been giving a splendidly bravura performance in the title role of Sartre's *Kean* (72). His daughter is the actress, SARAH BADEL.

BALL, WILLIAM (1931–). American actor and director. After acting in Shakespeare in many places in the U.S.A., has (since 58) concentrated on directing the classics and opera, including a very fine *Tartuffe* at Lincoln Center (65). Director of the American Conservatory Theater (since 65) now permanently in San Francisco.

BANNEN, IAN (1928–). British actor. The first British Jamie in *Long Day's Journey into Night* (58), Sergeant Musgrave in *Sergeant Musgrave's Dance* (59), Hamlet, Orlando, Mercutio and Iago at Stratford (61) and Orlando at the Aldwych (62). Brutus at the Royal Court (64).

BARDON, HENRY (1923–). Czech-born designer of plays, operas and ballets.

BARKER, HARLEY GRANVILLE (1877–1946). British director, playwright and writer whose work as a manager and director had an immense influence on the modern British theatre. Produced Shakespeare in the simple style of the Elizabethans, as advocated by William Poel, including a built-on apron stage without footlights. His *The Winter's Tale* and *A Midsummer Night's Dream* (14) were revolutionary in the day of Tree and his live rabbits. The creator of Marchbanks in *Candida*. With Vedrenne as joint manager at the Court and himself as director, staged plays by Ibsen, Euripides, Galsworthy and others, as well as sponsoring Shaw's own productions (04–7): he presented all Shaw plays (06–7). After 1921, he virtually retired, but wrote his influential *Prefaces to Shakespeare*.

BARRYMORE, JOHN (1882–1942). American actor and the most famous Hamlet of his day, in New York (22) and London (25), see beginning of chapter. Also a notable Richard III. Sadly for American theatre, his nature prevented him capitalizing on his role of a great classical actor, and, after Hamlet, he virtually gave up the theatre altogether. His sister ETHEL BARRYMORE (1879–1959) played with Irving in *The Bells*, and her parts included Nora in *A Doll's House* Portia, Juliet and Lady Teazle. Also see p. 149. For Lionel Barrymore, see p. 149.

BARTON, JOHN (1928–). British director and writer. Joined the Royal Shakespeare Co. in 1960. Co-directed and edited the text of *The Wars of the Roses* (63). Directed the most enchanting *Twelfth Night* since the war (Stratford, 69; Aldwych, 70) and a strikingly successful *Troilus and Cressida* (Stratford, 69; Aldwych, 70). Other productions have included *All's Well, Measure for Measure* and *Othello*, and, for Theatregoround, *Richard II* and *Henry V*. Devised the anthology *The Hollow Crown* (61).

BATES, ALAN (1934–). British actor (also see p. 150). At Stratford, Ontario (67), played Richard III and Ford. The only Hamlet (Nottingham and London, 71) in Eric Shorter's experience to look as if he could 'drink hot blood and do unnameable bitter deeds', the critic also noting his scorn and sarcasm.

BATES, MICHAEL (1920–). British actor. Stratford (48–52), where his comedy roles included Touchstone and Bardolph. In the first Stratford, Ontario, season (53), where his Lafeu in *All's Well* was much admired. Later played Sir Joseph Porter in *Pinafore* there. Old Vic (54). Other parts have been as the corrupt policeman in *Loot* (66) and Charles Bisley in *Forget-Me-Not Lane* (71).

BATESON, TIMOTHY (1926–). British actor whose riveting performance in *Waiting for Godot* as Lucky, the dumb but suddenly

eloquently incoherent slave (55) has been his most famous role. An Old Vic Osric (53), where his other parts included Trinculo. Tecnicus in *The Broken Heart* at Chichester (62) Belcredi in *Henry IV* at the Mermaid (65).

BAYLIS, LILIAN (1874–1937). British theatre manager who was directly responsible for creating three national theatres—the Old Vic, Sadler's Wells Opera and Sadler's Wells (now the Royal) Ballet. This earthy, invincible, God-intoxicated, anecdote-provoking, semi-educated, glorious woman first assisted her aunt, Emma Cons, in managing the Vic, then (14) took control. Having given Shakespeare and opera at popular prices, and already managed to attract up-and-coming actors and stars, despite minimal salaries, she rebuilt and reopened Sadler's Wells (31). See also p. 248. Her greatest gifts were courage, capacity for hard work and a genius for finding the right helpers. Her faults are easily ascertained; her achievements make her a theatre immortal.

BEATON, CECIL (1904–). British designer and photographer whose finest achievements have been in Wilde, Pinero, etc., and *My Fair Lady*. For the Vic designed *The School for Scandal* (49) and *Love's Labour's Lost* (54), *The Chalk Garden* in New York (55), where he has also designed musicals including *Saratoga* and *Coco* (69). In *Lady*

Windermere's Fan (46) in San Francisco and New York, played Cecil Graham as well as designing the play.

BELDON, EILEEN (1901–). British actress whose classical career ranges from Maria at the Old Vic (17) to Queen Elinor at Stratford (70), her other parts that season including Mistress Overdone. A regular Shavian between the wars at Birmingham, Malvern and in London.

BENNETT, VIVIENNE (1905–). British actress, hailed by Agate for her moving Desdemona at the Old Vic (35). Another of her finest roles was Sonia in *Uncle Vanya* (43). Too lightweight a Lady Macbeth (44) for Agate, she impressed many others in the role. Has toured widely abroad giving Shakespearean recitals.

BENSON, FRANK (1874–1937). British actor-manager. Though the great days of his famous touring company were before the span of this book, it survived until 1933 when he played Shylock for the last time. An unequalled trainer of actors in his day, as a glance at a list of Old Bensonians shows, and a popularizer of simple, direct Shakespeare all over Britain and, occasionally, abroad. Remembered at his best as a great actor who looked 'the noblest Roman of them all'. Jokes about his insistence on physical fitness fall flat today; he was in advance of his times. Knighted (16). See *Benson and the Bensonians* by J. C. Trewin.

BENSON, GEORGE (1911–). British actor whose career has ranged from Shakespeare to revue. Three times an Old Vic player, perhaps his most famous performance was a definitive Costard (49). The original Arthur Groomkirby in *One Way Pendulum* (59). Shallow and Gonzalo at the Mermaid (70).

BENTHALL, MICHAEL (1919–). British director, mainly of the classics and opera. Director of Productions at the Old Vic (53–9), during which all the plays of the First Folio were produced, many by Benthall himself. His productions are usually fast moving and are pictorially attractive, but not always renowned for fine verse-speaking. His reign at the Old Vic is remembered with some affection by the public and a wide range of players appeared there for him. Theatre historians of the future would do well to research it carefully, for some critics took it too much for granted. *Macbeth* in Lisbon and Chichester, and *Coco* in New York (69).

BERRY, ERIC (1913–). British actor, whose parts have included Falstaff at Stratford, Conn. (62), an impressive performance.

BLAKELY, COLIN (1930–). British actor. Hastings and

Touchstone at Stratford (61), Bottom at the Royal Court (62), then became a National Theatre player, playing Fortinbras in the opening production (63). Though this chunky, rich-voiced actor's biggest successes have usually been in comedy, notably Kite in *The Recruiting Officer* (63), Hobson in *Hobson's Choice* (63) and Ben in *Love for Love* (65), his most famous part has, perhaps, been as a tough and ultimately moving Pizzaro in *The Royal Hunt for the Sun* (64). A fine 'Paycock' (66). Astrov at the Royal Court (70). An admired, ferocious Titus Andronicus at Stratford (72).

BLOOM, CLAIRE (1931–). British actress. Stratford's very youthful Ophelia (48). Joined the Old Vic (52–7) where her finest performances were a much-acclaimed Juliet (52, 56, also in New York) and a sympathetic Helena in *All's Well*. A New York Nora in *A Doll's House* and Hedda (71). Her Isabelle in *Ring Round the Moon* (50) was a non-classical delight. Has appeared in many films. At the time of writing (73), a very fine Nora in London.

BOSCO, PHILIP (1930–). American actor who, especially at Stratford, Conn., has played a wide range of Shakespearean parts, including Bolingbroke, Kent, Pistol, Benedick, Claudius and Coriolanus. Is surely one of the only younger actors to have played Hawkshaw in *The Ticket-of-Leave Man* (61). Has frequently played with the Lincoln Center Rep. Theater (since 66), including Dunois in *St. Joan* and Hector in *Tiger at the Gates*.

BRETT, JEREMY (1935–). British actor, classically handsome and capable of passion and fire. Patroclus at the Old Vic (56), also Malcolm, Paris, Aumerle and Troilus. Has appeared in musicals, and been a fine Danilo on TV. Ron in *Variations on a Theme* (58) and Sebastian in *The Edwardians* (59). Hamlet at the Strand (61). At Chichester (63), parts included Dunois, Peter in *The Kitchen* and Maurice Sweetman in *The Workhouse Donkey*. Father Riccardo in *The Deputy* (New York, 64). Baliaev opposite Bergman in *A Month in the Country* (65). Joined the National (67), where his parts included Orlando, Berowne and a bounderish, bowler-hatted Bassanio.

BRITTON, TONY (1924–). British actor whose parts have included Mercutio and Thersites (Stratford, 54), Hotspur (Old Vic, 61). Lord Illingworth in *A Woman of No Importance* (67), etc.

BROOK, PETER (1925–). British director, equalled in Britain only by Guthrie in inventiveness, but less capricious. 'The greatest explorer among our directors' (Ronald Hayman). Two supreme achievements, *Titus* and the

Dream, are considered earlier in this chapter.

First made his name at Birmingham Rep (45) and Stratford (46–7): Barry Jackson called him 'the youngest earthquake I have known'. His *King John* (45) began his long association with Scofield. *Love's Labour's Lost* (46) à la Watteau is a theatre legend. *Romeo and Juliet* (47).

Director of Productions at Covent Garden (48–50) 20 years before his time, when faced with too young a company, an intractable Musical Director, critical attacks and his own inexperience that even a love of music and shafts of brilliance could not overcome.

Memorable productions of *Dark of the Moon* (49) and *Ring Round the Moon* (50) were followed by a sombre, powerful *Measure for Measure* (50), for which he also designed the set, costumes and composed a song. Ranging between the commercial and classical stage he directed *The Little Hut* (50), a delightful *Penny for a Song* (51) and the most successful *Winter's Tale* in memory (Stratford and London, 51). *Venice Preserved* (53), *The Dark is Light Enough* (54), *House of Flowers* in New York (54), *The Lark* (55) and Scofield's Hamlet. *The Power and the Glory* and *The Family Reunion* (56). Directed *Cat on a Hot Tin Roof* in Paris (56), *The Tempest* at Stratford and *Eugene Onegin* at the Met (57), since when his career has been increasingly international.

Staged the musical *Irma La Douce* gymnastically (London 58; New York 60). His famous, very controversial, Beckettian *Lear* (62) with Brook himself designing an apt landscape, marked his joining the Royal Shakespeare Co. as a Director. At this time came under Artaud's influence and the Theatre of Cruelty (see p. 276). Directed the ultimate Director's Theatre piece, *Marat-Sade* (London 64; New York 65). *US* (66), Brook's conception, was a sincere comment on the U.S. in Vietnam and the lack of involvement of 'us'. For some it was a triumph, for others, actorish, self-indulgent and far less effective than a good play would have been.

His superbly theatrical National Theatre production of Seneca's *Oedipus* (68) was followed by his historic *Dream* (see p. 77), since when his Parisian International Centre for Theatre Research has performed in Persia (72). *Orghast* the title of the piece, and the name of Ted Hughes' international language invented for the occasion, would seem from all accounts to be the next stage in an extraordinary career. His work will no doubt remain at once brilliant, controversial and often maddening, but always important and never at any point trivial. Finds time to direct films and write provocative and stimulating books, most notably *The Empty Space* (68).

BROOKES, JACQUELINE (1930–). American actress who has played most of Shakespeare's heroines including Desdemona, Constance, Beatrice, etc. at Stratford, Conn.

BROWN, PAMELA (1917–). British actress. Stratford's Juliet and deliciously lisping Cressida (36). Leading lady at Oxford Playhouse (40–1) where Agate extolled her Hedda. Goneril for the Old Vic at the New (46). The definitive Jennet Jourdemayne in *The Lady's Not for Burning* (London, 49; New York, 51). Mrs. Millimant and Aquilina in *Venice Preserved* for Gielgud (53).

BROWNE, CORAL (1913–). Australian-born British actress and wit. Her dominating personality and skill have added zest to many commercial successes (see p. 152). Also a strong classical actress culminating in one of the finest Lady Macbeths of modern times for the Old Vic (56) for whom she also played Emilia, Regan, Goneril, Gertrude and other roles. Mrs. Warren in *Mrs. Warren's Profession* at the National Theatre (70).

BRUCE, BRENDA. British actress. For many years in the commercial theatre, including revue, a highlight being her Mabel Crum in *While the Sun Shines* (43), also her Dolly Clandon in *You Can Never Tell* (47) and Victoria in *Home and Beauty* (50). Joined the Royal Shakespeare Co. (64),

where her parts have included Mistress Page, Paulina, Queen Elizabeth, Marina and Gertrude, and Paulina in Gorki's *Enemies*. One of the company's major assets.

BURRELL, JOHN (1910–72). British director. While at the B.B.C. staged *Heartbreak House* (43), then left to become one of the triumvirate, with Olivier and Richardson, of the great seasons of the Old Vic at the New Theatre (44–9). His own productions included *Arms and the Man, Richard III, Uncle Vanya, Henry IV* Parts I and II, all of which are now theatre legends, and *The Alchemist, The Taming of the Shrew, St. Joan, The Government Inspector, Dr. Faustus* and *The Way of the World.* Since 1955, Director of the Training Academy of the American Shakespearean Theater.

BURRELL, SHEILA (1922–). British actress who made her name as Barbara Allen in *Dark of the Moon* (49). Recent parts have included Constance at Stratford (70) and Lady Sneerwell at the National (72)

BURTON, RICHARD (1925–). British actor. Blessed with presence, fire and voice, this Welsh-born actor's two seasons at the Old Vic (53–4 and 55–6), though not universally admired, suggested to many that he was a great classical actor in the making. His parts, interestingly like the young Olivier's at the

Vic before the war, included Hamlet, Sir Toby, Coriolanus, the Bastard in *John*, Caliban, Henry V, Iago and Othello. Since then he has concentrated mainly on films, excepting his record-breaking Hamlet in New York (69) directed by Gielgud, an Anouilh lead, and Arthur in Camelot, also on Broadway, and a few performances of *Dr. Faustus* at Oxford. At the Vic his Coriolanus and Henry V received most praise. Arguments still rage as to whether he or John Neville was the more successful in their alternating Iagos and Othellos. Neville, perhaps the finer actor, was less well cast in both roles but was the better Iago. Burton's Othello, more passionate and intense as the run progressed, was yet another reminder of what the stage has lost to films.

BURY, JOHN (1925–). British theatre designer. With Joan Littlewood (46–61), since when he has been with the Royal Shakespeare Co. A belief in authentic materials for stage design stemming from his Theatre Workshop days reached its climax in the steel look of *The Wars of the Roses* (63) at Stratford, with iron props and furniture. Since then he has laid a new emphasis on lightness and mobility.

Among his theatre designs have been those for Hamlet (65), *The Homecoming* (65), *Landscape* and *Silence* (68) and the Broadway musical, *The Roths-childs* (71). Also notable have been his opera designs for Peter Hall productions, including *Moses and Aaron* (65) and *La Callisto* (70). An Associate Director of R.S.C., he believes his job is to provide a 'sounding board for the actor's imagination to supply him with the basic imagery that he needs'.

CALDWELL, ZOE (1934–). Australian-born actress who has played Shakespeare at Stratford and Stratford, Ontario (including Cleopatra, 67), Molière and Millimant in Minneapolis, Jean Brodie in New York (68) and Rattigan's Emma Hamilton in London (70).

CAMPBELL, DOUGLAS (1922–). British actor and director. Old Vic (51–3), where his parts included Othello and a Julius Caesar who for once made a memorable impression. Parolles and Hastings at the first Shakespeare Festival at Stratford, Ontario (53), to which he returned for a number of seasons playing a wide range of parts and directing regularly. Founded the touring Canadian Players (55). Bottom at the Old Vic (60). Director of the Tyrone Guthrie Theater, Minneapolis (65). His wife, ANN CASSON (1915–), daughter of Sir Lewis and Dame Sybil, was a notable Joan and an Old Vic player before going to Canada with her husband to play leading parts at Stratford and with the Canadian Players.

CAREY, DENIS (1909–). British director and actor who was in charge of the Bristol Old Vic (49–54), a most notable period in the Theatre's history, Carey having a particular gift for comedy. His *Two Gentlemen of Verona* (54) was later admired in London and he directed *An Italian Straw Hat* for both companies (53). Another stylish romp was *The Taming of the Shrew* at the Vic (54), while the author remembers *The Shoemaker's Holiday* at Bristol with particular affection: the cast included Douglas Campbell, John Warner, Alan Dobie, Norman Rossington, Basil Henson, Eric Porter, Michael Meacham, Dorothy Reynolds, Yvonne Coulette (his wife), Christine Finn, etc.! First director of the American Shakespeare Theater, Stratford, Conn. (55), since when he has directed in London, Dublin, Glasgow, etc., and led a British Council tour by the Bristol Old Vic to Asia (63). Has since directed at Bristol, Dublin and elsewhere.

CARIOU, LEN (1939–). Canadian actor whose many classical parts include Orlando in Minneapolis (66) and Henry V at Stratford, Conn. and New York (69). Bill Sampson in *Applause* (70).

CARNOVSKY, MORRIS (1898–). American actor and leading member of the Group Theater (see p. 244). One of the few American actors in modern times to have built up a successful repertoire of leading Shakespearean roles, especially (since 56) at Stratford, Conn., culminating in a magnificent Lear at Stratford, and later Chicago, Los Angeles and, again, at Stratford. Another of his major successes (since 57) has been Shylock. Also see p. 154.

CASS, HENRY (1902–). British director and actor. Director of the Old Vic (34–6). His chief successes were non-Shakespearean, including *Peer Gynt* (35). A regular director at the Westminster since 1963.

CASSON, LEWIS (1875–1970). British actor and director. His long and distinguished career, by no means overshadowed until towards the end by his wife, Sybil Thorndike, included seasons at the Court (04–07) with Granville Barker, where his parts included Octavius in *Man and Superman* and Laertes to H. B. Irving's Hamlet (05), and acting and directing for Miss Horniman at the Gaiety, Manchester (08–13). With Bruce Winston presented Greek tragedy (20). With Shaw, directed *St. Joan* (24) in which he played de Stogumber.

Other highlights between the wars included directing for the Old Vic in the late 30s, notably Olivier's Coriolanus (38) and directing, with Granville Barker, Gielgud's Lear (40) in which he played Kent. Toured Welsh coalfields during the war with his wife also worked for the Old Vic in London. Played Warwick to his daughter Ann Casson's St. Joan (45). Post-war parts included Professor Linden in Priestley's *The Linden Tree* (47) and—rare event—a delightful, totally unboring Friar Laurence (52). Still busy acting as Mr. Witherspoon in *Arsenic and Old Lace* in 1966. Knighted (45).

CHAMBERLAIN, RICHARD (1935–). American actor. An invitation from Birmingham Rep to play Hamlet (69) after he had become identified with TV's Dr. Kildare in the public mind, led to the discovery of that rarest of beings in modern times, a first-rate American Shakespearean romantic actor. Since then he has successfully played Richard II in America. His Thomas Mendip in *The Lady's Not for Burning* at Chichester (72) has been another success.

CHERRELL, GWEN (1926–). British actress who won a Clarence Derwent award for her Cherry in *The Beaux, Stratagem* (48). Old Vic (53–7), where her parts included Doll Tearsheet and a much more colourful Celia than usual. Recent parts have included Annie Parker in *When We Are Married* (70).

CHURCH, ESMÉ (1893–1972). British actress, director and teacher, particularly associated with the Old Vic and Bradford Civic Playhouse. An Old Vic Rosalind (28), she later directed the famous Evans *As You Like It*, also *Ghosts*, etc.

CHURCH, TONY (1930–). British actor. Royal Shakespeare Co. (60–65) where his parts included Quince, Holofernes, Polonius and (69) Pandarus. Director of the Northcott, Exeter (67–70). R.S.C. (72–73); Antonio in *The Merchant*, Kostylov in *The Lower Depths*, etc.

CHURCHILL, DIANA (1913–). British actress. Though much of her career has been in the commercial theatre, this excellent actress has given some fine classical performances, notably as one of the leading players of Hugh Hunt's much admired Old Vic Company at the New (49–50). Her parts included Rosaline, Kate Hardcastle, Lizaveta in *A Month in the Country* and Elise in *The Miser*. A pert, brittle Natasha in *The Three Sisters* (51). Her Stratford Gertrude (56) was described by Ivor Brown as 'taut, nervous, intelligent ... original and exciting.' Araminta in *The Farmer's Wife* and Lady Utterwood in *Heartbreak House* at Chichester (67). Her husband was BARRY K. BARNES.

CLEMENTS, JOHN (1910–). British actor, manager, director and Director of the Chichester Festival (see p. 241), 1966–73. Classical parts have included a fine Coriolanus for the Old Vic (48), after which came his production of *The Beaux' Stratagem*

(49) which broke all records for a classical revival, and which starred himself and his wife, Kay Hammond (see p. 165). as a delectable Mrs. Sullen. They also played *Man and Superman* together (50), once a week in its entirety. Presented a season of plays at the Saville (55): *The Wild Duck*, *The Rivals*, *The Doctor's Dilemma*, and *The Way of the World*, with Clements himself playing a splendid Sir Anthony and a stylish Mirabell. Macbeth, and the Earl of Warwick in *St. Joan* in New York with the Old Vic (61).

At Chichester, which under his banner has become a 'festival of acting', his productions have included *The Clandestine Marriage*, *The Cherry Orchard*, *Heartbreak House*, *The Beaux' Stratagem* and *The Magistrate*, and his roles have included Macbeth (66), Shotover (67), Prospero (68), Antony (69) and Sir Antony Absolute (71). For his long commercial career see p. 155. He has also appeared in many films. Something of a legend for his management of the Intimate, Palmers Green, founded by him (35). Played Hamlet there (37). Knighted (68).

CLUNES, ALEC (1912–70). British actor and director. A mainly classical career before the war, culminating in leads at Stratford (39), including Petruchio, Benedick and Coriolanus. His taking no part in the war was the theatre's gain, as he ran the Arts Theatre (42–50) with outstanding success, directing over 100 productions. Parts included Hamlet (45), much admired by Agate. The first Thomas Mendip in *The Lady's Not for Burning* (48). Orsino at the reopening of the Vic (50), where he later played a vigorous, ringing-voiced Henry V (51) and an amusing Ford (51). Took over Higgins in *My Fair Lady* from Rex Harrison (59). His later classical parts included a magnificent Claudius (55), also Brutus, the Bastard in *King John* and Caliban at Stratford (57).

COLICOS, JOHN. Canadian actor who has played major parts at both North American Stratfords including fine performances of Caliban, Petruchio, Timon and Lear at Stratford, Ontario. Churchill in *Soldiers* (Toronto, New York, London, 68).

COLLIER, PATIENCE (1910–). British actress, with the Royal Shakespeare Co. since 1961. Her parts have included Regan, Mistress Quickly, Charlotta in *The Cherry Orchard*, and (69–70) Dame Purecraft in *Bartholomew Fair* and Edna in *A Delicate Balance*, etc.

COMPTON, FAY (1894–). British actress (also see p. 155). Ophelia opposite Barrymore (25), the first of several beautiful performances of the part. Her many other classical parts have included a particularly fine season at the Vic (53–4): the

Countess in *All's Well*, Gertrude, Constance and Volumnia. Lady Bracknell at the Vic (59). Parts in the first two Chichester seasons included Marya in *Uncle Vanya* (62–3). Anna in *A Month in the Country* (65).

CONVILLE, DAVID (1929–). British actor and director who has run the Open Air Theatre, Regent's Park, since 1962, and presented *Toad of Toad Hall* annually in London since then. His often weather-beaten theatre remains a delight. Artistic Director since 1968, RICHARD DIGBY DAY (1940–).

COPLEY, PETER (1915–). British actor. His varied career included a period with the Old Vic at the New (45–50), where he played Edmund, Brother Martin, Sir Andrew and a highly effective, fanatical Ananias in *The Alchemist*. Many commercial parts since.

CORNELL, KATHARINE. See p. 156.

COTTRELL, RICHARD (1936–). British director, manager and dramatist. Director and Manager of the Prospect Theatre Co. (62–9). Director, Cambridge Theatre Co. (70–). Managed Hampstead Theatre Club (64–6). Now associated with the Actors' Company, whose first production, Feydeau's *Ruling the Roost*, he directed excellently at Edinburgh (72). Other productions have included *Richard II* (69), with McKellen in the title-role,

also *The Recruiting Officer*, etc. Has translated Chekhov and Feydeau, including the above.

COULOURIS, GEORGE (1903–). British actor whose long career in Britain and America has included Mark Antony for Welles's Mercury Theater (37) and other classical and modern leads. Sikorski in *Soldiers* (London, 68).

COURTENAY, TOM (1937–). British actor. Constantin in *The Seagull*, Poins and Feste for the Old Vic (60–1), since when his parts have included Trofimov in *The Cherry Orchard* and Malcolm at Chichester (66), Lord Fancourt Babberley and Peer Gynt for Manchester's 69 Theatre Co., and Young Marlow and Hamlet, the latter in Edinburgh (68). Currently (73) starring in *Time and Time Again*. A major film actor.

CROWDEN, GRAHAM (1922–). British actor whose wide range of parts for the National (65–8) included Colpoys in *Trelawny of the Wells*, Foresight in *Love for Love* and his bravura Player in *Rosencrantz and Guildenstern are Dead*. Henry IV and Prospero at the Mermaid (70).

CRUICKSHANK, ANDREW (1907–). British actor. Old Vic (37–40), where his parts included Banquo, Cassio, Cornwall and Claudius in *Hamlet*, one of the finest of modern times, in Guthrie's modern dress production (38).

Later classical roles have included Julius Caesar, Leonato, Kent and Angelo at Stratford (50), Morell in Candida (51) and Halvard Solness in *The Master Builder* at the Ashcroft, Croydon (62). Commercial successes have included Chief-Inspector Hubbard in *Dial 'M' for Murder* (52). Dr. Cameron in the TV *Dr. Finlay's Casebook*.

CUMMINGS, CONSTANCE (1910–). American actress, in Britain since 1934. The Old Vic's Juliet and St. Joan in 1939 to which she returned (71) as a National Theatre Player—after many West End leads—playing Volumnia in the misconceived *Coriolanus*, Leda in *Amphitryon* (38) and (72) Mary Tyrone in *Long Day's Journey into Night*, a magnificent performance for which she will always be remembered. Married to Benn Levy (see. p. 48).

CURRAN, PAUL (1913–). British actor. Joined the National Theatre (65), where his parts have included Sir William Gower in *Trelawny of the Wells* (65) Pizarro in *The Royal Hunt of the Sun* (66), etc., and a rich, crusty, utterly captivating Sir Peter Teazle (72).

CUSHING, PETER (1913–). British actor who, before becoming a master of the macabre in horror films, played in classical and commercial parts, including Joseph Surface and Clarence for the Old Vic (48–9), and Bel

Affris and Brittanus in *Caesar and Cleopatra* and Alexas Diomedes in *Antony and Cleopatra* in the Olivier productions (51).

DALE, JIM (1935–). British actor. After a debut as a comedian in 1951, which led to pantomime, films, etc., played Autolycus at Edinburgh (66), Bottom there (67) and in London, then, for the National, Barnet in *The National Health* (69), Costard (70), Launcelot Gobbo (70) and, for the Young Vic (70), Scapino and Petruchio.

DANEMAN, PAUL (1925–). British actor. Parts have included Mowbray and Carlisle in *Richard II* for Gielgud (52), Laertes and Sir Toby at the Embassy (53), his Richard parts in Bulawayo (53), then, for the Old Vic (53–5), Shallow, Feste, Tullus Aufidius in *Coriolanus*, Malcolm, etc., his Shallow being a particular success, a 'galvanized memorial brass', according to Trewin. Later performances for the Vic included Henry VI, Lear's Fool and Sir Toby (57–8) and Faustus, the Bastard in *John*, Malvolio and Richard III (61–2). Hook (67). Commercial parts have included Martin Eliot in *The New Men* (62).

DENCH, JUDI (1935–). British actress. First appearance on the stage was as Ophelia (57) for the Old Vic. Stayed with the Company four seasons, rapidly establishing herself as a leading young Shakespearean, her most acclaimed part being a youthful, ardent and impulsive Juliet in Zeffirelli's famous *Romeo* (60). Her mainly classical career has taken her to the States, Europe, and to West Africa with Nottingham Playhouse as Lady Macbeth (63). Other engagements in the 60s included seasons with the Royal Shakespeare Co., Oxford Playhouse, and her Lika in *The Promise* which won her a Variety Club award as the actress of the year (67), also Sally Bowles in *Cabaret* (68).

Now an Associate Artist of the Royal Shakespeare Co., her recent parts in Stratford and London have included a Viola (69–70) which, as J. W. Lambert noted, was sturdy, steadfast and spiritual at the same time, also an amusing Grace, the rustic bluestocking in *London Assurance* (70). A rare double was Hermione and Perdita in *The Winters' Tale* (69). A commanding, moving Duchess of Malfi (71). One of today's two or three finest younger actresses, she is married to MICHAEL WILLIAMS (1935–) of the R.S.C. whose parts have included Orlando, Troilus, Lear's Fool and Petruchio, and her brother is JEFFERY DENCH of the Company, whose parts have included Sir Andrew and Page in *The Merry Wives*.

DEVINE, GEORGE (1901–66). British director, actor and manager. The first Director of the English Stage Co. (see p. 242). His many classical roles included Sir Toby at the Queen's for Gielgud (38) and George Tesman in *Hedda Gabler* (54). Ran the original, excellent and now apparently forgotten Young Vic (46–50). Directed *Bartholomew Fair* at the Old Vic (50), also *King John*. Directed a number of productions at Stratford, including *Volpone*, *The Shrew*, a *Dream* which discarded Mendelssohn and had 'fairies closer to insects than human beings' (Ivor Brown), and an exciting controversial *Lear* (55) with Gielgud, and with sets and costumes by the Japanese American artist, Isamu Noguchi. Aiming to stress the timeless universal and mythical quality of the story, Devine and Noguchi convinced and thrilled many, distracted and shocked others, who spoke of science fiction and geishas. Directed *The Country Wife* (56), *Major Barbara* (58), *Rosmersholm* (59), *Platonov* (60) and *Twelfth Night* (62) for the English Stage Co. and was also a successful director of opera.

DEVLIN, WILLIAM (1911–). British actor. His long career, mainly in the classical theatre, was perhaps thrown off balance through no fault of his own by his astonishing and powerful Lear when he was only 22 (34). Played Lear again at the Vic (35) where he also played Cassius, Tusenbach in *The Three Sisters*, Banquo, Richard III, Dr. O'Meara in *St. Helena*, Leontes and Peer Gynt. Later Lears were at Bristol Old Vic after the war and at the Embassy (47), finally taking over at the Vic in an emergency (52), 'rich in voice and crumbling but unconquered virility' (Audrey Williamson). A magnificent player of small parts at the Vic and Stratford after the war, bringing real authority to roles like Antonio in *Twelfth Night* and the Duke of Verona in *Romeo and Juliet* at the Vic (52) when he also played the Chorus.

DEXTER, JOHN (1925–). British director of plays and operas, especially associated with the English Stage Company and the National Theatre. Renowned for organizing large scale business on stage since his production of Wesker's *The Kitchen* at the Court (61), where he staged the Wesker *Trilogy* (58–60) and *Chips with Everything* (63). His most famous productions at the National have been the Olivier *Othello* (64) and his vividly imaginative staging of *The Royal Hunt for the Sun* (Chichester and the National 64). Directed the New York production (65). Other productions at the National have included *St. Joan*, *Hobson's Choice*, *Black Comedy* and— creating a solid Tudor provincial world—*A Woman Killed with Kindness* (71). His latest productions at the time of writing in his second spell as an Associate Director of the National, are Goldsmith's *The Good-Natured Man* (71) and a brilliant *The Misanthrope* (73).

DIGNAM, MARK (1909–). British actor whose long career in classical and modern plays has ranged from touring with Ben Greet (31) to Menenius at Stratford (72).

DONAT, ROBERT (1905–1958). British actor and manager. A very fine actor and major star, especially in films, whose career was ruined by ill-health. At Buxton for the Old Vic he played Dick Dudgeon, Romeo and a particularly fine Honeywood in *The Good-Natured Man* (39), performances which never reached London because of the war. A notable Shotover in *Heartbreak House* (43). His Benedick (46) in a *Much Ado* staged by himself, was witty and beautifully spoken, this last being a feature of his moving, serene and strong Becket in *Murder in the Cathedral* at the Old Vic (53).

DOTRICE, ROY (1925–). British actor. Noted for his portrayals of old men, especially John Aubrey in *Brief Lives* (68), an extraordinary solo feat, and A. P. Herbert's Mr. Haddock on TV. Was also an unusually effective Julius Caesar at Stratford (63) and a strong Edward IV (63–4). The best known of his talented family, apart from himself, is his eldest daughter, MICHELE DOTRICE.

DUNLOP, FRANK (1927–). British director of the lively Young Vic Company (70–), see p. 255.

Associate Director of the National Theatre, where his productions (from 68) have included Brecht's (sic) *Edward II, Home and Beauty*, a highly effective and fantastical *The White Devil*, and *The Captain of Köpenick*. Previous work included his Pop Theatre (66) which staged classical productions at two Edinburgh Festivals. A key figure in the fight to attract younger, wider audiences to the theatre.

EASTON, RICHARD (1933–). Canadian actor who has played at both the North American Stratfords and toured Europe for Britain's (55) playing Claudio in *Much Ado* and Edgar. Nick in *Who's Afraid of Virginia Woolf?* (London, 64).

EDDISON, ROBERT (1908–). British actor whose very wide-ranging career has included a Witwoud in *The Way of the World* for the Vic (48) which was 'the very ecstasy of foppery' (Ivor Brown), and a Lightborn in *Edward II* (69) which won him a Clarence Derwent award. Well-known since the 30s for his Shakespearean and Restoration comedy work, his voice and presence helped make him an admirable Clarence and Cassius at the Vic (62). Also a fine Chekhovian.

ELLIOTT, MICHAEL (1931–). British director. After TV work, directed a famous *Brand* at the Lyric, Hammersmith (59), with Patrick McGoohan magnificent in the title role. Directed the Royal Shakespeare Co.'s magical *As You Like It* (61). Artistic Director of the Old Vic for its final and distinguished last season (62–3), his productions being *Peer Gynt*, *The Merchant of Venice* and *Measure for Measure*. *Little Eyolf* at Edinburgh (63). *Miss Julie* at Chichester (65). Helped found the 69 Theatre Co. of which he is Artistic Director (68–).

EVANS, EDITH (1888–). British actress (also see p. 159). Her classical career began with a Cressida for William Poel (12). Toured variety theatres playing Shakespearean scenes with Ellen Terry (18). After an early success as Cleopatra in Dryden's *All for Love* (22) followed by the Serpent and the She-Ancient in the first *Back to Methusalah* at Birmingham Rep (23), later seen in London, she gave one of the classic performances of the century as Millimant in *The Way of the World* (24) at the Lyric, Hammersmith. Agate described her in the role as 'a city in illumination'.

This was her first triumph in a classical high comedy role. Others have included Mrs. Sullen in *The Beaux' Stratagem* (27), her immortal Lady Bracknell (39) mercifully preserved on film and record, Mrs. Malaprop (45) and Lady Wishfort (48). Her Shakespearean career began to blaze when she joined the Old Vic (25–6), her parts included Portia, Katharina, Rosalind,

Beatrice, Queen Margaret, a first Nurse in *Romeo and Juliet* which foreshadowed her classic one for Gielgud (35) and a Cleopatra too fastidious for Agate, but happier than a later one (46), which was a rare mis-judgement in a supremely well-judged career. Her work in this first of four Vic seasons is remembered as one of the highlights of the Company's history. Returned for Emilia and Viola (32). Her later Rosalind (37), 'witty, charming and boyish' (Harcourt Williams), is now as legendary as her Millimant and her earthy 'massive, lumbering crone' of a Nurse (Trewin). Later parts have included Henry VIII's Katharine at the Vic (58), Volumnia at Stratford (59) and the Countess in *All's Well* in the same season.

Other parts have included two Chekhovian ones, Irena Arcadina (36) and Mme. Ranevsky (48) which divided the critics—'perhaps too irrepressibly mischievous' (Audrey Williamson)—but was warm and radiant; also several late Shavian roles (Shaw being a classic in this book), including Orinthia in *The Apple Cart* in Malvern and London (29) and Lady Utterwood in *Heartbreak House* (Malvern, 29; London, 32). D.B.E. (46).

EVANS, MAURICE (1901–). British actor resident in America since 1935. One of his earliest successes was as Raleigh in *Journey's End* (Stage Society,

CTT–G

28; Savoy, 29). Joined Vic/Wells Co. (34) where, after a fine Octavius, he made his name as Richard II. After a successful Hamlet, went to America to become her leading classical actor. Hamlet apart, two of his most notable parts were his John Tanner in *Man and Superman* and Dick Dudgeon in *The Devil's Disciple* (50). Has played Shakespearean roles on TV and made a film of Macbeth. See also p. 160.

EVERHART, REX (1920–). American actor whose many parts at Stratford, Conn., have included Dogberry, Junius Brutus and Grumio. Murray in *The Odd Couple* (London, 66).

FARRAH, ABD'ELKADER (1926–). Algerian designer and Associate Artist of the Royal Shakespeare Co. *Dr. Faustus* (68), *Richard III* (70), *Murder in the Cathedral* (72), etc. A chilling *Romeo* (73).

FERRER, JOSÉ (1912–). Puerto Rican-born American actor, producer and director. Played Iago opposite Paul Robeson at the Shubert Theatre for a record run (43). Other parts have included Cyrano, Richard III, Jeremy in *The Alchemist*, Face in *Volpone* and Lord Fancourt Babberley in *Charley's Aunt*, which he directed (53–54). Some of these parts were played in his two seasons directing at the City Center, New York (48/53–4). *Oedipus Rex* (Salt Lake City, 66). Also see p. 160.

FFRANGCON-DAVIES, GWEN (1896 –). British actress and singer who created the role of Etain in *The Immortal Hour* (19). The first Eve, Amaryllis and the Ghost of Eve in *Back to Methusalah* at Birmingham Rep (24). Other parts have included Shaw's Cleopatra and Eliza, Ophelia (30), Magda (30), Anne of Bohemia in *Richard of Bordeaux* (32), Elizabeth in *The Barretts of Wimpole Street* (30), Lady Macbeth (42) and Queen Katharine at Stratford and the Old Vic (50/3). Won an *Evening Standard* drama award for her very moving Mary Tyrone in *Long Day's Journey into Night* (58).

FICHANDLER, ZELDA (1924–). American director and producer. Founded, with Edward Magnum, the Arena Stage, Washington D.C. (50) for whom she has directed and produced an extraordinary range of classical and modern plays.

FINLAY, FRANK. British actor. Played Harry Kahn in *Chicken Soup with Barley* at Coventry, the Royal Court and in New York (58). Other parts before becoming a National Theatre player (63) included Percy Elliott in *Epitaph for George Dillon* (59), Private Attercliffe in *Sergeant Musgrave's Dance* (59), roles in the Wesker Trilogy at the Royal Court (60) and Corporal Hill in *Chips with Everything* (62). Parts at the National included the First Gravedigger and de Stogumber (previously played at Chichester, 63), a notable Willie Mossop in *Hobson's Choice* (64), and Iago to Olivier's Othello (64) at Chichester and the National. This was Iago the 'appalling practical joker' (W. H. Auden) and, for many, highly effective. Another notable performance was a garlic-scented Dogberry in *Much Ado* (65). A Major T.V. actor.

FINNEY, ALBERT (1936–). British actor who first became known for his work at Birmingham and Stratford. At the former (56–8) parts included Hamlet, Macbeth, Henry V and Face, and at Stratford (59), Edgar, Cassio and Lysander. Went on for Olivier as Coriolanus with great success. For the National, Don Pedro in *Much Ado*, Jean in *Miss Julie* and Harold in *Black Comedy* (65). His Victor and Poche in *A Flea in her Ear* for the National (66) won him an *Evening Standard* award. Also see p. 161.

FLEETWOOD, SUSAN. British actress whose notable performances have included Regan (68) and Portia (72) for the Royal Shakespeare Co. To play the Shrew at Stratford (73).

FLEMING, TOM (1927–). British actor and director, and founder of Edinburgh's Gateway Theatre (53). For the Royal Shakespeare Co. played Kent, Prospero, Brutus, etc. (62–4).

FLETCHER, ALLEN (1922–).

American director who, since his *King John* for the Oregon Shakespeare Festival (48), has directed classical and modern plays, also opera, in many parts of the U.S.A. Director of the American Conservatory Theater since 1970.

FLETCHER, ROBERT (1923–). American designer of classical and modern plays and opera, including two seasons at San Francisco's American Conservatory Theater (69–71), where he designed *Oedipus Rex, Hamlet, The Relapse*, etc.

FORBES-ROBERSTON, JEAN (1905–62). British actress, daughter of Sir Johnston. Her parts included Viola, Rebecca West, Hedda, Puck, Portia, also Kate in Priestley's *Time and the Conways* (37). The finest of all Peter Pans (nine seasons), eerie, boyish and utterly convincing. Her Viola, according to Agate, transcended in beauty any other rendering since Ellen Terry's. Married to the actor and director, ANDRÉ VAN GYSEGHEM (1906–). There daughter is JOANNA VAN GYSEGHEM.

FRENCH, LESLIE (1904–). British actor whose Shakespearian career dates from the Vic in 1929 to the present. Between the wars regarded by many as the finest Ariel and Puck of the day.

FURSE, ROGER (1903–73). British designer. Designed some famous Old Vic productions, including Guthrie's *Hamlet* (38), *King*

Lear (40), *Henry IV* (45) Olivier's Cleopatra plays (51) and his Shakespeare films, also operas, *The Mousetrap*, etc. *The Broken Heart* (Chichester, 62).

GASCON, JEAN (1921–). Canadian actor and director, Director of the Stratford, Ontario, Festival, where he has been staging plays since 1959, also operas (since 65). Directed and played Edgar in *The Dance of Death* (67) and has directed Shakespeare, Molière, Chekhov, etc.

GASKILL, WILLIAM. See p. 41.

GENN, LEO (1905–). British actor who, before becoming a film star, played a wide range of classical parts in the 30s at the Old Vic, including Horatio, Orsino, Brutus and Burgundy in *Henry V*. Trewin has called his voice 'tapestried'. Buckingham in *Henry VIII* at the Vic (53). Has also played many commercial parts.

GIELGUD, JOHN (1904–). British actor and director, and a leader of his profession for over 30 years. The most famous British Hamlet of modern times (see p. 72), his noble voice, emotional approach allied to keen intelligence, powerful presence and sheer dedication to his art have contributed to an extraordinary career and performances that have reached greatness.

Romeo for Barry Jackson in London (24). Played a number of commercial parts, see p. 162, also in Chekhov and Ibsen, including Oswald (28). Joined the Old Vic (29–31) for seasons that established his fame as a classical actor, in parts that included Romeo, Richard II, Macbeth, Hotspur and Hamlet.

His most famous early commercial success was in the title role of *Richard of Bordeaux* (32) which he also directed. Hamlet (34) and Noah (35) and, alternating with Olivier, Romeo and Mercutio (35). Trigorin (35) and Hamlet in New York (36). By now well-established as a director, including *Strange Orchestra* (32), he took over the management of the Queen's for a season which is regarded as laying the foundations of British ensemble acting (see p. 72). His own parts were Richard II, Joseph Surface, Vershinin and Shylock. His first John Worthing (39) sealed his reputation as a stylish comedian, and the same year saw another Hamlet.

His wartime seasons and tours included Lear and Prospero at the Old Vic (40) and the famous Haymarket season (44–5) of *Hamlet*, *Love for Love*, *The Circle*, *A Midsummer Night's Dream* and *The Duchess of Malfi*. Stratford (50), where, as well as Benedick, Cassius and Lear, he gave a cold, fanatical Angelo, a striking indication of his new range, which his tormented Leontes confirmed. A season at the Lyric, Hammersmith (52–3) included directing Scofield's Richard II and acting Mirabel and Jaffeir in *Venice Preserved*.

Performances at Stratford and the Old Vic during the 50s included Lear (55) and Prospero (57) at Stratford and later in London, and a successful debut as an opera director in Berlioz's colossal *The Trojans* at Covent Garden (57). His Wolsey at the Old Vic (58) was another highlight of the period, as was his first Shakespearian recital, *The Ages of Man* (New York 58), seen in several countries, including Britain.

Highlights of the 60s were his Gayev in *The Cherry Orchard* (61) at the Aldwych, Ivanov (65) Seneca's *Oedipus* at the National Theatre (68). His deeply moving performance in David Storey's *Home* at the Royal Court (70) was later seen in America. He has appeared in a number of films in one of which, *Julius Caesar*, his Cassius, as forceful as it was stylish, is fortunately preserved for posterity. Knighted (53).

GODFREY, DEREK (1924–). British actor. After appearing with the Young Vic and at Stratford in small parts, followed by Rep at Nottingham and Bristol Old Vic, joined the Old Vic (56) where his Iachimo, sardonic and striking, won him a Clarence Derwent award for the year's best supporting player. At Stratford and, later, the Aldwych (58–63), where his wide range of parts included a notable Proteus in *Two Gentlemen of Verona* (60), Henry in *Curtmantle* (62) and Macheath

(63). Returned to play Machiavel in *The Jew of Malta* (64). At the National (69–70) played Mirabell, Bracchiano in *The White Devil* and Don Quixote in *The Travails of Sancho Panza*. Trigorin at the Arts (70).

GOODLIFFE, MICHAEL (1914–). British actor who, after small parts at Stratford and the Old Vic before the war, was a striking Octavius Caesar of great authority in *Antony and Cleopatra* in London (47). Other roles have included a dangerous Don John in *Much Ado* at the Phoenix (52), Commander Wyburton in Morgan's *The River Line* (52), Dr. Rank in *A Doll's House* (54), the Inquisitor in *The Lark* (55) and, in New York, Michael Dennis in *The Living Room* (54). In the late 50s and 60s was mainly seen in films and on TV, but played Marlowe's Mephistopheles (61) and Hubert for the Vic, Robert Chilton in *An Ideal Husband* (66) and several non-classical parts.

GOOLDEN, RICHARD (1895–). British actor. The ancient 'ingenious and moving Fool' (Agate) to Wolfit's great Lear (44), who is also known to generations of children for his Mole in *Toad of Toad Hall*, a role for which his seemingly meek voice and personality are well-suited. His other roles for Wolfit included Polonius and Roderigo, and he also played at the Old Vic, including Sir Andrew (33), and in Regent's

Park (38). Has had long career in the commercial theatre (also on radio) a remembered joy being his downtrodden Author in *On Monday Next* (49). The Mayor in *Look after Lulu* at the Royal Court (59). Shallow in *The Merry Wives*, Old Gobbo and Verges in *Much Ado* in Regent's Park (68–70).

GORDON, RUTH (1896–). American actress, mainly in the commercial theatre (see p. 63). Her Mrs. Pinchwife in *The Country Wife* at the Old Vic (37), previously seen at Westport, Conn., and later on Broadway, was one of the classic comedy performances of its generation. In London it had the additional advantage of a Guthrie production and a very strong cast alongside its delicious star. Other classical parts have included Nora in *A Doll's House* (37), Natasha in *The Three Sisters* (42) and Natalie in *A Month in the Country* (49).

GORING, MARIUS (1912–). British actor, frequently at the Old Vic in the 30s, where his parts included Romeo, Epihodov, Feste and Hamlet. Has played Hamlet in French with the Compagnie des Quinze (34–5) and has acted in German in Germany. Other roles include Gregers in *The Wild Duck* at the Westminster (38) and John Rosmer and Trophimof at the Arts (48). At Stratford (53) his parts included Richard III, Octavius, Petruchio and Lear's

Fool. Has taken a company performing Shakespearean scenes to Paris, Holland, Finland and India (57–9) and has appeared in many commercial plays, including *Sleuth* (71), films and on TV where his ability and intellectual personality made him a major star as a pathologist in *The Expert*. Directed *The Bells* (68) in which he played Mathias. Married to the distinguished German actress, LUCIE MANNHEIM.

GREEN, DOROTHY (1886–1961). British actress of 'proud voice and bearing' (Trewin) whose career as a Bensonian, at the Old Vic and Stratford embraced practically the whole repertoire of Shakespearean women. One of the few women to succeed as Cleopatra, at Stratford (12) and the Old Vic (30). Later parts included Gertrude at the Vic (35), the Duchess of Gloucester in *Richard II* and Lady Sneerwell for Gielgud at the Queen's (37), Volumnia at Stratford (39), Dame Purecraft in *Bartholomew Fair* (50) and Isabel in *Henry V* (51) at the Vic. Mrs. Telfer in *Trelawny of the Wells* at the Lyric, Hammersmith (57) and a stylish Lady Sneerwell for Wolfit at the King's, Hammersmith (53).

GREET, PHILIP BEN (1857–1936). British actor, manager and director. Toured for many years in Britain and America with a repertoire of Shakespearean and other plays. As fine a trainer of young talent as Benson. One of the key figures in the founding of the Old Vic where between 1915–18 he produced 24 Shakespearean plays. Later he took Shakespeare to schools. A practical man-of-the-theatre. Knighted (29).

GRIFFITH, HUGH (1912–). British actor whose most famous role—an Oscar-winning performance in *Ben Hur* apart—has been General St. Pé in Anouilh's *The Waltz of the Toreadors* (56). Stratford (46) including Touchstone and a striking Mephistopheles. W. O. Grant in *Look Homeward, Angel* in New York (57), Count Cenci in *The Cenci*, Old Vic (59). Stratford's fine Falstaff (64) in both the *Henry IV* plays.

GUINNESS, ALEC (1914–). British actor of exceptional versatility. Joined the Old Vic (36) playing Osric and Sir Andrew. Played in Guthrie's complete, modern dress production of *Hamlet* (38), where he was acclaimed for his moving restraint rather than bravura. After the war rejoined the Old Vic (46–8) to play, amongst other parts, the finest Fool in *Lear* in living memory, Richard II, the Dauphin, and a definitive Menenius Agrippa in *Coriolanus*. After his delightful Herbert Pocket in David Lean's *Great Expectations*, films have claimed most of his time, but other notable stage roles have been Sir Henry in *The Cocktail Party*

(Edinburgh Festival, 49; New York, 50), the Cardinal in *The Prisoner* (54), Lawrence in *Ross* (60), the King in Ionesco's *Exit the King* (63), also Dylan Thomas in *Dylan* (New York, 64) and the Father in Mortimer's *A Voyage Round My Father* (71). Neither his Macbeth (67) nor, rather notoriously, his Hamlet (51), which he also directed with Frank Hauser, were successes.

Whether Guinness is a 'great actor' or not revolves round the old argument as to whether a major character actor who is rarely 'himself' can reach the heights in great roles that a major actor of exceptional personality can attain. This is for the individual to decide. Guinness's cool naturalism, high intelligence, dedication and authority (which is surely partly personality) are beyond dispute. Knighted (59).

GUTHRIE, TYRONE (1900–71). British director of astounding energy, also author, talker and theatre founder. Originally an actor, his 6 ft. 5 in. did not help his career. His first London productions included Bridie's *The Anatomist* (31) and Priestley's brilliant early play, *Dangerous Corner* (32). Became the Old Vic's youngest director in (33); returned (36–8). In sole charge of the Old Vic and Sadler's Wells (39–45). First director of the Stratford, Ontario, Festival (53) and later returned there. Director of the new theatre at Minneapolis (62–5) which bears his name. Also directed operas, *Oedipus Rex* in Hebrew at Tel Aviv, and plays in Australia, New Zealand, etc.

Though not the first major director in Britain, he was its first world-famous star director. Incapable of dullness, he could be capricious to a degree in Shakespearean plays he had directed more than once. No respecter of stars, and a tough taskmaster who remained an *enfant terrible* till he died, actors delighted in working for him. He practised ensemble before it was fashionable and was the leading, because most authoritative, advocate of the open stage, arena stage, theatre - in - the - round— anything except the proscenium theatre in which he also excelled. Amongst his most famous productions were his *Dream* (Old Vic, 37), *The School for Scandal* (37), *Peer Gynt* (Old Vic at the New, 44), *Tamburlaine* (Old Vic, 51) see p. 74, *Troilus and Cressida* (Old Vic, 56), also his *All's Well* (Stratford, Ontario, 53). His *A Life in the Theatre* and *Tyrone Guthrie on Acting* are strongly recommended. Author of the play, *Top of the Ladder* (50). Knighted (61).

HADDRICK, RON (1929–). Australian actor. Played Hubert, Tybalt, Horatio, etc. at Stratford (54). Parts in Australia have included Othello, Claudius, John Tanner and, for Guthrie, Oedipus (Sydney, 70).

HAGEN, UTA (1919–) German-born American actress, also p. 164. Her classical parts have included a fine Desdemona opposite Robeson (42), a stirring St. Joan (51) and Mme. Ranevskaya (68).

HALL, PETER (1930–). British director of plays, films and operas, and one of the most influential and successful figures in the modern theatre. Director of the Arts Theatre (55–6), where his productions, amongst others, included the historic first staging in Britain of *Waiting for Godot* (53), Anouilh's *Waltz of the Toreadors* and *Mourning Becomes Electra*. Worked at Stratford from 1956 onwards, his first production being *Love's Labour's Lost*. Became Director of the Royal Shakespeare Co. in 1960, the year Stratford found a permanent London base at the Aldwych.

A born administrator, his range as a director is as considerable as his ability. His famous Pinter productions, his unusually successful forays into the opera house to direct classical and modern works, and his major achievement at Stratford in producing all the seven histories, including the epic *Wars of the Roses* sequence with John Barton (see p. 76), are typical of a versatility which seems incapable of lapsing into routine or gimmickry. Gave up the post of Managing Director of the R.S.C. (69), but remained a director. His non-classical productions, Pinter apart, have

ranged from Livings's *Eh?*, Charles Dyer's *Staircase* and Albee's *A Delicate Balance* to Schoenberg's *Moses and Aaron*. His long partnership with the designer, John Bury, has produced remarkable results in the theatre and at Covent Garden where he was to have become co-director with Colin Davis. His cancellation of this appointment (71) was opera's cruel loss and the theatre's great gain. At the time of writing (72) has been appointed to succeed Olivier at the National Theatre.

HANDS, TERRY (1941–). British director and an Associate Director of the Royal Shakespeare Co. with which he started in 1966 as Artistic Director of the touring Theatregoround. Productions have included *Merry Wives, Pericles, Richard III, The Merchant,* Triana's *The Criminals* and, his finest achievement to date, a stunning realization of Genet's *The Balcony* (71). Directed *Richard III* at the Comédie Francaise with great success (72). A bizarre *Romeo* (73).

HANNEN, NICHOLAS (1881–1972). British actor whose long West End career did not prevent regular appearances in the classics, beginning with Lysander for Granville Barker in New York (15). These culminated in his work with the Old Vic at the New (44–7), including Buckingham in *Richard III* (44) and, most notably, that rather thankless part, Henry IV (45).

HARDWICK, PAUL (1918–). British actor, much of whose career has been spent with the Shakespeare Memorial Co., later the Royal Shakespeare Co. (48–65). This strong, reliable actor's parts have included Roderigo, Bottom, Buckingham in *The Wars of the Roses* and Pistol (in the *Henrys*). Played John of Gaunt and Maltravers in *Edward II* for Prospect Productions (Edinburgh, 69: London, 70). Dr. Relling in *The Wild Duck* (70).

HARDWICKE, CEDRIC (1893–1964) British actor who, while at Birmingham Rep, became the leading Shavian of his day. A member of the first Old Vic Company (14). Apart from his bowler-hatted Gravedigger for Sir Barry Jackson in London (24), his classical parts were few until rejoining the Old Vic at the New (48). His dry, underplayed Sir Toby was admired by many, his Faustus by few. His Gaev in *The Cherry Orchard* was his most successful performance of the season. See also p. 165. Knighted (34). His son, EDWARD HARDWICKE (1932–), when a National Theatre player, gave one of the comic performances of the decade as the cleft-palated Camille in *A Flea in her Ear* (66).

HARDY, ROBERT. British actor and medievalist. Stratford (49–51). Claudio in *Much Ado* at the Phoenix (51). Old Vic (53–5) where he quickly made his name as a fine actor with a considerable technique in a range of parts that included Laertes, Sebastian, Duncan, Hortensio, and Ariel in a production that did him no favours. A superb Prince Hal, though Tynan alleged too great a show of intelligence. At Stratford (59), played the King of France in *All's Well*, Sicinius Velutus in *Coriolanus*—'a slick and oily master of intrigue' (Ivor Brown)—and an unusually subtle Edmund. Rosmer in *Rosmersholm* in London (60). Henry V and Hamlet at the Ravinia Festival, Illinois (64). Sir Harry Wildair in *The Constant Couple* (67). His non-classical parts have included Martin in *Someone Waiting* on Broadway (56), Byron in *Camino Real* (57), the Count in Anouilh's *The Rehearsal* (61) and Martin Lynch-Gibbon in *A Severed Head* (63). Made the film *The Picardy Affair*, about Henry V and Agincourt. A major TV star.

HARE, ERNEST (1900–). British actor and, from 1924, a fine small part Shakespearean at Stratford, the Vic, etc. Played Kent, Sir Toby, etc., for Wolfit (53).

HARRIS, ROBERT (1900–). British actor whose fine voice and intelligence have contributed to his success in a wide range of Shakespearean parts, especially at the Old Vic. These include Hamlet (32), Shylock (61) and, at Stratford, Prospero and Richard II (47). Has appeared in many commercial successes. Toured the U.S.A. as More in *A Man for All Seasons* (63–4). Pope Pius XII in *The Deputy* (New York, 64).

HARRIS, ROSEMARY (1930–). British actress now resident in America. Her parts at the Old Vic in the 50s included Desdemona and Cressida, both notably successful. Ilyena at Chichester (63) which she repeated at the National, where she also played Ophelia. A wide range of classical parts in America for the Association of Producing Artists, including Lady Teazle, Viola, Nina and Mme. Arkadina. Also see p. 166.

HARVEY, LAURENCE (1928–). Lithuanian-born South African actor and film star. At Stratford (52 and 54). Parts included Orlando, Romeo and Troilus. Old Vic tour of U.S.A. (58–9) as Henry V. Leontes at Edinburgh (66) and in London. Sergius in *Arms and the Man* at Chichester (70).

HAUSER, FRANK (1922–). British director, notably at Oxford Playhouse (since 56), from which many of his productions have gone to London. Has taken the company abroad and directed elsewhere, notably for Sadler's Wells Opera, including the historic *Iolanthe* (62) the evening after the copyright expired, arguably the most enchanting G. and S. production ever staged in

Britain. Has directed *Hamlet* in Verona (63) and *Twelfth Night* in Stratford, Conn. (66).

HAWKINS, JACK (1910–). British actor. Before his notable screen career, this strong actor ranged between West End juveniles and classical roles in Regent's Park, and the Ghost and Claudius at Elsinore (39). His Edmund in the stellar Gielgud *Lear* at the Old Vic (40) was hailed by Agate as superb and the best performance in the production. Later parts included Mercutio (New York, 51) and Cymen in Fry's *Thor, with Angels* (51).

HAYES, GEORGE (1888–1967). British actor. Osric for Forbes-Robertson (12). Then became one of the leading Shakespeareans of his day at Stratford and the Old Vic, playing a colossal range of parts. A melodious speaker and a bold actor. 'On his night, a master', recalls Trewin.

HEELEY, DESMOND. British designer of plays, operas and ballets including many productions at Stratford, Ontario. For the National, designs include those for *Rosencrantz and Guildenstern are Dead* (67).

HELPMANN, ROBERT (1909–). Australian dancer, actor and director. Though principal male dancer of the Sadler's Wells Ballet for many years, as early as 1937 he made his name as an actor with his Old Vic Oberon, a finely-spoken 'strange, sinister stag-beetle' (Harcourt Williams). First played Hamlet at the New (44) with some pathos, but was swamped, according to Agate, by the production. However, Agate hailed his Flamineo in *The White Devil* (47) for its virtuosity, virility and 'a rare quality of verbal passion'. Alternated with Scofield as Hamlet at Stratford (48), where he also played Shylock, repeating it at the Vic (55) along with Angelo and Petruchio and (56–7) Saturninus in *Titus*, Richard III and a delightful Launce in *The Two Gentlemen of Verona*. Other parts have included Apollodorus and Octavius for the Olivier Cleopatra plays season (51) and the Doctor in *The Millionairess* (London and New York, 52).

He has directed a number of classical plays, including *Romeo*, *Antony and Cleopatra* and *As You Like It* at the Vic, where he also directed a much-praised *Murder in the Cathedral* (53), with Donat as Becket. Has also directed operas and appeared in films, and directed some commercial plays. Director of the Adelaide Festival of Arts (70). Knighted (68).

HEPBURN, KATHARINE (1909–). American stage and screen actress (see also p. 167). Between 1950–60 played Rosalind, Isabella, Portia, Viola, Beatrice, Katharina and, less fortunately, Cleopatra. Her Rosalind (New York, 50) and her Portia (Old

Vic tour, 57, of Australia and Stratford, Connecticut, 57) have perhaps been her most acclaimed roles, along with her Lady in *The Millionairess* (London and New York, 52).

HERLIE, EILEEN (1920–). British actress. With the Old Vic at Liverpool (44–5), where her parts included Paula Tanqueray and Anna Christie. A powerful actress, she made her name as the Queen in *The Eagle has Two Heads* (46). In America (since 55) her parts have included Emilia Marty in *The Makropoulos Secret* (57) and Gertrude in Gielgud's production of *Hamlet* in New York (64). Also Paulina and Beatrice at Stratford, Ontario (58).

HIRSH, JOHN (1930–). Hungarian-born Canadian director who has staged a number of plays at Stratford, Ontario, where he was Associate Director (67–9). Fine productions of *Yerma* and *Galileo*, etc., at Lincoln Center (66–).

HOGG, IAN (1937–). British actor. With the Royal Shakespeare Co. (since 64) has played Tybalt, Lavache in *All's Well*, etc., and the lead in *Coriolanus* (72), a surprising piece of casting which grew in performance.

HOLLOWAY, BALLIOL (1883–1967). British actor and a brilliant Shakespearean between the wars at the Old Vic and Stratford:

Richard III, Falstaff, Jacques, Angelo, Othello, etc. Returned to the Old Vic (at the New) as a wonderfully antique, resonant, fascinating Don Armado in *Love's Labour's Lost* (49).

HOLM, IAN (1931–). British actor. At Stratford (from 58) and the Aldwych for the Royal Shakespeare Co. his parts included an undemonic Richard III, a power game figure demanded by Hall and Barton, in *The Wars of the Roses* (63), well realized by the actor. Also Lenny in *The Homecoming* (65). His Henry V, with Barton and Nunn demanding a Henry for our times, unheroic (of course) with a tough job to do, won him, with his Lenny, the 1965 *Evening Standard* award. Malvolio (66) and Romeo (67). Nelson in *A Bequest to the Nation* (70).

HOPKINS, ANTHONY (1937–). British actor. As a National Theatre player he rapidly made his name in the late 60s after going on for Olivier in *The Dance of Death* (67). Since then he has played a wide range of parts including Andrei in *The Three Sisters* (67), Audrey in the all-male *As You Like It* (67), Frankford in *A Woman Killed with Kindness* (71), a powerful and moving performance, and a *Coriolanus* handicapped by a misconceived production. His Macbeth (72), ambitious, tough but scared, seemed destined to grow in stature.

HORDERN, MICHAEL (1911–). British actor. A leading player at Stratford and the Old Vic from the 1952 Stratford season onwards. Two particularly notable performances in the 50s at the Vic were his Parolles (53) and his frightening Macbeth (58). Sir Ralph Bloomfield Bonnington in *The Doctor's Dilemma* (55). An inspired comedian in parts ranging from Mr. Posket in *The Magistrate* (58) to the agnostic old vicar, Flint, in Mercer's play of that name (70) and, particularly, the moral philosopher in Stoppard's *Jumpers* for the National (72). Parts played at Stratford have included an especially fine Menenius (52) and, for the Royal Shakespeare Co. at the Aldwych, The Father in *Playing with Fire* and Harry in Pinter's *The Collection* (62), Ulysses in *Troilus and Cressida* (62) and the much-tried Tobias in Albee's *A Delicate Balance* (69). A master of frenzy, benevolence, timing and speaking, this superb and popular actor has also given a 'masterly show of clinical madness in clinically accurate and highly affecting terms' (Eric Shorter) in Jonathan Miller's quirky *Lear* (Nottingham, 69; London, 70).

HOUGHTON, NORRIS (1909–). American director and producer. Directed Macbeth (London, 47; New York, 48). With T. Edward Hambleton (see p. 250), founded and became managing director of the Phoenix Theater, New

York, presenting Webster, Brecht, Ionesco, Pirandello, Shaw, Shakespeare, etc., resigning in 1959. One of the plays he directed was *The Seagull* (54). They were brave years, with many successes despite financial worry.

HOUSE, ERIC. Canadian actor, who has played a wide range of parts at Stratford, Ontario, since 1953. Boyet in *Love's Labour's Lost* and the Dancing Master in *Le Bourgeois Gentilhomme* at Chichester (64).

HOUSEMAN, JOHN (1902–). Rumanian-born American director, notably for the Theater Guild and at Stratford, Conn. With Orson Welles, founded the Mercury Theater (37), see p. 245. In the late 50s, proceeded to redeem the Stratford, Conn., Festival from 'chronic provincialism' (Brooks Atkinson). Key positions in the 60s including Producing Director of A.P.A. Phoenix (67–). As well as Shakespeare and the classics and moderns, directs opera and produces films.

HOWARD, ALAN (1937–). British actor and a leading member of the Royal Shakespeare Co., where his performances since 1966 have included Benedick, Orsino, Lussurioso in *The Revenger's Tragedy*, Jacques, Achilles, Hamlet and Theseus/Oberon in Peter Brook's *Dream*. Won the *Plays and Players* London Theatre Critics

Award (69) as the most promising actor for his much-admired Achilles and Lussurioso. His leaden Benedick apart, he has shone in a taxing range of parts.

HOWARD, TREVOR (1916–). British actor. This superb film actor played Captain Plume in *The Recruiting Officer* (Arts 43) opposite his wife, HELEN CHERRY. Petruchio for the Old Vic at the New (47). Lopahin in *The Cherry Orchard* (54). The Captain in *The Father* (64).

HOWE, GEORGE (1900–). British actor, whose long career in supporting Shakespearean roles included a Polonius in several productions regarded as one of the finest in modern times. In the commercial theatre, had a very long run as the sorely tried Headmaster in *The Happiest Days of Your Lives* (48). Recently, parts have included Sir Paul Plyant in *The Double Dealer* at the Royal Court (69).

HUDD, WALTER (1898–1963). British actor and director. Creator of Private Meek in *Too True to be Good* (32): he looked amazingly like the part's inspiration, T. E. Lawrence. Particularly good in Chekhov, notably Trofimov in *The Cherry Orchard* (41) and Kouliguin in *The Three Sisters* (51). Definitive in that trying role, Boyet, for the Old Vic at the New (49). Directed *Richard II* and *Twelfth Night* at Stratford (47), follow-

110   *Shakespeare and the Classics*

ing a very imaginative *Dr. Faustus* (with Robert Eddison) the previous season. Also directed a double bill of *Titus Andronicus* and *The Comedy of Errors* at the Old Vic (57). Amongst his other achievements were several classical productions for the Icelandic National Theatre in the 50s.

HUNT, HUGH (1911–). British director. Directed at the Abbey Theatre, Dublin (35–8), including more than 30 Irish plays. Director of the Bristol Old Vic (45–8) for a notable period. His Old Vic season at the New (49–50) was a memorable one, especially for his enchanting *Love's Labour's Lost*. Director at the restored Old Vic (50–3), his most famous production perhaps being *Romeo and Juliet* (52) with Alan Badel, Claire Bloom and Peter Finch. Worked in Australia as Director of the Elizabethan Theatre Trust (55–60), directing the classics and opera. The first Professor of Drama at Manchester University (61). Author of several books, including *Old Vic Prefaces: Shakespeare and the Producer* (54). Became Artistic Director of the Abbey, Dublin, in 1969.

HUNT, MARTITA (1900–69). British actress, best known in London and New York for her Countess in *The Madwoman of Chaillot* (New York 48 and again 49; London, 51). Played three seasons at the Old Vic between 1929–38, her most

famous part being Gertrude opposite Gielgud (30), regarded by many as the finest they had seen. 'Brilliantly stupid', wrote Martin Browne. She was also a powerful Lady Macbeth (30). Her Miss Haversham in David Lean's *Great Expectations* is a Dickensian (and film) classic.

HURRY, LESLIE (1909–). British designer of plays, operas and ballets. From his *Hamlet* for Sadler's Wells at the New (42), he has designed many famous productions including *The Ring* for Covent Garden (54) and Guthrie's *Tamburlaine the Great* (Old Vic, 51; New York, 56). Has been particularly associated with the Old Vic and Stratford, Ontario.

HUTT, WILLIAM (1920–). Canadian actor who has graduated from supporting to the great parts at Stratford, Ontario, where (since 70) he is Associate Director of the Festival Theatre. Has played James Tyrone in *Long Day's Journey into Night* (59) at Bristol and Sir Epicure Mammon in *The Alchemist* at Chichester (70). A sensitive, poetic Lear (Stratford, Ont. 72) 'broken in its madness, healing in its desolate dignity' (Barnes).

HYMAN, EARLE (1926–). American actor whose parts have included Othello at Stratford, Conn. (57), and Antonio in *The Duchess of Malfi* (New York, 57), also Othello in Norwegian (Bergen, 63).

IDEN, ROSALIND (1911–). British actress and the leading lady of her husband, Donald Wolfit. Very successful as Viola, Portia, etc., and, especially, Rosalind. Gave many Shakespeare Recitals with Wolfit at home and abroad: her voice and diction are notably good. The first Shakespearean leading lady countless playgoers, this writer included, ever saw. Daughter of Ben Iden Payne (see p. 126).

INGHAM, BARRIE (1932–). British actor, much of whose work has been for the Royal Shakespeare Co. As Bill Cody, almost saved *Indians* against all obstacles (68), see p. 47. Other parts have included Lord Foppington, Leontes, Brutus and a Scottish Sir Andrew Aguecheek. Elsewhere, parts have included Jingle in *Pickwick* (64) and Clancy Pettinger in Ron Grainer's *On The Level* (66). His Dazzle in *London Assurance* (Aldwych, 70: New, 72) was dubbed by Hugh Leonard, 'Son of Mr. Jingle'.

IRVING, LAURENCE (1897–). British artist and designer and his grandfather's brilliant biographer. Has designed many classical and modern plays from farce (*Banana Ridge*, 38) to *Hamlet* at the Vic (50) and *The Wild Duck* (55).

JACKSON, GLENDA (1936–). British actress and a major film and TV star. For the Royal Shakespeare Co. parts included the Princess of France, Ophelia, and Charlotte Corday in *Marat-Sade* (London and New York, 65), a most striking performance. Masha in *The Three Sisters* at the Royal Court (67). Hobbies include telling the Press she hates going to the theatre: more seriously, this brilliant actress is too rarely seen on the stage. Returned in *Collaborators* (73).

JACOBI, DEREK (1938–). British actor. Hamlet for the National Youth Theatre. Jimmy Porter, Troilus, Henry VIII and Aaron at Birmingham Rep. At the National (63–72), played Laertes, Brother Martin, the perfect Cassio, Tusenbach in *The Three Sisters*, Touchstone, etc., and a touching Myshkin in a much-criticized *The Idiot* (70). At Birmingham (72), repeated Olivier's famous double, Oedipus and Mr. Puff, to much acclaim.

JACOBS, SALLY (1932–). British designer, especially noted for her work for the Royal Shakespeare Co. with Peter Brook. *The Screens* (64), *Marat-Sade* (64), *US* (67) and his *Dream* (70), see p. 77; also *Love's Labour's Lost* (64), *Twelfth Night* (66), etc.

JAMES, EMRYS (1930–). British actor. Since 1956 has played mainly in the classics at Bristol, the Vic and Stratford, culminating in a good, flamboyant Shylock (Stratford 71; Aldwych, 72) and a brilliant, daringly inventive Iago (Stratford, 71; Aldwych, 72) along cocky N.C.O. lines, who yet appeared 'honest'—just.

JAMES, GERALD (1917–). British actor whose career has mainly been at the Vic and the National. Parts have included Friar Laurence in Romeo (London, 60: New York, 62), Sir Hugh Evans, Fluellen, and, at the National, Leonato in *Much Ado* (65), Captain Jones-Parry in *H* (69), etc.

JAMESON, PAULINE (1920–). British actress. At the Vic (48–51), played Bianca, Maria, etc. Mrs. Page at Stratford, Ontario (56). The Abbess in *The Comedy of Errors* for the Royal Shakespeare Co. (64). Mrs. Allonby in *A Woman of No Importance* (67). At Chichester (68), played Lavinia in *The Cocktail Party* and Mrs. Antrobus in *The Skin of our Teeth*.

JEANS, ISOBEL (1891–). British actress, also see p. 169. This very stylish actress worked with Tree and Granville Barker. Her Margery Pinchwife in *The Country Wife* (24), sent Agate into ecstasies, as did her Lydia in *The Rivals* (25). Her Duchess of Berwick in *Lady Windermere's Fan* (66) had Caryl Brahms in the *Guardian* saying that 'her beauty, poise and brilliance lit the stage'. Then, out-Agating-Agate, she claimed (with reason), that Miss Jeans was no longer 'stylish—she was Style'.

JEANS, URSULA (1906–73). British actress, wife of Roger Livesey (see p. 173). Apart from her commercial successes, was an Old Vic player for several seasons in the 30s, her finest performances including Viola (33), Alithea in the now legendary Guthrie production of *The Country Wife* (36) and Katharine in *The Taming of the Shrew* (39). Her Dame Overdo in *Bartholomew Fair* and Mrs. Ford (51) were much enjoyed, her Lady Cicely in *Captain Brassbound's Conversion* in the same Old Vic season divided opinion. She was miscast and frivolous or utterly charming and convincing, depending which paper one read. Lady Markby in *An Ideal Husband* (65).

JEFFORD, BARBARA (1930–). British actress, one of the very finest younger classical players. Stratford, (50–4). Old Vic (56–62), where she played a range of parts as wide as any actress in earlier Old Vic generations. Among her most successful were Imogen (56) and a much-admired St. Joan (60), a part she later played at the City Center, New York (62). In recent years she has toured many parts of the world giving dramatic recitals with her husband, JOHN TURNER. She has also played Cleopatra at Oxford and Nottingham (66).

JOHNSON, CELIA (1908–). British actress (also see p. 170). Her classical parts have included a New York Ophelia (31), St.

Joan for the Old Vic (47), Olga in *The Three Sisters* (51) and, in striking contrast to these expected successes, a diffident, frigid Mrs. Solness in *The Master Builder* at the National Theatre (64), where she later took over Judith Bliss in *Hay Fever* from Edith Evans. Gertrude in *Hamlet* (71) opposite Alan Bates at Nottingham and in London. Her Joan was widely hailed as moving, radiant and deeply felt, if lacking 'the *strength* of Joan's passion' as Audrey Williamson put it.

JOHNSON, RICHARD (1927–). British actor. Small parts in Gielgud's famous Haymarket season (44). Laertes (Moscow and London, 55), Jack Absolute (56), then, at Stratford (57–9), his parts included Orlando, Mark Antony, Leonatus in *Cymbeline*, Sir Andrew, and Romeo, playing this last part in Russia. The first Grandier in *The Devils*, a most striking performance (Aldwych, 61), since when he has mainly been in films. Antony in *Julius Caesar* and *Antony and Cleopatra* at Stratford (72), both generally admired.

JONES, ROBERT EDMUND (1887–1954). American designer who 'turned scene design from a craft to an art by his use of colour, form and lighting' (Brooks Atkinson). This genius, whose settings included those for Barrymore's Richard III (20) and Hamlet (22), worked with

CTT–H

O'Neill—*The Great God Brown* (26), etc.—created fantastic sets for *The Green Pastures* (30) and fascinating, relevant designs, often revolutionary, for a host of other plays, giving the New York theatre of his day a visual excitement far ahead of London's, and inspiring a younger generation of designers.

KAHN, MICHAEL. American director. Since 1969, Artistic Director of the American Shakespeare Festival, Stratford, Conn., where (72) he directed *Julius Caesar* and *Antony and Cleopatra*. He 'has achieved a new level of interest in the festival' (Clive Barnes), his first production there being *The Merchant* (67).

KAY, CHARLES (1930–). British actor. Royal Shakespeare Co. (63–6), where his parts included Clarence in *The Wars of the Roses* (63). At the National (67–72) played Celia in the all-male *As You Like It* (67), Gaveston in (Brecht's) *Edward II*, etc.

KEACH, STACY (1941–). American actor and director whose very wide range of parts have included Falstaff and Edmund in New York (68), Buffalo Bill in *Indians* in Washington and New York (69), Jamie in *Long Day's Journey* (71) also in New York. Won awards for this performance as he had for his first major success in the title-role of *MacBird* (67). A much admired Hamlet at New Haven. Conn. (72).

KEEN, MALCOLM (1887–1970). British actor whose very successful career in the commercial theatre was interspersed with many Shakespearean performances. With Martin Harvey (15–16). Claudius to Barrymore's Hamlet (25). Old Vic (32), where his parts included Macbeth, Shylock, Sir Peter and Caliban. A notable Long John Silver (37–8). His son, GEOFFREY KEEN (1918–), before becoming a regular film actor and a TV superstar, was a Shakespearean at the Vic, Stratford, and with Wolfit. First appeared at the Vic as Florizel (36). Cassius and Iachimo at Stratford (57). His commercial parts have included the Turkish Military Governor in *Ross* (London, 60; New York, 61).

KENTON, GODFREY (1902–). British actor. Played at the Old Vic, Malvern and at Stratford between the wars. Parts at Stratford included Oberon and Edgar (37) and Romeo (40). With Wolfit (44–6). William Cecil in *The Young Elizabeth* (52). A regular radio acter.

KNIGHT, ESMOND (1906–). British actor. From his first appearance at the Old Vic (25) as Balthasar in *The Merchant*, has played a wide range of classical and commercial parts, except during the war, when he was almost blinded in the fight against the *Bismarck*. Has also sung in operas and musicals, including Strauss Junior in *Waltzes from Vienna* (31). Leontes, Gratiano, Sly and the Ghost in *Hamlet* at Stratford (48), and has since worked for the Royal Shakespeare Co. and the Old Vic, including the Troll King and Antonio in *The Merchant* for the latter (62). Work at the Mermaid has included Creon in the two *Oedipus* plays (65). Nicely cast as Admiral Lord Howe in *Spithead* at Greenwich (69). His wife is NORA SWINBURNE (1902–) who has enjoyed a long West End career and been in many films.

KNOX, ALEXANDER (1907–). Canadian actor. Old Vic (37–8), where his parts included a fine Snout and Dr. McGilp in Bridie's *The King of Nowhere*, which made his reputation. Also a noted Shavian. His Wolsey for the Vic (53) was impressive, but, at Guthrie's insistence, lacking in pathos and very secular. Arnold Rubek in *When we Dead Awaken* at Edinburgh (68).

KOHLER, ESTELLE (1940–). South African actress and a Stratford Ophelia, Olivia, Helena, Juliet, etc. (66–70). Juliet (73), her fine talents swamped by bizarre direction.

KOLTAI, RALPH (1924–). German-born designer, best known in Britain for many fine opera designs, including *The Ring*, also for his work for the Royal Shakespeare Co. including *The Jew of Malta* (64), *Little*

Murders and *As You Like It* (67). *Back to Methusalah* at the National (69).

KOMISARJEVSKY, THEODORE (1882–1954). Venetian-born Russian director and designer who became a naturalized Briton. After directing opera in Russia, Britain, Paris and New York, returned to Britain and produced Russian plays, notably in a small converted cinema at Barnes (25–6), with casts that included Gielgud, Laughton, Jean Forbes-Robertson and Martita Hunt. He insisted on depth and intensity in acting, plus the observation of some of Stanislavsky's methods. His Shakespearean productions were less successful because of his lack of interest in the texts, culminating in the monumental miscasting of a Russian Cleopatra at Stratford (36). But his settings were brilliant, stressing mood, not realism, and his lighting and groupings were worlds away from Stratford routine in the 30s. Gielgud called him a great *mêtteur en scene*, an inspiring teacher and a master of theatrical orchestration.

LACEY, CATHERINE (1904–). British actress whose distinguished career has ranged from playing with Mrs. Patrick Campbell in 1925 to leads with the Royal Shakespeare Co. (67–8), including Volumnia, the Countess in *All's Well* and the 3rd Witch. She had played the Countess, as well as a fine Cleopatra, Portia, etc., at Stratford in 1935, and other notable performances were her Helena in *All's Well* (40), Clytemnestra in *Electra* (Old Vic, 51) and Queen Elizabeth in *Mary Stuart* (Edinburgh and the Old Vic, 58), having previously played the title role at Edinburgh (54). Many commercial successes, including Lydia in *Judgement Day* (37) and Agatha in *The Family Reunion* (38).

LANG, MATHESON (1879–1948). British actor, manager and director of the very first Old Vic season in 1914. Earlier, he had toured widely, including overseas, with Shakespeare and modern plays, and later he had great successes with *The Wandering Jew* (20–) *Jew Suss* (29), etc.

LANG, ROBERT (1934–). British actor. National Theatre player (62–70), where his parts included Brazen in *The Recruiting Officer*, Roderigo, Mortimer in *Edward II*, William in *Home and Beauty* and a very fine performance as Havelock in *H* (69). Took over Shylock from Olivier (69).

LANGHAM, MICHAEL (1919–). British director associated with the Old Vic, Stratford, and, particularly, Stratford, Ontario, where he was Artistic Director from 1955–70. That the Festival has flourished down the years and that Canadianization of casts has been so successful, is in itself a tribute to him. Occasional forays into the commercial theatre have included directing *The Prime of Miss Jean Brodie* on Broadway (68).

LAUGHTON, CHARLES (1899–1961). British actor whose outsize personality, allied with remarkable powers of impersonation was only seen to its best advantage in his commercial career and some films. His rather tentative performances at the Old Vic (33–4) and Stratford (59) promised more than they achieved. An exception was his terrifying Angelo for Guthrie at the Vic. Adapted and played Galileo in New York (47). His wife is the actress ELSA LANCHESTER. See also p. 171.

LAURIE, JOHN (1897–). British actor, few of whose vast public for his part in TV's *Dad's Army* can know that he was once a leading Shakespearean, playing Hamlet at Stratford (27) and at the Old Vic (28). Played other leads including comic ones: Sir Andrew, Pistol, etc. Was Stratford's Othello and Richard III ('demonic', according to Trewin) in 1939. Gloucester in *Lear* for the Royal Shakespeare Co. (Aldwych, 64). His first wife, FLORENCE SAUNDERS, who died very young, was an Old Vic favourite of the 20s.

LE GALLIENNE, EVA (1899–). London-born American actress whose idealism led her to found the Civic Repertory Theater (26–33) and present and act in a whole series of foreign and American plays. With Cheryl Crawford and Margaret Webster, later founded the touring American Repertory Company (46). Her roles ranged from the great leads in Ibsen and Chekhov to Amanda in *Private Lives* and the White Queen in her own adaptation of *Alice*. Dedicated to fine plays, ensemble and repertory, this glamorous actress who could have become a film star or commercial favourite after her Julie in *Liliom* (21), became instead one of the greatest figures of the American theatre and a supreme player of Ibsen. In the 60s, she toured, acted and directed for the National Repertory Theater. The Countess in *All's Well* at Stratford, Conn. (70).

LEIGH, VIVIEN (1913–67). British actress (also see p. 173) whose major classical roles, Lady Macbeth, Cleopatra, etc., divided opinion, but who was very successful as Titania (37), Mrs. Dubedat (42), a sophisticated Lady Teazle (49), etc.

LEIGHTON, MARGARET (1922–). British actress (also see p. 173). Birmingham Rep (42–4), having originally begun there at 16. Joined the Old Vic at the New (44–7), where her glamour and talent shone in that legendary company in such parts as Yelena in *Vanya*, Lady Percy, and Roxane in *Cyrano*. Also played a superb Regan that was 'like honey turned rancid' (Audrey Williamson). An unforgettable Masha in *The Three Sisters* (51), and a delightful Rosalind at Stratford (52). Since then her classical parts have included Beatrice in New York, Ellida in *The Lady from the Sea* and, at Chichester (69), a much-acclaimed Cleopatra.

LUCKHAM, CYRIL (1907–). British actor. Now a TV regular, his commercial and classical career has included seasons at Stratford (57–8), playing Julius Caesar, Feste, Polonius, Parolles, etc.

MCCALLIN, CLEMENT (1913–). British actor, much of whose career has been in the classics, including Henry V at Stratford and Orsino for Wolfit (37). The Ghost, First Player and Fortinbras at Sydney (57). With the Royal Shakespeare Co. (70–), where his parts have included the Duke in *The Two Gentlemen of Verona* and a fine Cominius in *Coriolanus* (72).

MCCOWEN, ALEC (1925–). British actor, excelling in comedy. 'The most subtle actor since Michael Redgrave' (Frank Marcus). An early success was as Daventry in *Escapade* (53). Old Vic (59–61) where his roles included Touchstone, the Dauphin in *St. Joan*, an electric Mercutio, Oberon and a sharp Malvolio. His Antipholus of Syracuse in *The Comedy of Errors* (62) at Stratford looked

'like a cat about to sneeze' (Trewin). A movingly sad Fool to Scofield's Lear (62/64), Ronald Gamble in *Thark* (65). A cool Hamlet at Birmingham and the misunderstood philologist hero of *The Philanthropist* (70). His most famous performance in recent years has been in the lead in *Hadrian VII* (68).

MCENERY, PETER (1940–). British actor whose parts have included Laertes and Clarence (Stratford, 61), Konstantin in *The Seagull* (64) and Hamlet at Leicester (70).

MCEWEN, GERALDINE (1932–). British actress. After several West End comedy successes, played The Princess in *Love's Labour's Lost* at Stratford (56) and Olivia the next season. Appeared with the Company again (58–60). Joined the National Theatre Company (65), since when, apart from expected successes in roles which suit her gift for comedy and her high, cooing voice—Angelica in *Love for Love* (65), Raymonde in *A Flea in her Ear* (66), Victoria in *Home and Beauty* (68) and Almena in *Amphitryon 38* (71)— she gave a performance of power and bitterness as Alice in *The Dance of Death* (67) opposite Olivier, and was a striking Vittoria in *The White Devil* (69). Her husband, the director HUGH CRUTTWELL (1918–), has been Principal of RADA since 1965.

MCKELLAN, IAN (1939–).

British actor who made a spectacular success in Guthrie's production of *Coriolanus* at the opening of the new Nottingham Rep (63). Became a major star at the 1969 Edinburgh Festival, playing Marlowe's Edward II and Shakespeare's Richard II. In Richard, the finer of the two performances, the self pity was less in evidence than 'sardonic bite and hysterical anger' (Irving Wardle). Scarcely less fine, his Edward, ringing the changes from boyish lover to a ruined creature in a cesspool at Berkeley, endured one of the most terrifyingly realistic death scenes ever staged. His Hamlet (71) was performed in the wake of such statements as 'the Olivier from Wigan' and—from a critic who should have known better—'the greatest Shakespearean actor alive', and so was judged very harshly and was underpraised. It promised great things for the future. Since then, has been the begetter of the splendidly conceived Actors' Company. Giovanni for them (at Edinburgh, 72) in *'Tis Pity She's a Whore*, a striking 'splendidly steamy' performance (Eric Shorter).

MCKENNA, SIOBHAN (1923–). Irish actress whose most famous role is St. Joan (London, 54; Cambridge, Mass. and New York, 56), possibly its finest exponent since Sybil Thorndike, and one that left audiences in no doubt that her voices were real. Other parts have included Viola, Lady Macbeth and a notable Pegeen in *The Playboy of the Western World* (Dublin and London, 60). More recent parts have included Juno (66) and Mme. Ranevsky (68).

MCKENNA, VIRGINIA (1931–). British actress. The perfect Perdita (51). Old Vic (54–5), including Rosaline and Rosalind. Sister Jeanne in *The Devils* (61) and Lucy Lockit (63) for the Royal Shakespeare Co. Married to BILL TRAVERS.

MCKERN, LEO (1920–). Australian actor who from 1949 onwards frequently appeared at the Old Vic and Stratford. His first major success was at the Old Vic with a performance of grandeur as the Old Tutor in *Electra* (51). He has played several of the great Clowns and was a fine Iago, dangerous and bantering, at the Old Vic (63). Peer Gynt (62). Parts since have included Volpone (Oxford and London, 66–7).

MACLIAMMÓIR, MICHEÁL (1899–). Irish actor, dramatist, director and designer. After working in England, then playing leads for Anew MacMaster, he established, with Hilton Edwards (see p. 38), the Dublin Gate Theatre. His most notable parts included Hamlet, Robert Emmett in *The Old Lady Says No!*, Othello, and Oscar Wilde in his compilation, *The Importance of being Oscar*, which was a popular success in London (60). Helped make the Gate Ireland's most exciting theatre between the wars. Apart from a number of plays, including *Ill Met By Moonlight* (46), has written a theatre classic, his autobiography, *All for Hecuba.*

MACMASTER, ANEW (1895–1962). Irish actor and manager, little known in England apart from a single season at Stratford (37). On his night, reached true greatness in the supreme Shakespearean roles, as Harold Pinter, and others who acted with him and saw him, have recalled. Stories about him, especially on off-nights, would seem unbelievable if not vouched for by reliable witnesses who toured round Ireland with him. Ireland's erratic and glorious Chaliapin of the drama.

MALLESON, MILES (1888–1969). British actor and dramatist. Known to millions for his comedy roles in films and his lack of—or collapsed—chin, his theatrical career was rich in eccentrics, including Sir Andrew, Quince, Snout and, definitively, Nathaniel in *Love's Labour's Lost* (Old Vic at the New, 49), an elderly puppy, desperately anxious to please. His Molière translations are more successful than most.

MARCHAND, NANCY (1928–). American actress who has played many classical parts including a spirited Mrs. Page at Stratford, Conn. (59), Doll Common in *The Alchemist* (New York, 66), etc.

MASON, BREWSTER (1922–). British actor whose Shakespearean parts have included Kent (62), Warwick (63–4) in *The Wars of the Roses,* Claudius, the Ghost and Sir Toby (66), Banquo (67) and Othello (71) all for the Royal Shakespeare Co. A commanding actor, though his Othello lacked passion. His commercial parts have included General Allenby in *Ross* (60) and Sir Lewis Eliot in *The Affair* (New York, 62).

MASSEY, RAYMOND (1896–). Canadian actor. Though most of his career was in non-classical roles (see p. 176), he played a very energetic Hamlet on Broadway (31), and Brutus and Prospero at Stratford, Conn. (55).

MERCHANT, VIVIEN (1929–). British actress famous for her performances in plays by her husband, Harold Pinter, including Ruth in *The Homecoming* (65) and Anna in *Old Times* (71), both for the Royal Shakespeare Co. A widely experienced actress in Rep before this, much admired by her colleagues. Other parts have included Lady Macbeth (67), a moving Bertha in Joyce's *Exiles* (Mermaid, 70; Aldwych, 71) and Mrs. Loveit in *The Man of Mode* (71).

MICHELL, KEITH (1928–). Australian actor whose first London appearance was as Charles II in the Pepys musical by Vivian Ellis, *And So To Bed*

(51). Later joined the Stratford Company, where early successes included Macduff and Petruchio (54). At the Old Vic (56–7) his parts included Benedick, Mark Antony, Proteus and Aaron. His Antony (in *Antony and Cleopatra*) was so good that a comparable Antony in the 70s is something to be hoped for. Played and sang in *Irma La Douce* in London and New York (58, 60). In the original Chichester Festival Company (62). Robert Browning in *Robert and Elizabeth* (64), Don Quixote in *Man of La Mancha* (68), Hamlet at the Bankside Globe Playhouse (72). Has also appeared in films and on TV, becoming an international star with his Henry VIII. An actor of style, panache and ability. Chosen to succeed Clements at Chichester (74). Married to JEANNETTE STARKE.

MILES, BERNARD (1907–). British actor, director and manager and founder of the Mermaid Theatre (see p. 246). Received a good grounding in theatrecraft by working in Rep for five years as a designer, stage manager, carpenter, props and actor. His most notable role before his Mermaid venture was his Iago for the Old Vic (Tour, 41; New Theatre, 42). Parts at the Mermaid have included Oedipus, Falstaff and Long John Silver. Knighted (69).

MILLER, JONATHAN (1934–). British director. One of the original cast of *Beyond the Fringe* (61). An extraordinary (albeit striking) interpreter who has produced *The Tempest* (70) as a comment on Colonialism, *Lear* (Nottingham, 69; London, 70) as a 'clinical study of senility' (Benedict Nightingale), and a *Hamlet* inspired by Proust, Frazier and Freud (70). Fortunately his distorted *Merchant* at the National (70) worked quite delightfully. Even those who cannot accept the director's vivisectionist, revisionist ideas, more drastic than any mere old-time actor-manager, could welcome his superb *Danton's Death* for the National (71), also his splendidly down-to-earth *The School for Scandal* there (72).

MILTON, ERNEST (1890–). American-born British actor and one of the great Old Vic players of his (splendidly long) day. An unforgettably intense, passionate Hamlet (18 onwards) who also had success in major comedy roles. Lear was another of his finest portrayals. In the 50s a new generation were able to glimpse his prowess in two performances opposite Wolfit: Lorenzo Querini in *The Strong Are Lonely* (55) and Pope Paul in *Malatesta* (57). Harwood, in his Wolfit biography, calls his performance in the latter 'gloriously baroque', an apt description of the Milton legend that has grown down the years.

MIRREN, HELEN (1946–). British actress. Started with the National

Youth Theatre, where her roles included Cleopatra. After joining the Royal Shakespeare Co. (67), this very fine and exciting young actress played a wide range of parts, including Cressida, Hero, Ophelia, Harriet in *The Man of Mode*, Tatyana in Gorky's *Enemies* and a magnificent Miss Julie (71), which Hobson hailed as definitive.

MOFFAT, DONALD (1930–). British actor and director, resident in the U.S.A. since 1956, where he has acted in, and directed, many Shakespearean and other productions. Has played Macbeth, Touchstone, Richard II, Henry V, etc., at various festivals, also in Shaw, Ibsen and Pinter.

MOFFATT, JOHN (1922–). British actor whose 2nd Lord in *The Winter's Tale* (3rd Gent, in most editions) was one of the most memorable cameos of modern times (51). Parts since have included Mr. Sparkish in *The Country Wife* (New York, 57), de Stogumber and Dr. Caius (Old Vic, 59), Algernon at the Vic (60), Cardinal Cajetan in *Luther* (61), which won him a Clarence Derwent award, and Lord Foppington at the Mermaid (63). Played in *Luther* in New York (63), since when, parts have included Kulygin in *The Three Sisters* at Oxford, and, for the National, Fainall in *The Way of the World*, Judge Brack in *Hedda*, etc. Has appeared in a *Victorian Music*

Hall of his own devising and is a regular pantomime Dame. Currently (72–73) in *Cowardy Custard* at the Mermaid.

MOISEIWITSCH, TANYA (1914–). British designer, daughter of the great Benno. Though much of her career has been with the Old Vic, including designs for such legendary productions as *Uncle Vanya* and *The Critic* (New Theatre, 45–6), plus work at Stratford, including *Henry VIII* (49), and in the commercial theatre, her unique sphere of influence has been Stratford, Ontario. With Guthrie, designed the original Festival Tent there, and, including the first productions, has designed a score of plays since. Has also designed for the Tyrone Guthrie Theater, Minneapolis: *Hamlet*, *St. Joan*, etc.

MORELL, ANDRÉ (1909–). British actor. Tom Wrench at the Old Vic (38), also Horatio, Mercutio, etc., since when his performances there have included Kent in *Lear* (52), also Timon in London and Zurich. Edward Fairfax Vere in *The Good Sailor* (56), a notable Brack in *Hedda* (Oxford, 62; London, 64), and a member of the first Chichester company (62). Married to Joan Greenwood (see p. 164).

MORLEY, CHRISTOPHER. Head of Design for the Royal Shakespeare Co. A master of colour and, on occasion, of extraordinary effects in simple, box-like sets. Some of his finest work has been with Trevor Nunn, including *The Revenger's Tragedy* (66), with ashen-faced courtiers in white wigs greatly adding to the play's sense of festering corruption. With Nunn, has also designed *Much Ado*, *Hamlet*, *The Winter's Tale* and *The Relapse*, and the Roman season (72). Designed the enchanting Barton *Twelfth Night* (69).

MOTLEY. Firm of British designers, SOPHIA HARRIS (1901–1966), MARGARET HARRIS (1904–) and ELIZABETH MONTGOMERY (1902–). The last is now permanently in New York. Their first designs were for the O.U.D.S. *Romeo and Juliet* (32), since when they have designed innumerable classical and commercial productions, including musicals and operas, on both sides of the Atlantic. Sometimes labelled 'tasteful' and 'safe' in these days of 'daring' designs, the firm's record speaks for itself: designed the entire, historic Gielgud season at the Queen's (37), and many plays at the Old Vic and Stratford. *Hobson's Choice*, *Hay Fever*, *Trelawny of the Wells* and *The Dance of Death* at the National.

MURRAY, BRIAN (1937–). South African-born British actor. With the Royal Shakespeare Co. (61–4) his parts included Horatio, Romeo, Cassio, Lysander and Edgar. Tolen in *The Knack* (New York, 64). Bassanio and Claudio in *Measure for Measure* at Bristol (66), since when his successes have included Mike in *Wait until Dark* in London (66) and Rosencrantz in *Rosencrantz and Guildenstern are Dead* on Broadway and on tour (67–8).

MURRAY, STEPHEN (1912–). British actor and director. Worked at Birmingham, Malvern, in London and at the Vic (36–7) before the war, giving notably good performances as Roderigo, and the Duke in *Measure for Measure* at the Vic and in the title-role of Drinkwater's *Abraham Lincoln* at the Westminster (40). Had the misfortune to play Lear (52) when Wolfit left the Vic in mid-season, in a production less good than Hugh Hunt's usual high standard. Since then parts have included Sir Peter Teazle at Stratford, Ontario (70).

NEILSON-TERRY, PHYLLIS (1892–). British actress, daughter of Fred Terry and Julia Neilson. After success as Rosalind and Juliet (11) was an exquisite Desdemona opposite Tree (12). Her long career in London, on tour and abroad, included many performances of Trilby. In the first season at the Open Air Theatre, Regent's Park, and later seasons (33–6). Wolfit's first leading lady (37). Stratford's Lady Macbeth (38). Amongst her very many commercial roles a post-war performance that stands out was her Mrs. Railton-Bell in *Separate*

Tables (London, 54; New York, 56).

NEVILLE, JOHN (1925–). British actor. Birmingham Rep and Bristol Old Vic (49–53), then joined the Old Vic where he remained for six years and established himself as one of the finest classical actors in the country and a romantic favourite in the Gielgud tradition. Particularly notable performances included a Richard II (55) that made him a Shakespearean star, an uproarious Pistol, his beautiful voice suitably coarsened, a fine Romeo and a 'loving, lonely Hamlet' (Trewin). His celebrated alternation of Othello and Iago with Burton (56) causes pleasant arguments even today. The author, who was in Rep at the time, can only record that opinion seems to have generally favoured Neville as Iago. In these seasons he learnt between 8 and 9 thousand lines.

His most notable achievement in the 60s was his period as Director of the Nottingham Playhouse (63–8), see p. 259. Parts during this period, Nottingham apart, included a haunting, sombre Stranger in *The Lady from the Sea* (61), Alfie at the Mermaid (63), Don Frederick in *The Chances* and Orgilus in *The Broken Heart* at the first Chichester Festival (62) and a stylish King Magnus in *The Apple Cart* at the Mermaid (70). Macheath at Chichester (72).

NEY, MARIE (1895–). British actress. As well as work in the commercial theatre, including the original Freda in *Dangerous Corner* (32), was at the Old Vic (24/35/39/52). Her parts included Desdemona and Lady Macbeth (24), Olga in *The Three Sisters* (35) and Marte in *The Other Heart* (52). A particular success was her Mrs. Alving in *Ghosts* at the Vaudeville (37).

NICHOLLS, ANTHONY (1907–). British actor who, since his Lysander at the Vic (38) has played many Shakespearean parts including Antonio in *The Merchant of Venice* at Stratford (56) and the National (69) and Kent and Aufidius at Stratford (59). Parts for the National have included Warwick in *St. Joan* and the Duke in *The White Devil*.

NICHOLSON, NORA (1892–). British actress. An Old Bensonian (12–13) and original Old Vic player (14–15) where her parts included Ariel and Titania, this delightful and charming actress has had a long career in commercial and classical plays, including spells with Sir Barry Jackson, the Playhouse, Oxford, and the Bristol Old Vic. A particular joy for post-war theatre-goers was her Margaret Devize in *The Lady's Not for Burning* (London, 49; New York, 50).

NUNN, TREVOR (1940–). British director. Since 1968 Artistic Director of the Royal Shakespeare Co. After being resident producer at the Belgrade. Coventry, became an associate producer of the R.S.C. (65) when, with John Barton, he directed *Henry V*. Made his name with a magnificent production of *The Revenger's Tragedy* (66) at Stratford, later seen in London, since when his work has included *Hamlet, Lear, Henry VIII, Much Ado, The Relapse, The Shrew, The Winter's Tale*. Director of the Roman plays (72). Married to Janet Suzman (see below).

O'BRIEN, TIMOTHY (1929–). British designer of plays and operas and (since 66) Associate Artist of the Royal Shakespeare Co. for whom his productions include *All's Well, Troilus and Cressida, Pericles, The Man of Mode* and *Enemies* (71). Designs for other plays include *Entertaining Mr. Sloane*. Uses the most modern material now as opposed to mere decoration. His two most famous opera designs have been for *The Flying Dutchman* (58) at the Wells, first rate traditional realism and, perhaps the most brilliant of his career, his sets for *The Knot Garden* at Covent Garden (70).

O'CONOR, JOSEPH (1916–). Irish-born British actor and director who, before his sympathetic Old Jolyon in TV's *Forsyte Saga* made him world famous, had played a wide variety of classical as well as modern parts, including Orlando and The Bastard at Regent's Park (48) and Othello, Iago and Hamlet for Wolfit at the Bedford, Camden Town, alternating the first two roles, and offering a Hamlet (with Wolfit as First Gravedigger) which was straightforward and convincing. Has also played Shakespeare in leading Reps, including Glasgow Citizens' and Bristol Old Vic. Also remembered for his bluff Thomas Seymour in *The Young Elizabeth* (52). Author of the play, *The Iron Harp*. Director of Michael York's Hamlet at the Thorndike Theatre, Leatherhead (70), where he has also played Lear.

OLIVIER, LAURENCE (1907–). British actor, director and manager and the Director of the National Theatre. First spotted as a schoolboy by Ellen Terry who saw him play Brutus, then Katharina in *The Shrew* at 14. Birmingham Rep (26–8), then West End leading actor (see p. 180) in romantic drama and comedy. Alternated with Gielgud as Mercutio and Romeo (37), his romantic fire compensating for alleged deficiencies of verse-speaking. Joined the Old Vic (37), where his progress over two seasons, in parts which included Hamlet (complete), Sir Toby, Macbeth, Iago and Coriolanus (a particular success), proved that he was a great actor in the making. Films and war service followed.

In 1944, became, with Richardson and John Burrell, a co-director of the Old Vic in its legendary seasons at the New

(44–8). For his Richard III, see p. 73. Other parts included the Button Moulder, Sergius, Dr. Astrov, the perfect Hotspur, an amusing Shallow that some said was not of the country; also an Oedipus whose great cry of anguish is said to haunt the rafters of the New still, and, in the same incredible evening, Mr. Puff. His magnificently conceived Lear (48) for all its desolation, lacked, for some, ultimate emotional impact. When he left the Vic (49) he had added several more roles to his repertoire, including a delightfully warm, crusty Sir Peter Teazle.

Became an actor-manager at the St. James where, in a lull from greatness, acted in Fry, Rattigan and as Shaw's Caesar and Shakespeare's Antony (an underrated performance) opposite his then wife, Vivien Leigh. Then came the historic Stratford season of 1955: Macbeth, Malvolio and Titus Andronicus (see p. 75). His Macbeth, one of the few to be almost universally acclaimed, began quietly and 'presented frighteningly the death of a soul' (Trewin). There followed his brazen, virtuoso Archie Rice in *The Entertainer* (57), an electrifying Coriolanus at Stratford (59), Berenger in Ionesco's *Rhinoceros* (60), and Becket, then Henry, in Anouilh's *Becket* (New York, 61). The first director of the Chichester Festival (62). The first director of the National Theatre (63), where his roles have included Astrov, the Master Builder,

Shylock, the Captain in *Dance of Death*, a preening, bussing Brazen in *The Recruiting Officer*, an ultimate fop of a Tattle in *Love for Love*, and the most acclaimed Othello since Kean's. An actor's director, among his many fine productions has been *Juno and the Paycock* at the National and, especially, *Uncle Vanya* at Chichester and the National (63). Two of his three Shakespeare films, *Henry V* and *Richard III*, are classics, and his more controversial *Hamlet* is, by any standards, an achievement.

As an actor he is blessed with major assets: striking eyes, a commanding trumpet-like voice and looks which earlier made him one of the only great actors ever to be a romantic film star in the old sense (the perfect Heathcliff, etc.). Unselfish as an actor, he attracts all eyes. He brings a sense of danger into the theatre as well as electric excitement. Like Callas, he can turn a word or phrase in such a way that it is never forgotten. A born comedian, he made himself a tragedian capable of effects that have taken their place in theatre history, one of many of which was a supreme moment in *Othello* when, at 'Now, by yon marble heaven', he tore the crucifix from his neck and crouched on the ground to make his vow, an obsessed vision of black power, bowing down to ancient, terrible gods. At the time of writing (72), he has added a magnificently powerful, tormented James Tyrone in *Long*

Day's Journey into Night to his roles. Knighted (47). Became a Life Peer—the first actor Peer—(70).

O'TOOLE, PETER (1932–). Irish actor. At the Bristol Old Vic (55–8), his parts included Jimmy Porter, John Tanner and Hamlet. Shylock, Petruchio and Thersites at Stratford (60). Hamlet at the National Theatre (63). In Dublin, at the Gaiety, has played Jack Boyle in *Juno* (66), and John Tanner and Vladimir in *Godot* (69). A major film star. His wife is SIAN PHILLIPS, a fine actress and a beauty, whose parts have included Julia in *The Duchess of Malfi* at the Aldwych for the Royal Shakespeare Co. (60), Hannah Jelkes in *The Night of the Iguana* (65), Ann Whitefield (65) and the Strange Lady in *The Man of Destiny* at the Mermaid (66).

PAPP, JOSEPH (1921–). Producer and director of the New York Shakespeare Festival (see p. 247), also of the Public Theatre, which he founded in 1967, where shows have ranged from (the original) *Hair* to *Hamlet*. Everything he touched in 1971–2 seemed to turn to awards including the hit musical, *The Two Gentlemen of Verona*. At the time of writing (73) has just been appointed Director of both the Vivian Beaumont Theater and the Forum Theater at the Lincoln Center.

PASCO, RICHARD (1926–).

British actor who has worked at the Old Vic, Birmingham Rep and the Bristol Old Vic, where he has played Hamlet (65, 66). One of the first to play Jimmy Porter (Royal Court, 57). Archie Rice in *The Entertainer* (57). Polixenes, Proteus, etc., for the Royal Shakespeare Co. His Orsino at the Aldwych (70), virile and poetic, was the finest for many years. Eliot's Becket in *Murder in the Cathedral* (72). At the time of writing (73) due to alternate Richard II and Bolingbroke with Ian Richardson.

PATTERSON, TOM (1920–). Founder of the Stratford Shakespearean Festival of Canada (see p. 253) and therefore a resounding figure in North American theatre history and, indeed, in Shakespearean history. With Douglas Campbell, helped found the Canadian Players (54).

PAYNE, BEN IDEN (1888–). British director and actor, and disciple of William Poel. Miss Horniman's director and producer at the Gaiety, Manchester (07–11). Directed mainly in America in the 20s. Director of the Shakespeare Memorial Theatre (42–3). Since the war has directed many Shakespearean performances and festivals in the U.S.A., where he has been awarded many honours. Rosalind Iden (see above) is his daughter.

PAYNE, LAURENCE (1919–). British actor. Joined the Old Vic (39), appearing for a number of seasons. Stratford's Romeo and Berowne (47). A highly praised 'spitfire' Tybalt at the Vic (52), and a dazzling Ferdinand the same season in *The Italian Straw Hat*.

PETHERBRIDGE, EDWARD (1936–). British actor. National Theatre player (64–70) where he was the original scared, sardonic Guildenstern in *Rosencrantz and Guildenstern Are Dead* (67). Joined the Actors' Company (72).

PHILLIPS, ROBIN (1942–). British actor and director. Acted and directed at Bristol Old Vic. Royal Shakespeare Co. as actor and director (65) where he assisted with Schlesinger's *Timon of Athens* and Hall's *Hamlet*. Since then he has directed Chekhov and *The Beggar's Opera* at Exeter, *Tiny Alice* and *Two Gentlemen of Verona* for the R.S.C., a controversial *Caesar and Cleopatra* at Chichester (71) and Anouilh's *Dear Antoine* the same season. Directed the major West End success, *Abelard and Heloise* (70). Starred in the films, *Decline and Fall* and the inferior remake of *David Copperfield*. Now an established and major director. Successfully staged *The Lady's Not for Burning* at Chichester (72). His most acclaimed production has been *Miss Julie* (71) at the R.S.C.'s The Place 'both intensely realis-

tic and . . . powerfully symbolic' (Harold Hobson). Currently (73), has begun an exciting season at Greenwich with a starry *The Three Sisters*.

PICKUP, RONALD (1941–). British actor and National Theatre player. Played Rosalind in the all-male *As You Like It* (67). An actor of striking promise, as his Edmund in *Long Day's Journey* showed (72). An admired Richard II (72).

PLAYFAIR, NIGEL (1874–1934). British manager and director who ran the Lyric, Hammersmith (18–34). Presented Drinkwater's *Abraham Lincoln* (18). His production of *The Beggar's Opera* (20) ran 1,463 performances. *The Way of the World* (24) made Edith Evans as Millimant a major star. She also played in *The Beaux' Stratagem* (27) for him. *The Importance of Being Earnest* (30) had Gielgud as Jack Worthing. Playfair, who began his career with Benson, Tree, and as Bottom in Granville Barker's historic *Dream* (12), also acted at the Lyric, which he made one of the most famous theatres in Britain. Knighted (28).

PLOWRIGHT, JOAN (1929–). British actress. After Rep at the Bristol Old Vic, etc., and touring with the Old Vic (52), played Donna Clara in *The Duenna* (54). Joined English Stage Co. (56) where her first major success was as Marjery Pinchwife in *The Country Wife* (56). At Coventry and the Royal Court, created the role of Beatie in *Roots* (59). A leading member of the first Chichester Festival company (62) and the National Theatre (63–), where her parts have included St. Joan, Maggie in *Hobson's Choice*, Sonya, Hilda Wangel, Masha, Portia and Anne in *A Woman Killed with Kindness*. Her Chekhovian performances have perhaps been particularly successful. The wife of Laurence Olivier.

PLUMMER, CHRISTOPHER (1929–). Canadian actor. The first native star Shakespearean actor to rise to fame at the Stratford, Ontario, Festival where his parts (from 56) have included Henry V, Hamlet, Richard III, Benedick, Sir Andrew, the Bastard, Mercutio, Macbeth, etc., Henry and Benedick being particular successes. Other parts in this period outside Stratford included King Henry in *Becket* (London, 61) and Pizarro in *The Royal Hunt of the Sun* (New York, 65). A National Theatre player in 1971 where he had the wisdom to withdraw from *Coriolanus*, as mis-interpreted by its directors. His finest performance for the company was as Danton in *Danton's Death* (71). 'Character brings out his best: humour, detail, precision,' as Ronald Bryden wrote in *The Observer*. His Henry in *Becket* won an *Evening Standard* award. Has appeared in many films.

POEL, WILLIAM (1852–1934). British actor and director. Though the key period of his career pre-dates the time span of this book, he was a pioneer of modern Shakespearean staging. In the age of Tree and live rabbits, tried to perform Shakespeare as nearly as possible in the Elizabethan manner. Founded the Elizabethan Stage Society (94) then performed *Twelfth Night* (95) on an Elizabethanstyle stage. Produced many other Elizabethan and Jacobean plays before the Society closed in 1905.

POLLOCK, ELLEN (1903–). British actress and director. A powerful actress of considerable range down the years, including light comedy and Grand Guignol performances, Jocasta, Regan, Maria, etc. for Wolfit (53) and many Shavian parts. These have included the Nurse in *Too True to be Good* in Malvern and London (32), Aloysia Brollikins in *On the Rocks* (33), directing and playing in *Too True to be Good*, *Pygmalion* and *A Village Wooing* at the Lyric, Hammersmith (44) and, for the Shaw Centenary, playing Mrs. Warren at special Royal Court matinées (56). Has directed many plays, including Grand Guignol.

PORTER, ERIC (1928–). British actor with a fine theatrical reputation before he became literally world-famous as Soames in the TV *Forsyte Saga*. One of the strongest classical actors to emerge since the war, noted, even early in his career, for his middle-aged parts. Toured with Wolfit. Rep at Birmingham and the Bristol Old Vic. Bolingbroke to Scofield's Richard II at the Lyric, Hammersmith (52), a part he repeated, with Henry IV, at the Old Vic (55). Since 60, has been one of the leading members of the Royal Shakespeare Co., for whom his roles have included Antonio in *The Duchess of Malfi*, a bravura Barabas in Marlowe's *The Jew of Malta*, Shylock, Macbeth and King Lear. Captain Hook (71).

PRIDE, MALCOLM (1930–). British designer of plays, musicals and operas, especially noted for his famous and witty sets and costumes for the Wells' *Orpheus in the Underworld* (59–). *The Chances* at Chichester (62). *Measure for Measure* (63), the last production of the Old Vic Company. Other designs include those for *Catch My Soul* (70).

PURNELL, LOUISE (1942–). British actress, who has become a leading member of the National Theatre company since her Sorel in *Hay Fever* and her Rose Trelawny (65). Other parts have included Irina in *The Three Sisters* and the Princess in *Love's Labour's Lost*. Recently (72), followed a fine Juliet for the Young Vic with a very knowing, very country girl of a Lady Teazle.

QUAYLE, ANTHONY (1913–).
CTT–I

British actor and director, whose mainly classical career (until the 60s) included a very successful spell as Director of Productions at Stratford (48–56). A pre-war Old Vic player, parts including Laertes at Elsinore (37) and John Tanner (38). His excellent Enobarbus (46) was the first of many post-war successes. His most famous parts have been Iago, Falstaff, Othello and Aaron in *Titus* (55): Tynan wrote of its 'superbly corrupt flamboyance'. Other parts have included a powerful James Tyrone in *Long Day's Journey into Night* (Edinburgh and London, 58), Sir Charles Dilke in *The Right Honourable Gentleman* (64), Leduc in *Incident at Vichy* (66) and Andrew Wyke in *Sleuth* (London, 70; New York, 71). The only living British actor to have played Tamburlaine (?) (New York, 56).

QUILLEY, DENIS (1927–). British actor and singer. After Birmingham Rep and classical parts, including Gratiano for the Young Vic (51), made his name mainly in musicals, including an ideal performance in the title-role of *Candide* (59), Nestor-le-Fripe in *Irma La Douce* (London, 60; New York, 61). Archie Rice and Macbeth at Nottingham (69). A National Theatre player since 1971, his reputation growing with each performance. Parts have included Aufidius, Jamie in *Long Day's Journey*, Bolingbroke, Banquo and Hildy Johnson in *The Front Page* (72). At the time of writing (73), about to play Macbeth.

RABB, ELLIS (1930–). American actor, director and producer. Founder of the A.P.A. (Association of Producing Artists) in 1960. See PHOENIX THEATER, p. 250.

RAIN, DOUGLAS. Canadian actor and an outstanding member of the Stratford, Ontario, company from its inception (53). Among his many successes have been his Iago (59) and King John (60). Appeared at Chichester with the company (64) where his parts included M. Jourdain in *Le Bourgeois Gentilhomme*. Giovanni Mocenigo in *The Heretic* (London, 70).

RATHBONE, BASIL (1892–1967). South African actor who, apart from his villainy in Errol Flynn films and being the finest screen Sherlock Holmes, was once a Bensonian of fire and presence. One of the only completely successful Romeos of modern times, though not his last assumption, opposite Cornell (34), which was less acclaimed. Dr. Sloper in *The Heiress* (47).

RAWSON, TRISTAN (1888–). British actor. From his Silvius (20) at the Lyric, Hammersmith, has played a huge range of classical and modern parts, and was a Regent's Park regular from 1938 to the early 60s, including Malvolio, etc. (53).

Also a regular Dr. Livesey in *Treasure Island* (46–50).

REDGRAVE, MICHAEL (1908–). British actor, dramatist and director. After being a schoolmaster, joined Liverpool Rep (34). Old Vic (36–7), where his parts included Mr. Horner in *The Country Wife*, Orlando and Charles Surface. With Gielgud's famous Queen's Co. (37–8), where his parts were Bolingbroke, Charles Surface and the Baron in *The Three Sisters*. Macheath in *The Beggar's Opera* (40) and Charleston in *Thunder Rock* (40).

This very intelligent, stylish and subtle actor then went through a period when he was considered too intellectual by half and unable to play comedy (according to Agate). Notably successful, however, as Ratikin in *A Month in the Country* (43), in *Uncle Harry* (44) and as the Captain in *The Father* (48). Criticism ceased after his romantic, witty Berowne for the Old Vic at the New (49), followed by Marlow in *She Stoops*, Ratikin, and a straightforward, believable Hamlet.

These followed seasons at Stratford (51 and 53), where his parts included a convincing Richard II, a tough, unromantic, Northumbrian Hotspur and a fine Prospero (51) and, even finer (53), a trio of magnificent performances, Shylock, Lear and Antony, which lifted him to the very peak of his profession. Most notable was his Antony in which actors rarely achieve Shakespeare's demands because, in the play, Antony does not demonstrate his superhuman qualities. Redgrave, entering with 'a careless laughing and abandoned magnificence' (Richard Findlater) finally buried the legend of a technique-conscious intellectual. This was Antony indeed. Another Hamlet (58), at Stratford, more moving than before, also a delightful Benedick. For his commercial successes during this period see p. 182.

At Chichester (63) played Vanya. For the National Theatre (64) played Vanya, Solness and Hobson. The first, by no means obvious casting, was particularly fine. Director of the first season at Guildford's Yvonne Arnaud Theatre (65). Recently mainly in films, in which, down the years, he has given many memorable performances. In *The Old Boys* (71) at the Mermaid. Author of *The Actor's Ways and Means* and *Mask or Face*. Knighted (59).

His mother, MARGARET SCUDA-MORE, was a striking actress of the school of Mrs. Kendal (Agate). His wife, RACHEL KEMP-SON (1910–), has given many fine performances since her enchanting Juliet at Stratford (33). VANESSA REDGRAVE (1937–), though now mainly in films, made her name as Stella in *The Tiger and the Horse* (60) and as the most admired Rosalind for many years (Stratford and London, 62). Other parts have included Imogen and memorable

performances in *The Lady from the Sea* and as Nina in *The Seagull* (64), also Jean Brodie (66). Her return to the stage from films in Robert Shaw's *Cato Street* (71) was handicapped, for all her revolutionary fire, by major production troubles. LYNN REDGRAVE (1944–) has had film and stage successes, including the female lead in the two-hander by Michael Frayn, *The Two of Us* (70), and CORIN REDGRAVE (1939–), the last of the family to go on the stage, made his debut as Lysander at the Royal Court (62). Octavius in *Julius Caesar* and *Antony and Cleopatra* at Stratford (72).

REDMAN, JOYCE (1918–). Irish-born actress who graduated from Alice and being the best of all Wendys (42) to leading parts with the Old Vic at the New (44–7). Among her most successful parts were Solveig, Louka in *Arms and the Man*, Sonia and Doll Tearsheet (or, rather, Doll O'Tearsheet). Her commercial parts have included *Anne of the Thousand Days* (New York, 48). Helena in *All's Well* and Mrs. Ford at Stratford (55). Titania at the Old Vic (57). A National Theatre player (64–6), where her parts included a striking Emilia, an unequalled Mrs. Frail in *Love for Love* and a Juno of quite exceptional emotion and power which surprised even her many admirers. Mrs. Waters in the most famous scene in *Tom Jones*.

REVILL, CLIVE (1930–). New Zealand-born actor. Stratford (56–7) where he was much praised in parts which included Costard, Barnardine, an odious Cloten and an amusing Trinculo. A wildly funny Koko in the Wells' *Mikado*. Fagin in *Oliver* in New York. The title role in *The Jew of Malta* (Aldwych, 64), and, also for the Royal Shakespeare Co., Marat in *Marat-Sade* (64). Caliban and Mr. Antrobus in *The Skin of our Teeth* at Chichester (68).

RICE, PETER (1928–). British designer of plays, operas and ballets at the Old Vic, Chichester, the Wells, etc., and much in demand also for commercial plays. A designer of range and extreme charm where necessary, his Chichester productions in 1965 included *The Farmer's Wife*, *The Beaux' Stratagem*, *Heartbreak House* and *An Italian Straw Hat*.

RICHARDSON, IAN (1934–). British actor. Birmingham Rep, where he played a brilliant Hamlet (59), Stratford (60), where his parts for the Royal Shakespeare Co. have included Oberon, Edmund, Antipholus of Ephesus, Marat (in New York and on film) in *Marat-Sade* and Coriolanus. A fine actor blessed with voice and striking eyes, his parts in the 1970 season included Angelo, Buckingham, Proteus and Prospero. Tom Wrench in the musical, *Trelawny* (72). Currently (73) due to alternate Richard II and Bolingbroke with Richard Pasco at Stratford.

RICHARDSON, RALPH (1902–). British actor capable of greatness, whose rich personality, comedy gifts, emotional power and range have made him a leading player for almost half a century. An extraordinary actor renowned for playing the ordinary man, and the possessor of a distinctive voice and delivery which for some of his admirers is uniquely fascinating.

First noted for his work at Birmingham Rep, he played leads at the Old Vic (30–2), notably Prince Hal, Sir Toby, Bluntschli, Petruchio, Bottom and Henry V. Other parts before his war service included Mercutio in New York (35), Bottom (37) and Othello (38). One of the pillars of the great Old Vic seasons at the New (44–7) with Olivier. His parts included Peer Gynt, Uncle Vanya, Cyrano and the finest Falstaff in living memory.

For some of his many commercial successes before and since the war, culminating in his Jack in *Home* and Wyatt Gillman in *West of Suez*, see p. 183. His classical roles have included Vershinin (51), Prospero, Volpone and—a rare failure—Macbeth (Stratford, 52), and Timon of Athens at the Old Vic (56). Has also played Bottom and Shylock abroad (64). Innumerable films. Knighted (47).

RIGG, DIANA (1938–). British actress who played Bianca, Cordelia, etc., with the Royal Shakespeare Co., then became a TV superstar in *The Avengers* and is currently (72) stunning as Dorothy in *Jumpers*. Hippolita in *'Tis Pity She's a Whore*, the National's first Mobile Production. A very striking and successful Lady Macbeth (72).

ROBERTS, RACHEL (1927–). British actress whose parts have included Mistress Quickly at the Vic (55)—'perfection' (Tynan), Anna in *Platanov* (60) which won her a Clarence Derwent award and the lead in *Maggie May* (64). A brilliant performance opposite Albert Finney in *Alpha Beta* (72).

ROBERTSON, TOBY (1928–). British director. Artistic Director of Prospect Theatre Company since 1964, which has performed in Edinburgh, London and elsewhere, and for which he has directed over 20 productions. These have included an excitingly wide range of plays, including the McKellen *Edward II*, *The Beggar's Opera* and *Venice Preserved*. Also a TV director.

ROBESON, PAUL (1898–). American singer and actor. His first great successes were as Jim Harris in *All God's Chillun Got Wings* (24) and Brutus Jones in *The Emperor Jones* (24). The legendary Joe of the original London *Show Boat* (28). Played Othello three times, in London (30), New York (43), for 295 performances, the longest Shakespearean run in America, and at Stratford (59). His magnificent voice—without exaggeration one of the great voices of the century—and his fine appearance could not disguise a lack of vocal variety and the technique and fire needed for the role, but for many people his monumental performance was very stirring.

ROBEY, GEORGE (1869–1954). British comedian and star of the music-hall and revue (see p. 217). His one venture into Shakespeare was a triumph: Falstaff in *Henry IV Part 1* (35). Later he appeared briefly and silently as the dying Falstaff in Olivier's film of *Henry V*. Knighted (54).

ROBSON, FLORA (1902–). British actress. Her classical roles have included Varya in *The Cherry Orchard*, Queen Katharine, Isabella and Lady Macbeth (Old Vic, 33–4), Lady Cicely in *Captain Brassbound's Conversion* (48), Paulina in *The Winter's Tale* (51), Mrs. Alving (Old Vic, 58) and Mrs. Borkman (63). An actress of exceptional emotional power, for her commercial career see p. 185. D.B.E. (60). A theatre at Newcastle was named after her (62).

RODWAY, NORMAN (1929–). Irish actor. The title part in *Stephen D* (Dublin, 62; London, 63). A notable member of the Royal Shakespeare Co. (66–)

where his parts have included Hotspur, Feste, Thersites, Richard III, etc.

ROGERS, PAUL (1917–). British actor, who at the Old Vic in the 50s established himself as one of the finest Shakespearean actors of the day. His parts there included a richly Devonian Bottom (51), a passionate Shylock (53) that was widely acclaimed, and a Macbeth (54) which received much praise, and which ended with the actor like a 'starved grey wolf' (Trewin). Among other notable performances were his Touchstone and a memorable Falstaff (54–5). Played Falstaff again for the Royal Shakespeare Co. (66), as before, in both the *Henry IV* plays, also Max in *The Homecoming* (65) which later won him a 'Tony' on Broadway. Many commercial successes.

ROSE, GEORGE (1920–). British actor, now mainly working in America. Old Vic (44–8). Stratford (49–50). Remembered especially for four bravura performances: a happily snobbish spectator at Henry VIII's Coronation (49), a spivish Pompey in *Measure for Measure* (50), a richly wheezing—some said too wheezing—Dogberry (50) and an excellent Autolycus (51), this last in London. Parts in America have included Dogberry (59), the First Gravedigger (64), Martin Ruiz in *The Royal Hunt of the Sun* (66) and Louis Greffin in *Coco* (69).

ROSMER, MILTON (1882–1971). British actor and director. Worked with Martin Harvey, and for Miss Horniman at the Gaiety, Manchester. The first British Giles de Rais in *St. Joan* (24) and a notable player of Shakespeare and Ibsen. His record of serious work in the 20s was a fine one, culminating in the management, with Malcolm Morley, of the Everyman, where, amongst other plays, he directed *The Father* (29). He had the misfortune to fail to grasp the biggest chance of his life as Director at Stratford (43). His productions there were pictorially reactionary and, more seriously, unsuccessful.

RYLANDS, GEORGE (1902–). British director and Shakespearean scholar. Director of many plays for the Cambridge A.D.C. and the Marlowe Society, also directed the whole of Shakespeare on records. Directed *Hamlet* and *The Duchess of Malfi* for Gielgud (44–5) in the famous Haymarket season. Selections from his anthology, *The Seven Ages of Man*, were used by Gielgud for his Shakespearean recitals in the 60s.

SAINT-DENIS, MICHEL (1897–1971). French director whose influence on the British theatre was immense. Settled in London (36) after the closing of his *Compagnie des Quinze*. Directed *Macbeth* (37) at the Old Vic, *The Three Sisters* (38), see p. 72, and other plays, and founded the

London Theatre Studio. Head of the Old Vic Theatre School (46–52), see p. 249. Productions included *Oedipus Rex* (45) and Stravinsky's *Oedipus Rex* (60), also *Electra* (51), and *The Cherry Orchard* (62) for the Royal Shakespeare Co., of which he was a director. A consultant for the Lincoln Center Repertory and Dramatic School, New York.

SCOFIELD, PAUL (1922–   ).British actor, considered by many to be the finest to appear since the war, and one who, on occasion, and in the strictest sense of the word, can be termed great. For his non-classical career see p. 186.

Birmingham Rep (44–6), where he first began his endlessly fruitful partnership with Peter Brook, playing the Bastard in *King John*. Stratford (46–8) where his early parts were Lucio, Malcolm, Cloten, Henry V (his only less-than-striking performance) and a still famous Don Armado in Brook's *Love's Labour's Lost*. This was 'faintly reminiscent of an overbred and beautiful old borzoi' (Philip Hope-Wallace). New roles (47) were Pericles, Mercutio, Sir Andrew and a tormented, heart-rending Hamlet (48), also Troilus, Bassanio, Roderigo and the Clown in *The Winter's Tale*.

Pericles at the Rudolph Steiner Hall (50). Don Pedro at the Phoenix (52). Richard II, Witwoud in *The Way of the World* and Pierre in *Venice Preserved* for Gielgud at the Lyric, Hammersmith (52–3). His Hamlet for Brook at the Phoenix (56) was too restrained for some tastes; the triumph of this season was his whisky priest in *The Power and the Glory*. Lear for the Royal Shakespeare Co. (62) in Brook's famous, though controversial Beckettian production, later seen in many European and American cities. The performance was earthy, pathetic, detailed in its description of old age, primitive and magnificent, and was astonishing, like the production. His Macbeth (67–8) for the R.S.C. finally became a thrilling whole when Scofield was able to give the soldierly side of the character its due. Uncle Vanya (70) at the Royal Court. Joined the National Theatre (71) where he brilliantly played Leone in *The Rules of the Game* and Voigt in *The Captain of Köpenick* (71), a witty triumph, not least for his transformation from a short, whining ex-convict to a captain who 'at once seems two feet taller' (Ronald Bryden).

This 'working actor', as he describes himself, often begins preparing a role by finding a voice for it. His own is flexible to a degree, glittering, sombre and unique, but he prefers accuracy, even ugliness, to beauty of tone. To this superb instrument is added an exceptionally magnetic personality, deep seriousness, authority, emotional strength, stillness and the power to surprise. His critics have occasionally found too much stillness and understatement, even flatness of delivery. This writer has never been aware of these flaws.

Fortunately for the theatre, he has only made occasional films, including repeating his More in *A Man for All Seasons*, and playing Lear in an essentially filmic version of the play directed by Brook.

SEALE, DOUGLAS (1913–). British director of plays and operas on both sides of the Atlantic. Two particular highlights of his career have been his Trilogy of *Henry VI* plays for Birmingham Rep, which were seen at the Old Vic (53) and both the *Henry IV* plays at the Vic (55).

SELBY, NICHOLAS (1925–). British actor who joined the Royal Shakespeare Co. in 1963, playing a wide range of parts, including Casca and Winchester in *Henry VI* (63), Junius Brutus in *Coriolanus*, the Duke in *The Revenger's Tragedy* and Camillo in *The Winter's Tale* (68–9), also modern parts.

SHAW, GLEN BYAM (1904–). British director and actor, co-director, with Anthony Quayle, of the Shakespeare Memorial Theatre, (53–6), sole director (56–9). Director of Productions at Sadler's Wells Opera since 1962. An actor until the mid-30s, his roles included Armand Duval (30), Laertes (34), Oswald (35) and Horatio (Lyceum and Elsinore, 39). Unlike some erratic

director-geniuses, his work has always been distinguished for respect for the author and help for actors. As befits one of the directors of the Old Vic School and Theatre Centre (see p. 249), he is renowned as a teacher—of young actors and also of opera singers. Stratford productions included the famous Ashcroft/Redgrave *Antony and Cleopatra* (53), and for the National he directed *The Dance of Death* (67). Has directed many commercial successes, including *The Winslow Boy* (46). His wife is ANGELA BADDELEY, see above.

SHAW, ROBERT (1927–). Strong British actor also novelist and playwright. Edmund (53) etc. at Stratford. Major film actor. His wife, MARY URE, was the first Alison in *Look Back in Anger*. Desdemona etc. at Stratford (59)

SHAW, SEBASTIAN (1905–). British actor. After a successful career mainly in the commercial theatre and in films, joined the Royal Shakespeare Co. (67), bringing a much needed authority and weight to a range of parts that have included Ulysses, Leonato, Duncan, Friar Laurence and Sir Gerald in *Belcher's Luck*.

SINDEN, DONALD (1923–). British actor, whose cheering career has embraced Shakespeare at Stratford, Bristol and London after the war, years as film star, Hook (60), and a decade of alternating between commercial hits and major performances with the Royal Shakespeare Co. Roles have included a powerful York in *The Wars of the Roses* (63), an hilariously prim, alarming Malvolio (69, 70) and a vastly entertaining Sir Harcourt in *London Assurance* (70, 72) who resembled, as Harold Hobson wrote, 'Oscar Wilde simultaneously playing George IV and the Apollo Belvedere'. Henry VIII (71). Also see p. 187.

SLATER, DAPHNE (1928–). British actress. Stratford's Juliet, Olivia, Miranda and, most notably, Marina in *Pericles* (47). The first Alizon in *The Lady's Not for Burning* (48). Her Cordelia was one of the few successes in the unfortunate Old Vic *Lear* (52).

SMITH, MAGGIE. British actress who, after appearing in revue and becoming a well-known comedienne (see p. 187), joined the Old Vic (59–60) and, later the National Theatre (63). Her comedy roles, notably Silvia in *The Recruiting Officer* (63) and Myra in *Hay Fever* (64) have not overshadowed her serious roles, especially her touching, dignified Desdemona (64) and, in the opinion of this writer, her Hilde Wangel in *The Master Builder* (64). Married to Robert Stephens (see below), with whom she played *The Beaux' Stratagem* in Los Angeles (70) on a National Theatre tour. Her performance as Mrs. Sullen ought to have been filmed, according to *Time*'s critic, as an instructional visual

aide for American actresses.

SOFAER, ABRAHAM (1896–). British actor and a leading Shakespearean of the 30s and 40s. A much-praised Othello at the Old Vic (34). Disraeli in *Victoria Regina* in New York and on tour (36), also directing *The Merchant* for Helen Hayes and playing Shylock. Stratford's Lear, Othello, Iago, Leontes, etc. in 1943, Trewin considering his Lear 'much too shrewd to have yielded his throne'. In many films.

SPEAIGHT, ROBERT (1904–). British actor and author of a number of books including *William Poel and the Elizabethan Revival*. In the Vic-Wells company (31–2) where he gave a splendid Fluellen, a fiery Cassius and a vigorous Hamlet, etc. Since then, has worked in many countries, directing as well as acting, his most famous part having been Becket in *Murder in the Cathedral*, creating the role in Canterbury Cathedral (35) and playing it in London, New York, London again (48) and Sydney (60), also directing it and Romeo in French in Montreal (50).

SPRIGGS, ELIZABETH (1929–). British actress who, after Rep, including Birmingham, joined the Royal Shakespeare Co. (62), coming into her own in the late 60s with performances which have established her as a leading actress of the day. Apart from her splendid Nurse in *Romeo*

(67) and her Claire, the charming alcoholic in Albee's *A Delicate Balance* (68), which won her a Clarence Derwent award, her parts have included a prim Edinburgh Maria, an exhilarating, sporting Lady Gay Spanker in *London Assurance*, Beatrice and a memorable Emilia. Never a juvenile, as she herself admits, she is now in a high summer spell which has audiences and critics basking in its warmth.

SQUIRE, WILLIAM (1920–). British actor. From 1948, this excellent actor has played a huge range of parts at Stratford and the Old Vic, including Mowbray, Glendower, Suffolk and Buckingham in the 1964 Histories cycle at Stratford. The delightful Captain Cat of *Under Milk Wood* (56). Other parts have included Timothy in *A Penny for a Song* and Arthur in *Camelot* on Broadway and on tour.

STEPHENS, ROBERT (1931–). British actor and director. English Stage Co. (56) where his most famous role was the lead in *Epitaph for George Dillon* (London and New York, 58). Peter in Wesker's *The Kitchen* (59 and 61). After his Dauphin in *St. Joan* at Chichester (63) joined the National, where he became an Associate Director. His most notable parts were Captain Plume in *The Recruiting Officer* (63) and his virtuoso Atahuallpa in *The Royal Hunt of the Sun* (64), also Kurt in *The Dance of Death*, Tom Wrench, Vershinin, Archer in *The Beaux' Stratagem* and parts in Maugham and Coward. Married to Maggie Smith (see above) with whom he played in *Design for Living* in America after leaving the National (71) and in *Private Lives* (72).

STEWART, PATRICK (1940–). British actor whose parts with the Royal Shakespeare Co. (since 66) have included Galileo, Shylock, King John, Tullus Aufidius and Cassius.

STRIDE, JOHN (1936–). British actor. Now a TV superstar, he made his name as Romeo at the Vic in the Zeffirelli production with Judi Dench as Juliet (60). Played it in New York (62). Other Old Vic parts included Prince Hal. A National Theatre player (63), his parts included Dunois, Valentine in *Love for Love*, Rosencrantz in *Rosencrantz and Guildenstern are Dead*, Audrey in the all-male *As You Like It* and Edward II (Brecht's, not Marlowe's).

SUZMAN, JANET (1939–). South African-born actress. Joined the Royal Shakespeare Co. (63) to play Joan of Arc and Lady Anne in *The Wars of the Roses*, since when this excellent actress, married to Trevor Nunn, has played Ophelia, Rosaline, Berinthia in *The Relapse*, Rosalind, Beatrice, etc. Her Cleopatra (72) was widely praised.

SWINLEY, ION (1891–1937). British actor widely regarded as one of the supreme Shakespeareans of the century. Never fully recovering from shellshock in the First World War, he gave haunting, memorable performances at the Vic and elsewhere of Hamlet, Romeo, Prospero, Henry V, Cassius, the Button Moulder, etc. 'A fine actor in any part' wrote Harcourt Williams in *Old Vic Saga*. His voice was as memorable as his personality and ability.

SYDNEY, BASIL (1894–1968). British actor whose long career included Oswald in *Ghosts* (17), Mercutio (New York, 22), Higgins in *Pygmalion* (39), Salvatore in *A Man about the House* (46) and Claudius in Olivier's film of *Hamlet*.

TANDY, JESSICA (1909–). Anglo-American actress (also see p. 189). Her classical parts have included a very fine Viola (and Sebastian) at the Old Vic (37), a moving Cordelia there (40), and, at Stratford, Conn., Lady Macbeth (61). At the Tyrone Guthrie, Minneapolis, parts have included Gertrude, Olga in *The Three Sisters*, Mme. Ranevskaya, Lady Wishfort, etc. (63 and 65).

TEARLE, GODFREY (1884–1953). British actor. Began in his father, Osmund Tearle's, Shakespearean company. In the 20s, when this handsome, magnificently voiced actor should have been in his classical prime, Shakespeare was out of fashion in the West End, and Tearle spent the major part of his career in the commercial theatre. Commander Edward Ferrers in *The Flashing Stream* (38). Henry V and Antony (34). His Antony (46) in Glen Byam Shaw's production of *Antony and Cleopatra* was a majestic performance with the verse given its full splendour. His Othello (48) at Stratford looked 'a fine fighting animal built for leadership and instant decision' noted *The Times*. This anguished portrayal only lacked the supreme passion of the part, and again, the verse was regally spoken. Less successful was his Macbeth (49). Though perhaps too lacking in theatrical ambition (to play at the Old Vic and Stratford between the wars), not the least of his achievements was to become the first President of Equity (32). Knighted (51).

THATCHER, TORIN (1905–). British actor. Doubled the Ghost and Claudius (Old Vic and Elsinore 37). Has played on Broadway and in many films.

THESIGER, ERNEST (1879–1961). British actor. Fortunately films will preserve the unique flavour of this witty, sharp-faced, clever actor who was the first British Dauphin in *St. Joan* (24)—and the 1st Witch in *Macbeth* (42). A great Shavian and major personality, his entry in *Who's Who in the Theatre* (13th edition) was one of the longest and most far-ranging in the book. In the 30s alone his Shaw parts included the Dauphin, Higgins, Sir Orpheus in *Geneva*, Charles II in *In Good King Charles's Golden Days* and the Monster in *Too True to be Good*, while 1955 found him playing Polonius in Moscow—'an annoyingly restrained performance', lamented Tynan.

THOMPSON, SADA (1929–). American actress who has played a wide range of classical parts including Dorine in *Tartuffe* which won her an Obie Award. Her stunning Beatrice in *The Effect of Gamma Rays on Man in the Moon Marigolds* (70) won her two awards.

THORNDIKE, RUSSELL (1885–1973). British actor, director and novelist. Played a huge range of Shakespearean roles for Ben Greet in Britain and America before the First World War. Also acted with Matheson Lang and for Miss Horniman at Manchester. A pillar, with his sister Sybil, of the Old Vic in its earliest days, directing as well as acting. His most famous performance was as Peer Gynt (22) in the first British production of the play. Very well cast: as Lilian Baylis remarked: 'You see Russell is Peer Gynt, a born romancer.' A stalwart of the Open Air Theatre, Regent's Park, for many years. Also known to hundreds of thousands of playgoers, young and old, as *the* Smee in *Peter Pan*.

THORNDIKE, SYBIL (1882–). British actress. Toured America for three years with Ben Greet (04–7), then with Miss Horniman at Manchester (08). At the Old Vic in its infancy (14–18), where she played nearly all Shakespeare's female roles as well as Prince Hal, owing to the shortage of men. A great success as Hecuba in *The Trojan Women* (19, 20). A famous Medea (20). Played in a number of Grand Guignol pieces (20–22). In 1924 became the first British and greatest St. Joan (see p. 15).

Other notable roles between the wars were as Judith in *Granite* (26), Volumnia (Old Vic, 38) and Miss Moffat in *The Corn is Green* (38). With her husband, Lewis Casson, (see p. 89), she toured mining villages, etc., during the War with Medea, Lady Macbeth and Candida; later joined the Old Vic Company at the New (44–6), where her parts included Aase, Queen Margaret, Mistress Quickly and Jocasta.

Since the War, she has appeared in a number of commercial plays (see p. 189). She also gave recitals with her husband and has appeared in many films. Her vitality is as notable as her ability. With her brother, wrote a biography of Lilian Baylis (38). D.B.E. (31).

TUTIN, DOROTHY (1930–). British actress. Bristol Old Vic (50–1) where her parts, which included Katharine in *Henry V*, gave no hint of the shattering power and emotion of her Rose in Graham Greene's *The Living Room* (53). Other notable performances before joining the Stratford company (58) included her Sally Bowles in *I Am a Camera* (54), a very moving Hedvig in *The Wild Duck* (55), Joan of Arc in Anouilh's *The Lark* (55) and Jean Rice in *The Entertainer* (57). At Stratford her parts have included Juliet, Ophelia and especially fine performances of Viola and Cressida. A powerful, tormented Jeanne in *The Devils* (61). Queen Victoria in William Francis's *Portrait of a Queen* (65), with her husband, DEREK WARING, as Albert. Rosalind at Stratford (67), then repeated her Victoria in New York (68). Her Kate in Pinter's *Old Times* (71) had critics reaching for the superlatives once more, as did her Peter Pan (71–2), a vigorous, yet remote, and utterly convincing performance, hailed as the finest since Jean Forbes Robertson's.

VALK, FREDERICK (d. 1956). German actor forced first to flee to Czechoslovakia, then to Britain where his titanic Othello (42) opposite Bernard Miles as a chilling Iago, was followed by a fine Shylock (43), both for the Old Vic at the New. His Othello (46) opposite Wolfit at the height of his powers as Iago is remembered with awe by all who saw it. The young Tynan recorded how he had lived for two hours on the red brink of a volcano during the performance.

Rosalind Iden, the Desdemona, was lucky to survive her death scene.

VAUGHAN, STUART (1925–). American director whose many Shakespearean productions have included *The Wars of the Roses* and *Richard III* in New York (70).

WALLER, DAVID (1920–). British actor whose performances with the Royal Shakespeare Co. have included Harry Belcher in Mercer's *Belcher's Luck* (66), Pastor Manders, Duff in Pinter's *Landscape*, a brutal Claudius, Dr. Faustus (Theatreground) and a marvellously rich Bottom in Brook's *Dream* (70).

WANAMAKER, SAM. See p. 266.

WARNER, DAVID (1941–). British actor, especially famous for his very moving Henry VI at Stratford (63 and 64). Richard II (63), Hamlet in Peter Hall's production (65), a striking performance admired by many, though some complained it was not princely. ('How the hell do I know what princely is?' he asked in *The Times*, 4 March 72, a thought-provoking query.) The Postmaster in *The Government Inspector* and Sir Andrew (66). Films include *Morgan, a Suitable Case for Treatment* and Blifil in *Tom Jones*.

WARRE, MICHAEL (1922–). British actor, director and designer. With the Old Vic at the New (44–7) where his roles included Prince Hal (up against Olivier, the most formidable Hotspur since the original) and Edgar. A fine Andrey in *The Three Sisters* (51). Clarence at Stratford (53), also Albany in *Lear* (53) for which he arranged the fights. Eilert Lovborg in *Hedda Gabler* (54), Captain Hook (57).

This all-round man-of-the-theatre has designed many productions including *Twelfth Night* for the Old Vic (48), directed in Holland as well as Britain, designed the flexible and experimental L.A.M.D.A. theatre, appeared in films and written *Designing and Making Stage Scenery* (68).

WATSON, DOUGLASS (1921–). American actor whose many classical parts have included Richard III (64) and Brutus (66) at Stratford, Conn.

WEBSTER, MARGARET (1905–72). Anglo-American actress and director, daughter of Ben Webster and Dame May Whitty. Her long career began in the Chorus of *The Trojan Women* (24) with Sybil Thorndike. Worked with the Macdona Players, Fagan, Ben Greet and in commercial plays before joining the Vic (29–30), where she played Hermia, Audrey, etc. Lady Macbeth there (32). Went to America in 1938, having begun to direct in Britain. Staged the long-running Robeson *Othello* (43), playing Emilia. With Eva Le Gallienne and Cheryl Crawford founded the American Repertory company (46).

Since then she has staged (and sometimes presented) Shakespeare, Shaw, Ibsen, organized Shakespeare tours and directed operas in New York. Has also worked in Britain again, including *The Merchant* at Stratford (55), *Waiting in the Wings* (60) and *Mrs. Warren's Profession* at Guildford (70). Made theatre history as Lady Macbeth by having three husbands in three weeks: Malcolm Keen slipped while fighting, Marius Goring playing at a moment's notice was only 20, so John Laurie concluded the engagement. Miss Webster fortunately survived.

WELLES, ORSON (1915–). American actor, producer and director whose Shakespearean roles have included Hamlet, Lear, Mercutio, Brutus and Othello, the last being seen in London (51), his thrilling production compensating for a lack of power and range in himself. Forced to play his Lear (56) in a wheelchair. This theatre giant who all-too-rarely works in the theatre has presented a Negro *Macbeth* (36), staged a modern dress *Caesar* at his Mercury Theater (see p. 245), where he also presented Dekker, Shaw, etc., and directed and designed *Rhinoceros* in London (60). For details of his Dublin debut see Macliammóir's *All for Hecuba*.

WEST, TIMOTHY (1934–). British actor. After playing a variety of parts for the Royal Shakespeare Co. (64–6), played Dr. Johnson for the Prospect Theatre Company, then Bolingbroke and Marlowe's Mortimer (69) in Edinburgh and London, and other parts culminating in Lear (72), 'a very English Lear ... a well-fed, self-indulgent, obstinate old man' noted John Mortimer in *The Observer* and said he had never seen the King's death played so realistically. West's father is the actor, LOCKWOOD WEST, and his wife, the actress PRUNELLA SCALES, a Stratford Nerissa (56). She played Cherry in *The Beaux' Stratagem* at Chichester (67) and the Wife in *The Unknown Soldier and his Wife* the following year.

WESTBROOK, JOHN (1922–). British actor whose fine voice has been used to great effect as the Narrator in *The Play of Daniel* (from 60 in Britain, 61 in America). Has played Eliot's Becket in Canterbury Cathedral (70) and elsewhere, Comus (53) and Edward II and Samson Agonistes (56) at Ludlow Castle. Christ in the York Mystery Plays at York (66).

WHITELAW, BILLIE. British actress who, while a National Theatre player (64–5), showed her considerable ability in a wide range of parts: Desdemona, Francischina in *The Dutch Courtesan*, Maggie in *Hobson's Choice* and a vintage Avonia Bunn in *Trelawny of the Wells*. Clare in *After Haggerty* for the Royal Shakespeare Co. (71).

WICKWIRE, NANCY (1925–). American actress whose many classical parts have included Rosalind, Helena in *All's Well*, St. Joan, Rebecca West, etc.

WILLIAM, DAVID (1926–). British actor and director. An Old Vic and Stratford player in the 50s, began a long association with the Open Air Theatre, Regent's Park, with his production of *The Tempest* (55). Artistic Director of the Ludlow Festival (58–63). Toured abroad as Richard in his own production of *Richard II* (64). Artistic Director of the Glasgow Citizens' (65–6) and the National Theatre of Israel (68–70) and has also directed at Stratford, Ontario, and in Washington, etc. Has directed several operas. Directed *Richard II* for the National (72), a good, straightforward reading.

WILLIAMS, CLIFFORD (1926–). British director, with the Royal Shakespeare Co. since 1961, where he has twice (65 and 72) shown that *The Comedy of Errors* is a major play and had the courtesy to the author not to change his views the second time around for the sake of change. This sparkling, athletic, invigorating display of ensemble and fun apart, he has directed *The Jew of Malta, The Merchant, The Representative*, etc., and elsewhere, *The Soldiers* in Canada, New York and London (68), the historic all-male *As You Like It* at the National (67), also *Back to Methusalah* there (68). *Sleuth* in London, New York and Paris (69) and a *Flying Dutchman* at Covent Garden (66) which provoked uproar, abuse and cheers because of Kenny's sets. This man of parts also directed *Oh! Calcutta!* (69).

WILLIAMS, EMLYN (1905–). British actor, dramatist and director. In this second of four entries in the book must be recorded his chilling Angelo and powerful Richard III at the Vic (37), his Hjalmar Ekdal in *The Wild Duck* (55) and his Stratford season (56): Shylock, Angelo and a superbly dangerous Iago. Internationally renowned for his Dickens recitals.

WILLIAMS, HARCOURT (1880–1957). British actor and director. Appeared with Benson, H. B. Irving, etc., and as the Player King to Barrymore's Hamlet (25) and often at the Old Vic, including the historic 1944–46 seasons at the New. But his claim to theatrical immortality rests on his term as Director of the Old Vic from 1929–33, when his players included Gielgud, Richardson, Edith Evans, Wolfit, Ashcroft, etc. Fortunately, he wrote *Four Years at the Old Vic* about this great period, and, later, *Old Vic Saga*, the history of the Vic up to 1949.

WOLFIT, DONALD (1902–1968). British actor-manager. When he formed his Shakespearean company (37), he was known—and highly regarded—by Agate and others as one of the finest young supporting and leading actors of the day, notably at the Old Vic (29–30) and Stratford (36–7). At the Vic, he had been an admired Macduff and Cassius, and a Claudius (opposite Gielgud) who gained universal praise. At Stratford his parts included a superb Kent, a fine Ulysses, and his first (and only acclaimed) Hamlet.

His career as a touring actor-manager, which lasted until the 50s, brought Shakespeare to millions in Britain and overseas, and revealed him in London (44) as the greatest Lear of modern times, also a very notable Richard III. Other noted performances were as the Master Builder, Touchstone, Shylock, Iago, opposite Valk, and especially, Volpone. His much-abused company suffered from his actor-managerial ways; this period can only be understood by referring to Ronald Harwood's masterly, critical, but affectionate biography (71). For his Tamburlaine at the Old Vic see p. 74. This was followed by his famous Lord Ogleby and his equally famous walk-out from the company.

His later roles included Oedipus Rex and Oedipus at Colonus, Captain Hook, Father Fernandez in *The Strong are Lonely*, Pastor Manders, John Gabriel

Borkman, roles in two plays by Montherland, *Malatesta* and *The Master of Santiago*, Long John Silver, etc. He also gave Shakespearean recitals abroad with his wife, Rosalind Iden (see above) and gave some memorable film performances.

His main assets were a supremely good voice, magnificently used, extraordinary power, the courage to risk the most dangerous effects, and a capacity for hard work. His defects lay, not in his acting, but in his personality and in his attitude as an actor-manager who had to be in the limelight. A theatre giant, impossible and splendid, he richly deserved (and enjoyed) his knighthood (57).

WOOD, JOHN. British actor who, since joining the Royal Shakespeare Co. (71), has brilliantly played a wide range of parts, including Sir Fopling Flutter in *The Man of Mode*, Yakov Bardin in *Enemies* and Richard Rowan in *Exiles*, also Brutus, Antipholus of Syracuse in *Titus* (72).

WOODTHORPE, PETER (1931–). British actor. King Lear at Cambridge. The first British Estragon in *Waiting for Godot* (55) (see p. 20). Professor Müller in Durrenmatt's *Time and Again*, called *The Visit* in London (New York, 58). Stratford (59), as Flute, Roderigo and Junius Brutus in *Coriolanus*. His riveting Aston in *The Caretaker* (60) won him a Clarence Derwent award. The Clown in *The Chances* at Chich-

CTT–K

ester (62) also Phulas in *The Broken Heart* and Yefim in *Uncle Vanya*. Toad in *Toad of Toad Hall* (62 and 72 at Stratford). Dogberry, etc. (71).

WOODVINE, JOHN (1929–). British actor whose classical parts have included Macbeth at the Mermaid, also Simon Eyre in *The Shoemaker's Holiday* (64) and Claudius opposite McKellen (71). A TV star.

WOODWARD, EDWARD (1930–). British actor who, before achieving colossal TV fame as Callan, played Mercutio, Laertes, Thaliard in *Pericles* and Claudio in *Much Ado* at Stratford (58) with notable success. Played Percy in Dyer's *The Rattle of a Simple Man* (Johannesburg, 61; London, 62; New York, 62). Has also appeared in musicals, including Charles Condomine in *High Spirits* (New York, 65) and *A Tale of Two Cities* in London (69). Joined the National Theatre to play Flamineo in *The White Devil* finely (69), but his potentially magnificent Cyrano (70), touching and big, was spoilt by a wayward production.

WORDSWORTH, RICHARD (1915–). British actor whose wide range of classical parts have included Antonio in *Venice Preserved* (53) with which he won a Clarence Derwent award, and the definitive Roderigo: 'a wholly credible ninny' wrote Tynan (Old Vic, 56). Other notable roles have included

Justice Squeezum in *Lock Up Your Daughters* and Captain Hook.

WORTH, IRENE (1916–). American actress much of whose career has been in Britain. Only became an actress in 1942. The first Celia in *The Cocktail Party* (49). Her Desdemona at the Old Vic (51) drew superlatives: 'Truly tragic ... the best,' (Darlington), 'Almost burnt up Desdemona with her warmth,' (Hobson). Other admired performances of that period included Portia (53) and Helena in *All's Well* at Stratford, Ontario (53), where she later played Rosalind (59) and a magnificent Hedda Gabler (70).

Other parts have included Argia in *The Queen and the Rebels* (55), Schiller's Mary Stuart in New York (57) and Edinburgh and the Old Vic (58), Sara Callifer in *The Potting Shed* (58), Albertine in *Toys in the Attic* in New York (60), Lady Macbeth and Goneril at Stratford (62), Mathilde in *The Physicists* (63) and a performance of Alice in *Tiny Alice* (64) which won her the New York Drama Critics award. More recent roles have included a magnificent tragic performance as Jocasta in Seneca's *Oedipus* at the National (68), directed for

Brook, for whom she has since worked at his Parisian Theatre Research Centre.

WYNYARD, DIANA (1906–64). British actress whose career between the wars was mainly in the commercial theatre, an Old Vic Eliza Doolittle apart (37). Played Gilda in *Design for Living* (39). A notable beauty, she also appeared in many films. Joined the Stratford company (48), where her roles included Gertrude, Portia, Katharine in *The Shrew*, Helen, Desdemona and Lady Macbeth, too steely a part for her. Her moving Hermione (48) and radiant Beatrice were later seen in London opposite Gielgud. Marguerite Gautier in *Camino Real* (57). Andromache in *The Trojans* (60), a mime-role, beautifully done. Gertrude in The National Theatre's opening production, she died before playing the lead there in *Hay Fever* as planned.

YURKA, BLANCHE (1887–). American actress who has played many of the Greek classical roles. Gertrude opposite Barrymore (22) Hedda (29), which she directed. The Nurse (35). Jocasta (45). Many non-classical successes Particularly fine in Ibsen.

WEST END AND BROADWAY

Some stars, matinée idols, major talents and popular
favourites

This chapter, unlike the other major ones in the book, is solely
about people and consists only of a Who's Who section.
There are two reasons for this, firstly because some of the
plays which would be featured occur at the start of Chapter
I, and secondly because of the sheer impossibility of selecting
specimens from a flood of pleasant light comedies and dramas
—highbrows would say the inadvisability. A list of long runs
would perhaps have been a reasonable substitute, but that
would have done less than justice to earlier days when runs
were shorter but the theatre was indisputably more generally
popular than it is today. The interested can consult *Who's
Who in the Theatre* for a huge and definitive list of long runs
in the West End and on Broadway. And now to our stars and
other worthies, a number of whom have already appeared in
this book in classical guise. . . .

ADLER, LUTHER (1903–). American actor. With the Group Theater (32–40), for whom his parts included Joe Bonaparte in *Golden Boy* (New York, 37; London, 38). Later parts have included Shylock and Tevye in *Fiddler on the Roof* (65). His sister, STELLA ADLER (1902–), was also with the Group: Bessie Berger in *Awake and Sing* (35) etc. Madame Rosepettle in *Oh Dad, Poor Dad* ... (London, 61). A distinguished teacher of drama.

AHERNE, BRIAN (1902–). British stage and screen star, whose best known Broadway part has been Robert Browning in *The Barretts of Wimpole Street* (31) opposite Katharine Cornell.

ALBANESI, MEGGIE (1899–1923). British actress destined, according to Masefield, to become 'the wonder of our stage', but who died tragically young. One of her great successes was as the daughter in *A Bill of Divorcement* (21). 'Remember Meggie Albanesi' urges a plaque at the St. Martin's, but no one who saw her will ever forget her.

ARNAUD, YVONNE (1892–1958). French actress who, after being a child piano prodigy, became one of the West End's most popular actresses. Her parts ranged from juveniles in Aldwych farces, through leading roles, including Lady Catherine in *The Circle* (44), to Mme. Alexandra in *Colombe* (51). Her extreme charm sometimes got in the way of sharp characterization. Guildford's theatre is named for her.

ASHCROFT, PEGGY (1907–). British actress whose wonderful career is dealt with at length in the previous chapter. Her first great commercial success was as Naomi in *Jew Suss* (29) and, since then, her most famous non-classical parts have included Evelyn Holt in *Edward, My Son* (London, 47; New York, 48), Catherine in *The Heiress* (49) and Hester in *The Deep Blue Sea* (52). Returned to the commercial theatre as the wife in *Lloyd George Knew My Father* (72).

BACALL, LAUREN (1924–). American actress who, since returning from Hollywood, has had Broadway successes culminating in her stellar performance as Margot Channing in *Applause* (New York, 70; London, 72).

BAILEY, ROBIN (1919–). British actor in many West End successes. Australia's Higgins in *My Fair Lady* (59/70). Among his classical parts, his Faulkland in *The Rivals* (48) won him a Clarence Derwent award.

BALSAM, MARTIN (1919–). American actor, well known to British filmgoers, whose three roles in *You Know I Can't Hear You When The Water's Running* (67) won him major awards.

BANCROFT, ANNE (1931–). American actress, whose Gittel in *Two for the Seesaw* (58) and Annie Sullivan in *The Miracle Worker* (59), for which she won the New York Critics award, proved that a major talent had arrived. Her film performances have increased her stature. The title-role in *Mother Courage* (63), the Princess in *The Devils* (65), Regina in *The Little Foxes* (67), Anne in *A Cry of Players* (68).

BANKHEAD, TALLULAH (1903–68). American actress and London's darling in the 20s when her beauty, the 'smoky huskiness of her voice' (Trewin) and her considerable abilities were displayed as *femmes fatales* and, occasionally, worthy comedy roles like Julia in Coward's *Fallen Angels*. Her American parts include a notorious Cleopatra (37)—she used to read her reviews out publicly—a vicious Regina in *The Little Foxes* (42) and Blanche in *A Streetcar named Desire* (56). Her autobiography, *Tallulah*, is a riot and a joy.

BANKS, LESLIE (1890–1952). A fine British actor whose popularity with play- and film-goers was immense. His parts included Lester Faraday in *The Moon and Sixpence* (25), Nelson in *Emma Hamilton* (29), Clive in *Clive of India* (34), Mr. Chips in *Goodbye Mr. Chips* (38), the Duke in *The Duke in Darkness* (42), Claudius (44), Father in *Life with Father* (47) and Aubrey Tanqueray (50), etc. Blessed with a strong but sympathetic

personality and a distinctive but unaggressive voice, he survived a facially disfiguring war wound which might have held back a lesser actor and a lesser man.

BARRYMORE, ETHEL (1879–1959). American actress whose career ranged from appearing with Irving in *The Bells* to playing a centenarian in *Whiteoaks* (36). Extremely beautiful in her youth, her first success was in *Captain Jinks of the Horse Marines* (01). As well as numerous commercial successes, she played a number of major classical roles (see p. 82) and appeared in many films. She served the theatre for longer than her brothers, and among her most famous roles were Maugham's Lady Frederick and his Constant Wife, Sister Garcia in *The Kingdom of God* (28) with which the Ethel Barrymore Theater opened, and, after a spell in indifferent plays, a magnificent Miss Moffat in *The Corn is Green* (40).

BARRYMORE, JOHN (1882–1942). Younger brother of Ethel and the possessor of a famous profile, remarkable talents and a genius for living it up. For his few great classical performances before he deserted the theatre for films see p. 82. One of his best non-classical performances was as Falder in *Justice* (16) and he was also very fine as Peter Ibbetson (17) and in *Redemption*.

BARRYMORE, LIONEL (1878–1954).

The oldest of the Barrymores, who was the first to give up the stage for films, not before making his mark in *The Copperhead* (18) and other plays. After a dismal Macbeth and a success in *The Claw* he left Broadway for Hollywood (25).

BATES, ALAN (1934–). British actor. The original Cliff in *Look Back in Anger* (London, 56; New York, 58). The first British Edmund Tyrone in *Long Day's Journey into Night* (58), for which he won a Clarence Derwent award. The first Mick in *The Caretaker* (London, 60; New York, 61) Adam in *The Four Seasons* (65). His bravura and witty performance in the title-role of Simon Gray's *Butley* (71) won him an *Evening Standard* award (72) for the year's best actor. Has become a major film actor. Also see p. 83.

BAXTER, JANE (1909–). British actress who graduated from understudying in *Rookery Nook* (26) to become a popular West End juvenile and leading lady (with a particularly attractive voice). Parts have included Frankie in *George and Margaret* (37), Lady Elizabeth in *While the Sun Shines* (43), Jenny in *The Holly and the Ivy* (50) and Sheila in *Dial 'M' for Murder* (52). Classical parts have included Cecily in *The Importance of Being Earnest* (New York, 47) and Viola (Old Vic at the New, 48). More recent parts have been Laura in *The Shadow of Doubt*

(55), Jane in *The More the Merrier* (60), Gabriel in *Dear Antoine* at Chichester (71). The Mother in *A Voyage round my Father* (72).

BEDFORD, BRIAN (1935–). British actor. After work at Stratford, etc., made his name as Clive Harrington in *Five Finger Exercise* (London, 58; New York, 59). Since then, parts have included Louis Dubedat (63) and, in New York, Tchaik in *The Private Ear* (63), Tom in *The Knack* (64), Edward in *The Cocktail Party* (68) and Elyot in *Private Lives* (69).

BEL GEDDES, BARBARA (1922–). American actress whose parts have included Genevra Langdon in *Deep are the Roots* (45), Patty in *The Moon is Blue* (51) and powerful performances as Rose in *The Living Room* (54) and Margaret in *Cat on a Hot Tin Roof* (55). Played Mary in *The Sleeping Prince* (56), Katherine in *Silent Night, Holy Night* (61), the title role in *Mary, Mary* (61), etc., and Jenny in *Everything in the Garden* (67).

BENNETT, JILL (1931–). British actress, who first made a mark as Anni in *Captain Carvallo* (50). Since then her parts have included Masha in *The Seagull* (56), Isabelle in *Dinner with the Family* (57) Countess Sophia in *A Patriot for Me* (65), Katerina in *The Storm* at the National (66) and, stunningly, Pamela in *Time Present* (68), by her husband,

John Osborne, a performance which gained her *Evening Standard* and Variety Club awards. Again very fine as Frederica in *West of Suez* (71), and as Hedda (72).

BERGNER, ELIZABETH (1900–). Viennese and international actress who, after playing major classical parts in Germany, had a colossal success in London as Gemma in *Escape Me Never* (33). Such was her magic that Agate was abused for claiming she had not proved herself a great actress. Played the part in New York (35). Other parts in Britain included the title-role in the ill-fated *The Boy David* (36), St. Joan at Malvern (38), Tionette in *The Gay Invalid* (50) and The Countess in *The Madwoman of Chaillot* at Oxford and Guildford (67). A major hit on Broadway was her Sally in *The Two Mrs. Carrolls* (43), which she has also played in Australia (50). Has frequently appeared in Germany and Austria since the war.

BIRD, RICHARD (1894–). British actor and director. Apart from his busy West End acting career, has directed many successes including *George and Margaret* (37), *The Happiest Days of your Life* (48) and several classic farces by Vernon Sylvaine. The original Robert in *Dangerous Corner* (32). His wife is the actress JOYCE BARBOUR (1901–), who has also played many leads in musicals and revues.

BOOTH, JAMES (1933–). British actor whose parts have ranged from Tosher in *Fings Ain't Wot They Used T'Be* (Stratford East, 59; Garrick, 60) to Edmund at Stratford (62). Other parts have included A.C.2 Harrison in *Nil Carborundum* (Arts, 62) and Robin Hood in *Twang* (65), also Face in *The Alchemist* at Chichester (70).

BOOTH, SHIRLEY (1907–). American actress who after years of being cast as an 'expert character actress of sardonic hussies' (Brooks Atkinson), became a major star for her famous performance as Lola in *Come Back, Little Sheba* (50). Another great success was her Leona in *The Time of the Cuckoo* (52), since when her parts have included the title-role in *Nina* (60) and Judith Bliss in *Hay Fever* (70).

BOWERS, LALLY (1917–). British actress. A much-admired supporting player who won a Clarence Derwent award for her Mme. de Montrachet in *Dinner with the Family* (58).

BRAITHWAITE, LILIAN (1873–1948). British actress renowned for her work in classical and modern plays and for her scorching wit. A Bensonian before 1914, who also worked with Alexander. Two of her most famous later parts were as Florence Lancaster in *The Vor-*

tex (London, 24; New York, 25) and Abbey Brewster in *Arsenic and Old Lace* (42). D.B.E. (43). Her daughter is the actress, JOYCE CAREY (1898–) who has appeared in many Coward plays, including *Present Laughter*, as Liz Essendine (London, 43: New York, 58).

BRIERS, RICHARD (1934–). British actor. An excellent comedian and farceur who first appeared in London as Joseph Field in *Gilt and Gingerbread* (59). Parts have included Gerald in *Rookery Nook* (Tour, 64), Roland Maule in *Present Laughter* (65), Mortimer Brewster in *Arsenic and Old Lace* (66). Starred with Lynn Redgrave in the triple bill, *The Two of Us* (70). A very effective non-comedy performance was his Falder in *Justice* (68). Took over the title-role of *Butley* (72). Has startled his many admirers by giving a fine Richard III (72). A very popular TV actor.

BROOK, CLIVE (1887–). British actor and a major film star between the wars. Parts have included Michael Wentworth in *The Years Between* (45), Henry Hutton in *The Gioconda Smile* (48) and Josiah Bolton in *Second Threshold* (New York, 51; London, 52). His daughter is the actress FAITH BROOK (1922–), an Old Vic Millimant and Olivia (48–9), Gertrude (71) opposite McKellen. She has also given notably good emotional performances in non-classical roles on stage and on TV. His son the actor LYNDON BROOK.

BROWNE, CORAL (1913–). British actress and wit for whose classical performances see p. 87. This stylish, commanding Australian-born star has enhanced many a commercial play including the title-roles in *The Last of Mrs. Cheyney* (44) and *Lady Frederick* (46). 'Boss' Trent in *Castle in the Air* (49), Constance in *Affairs of State* (54), Laura in *Simon and Laura* (54), Katherine in *The Pleasure of his Company* (60), Marie in *Bonne Soupe* (61), the Countess in *The Rehearsal* (New York, 63), Mrs. Rossiter in *The Right Honourable Gentleman* (London, 64; New York, 65), etc.

BRYANT, MICHAEL (1928–). British actor who, after playing Willie Oban in *The Iceman Cometh* (58), made his name as Walter in *Five Finger Exercise* (London, 58; New York, 59). The title-role in *Ross* (61), since when his parts have included Jacko in *Gentle Jack* (63) and, for the Royal Shakespeare Co., the Dauphin in *Henry V* and Teddy in *The Homecoming* (65). Johnson in *This Story is Yours* at the Royal Court (68). Many TV appearances.

BULL, PETER (1912–). British actor and author. The original Tappercoom in *The Lady's Not For Burning* (48), Pozzo in *Waiting for Godot* (55) and Tetzel in *Luther* (61), etc. Has writ-

Tyrone Guthrie rehearsing *Othello* at the Old Vic in 1938, not, as is
usually supposed, the '*Dream*'. Those in the picture include (left to
right) Stephen Murray (Roderigo), Laurence Olivier (Iago), Michael
Goodliffe (Montano), Guthrie, Timothy [*sic*] Kearse (Bianca), and
Anthony Quayle as Cassio. The author's thanks are due to Stephen
Murray, Anthony Quayle and Sir Ralph Richardson (who played
Othello) for solving most of the picture's problems for him.

Above left: Lilian Baylis, founder of three national theatres.
Above right: Elia Kazan, most influential of American directors.
Below left: Peter Brook, master of excitement, unease and total theatre.
Below right: Peter Hall, man of superlative theatre talents.

Ivor Novello was the ultimate matinée idol of his day. He is seen here in his own hugely popular *King's Rhapsody*, gazing at Vanessa Lee.

Right: Flora Robson as Alicia Christie in Lesley Storm's *Black Chiffon*, one of her greatest successes.

Below: Edith Evans and John Gielgud first played opposite each other in *The Importance of Being Earnest* in 1939. Her 'A hand-bag?', an aria in three syllables, is fortunately preserved for posterity on both record and film.

Above: Two superstars, Noël Coward and Vivien Leigh.

Below: Robertson Hare and Ralph Lynn, masters of farce, Aldwych style.

Peggy Ashcroft and Ralph Richardson in *The Heiress*.

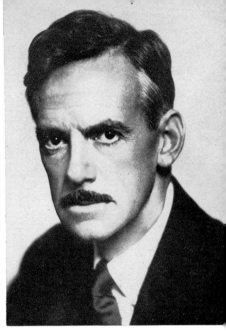

Above left: Sean O'Casey.   *Above right:* Eugene O'Neill.

Below left: Arthur Miller.   *Below right:* Tennessee Williams.

Above: John Gielgud's production of *The Lady's Not for Burning.*
Left to right: Claire Bloom, Nora Nicholson, John Gielgud, Pamela
Brown, David Evans, Harcourt Williams, Richard Burton, Richard
Leech.
Below left: Joyce Redman as Juno.   *Below right:* Joan Plowright as
Sonya.

Laurence Olivier as Othello.

Kay Hammond and John Clements in *Man and Superman*.

Left: Richard Rodgers and Oscar Hammerstein II.

Below: The splendid and influential Shakespearean Festival Theatre at Stratford, Ontario.

Right: Robert Morley as the Prince Regent in Norman Ginsbury's *The First Gentleman.*

Below: Morris Carnovsky as King Lear at the Stratford Shakespeare Festival, Connecticut, one of the finest and most acclaimed performances of a Shakespearean role by an American in this century.

The opening scene of Michel Saint-Denis's production of *Oedipus Rex* for the Old Vic at the New Theatre, with Laurence Olivier as Oedipus. Setting: John Piper.

Right: The death of Atahuallpa (Robert Stephens) in John Dexter's production for the National Theatre of Peter Shaffer's *The Royal Hunt of the Sun.*

Below: A scene from Harold Pinter's *The Caretaker.* Left to right: Peter Woodthorpe, Donald Pleasance, Alan Bates.

Judi Dench and Donald Sinden in *London Assurance*.

Above: A scene from John Osborne's *A Hotel in Amsterdam*, with Paul Scofield and Judy Parfitt on the sofa, and David Burke behind it.

Below: A model of The National Theatre due to be opened in 1974.

ten two essential, light-hearted theatre books, *I Know the Face but—* and *I Say, Look Here!*

BUNNAGE, AVIS. British actress who played a huge range of parts for Joan Littlewood at Stratford East, including Helen in *A Taste of Honey* (58). Meg Dillon in *The Hostage* (London, 59; New York, 60) and Marie in *The Marie Lloyd Story* (67). Golde in *Fiddler on the Roof* (69).

BURDEN, HUGH (1913–). British actor whose wide range of West End parts has included a powerful Unknown Man in *The Paragon* (48) and Vladimir in *Waiting for Godot* (55). Has written a number of plays and is TV's Mr. Reeder, Edgar Wallace's anti-detective with 'The Mind'.

BURKE, BILLIE (1885–1970). American actress. A star of Broadway and the West End before 1914 and a film star from 1916. The very pretty wife of the great Ziegfeld. The shows in which she appeared are nearly all forgotten; her charm is not.

CADELL, JEAN (1884–1967). British actress whose distinguished career included one very famous performance, her Miss Shoe in *At Mrs. Beam's* (London 23, 24, 32; New York, 26). Other parts included May in *The Old Ladies* (35 and 50), Goudie in *Suspect* (37), Mrs. Higgins and Mistress Overdone at the Old Vic (37) and Miss

Prism (London, 42; New York, 47).

CALHERN, LOUIS (1895–1956). A popular Broadway and film actor for many years whose Lear (40) was acclaimed by many, though not by Nathan.

CALVERT, PHYLLIS (1915–). British actress who after being a popular film star in the 40s, has played West End leads including Mary in *The Complaisant Lover* (59), Liz in *Present Laughter* (65) and Ruth in *Blithe Spirit* (70).

CAMPBELL, JUDY (1916–). British actress and noted beauty of her day, particularly associated with Noel Coward plays, notably her Joanna in *Present Laughter* and Ethel in *This Happy Breed* at the Haymarket (43) and Miranda Frayle in *Relative Values* (51). Joanna in *Book of the Month* (54), Mrs. Clandon in *You Never Can Tell* (66), Sheila in *Relatively Speaking* (67).

CARMICHAEL, IAN (1920–). British actor who became famous in post-war revues, notably *The Lyric Revue* (51) and *The Globe Revue* (52). Soon after this, films made use of his excellent comedy technique and personality, but he has appeared in a number of plays, notably Augie Poole in *The Tunnel of Love* (57), Elliot Nash in *The Gazebo* (60) and Robert in *Boeing-Boeing* (New York, 65). St. John Hotchkiss in *Getting Mar-*

ried (67). Michael in *I Do! I Do!* (68). A very popular film and TV comedian.

CARNOVSKY MORRIS (1896–). American actor. One of the few living Americans to have triumphed in Shakespeare (see p. 89), his long career has included the original La Hire in *St. Joan* (23) and other performances for the Theater Guild, and membership of the Group Theater for which he played a wide range of parts including Robert Connelly in *The House of Connelly* (31) and Mr. Bonaparte in *Golden Boy* (New York, 37; London, 38).

CARRADINE, JOHN (1906–). American actor, who, his many film parts apart, has run a Shakespearean touring co., playing Hamlet, Shylock, etc., toured in other plays, and, on Broadway played the Inquisitor in *Galileo* (47), the Ragpicker in *The Madwoman of Chaillot* (48) and Lycus in *A Funny Thing Happened on the Way to the Forum* (62), etc.

CARROLL, LEO G. (1892–1972). British-born actor whose career (from 24) was on Broadway and in films. Parts included Private Meek in *Too True to be Good* (32), Inspector Rough in *Angel Street* (*Gaslight*) (41) and a very funny George in *The Late George Apley* (44), etc.

CHAPMAN EDWARD (1901–). British actor well-known for his blunt, no-nonsense North Country characterizations. The first Jess Oakroyd in *The Good Companions* (31).

CILENTO, DIANE. Australian-born actress, whose West End parts have included Helen in *Tiger at the Gates* (55), also in New York, the title-role of *Zuleika* (57), Leni in *Altona* (61) and Beatrice in *The Four Seasons* (65). On Broadway, played Ellie in *Heartbreak House* (59) and Marie-Paule in *The Good Soup* (60). Recent parts have included Nastasya in *The Idiot* (70) at the National.

CLAIRE, INA (1892–). American actress and beauty who was impersonating Harry Lauder in 1909 and starring in musical comedies in the next decade. Played Jerry in *The Gold Diggers* (19–21), and later parts included Mrs. Cheyney (25) and Marion in *Biography* (New York, 32; London, 34). Lady Elizabeth in *The Confidential Clerk* (54), a performance which moved John Mason Brown to call her the Comic Spirit incarnate.

CLARE, MARY (1894–1970). British actress, whose parts included Mary Fitton in *Will Shakespeare* (21), Tondeleyo in *White Cargo* (24), a famous performance in a now legendary play, and Jane Marryot in *Cavalcade* (31). Later parts included Ellen Creed in *Ladies in Retirement* (39, 41) and Almina in *Waiting in the Wings* (60).

CLARK, ERNEST (1912–). British actor, whose many West End parts have included Dr. Skillingworth in *Escapade* (53), which won him a Clarence Derwent award, Lewis Eliot in *The New Men* (62) and Sir Dymock in *The Jockey Club Stakes* (70). Currently President of Equity.

CLEMENTS, JOHN (1910–). British actor-manager whose achievements in the classics (see p. 90) and at Chichester have not dimmed his commercial career, which has included his founding and brilliantly running the Intimate Theatre, Palmers Green (35–40), and his Elyot in *Private Lives* (44) opposite his wife, Kay Hammond (see below). His modern parts have included Henry in *The Happy Marriage* (52) which he presented, and Arthur in Norman King's fine *The Shadow of Doubt* (55) which he also presented. Heracles in *The Rape of the Belt* (57), Charles in *Gilt and Gingerbread* (58), Paul in *The Marriage-Go-Round* (59), Sir Lewis in *The Affair* (61), Colin Elliot in *The Tulip Tree* (62), Paul in *The Masters* (63) and Edward Moulton Barrett in *Robert and Elizabeth* (64). Knighted (68).

COBB, LEE J. (1911–). American actor. Joined the Group Theater in 35 when his many roles included Papa Buonaparte and Mr. Carp in *Golden Boy*. The latter part in London (38). The creator of Willie Loman in *Death of a Salesman* (49). A distinguished film actor.

COLBERT, CLAUDETTE (1905–). American actress and a Broadway favourite of the 20s. Film stardom followed, since when her stage parts have included Hedda in *The Irregular Verb to Love* (63).

COLE, GEORGE (1925–). British actor who, his film and TV appearances apart, is best known for his many Bridie performances since his Cohen in *Mr. Bolfry* (43). George Tesman in *Hedda Gabler* (64), Sergeant Fielding in *Too True to be Good* (65). At the time of writing (72), starring in *The Philanthropist*.

COMPTON, FAY (1895–). British actress (also see p. 91). Her most famous non-classical parts have included Mary Rose (20), the Lady in *The Man with a Load of Mischief* (25), Fanny in *Autumn Crocus* (31), Ruth in *Blithe Spirit* (41), Regina in *The Little Foxes* (42), the Virgin Mary in *Family Portrait*, etc.

COOPER, GLADYS (1888–1971). British actress. From her days as a chorus girl and picture postcard queen, she graduated to become the highly efficient artist she remained on both sides of the Atlantic on stage and in films. Two of her most famous roles were Mrs. Cheyney in *The*

Last of Mrs. Cheyney (25) and Leslie Crosbie in *The Letter* (27). Later performances included Felicity in *Relative Values* (51) and Mrs. St. Maugham in *The Chalk Garden* (New York, 55; London, 56, for three weeks). She was also Peter Pan, a New York Desdemona (35) and a Regent's Park Rosalind and Oberon (38). D.B.E.

COOPER, MELVILLE G. (1896–). Anglo-American actor. The first Trotter in *Journeys End* (28–9), his Broadway roles have included Doolittle in *Pygmalion* (45) and Pickering in *My Fair Lady* (59), etc.

CORNELL, KATHARINE (1898–). American actress and a major figure in the American theatre for many years. After an early success as Jo in *Little Women* (19), played Sydney in *A Bill of Divorcement* (21), and another great success was her Iris in *The Green Hat* (25). Two of her most famous roles have been Elizabeth in *The Barretts of Wimpole Street* (31 and revivals) and Candida (24 and revivals). At the height of the Depression (33–34) she toured 75,000 miles with these parts, as well as playing Juliet. A less fortunate assumption was her later Cleopatra. Perhaps the 30s was her finest period during which she and her husband, the director GUTHRIE MCCLINTIC (see p. 49), did so much to raise the standards of the American theatre. To this period belong her St.

Joan, Linda in *No Time for Comedy*, Elsa in *Alien Corn*, as well as those performances listed above, but her whole career, like that of Helen Hayes, has shown a devotion to the theatre which, for whatever reason, no longer exists on Broadway. Many of her greatest successes were directed by her husband.

COTTEN, JOSEPH (1905–). American actor. With Welles's Mercury Theater (37–8). C. K. Dexter Haven in *The Philadelphia Story* (39). Linus Larrabee Jnr. in *Sabrina Fair* (53), etc., and many major film roles.

COWARD, NÖEL (1889–1973). British master entertainer, whose achievements are scattered through this book. Acted in many of his own plays, including Nicky in *The Vortex* (24), Elyot in *Private Lives* (30) and Gary Essendine in *Present Laughter* (42), also in many films. Knighted (70).

CROMWELL, JOHN (1887–). American actor, producer and director of plays and films, whose long Broadway career included John Gray in *Point of No Return* (51) which won him a 'Tony' award.

CRONYN, HUME (1911–). Canadian-born actor whose many Broadway parts have included Michael in *The Fourposter* (51), etc. Played Jimmie in *Big Fish, Little Fish* (New York, 61; London, 62). His Polonius in

Gielgud's production of *Hamlet* (64) won him a 'Tony' and his parts at the Tyrone Guthrie Theater, Minneapolis, have included Richard III, Harpagnon in *The Miser* (65), etc. Married to Jessica Tandy, see below and previous chapter.

CUKA, FRANCES (1936–). British actress. The first Josephine in *A Taste of Honey* (58). Becky Sharp in *Vanity Fair* (62). Recent parts have included Ellen in *Silence* and Mrs. Foran in *The Silver Tassie* (69) for the Royal Shakespeare Co.

CULVER, ROLAND (1900–). British actor. His many films apart, his best-known roles have been the Commander in *French Without Tears* (36), William Collyer in *The Deep Blue Sea* (52) and Stanley Harrington in *Five Finger Exercise* (London, 58; New York, 59). Lebedev in *Ivanov* (65). His son is the actor, MICHAEL CULVER.

CUSACK, CYRIL (1910–). Irish actor and manager, who has played many leading parts in O'Casey, Shaw, O'Neill etc. in Ireland and Britain, including Dubedat at the Haymarket (42). Has played Christy in *The Playboy* in London (39) presented the play in Paris (54) and presented the première of *The Bishop's Bonfire* (O'Casey) at the Gaiety (55). The title role in *Hadrian VII* at the Abbey (69). Has played Romeo and Hamlet and, for the Royal Shakespeare

Co., Cassius and Johan Stettler in *The Physicists* (63). His daughter is the actress, SINEAD CUSACK.

DENISON, MICHAEL (1915–). British actor who has appeared with his wife, DULCIE GRAY (1919–) in many plays, including *The Fourposter* (52) and *Where Angels Fear to Tread* (63). Sir Andrew and Bertram at Stratford (55), and, more recently, with his wife, has toured widely in revivals of *A Village Wooing*, *The Clandestine Marriage*, *Dandy Dick*, etc. Both appeared in London in *Out of the Question* (68) and *The Wild Duck* (70). Miss Gray is a successful thriller writer.

DENNIS, SANDY (1937–). American actress who won 'Tonys' for her Sandra in *A Thousand Clowns* (62) and Ellen in *Any Wednesday* (64). Other parts have included Teresa in *How the Other Half Loves* (71). Won an Oscar for her Honey in *Who's Afraid of Virginia Woolf?*

DEWHURST, COLEEN. American actress who, via off-Broadway, has established herself as one of the finest younger performers in the States. Her successes have included Mary Follet in *All the Way Home* (60), Amelia in *The Ballad of the Sad Café* (63) and Sara in *More Stately Mansions* (67). Classical parts include Lady Macbeth, Cleopatra and Mrs. Squeamish in *The Country*

Wife. Played Shen Teh in *The Good Woman of Setzuan* (70).

DOBIE, ALAN. British actor, Old Vic, London and Bristol (53–7), since when his parts have included Col in *Live Like Pigs* (58), Bernard Ross in *No Concern of Mine* (58), Capt. Morgan in *The Rough and Ready Lot* (59) Private Hurst in *Sergeant Musgrave's Dance* at the Royal Court (59), Macbeth at Ludlow (61), Donald Howard in *The Affair* (61) and Becket in *Curtmantle* (62). Later parts have included Corporal Hill in *Chips with Everything* (63), Bill Maitland in *Inadmissible Evidence* (65), Captain Delano in *Benito Cereno* (67) and Henri Perrin in *The Hallelujah Boy* (70).

DONALD, JAMES (1917–). British actor. The original Ronald Maule in *Present Laughter* (43) and Billy in *This Happy Breed* (43). Later parts have included Valentine in *You Never Can Tell* (47), Morris in *The Heiress* (49), the title-role in *Captain Carvallo* (50), Richard in *The Dark is Light Enough* (54), David in *Write Me a Murder* (New York, 61) and Sir Colenso Ridgeon in *The Doctor's Dilemma* (63).

DONLAN, YOLANDE. American actress whose Billie Dawn in *Born Yesterday* (46) and Myrtle in *To Dorothy, A Son* (50), were major hits in the West End.

DOUGLAS, MELVYN (1901–).

American actor. Only known to British audiences as a fine film actor, his long Broadway career culminated in his performance as William Russell in Gore Vidal's *The Best Man* (60) for which he won a 'Tony' award.

DOUGLAS, ROBERT (1909–). British actor and director who has also acted and directed in New York and appeared in Hollywood films. His most famous role was Colin Derwent in *Ten Minute Alibi* (33).

DOWLING, EDDIE (1894–). American actor, director and dramatist. Joe in *The Time of Your Life* (39), which he also directed. Directed the famous first production of *The Glass Menagerie* (45) and played the Son. This ex-cabin boy's notable Broadway career also included directing *The Iceman Cometh* (46).

DRESDEL, SONIA. British actress. After acting with the Old Vic, was a striking Hedda (42, 43), then had a huge success as Olivia in *This Was a Woman* (44). A superb Nurse Wayland in *The Sacred Flame* (45). More recent parts have included Christine in *Mourning Becomes Electra* at the Old Vic (61), Varvara in *The Possessed* (63) and Jocasta (65) at the Mermaid, and Georgiana Tidman in *Dandy Dick* (65).

DU MAURIER, GERALD (1873–1934). English actor and leading exponent of underplaying in his time, the difference between himself and many of his imitators being that he was an immaculate performer. The original Captain Hook (04), which was not underplayed. His most famous roles included Bulldog Drummond (21) and Lord Dilling in *The Last of Mrs. Cheyney* (25). Also a leading actor-manager and director, especially at Wyndham's, 1910–25. A remarkable biography of him, *Gerald* was written by his daughter, Daphne du Maurier. Knighted (22).

DUNNOCK, MILDRED. American actress whose most famous role has been the original Linda in *Death of a Salesman* (49). Big Mama in *Cat on a Hot Tin Roof* (55). Has appeared at Stratford, Conn. (56) as Constance, and in Montreal as Mary Tyrone in *Long Day's Journey into Night* (59). Vera in *The Milk Train Doesn't Stop Here Any More* (Spoleto, 62; New York, 63). Madame Renaud in *Traveller Without Luggage* (64). Since then her parts have included Amanda Wingfield in *The Glass Menagerie* and Sido in *Collette* (70).

ELLIOTT, DENHOLM (1922–). British actor whose parts have included two award-winning performances, his Edgar in *Venus Observed* (49) winning a Clarence Derwent award and, in New York, his twins in *Ring Round the Moon* (50) which won him a Donaldson award. His

other parts have included Colly in *The Confidential Clerk* (53) and Bassanio, Troilus and Valentine at Stratford (60). A recent West End success was in the Mortimer quartet, *Come As You Are* (70). Has been notably successful in supporting roles in films and has toured America with the National Rep Theater as Trigorin, and Rev. John Helm in *The Crucible* (63). Playing for A.N.T.A. his parts included Cornelius Melody in *The Touch of the Poet* (67).

EPSTEIN, ALVIN (1925–). American actor and mime whose parts have included a superb Lucky in *Waiting for Godot* (56).

EVANS, EDITH (1888–). British actress for whose classical career see p. 96. The commercial successes of this magnificent actress and major star have included her Irela in *Evensong* (London, 32; New York, 33), Gwenny, the Welsh maid, in *The Late Christopher Bean* (33), Sanchia Carson in *Robert's Wife* (37), Lady Pitts in *Daphne Laureola* (London, 49; New York, 50), Helen Lancaster in *Waters of the Moon* (51), a superb portrait of a dominating woman, the Countess in *The Dark is Light Enough* (54) and Mrs. St. Maugham in *The Chalk Garden* (56), also Mrs. Forest in *The Chinese Prime Minister* (65). D.B.E. (46).

EVANS, JESSIE (1918–). British actress whose wide range of parts has included Miriam in

The Keep (61), which won her a Clarence Derwent award, and The Wife of Bath in *The Canterbury Tales* (68).

EVANS, MAURICE (1901–). British-born American actor for whose distinguished classical career see p. 97. The original Raleigh in *Journey's End* (28, for the Stage Society; 29 at the Savoy). His many commercial roles in America include Andrew Crocker-Harris in *The Browning Version*, Arthur Gosport in *Harlequinade* (49) and Tony Wendice in *Dial 'M' for Murder* (52), also H. J. in *The Aspern Papers* (62).

EWELL, TOM (1909–). American actor whose Broadway comedy successes include Richard Sherman in *The Seven Year Itch* (52), Augie Poole in *The Tunnel of Love* (57), the revue *The Thurber Carnival* (New York, 60; London, 62) and Edward T. Wellspot in *Xmas in Las Vegas* (65). Four parts in *You Know I Can't Hear You When the Water's Running* (London, 68).

FERRER, JOSÉ (1912–). Puerto Rican-born American actor and director (also see p. 97). His classical performances apart, his roles have included Victor d'Alcala in *Key Largo* (39), Jerry Walker in *Let's Face It* (43), Oscar Jaffe in *Twentieth Century* (51) and Jim Downs in *The Shrike* which he also directed (52, 54), and the title-role in *Edwin Booth* (58). Starred in *The*

Girl Who Came to Supper (63). Plays directed include *Stalag 17* (51) and *The Andersonville Trial* (60). Has appeared in many films and in opera and ballet!

FFRANGCON-DAVIES, GWEN (1896–). British actress and singer (see also page 98), whose first great success was as Etain in *The Immortal Hour* (20 and revivals). Among her many non-classical roles have been Elizabeth Moulton-Barrett in *The Barretts of Wimpole Street* (30), Anne of Bohemia in *Richard of Bordeaux* (32), Mary Stuart in *Queen of Scots* (34), Mrs. Manningham in *Gaslight* (39), Lucia in *Charley's Aunt* (54), Mrs. Callifer in *The Potting Shed* (58) and most memorably, Mary Tyrone in *Long Day's Journey into Night* (58) for which she won an *Evening Standard* award (59). Amanda Wingfield in *The Glass Menagerie* (65).

FIELD, BETTY (1918–). American actress whose many Broadway appearances have included one particularly memorable performance as Georgiana Allerton in *Dream Girl* (45). Mme. Arkadina in *The Seagull* (56), Mlle de St. Euverte in *The Waltz of the Toreadors* (58). Later parts have included Mrs. Amis in *Strange Interlude* (62) and Amanda Wingfield (Boston, 64). Mrs. Bigelow in William Inge's *Where's Daddy?* (66).

FINCH, PETER (1916–). Australian actor who made a very

successful London debut as Ernest Piaste in *Daphne Laureola* (49). Professor Winke in *Captain Carvallo* (50), Papa in *The Happy Time* (52), Jerry Ryan in *Two for the Seesaw* (58), Trigorin in *The Seagull* (64). His staccato Iago opposite Welles (51) was as unmemorable as his Mercutio at the Old Vic (52) was superbly vigorous, a Renaissance man on the spree. Also played M. Beaujolais in *An Italian Straw Hat* (52). A major film actor.

FINNEY, ALBERT (1936–). British actor (also see p. 98). His non-classical parts include Ted in *The Lily-White Boys* at the Royal Court (60), the title-role in *Billy Liar* (60) and Martin Luther in *Luther* (London, 61; New York, 63). John Armstrong in *Armstrong's Last Goodnight* at Chichester and the National Theatre (65), where his other modern part was Harold Gorringe in *Black Comedy* (65). Played the title-role in Pirandello's *Henry IV* at Glasgow Citizens (63) and the husband in *Alpha-Beta* (72). A brilliant and inventive actor. His most famous film role has been as Tom Jones.

FITZGERALD, WALTER (1896–). British actor. A long West End career has included many strong performances, notably the Duke of Lamorre in *The Duke of Darkness* (42), Mr. Bolfry (43), Captain Hook (44), Sir Robert in *The Paragon* (48). A particularly fine Shotover in *Heart-*break House* (50). Father James in *The Living Room* (London, 53; New York, 54), Ulysses in *Tiger at the Gates* (London and New York, 55), Sir Hamish in *The Amorous Prawn* (59), Juror No. 4 in *Twelve Angry Men* (64).

FLEMYNG, ROBERT (1912–). British actor who has appeared in many West End leading parts including Kit (36) and Alan (49) in *French Without Tears*, Nigel in *The Guinea Pig* (46), Algernon in *The Importance of Being Earnest* (New York, 47), Rowlie in *People Like Us* (48), Philotas in *Adventure Story* (48), Edward in *The Cocktail Party* (New York, 50), David in *The Moon is Blue* (53), Rupert Forster in *Marching Song* (54), James Callifer in *The Potting Shed* (New York, 57). Has appeared in many films.

FONDA, HENRY (1905–). American actor. His first great stage success was as Dan Harrow in *The Farmer Takes a Wife* (34), soon after which he entered films to become a major star. Lieutenant Roberts in *Mister Roberts* on Broadway (48). Charles Gray in *Point of No Return* (51), Lieut. Greenwald in *The Caine Mutiny Court Martial* (54), Jerry Ryan in *Two for the Seesaw* (58), etc. The Stage Manager in *Our Town* (69). His daughter, JANE FONDA (1937–) has also appeared in New York: Madeline Arnold in *Strange Orchestra* (63), etc.

CTT–L

FONTANNE, LYNN. See LUNT, ALFRED.

FORBES, BRENDA (1909–). American actress whose best known part has been Wilson in *The Barretts of Wimpole Street*, with Katharine Cornell. Directed the play (65).

FORD, RUTH (1920–). American actress. With Orson Welles's Mercury Theater (37–8). A fine Estelle in *No Exit* (46). Mrs. Gowan Stevens in *Requiem for a Nun* (London, 57) Hattie in *Dinner at Eight* (66), etc.

FOSTER, BARRY. British actor. Parts have included Hank in *The Desperate Hours* (55), Cornelius Christian in *Fairy Tales of New York* (61), Ted in *The Private Ear* and Julian in *The Public Eye* (New York, 63), etc. Recent parts have included Stott in *The Basement* and Willy in *Tea Party* (70), also King John and Macbeth at Nottingham.

FRENCH, HAROLD (1897–). British actor and director, and author of the hugely enjoyable, *I Swore I Never Would*. Most famous part: Dick in *The Blue Lagoon* (20). Later turned to directing films and plays, including *French Without Tears* (36) and *Gilt and Gingerbread* (49), etc.

GABEL, MARTON (1912–). American actor, director and producer, and the Cassius, and Danton in *Danton's Death* (37–38), for Welles's Mercury Theater. Won a 'Tony' for his Basil Smythe in *Big Fish, Little Fish* (61), also the Critics award. Has presented plays on Broadway and in London. His wife is ARLENE FRANCIS, also with Welles, and later in many Broadway plays, including Dolly in *Once More with Feeling* (58), which her husband co-produced in New York and London.

GARFIELD, JOHN (1913–53). American actor of stage and screen, who made his name with the Group Theater, then achieved fame in Hollywood. Starred in *The Big Knife* (49) and in *Golden Boy* just before he died, sadly young.

GAZZARA, BEN (1930–). American actor. His Jocko de Paris in *End as a Man* (53), later filmed, won him major awards. Later parts have included Brick in *Cat on a Hot Tin Roof* (55), Johnny Pope in *A Hatful of Rain* (55), Edmund in *Strange Interlude* (63) and Gaston in *Traveller without Luggage* (64).

GEER, WILL (1902–). American actor whose long career has included Slim in *Of Mice and Men* (37), Mr. Mister in *The Cradle will Rock* (38) and many classical parts at Stratford. Conn. and elsewhere. Toured in readings from Mark Twain (60–62).

GIELGUD, JOHN (1904–). British actor. Though his incomparable classical career is dealt with on p. 99 and elsewhere, he cannot be left out of this chapter, having served as a West End leading man in his time: Coward's successor as Nicky in *The Vortex* (25), again Coward's successor as Lewis Dodd in *The Constant Nymph* (27), Inigo Jollifant in *The Good Companions* (31), Joseph Schindler in *Musical Chairs* (32), the year of his famous *Richard of Bordeaux*, and, proposing the famous toast, Nicholas in *Dear Octopus* (38). Two post-war successes of particular note were his Thomas Mendip in *The Lady's Not for Burning* (49) and Julian Anson in *A Day by the Sea* (53), though for some the Terry voice was almost too rich for so dry a character.

His many productions in the commercial theatre include *Strange Orchestra* (32), *Sheppey* (33), *The Glass Menagerie* (48), *The Heiress* (49), *Five Finger Exercise* (59) and *Private Lives* (72). Knighted (53).

GILBERT, LOU (1909–). American actor whose career in New York and elsewhere has included forming and running the Chicago Repertory Group (31–41).

GILFORD, JACK. American actor whose parts have included Mr. Dussel in *The Diary of Ann Frank* (55) and Herr Schutz in *Cabaret* (66).

GILLMORE, MARGALO (1897–).

British-born American actress, for many years a Broadway leading lady, her memorable performances including Sylvia in *The Famous Mrs. Fair* (19), Venice Pollen in *The Green Hat* (25) and Mary Haines in *The Women* (36). A distinguished player for the Theater Guild in the 30s. Appeared in London as Kate Keller in *All My Sons* (48), also Monica Breedlove in *The Bad Seed* (55) and Muriel Chadwick in *Roar Like a Dove* (58). Mrs. Van Mier in *Sail Away* (61).

GORDON, COLIN (1911–72). British actor. An excellent comedy actor, his first success was as Rupert Billings in *The Happiest Days of Your Life* (48), which won him a Clarence Derwent award. His Colonel Rinder-Sparrow in *The Love of Four Colonels* (51) was another gem. Recent parts included Thomas Empton in *Alibi for a Judge* (65) and Philip in *Relatively Speaking* (67). Many film and TV appearances.

GORDON, RUTH (1896–). American actress advised to avoid the stage by her drama director and lacking in obvious glamour, who has, nevertheless, enjoyed a brilliant career. Early successes included Bobby in *Saturday's Children* (27), a vivid Lily Malone in *Hotel Universe* (30) and her memorable gauche and plain Mattie in *Ethan Frome* (36). Her celebrated Mrs. Pinchwife followed (see p. 101). A later, much enjoyed perform-ance was her Mrs. Levi in *The Matchmaker* (London, 54; New York, 55). The husband of this very versatile and skilled actress is Garson Kanin (see p. 46), the playwright and director. She herself has written several plays, including *Over 21*, *Years Ago*, and *The Leading Lady*.

GOUGH, MICHAEL (1917–). Brit-ish actor whose first great suc-cess was in *Crime Passionel* (48). Julien in *Colombe* (51), Nicky in *The Vortex* (52), a very fine Gregers in *The Wild Duck* (55), the Stage Manager in *Six Characters in Search of an Author* (63). Theo in *Maigret and the Lady* (65) Dr. Parks in *Captain Oates' Left Sock* (69), etc.

GREENWOOD, JOAN (1921–). British actress whose delectably creamy voice and equally delec-table appearance, allied to comedy skill, have been seen to advantage in films and on stage in such roles as Gillian in *Bell, Book and Candle* (55) and Hattie in *The Grass is Greener* (58). The title-role in *Lysistrata* (57), another success. Has played both Peter Pan and Wendy, and, surprisingly to those who are unaware of her classical past, was an intense Hedda Gabler at Oxford (60), where she had earlier played Lady Teazle, Cleopatra and Nora in *A Doll's House*. An Old Wolfitian, play-ing Ophelia and Celia for him. Recent parts have included

Julia in *Fallen Angels* (67) and Miss Marigold in *The Chalk Garden* (70). Married to André Morell (see p. 121).

GRIMES, TAMMY (1934–). Am-erican actress and a Broadway star whose parts have included Lulu in *Look after Lulu* (59), Molly in *The Unsinkable Molly Brown* (60), which won her major awards, Elvira in *High Spirits* (64), and a scintillating performance as Amanda in *Private Lives* (69), which again won her awards.

GRIZZARD, GEORGE (1928–). American actor. His Broadway parts have included an award-winning performance as Hank Griffin in *The Desperate Hours* (55) and Nick in *Who's Afraid of Virginia Woolf?* (62). Jules Ros-enberg in *Inquest* (70). His classical parts have included major roles at the Guthrie Theater, Minneapolis: Hamlet, Henry V, Richard II and a par-ticularly fine Dauphin in *St. Joan* (64).

HAGEN, UTA (1919–). German-born American actress (also see p. 103). Her most famous non-classical parts include Blanche in *A Streetcar Named Desire* (48), succeeding Jessica Tandy and then touring, Georgie in *The Country Girl* (50) and Martha in *Who's Afraid of Virginia Woolf?* (New York, 62; London, 64).

HAGGARD, STEPHEN (1911–43).

British actor whose death in the Second World War robbed the theatre of what Agate called a 'charming *little* actor' who could play nervous emotion exquisitely. He called him 'a combination of scarecrow and eaglet'. His first great success was as Rene Latour in *The Laughing Woman* (34) which was followed by his gauche Glaswegian George in Bridie's *The Black Eye* (35). Later parts included a perfect Marchbanks and, finally, the Fool in the Old Vic's famous 1940 *Lear* in which his performance divided the critics, but now haunts the memory of all who saw it. Wrote the moving *I'll Go to Bed at Noon* for his two sons, which was published posthumously.

HAIGH, KENNETH. British actor and creator of Jimmy Porter in *Look Back in Anger* (London, 56; New York, 57). The title role in Camus's *Caligula* (New York, 60; London, 64), a powerful portrayal of a mad, logical monster. Jerry in *The Zoo Story* (London, 60). The Friend in *Playing with Fire* and James in *The Collection* for the Royal Shakespeare Co. (62), Mark Antony at Stratford (63), Patrick Casey in *Maggie May* (64), The Burglar in *Too True to be Good* (65), Laurie in *The Hotel in Amsterdam* (69). Has made a number of films and is a major TV star.

HAMMOND, KAY (1909–). British actress, whose seductive,

sugar-plum drawl of a voice, allied to fine comedy technique, made her a major star until ill-health halted her. Remembered especially for her Diana in *French Without Tears* (36), Elvira in *Blithe Spirit* (41) and Mrs. Sullen in *The Beaux' Stratagem* (49). The wife of John Clements (see p. 90) and mother of that fine actor John Standen.

HANCOCK, SHEILA. British actress who has played in revue, also Cyrenne in *The Rattle of a Simple Man* (62) Kath in *Entertaining Mr. Sloane* (New York, 65), Julia in *A Delicate Balance* (69), etc.

HANDL, IRENE (1901–). British actress and popular comedienne of stage, screen and TV, first attracting attention as Bear in *George and Margaret* (37).

HARDWICKE, CEDRIC (1893–1964). British actor whose career in Shakespeare and Shaw, etc. is discussed on p. 105. His West End parts included Churdles Ash in *The Farmer's Wife* (24), Richard in *Yellow Sands* (26), Captain Andy in *Show Boat* (28) and his famous Edward Moulton-Barrett in *The Barretts of Wimpole Street* (30). He appeared a number of times on Broadway, including the title-role in *The Amazing Doctor Clitterhouse* (37), and in some of his Shavian parts, and also directed there and toured. A notable success was his Koicni Asano in *A Majority of One* (59).

Few of his films did this very fine actor justice. Knighted (34).

HARE, ROBERTSON. See p. 228.

HARRIS, JULIE (1935–). American actress. An early success was in *Montserrat* (49) followed by her notable performance as Frankie in *The Member of the Wedding* (50). Sally Bowles in *I Am a Camera* (51), Joan of Arc in *The Lark* (55). Has played Juliet at Stratford, Ontario, also Blanche in *King John*. A versatile actress whose range extends from tragedy to farce, though British audiences only know her from delightful performances in films. Recent parts have included Ann Stanley in *Forty Carats* (68) which won her a 'Tony' award, and Mrs. Lincoln in *Last of Mrs. Lincoln* (72).

HARRIS, ROSEMARY (1930–). British actress, now a Broadway star (see also p. 106). Her non-classical parts have included the Girl in *The Seven Year Itch* (London, 53), Lennie in *The Tumbler* (New York, 60), Alice in *You Can't Take It With You* (New York, 65) and Eleanor in *The Lion in Winter* (66) which won her a 'Tony' award. Recent parts have included Karen, Muriel and Norma in *Plaza Suite* (London, 69) which won her an *Evening Standard* award, and Kate in *Old Times* (New York, 72).

HARRISON, KATHLEEN (1898–). British actress. This popular character star's successes have included Mrs. Miller in *Flare Path* (42), Violet in *The Winslow Boy* (46), Mrs. Ashworth in *Waters over the Moon* (51), the Nannie in *All for Mary* (54) and Cherry-May in *Nude With Violin* (56). Mrs. Frush in *Thark* (65). Has appeared in many films.

HARRISON, REX (1908–). British actor whose superb technique and crustily attractive personality have made him a major star since the first night of *French Without Tears* (36). Later successes have included Henry VIII in *Anne of a Thousand Days* (New York, 48), the Unidentified Guest in *The Cocktail Party* (London, 50), Shepherd Henderson in *Bell, Book and Candle* (New York, 50; London, 54), Hereward in *Venus Observed* (New York, 52), the definitive Henry Higgins in *My Fair Lady* (see p. 201) and Platanov at the Royal Court (60), which won him an *Evening Standard* award. Also at the Royal Court, Sir Augustus in *August for the People* (61). Has directed plays including *Bell, Book and Candle* (London) and *The Love of Four Colonels* (New York, 53) in which he played the Man. A film superstar.

HAVOC, JUNE (1916–). American actress. The original Gladys in *Pal Joey* (40), Sadie Thompson (44), etc. Director of the Repertory Theater, New Orleans (69), where she has directed *Streetcar Named Desire*, *The Skin of Our Teeth* (playing Sabina), etc.

HAYES, HELEN (1900–). Considered by many to be America's leading actress, she began on the stage at 5. Early successes included Polyanna (17) and Margaret in *Dear Brutus* (18), and later came Shaw's Cleopatra (25), Mary in Maxwell Anderson's *Mary of Scotland* (34) etc., and Victoria in *Victoria Regina* (35–8), a colossal triumph: 'Her masterpiece' wrote Brooks Atkinson. Post-war performances have included Amanda Wingfield in *The Glass Menagerie* (London, 48; New York, 56), the Duchess in *Time Remembered* (57) Nora Melody in *A Touch of the Poet* (58) and Mrs. Grant in *The Front Page* (69). She and James Stewart starred in a delightful revival of *Harvey* (70). As befits one who has done so much for the theatre, a Broadway theatre bears her name. Her husband was Charles MacArthur (see p. 49).

HECKART, EILEEN (1919–). American actress whose award winning performances have been Rosemary Sidney in *Picnic* (53), Mrs. Daigle in *The Bad Seed* (54) and Lottie Lacey in *The Dark at the Top of the Stairs* (57). Other parts have included Harriet, Edith and Muriel in *You Know I Can't Hear You When the Water's Running* (67). Has won two major TV awards.

HEPBURN, KATHERINE (1909–). American actress and major film star. Her most famous non-classical role has been Tracy Lord in *The Philadelphia Story* (37). Also see p. 107. The lead in *Coco* (69).

HICKS, SEYMOUR (1871–1946). British actor, director and dramatist. A famous comedian and man of the theatre who was one of the authors of London's first revue, *Under the Clock* (1893), who built the Aldwych and the Globe Theatres, and who opened the Garrick with his own adaptation from the French, *The Man in Dress Clothes* (22). A triumph in a serious role was the lead in Gladys Unger's *Edmund Kean* (11). Knighted (35). Books included *Twenty Years of an Actor's Life*. His beautiful wife, ELLALINE TERRISS (1871–1971) acted opposite him in many of his successes.

HILL, ARTHUR (1922–). Canadian actor whose parts have included Cornelius Hackl in *The Matchmaker* (London, 54; New York, 55) and George in *Who's Afraid of Virginia Woolf?* (New York, 62; London, 63) which won him major awards on Broadway.

HILLER, WENDY (1912–). British actress whose first major success was as Sally in *Love on the Dole* (35). Played St. Joan and Eliza Doolittle at the 1936 Malvern Festival, and amongst her other roles have been Tess of the D'Urbervilles (46), Ann Veronica (49) and Hermione and Portia at the Old Vic (55–6). Notably successful in emotional parts, including the frustrated Evelyn Daly in *Waters of the Moon* (51). Later parts have included Josie in *A Moon for the Misbegotten* (New York, 57), Isobel Cherry in *The Flowering Cherry* (London, 58; New York, 59), Miss Tina in *The Aspern Papers* (New York, 62) and Enid in *The Battle of Shrivings* (70). Played the leads in the films, *Major Barbara* and *Pygmalion*.

HOFFMAN, DUSTIN (1937–). American actor. After playing in Behan, Beckett, Pinter, etc. with the Theater Company of Boston (64), established himself by a series of Off-Broadway performances and in the title-role of *Jimmy Shine* (68). Now a major film actor.

HOLBROOK, HAL (1925–). American actor best known, since 1955, for his very fine *Mark Twain Tonight* one-man-shows, also for an excellent Lincoln in *Abe Lincoln in Illinois* (63). Other parts have included a vigorous Hotspur at Stratford, Conn. (62), Quentin in *After the Fall* (64) and Cervantes and Don Quixote in *Man of La Mancha* (68).

HOLM, CELESTE (1919–). American actress, the original Ado Annie in *Oklahoma!* (43). Other parts have included Mary L. in *The Time of Your Life* (39), Irene in *Affairs of State* (50), written for her by Louis Verneuil (50), Mame (68) and Candida (70). A very popular film star.

HOWARD, LESLIE (1893–1943). British actor, remembered today as a great romantic film star and by older Anglo-Americans as a stage actor and popular matinée idol. Two great successes were his André in *Her Cardboard Lover* (New York, 27; London, 28) and, especially, Peter Standish in *Berkeley Square* (29). Played Alan Squier in *The Petrified Forest* (New York, 35), which was to be one of his many screen roles (Romeo, Ashley in *Gone with the Wind*, etc.).

HUNTER, IAN (1900–). Popular South African-born stage and screen leading man from the early 20s. Post-war parts have included Edward Chamberlayne in *The Cocktail Party* (50), the Governor in *South Sea Bubble* (56), etc.

HUNTLEY, RAYMOND (1904–). British actor, well known on stage and screen. Parts have included Alan in *Time and the Conways* (37), Henry Martin in *The Late Edwina Black* (49), Manning in *The Shadow of Doubt* (55) and the Earl of Caversham in *An Ideal Husband* (66), etc.

HUSTON, WALTER (1884–1950). Canadian-born American actor

among whose many fine performances were his old Eben in *Desire under the Elms* (24), the title-role in *Mr. Pitt* (24) and Lewis Dodsworth in Sidney Howard's *Dodsworth* (34), Was a joy in *Knickerbocker Holiday* (38) of 'September Song' fame. Known in Britain for many superb film performances. The father of JOHN HUSTON.

HYDE-WHITE, WILFRID (1903–). British actor who came into his own after the war as a superb light comedian with a cheerful, knowing personality. Very popular in films, his stage parts have included Jimmy Broadbent in *The Reluctant Debutante* (London, 55; New York, 56), probably his most famous role. Henry in *Hippo Dancing* (54), Andrew Bennett in *Not in the Book* (58), etc., and two Shavian gems, Brittanus for Olivier (London and New York, 51) and Sir Ralph Bloomfield-Bonnington (63). Currently (73) starring in *The Jockey Club Stakes* in New York.

JACKSON, FREDA (1909–). British actress whose parts have ranged from Lucy in *The Country Wife* (Old Vic, 36), leads at Stratford (40–41) to Mrs. Hitchcock in *Sergeant Musgrave's Dance* (59) and Maria in *When We Are Married* (70). Her most famous—and striking—performance was as Mrs. Voray in *No Room at the Inn* (45).

JAFFE, SAM (1893–). American actor. A long and distinguished career in modern and classical plays, also films. Yudelson in *The Jazz Singer* (25), Kringelein in *Grand Hotel* (30). Co-founder of the Equity Library Theater (44) Tartuffe is, perhaps, his most famous classical role.

JEANS, ISABEL (1891–). British actress. Her incomparable style is discussed p. 112. Her many commercial parts have included Zelie in *The Rat* (24), Victoria in *Home and Beauty* (42), the Countess in *Ardèle* (51), Florence Lancaster in *The Vortex* (52), Lady Elizabeth in *The Confidential Clerk* (53) and Mme. Desmortes in *Ring Round the Moon* (68).

JENKINS, MEGS (1917–). British actress. Parts have included Fan in *The Light of Heart* (40), Bet in *The Wind of Heaven* (45), Miss Mathieson in *A Day by the Sea* (London, 53, New York, 55), Beatrice in *A View from the Bridge* (56), which won her a Clarence Derwent award, May Godboy in *Dutch Uncle* (69) for the Royal Shakespeare Co. and Grace Winslow in *The Winslow Boy* (70). A popular character actress with a warm personality.

JOHNS, GLYNIS (1923–). British actress whose parts have ranged from appearances as a child, including Miranda in *Quiet Wedding* (38) to four roles in John Mortimer's *Come As You Are* (71). Other parts have included Peter Pan (43), Pam in

Fools Rush In (46) and Major Barbara (New York, 56). Has appeared in many films, as has her father, MERVYN JOHNS (1899–), the first Ernest Beevers in *Time and the Conways* (37) and a noted Shavian, including Shotover (43) and Doolittle (47).

JOHNSON, CELIA (1908–). British actress and a major star since the 30s, with an enormous following for her stage and screen performances. These have included Elizabeth Bennet in *Pride and Prejudice* (36), Sheila Broadbent in *The Reluctant Debutante* (55) and Hilary in *The Grass is Greener* (58). For her classical performances see p. 112.

JONES, EMRYS (1915–72). British actor whose starring parts included Teddy in *Flare Path* (43), Lachlen McLachlen in *The Hasty Heart* (45), Tony Wendice in *Dial 'M' for Murder* (52) and Sir George in *The Claimant* (64).

JONES, GRIFFITH (1910–). British actor. Regularly in the West End from the 30s, including Caryl Sanger in *Escape Me Never* (London, 33; New York, 35), Marco Polo in *Marco's Millions* (38), Lord Darlington in *Lady Windermere's Fan* (45), Robert in *Dead on Nine* (55) and the title-role in *The Home Secretary* (64). His daughter is the actress, GEMMA JONES (1942–), whose parts in London have included Adele in *The Cavern* (65), for which she won a

Clarence Derwent award, and Helen in *Howard's End* (67).

JONES, JAMES EARL (1931–). American actor whose performance as Jack Jefferson in *The Great White Hope* (68) won him a 'Tony' award. His classical parts have included a very striking Othello (64).

KENDALL, HENRY (1897–1962). British actor and director. A fine comedian who played in many commercial comedies between the wars and the occasional serious part—Major Chappel in *Havoc* (23/24). A leading revue artist in the 40s and a memorably distraught Harry Blacker in *On Monday Next* (49). From 1939 regularly directed West End comedies including the classic Philip King *See How They Run* (35). Wrote a delightful autobiography, *I Remember Romano's*. His brother WILLIAM KENDALL (1903–) is also a fine comedian.

KENNEDY, ARTHUR (1914–). American actor. His most famous roles have been Chris Keller in *All My Sons* (47) and Biff in *Death of a Salesman* (49). Another notable performance was as John Proctor in *The Crucible* (53). Played the title-role of *Becket* on tour and in New York (61) Walter in *The Price* (68). Has appeared in many films.

KENT, KENETH (1892–1963). British actor best known for two

famous performances, his Napoleon at the Old Vic in *St. Helena* (36) and Descius Heiss in *The Shop at Sly Corner* (44). At the Old Vic where he established himself as one of the leading character actors of the day, his parts included the Button-Moulder, Casca, Andrei in *The Three Sisters* and Sir Oliver in *The School for Scandal*, on which Audrey Williamson commented: 'I cannot imagine it bettered in any age'.

KING, DENNIS. See p. 211.

LANDON, AVICE (1910–). British actress, especially well known for her comedy performances. These have included her Sylvia in *Not in the Book* (58), which won her a Clarence Derwent award.

LANSBURY, ANGELA (1925–). British actress. Her Broadway parts have included Marcelle in *Hotel Paradise* (57), Helen in *A Taste of Honey* (60), Mame (66), which won her a 'Tony' award, the Countess in *Dear World* (69), which won her another. Has appeared in many pictures.

LAUGHTON, CHARLES (1899–1962). British actor. For his classical career see p. 116. Most of his finest achievements were in the commercial theatre and in a few films. First success: Frank Pratt in *The Happy Husband* (27). At this period he ranged from a Russian general and Hungarian tramp to a sadist in *The Man with Red Hair* (28), and from Hercule Poirot in *Alibi* to Harry Heegan, the footballer hero of O'Casey's *The Silver Tassie* (29), a triumph of miscasting. His Chicago gangster, Tony Perelli, in Wallace's *On The Spot* (31) and murderer in *Payment Deferred* (London and New York, 31) completed an astonishing range of performances which made him the finest character actor in Britain. Despite occasional later successes, and fame in films, he never reached these heights again, but he made history by playing an act of *Le Médicin Malgré Lui* in French at the Comédie Française, playing Sganerelle. His wife is the actress ELSA LANCHESTER, an Old Vic Ariel, who appeared with him in many films.

LAWRENCE, GERTRUDE (1898–1952). British superstar before the word was coined, in revue, musicals and plays (see also p. 212). Her most famous straight role was as Amanda in *Private Lives* (London, 30; New York, 31) with—in Coward's words—'witty quick-silver delivery of lines', its 'romantic quality tender and alluring.' Played opposite him in London and New York in *Tonight at 8.30* (36). A wonderful Eliza in *Pygmalion* (New York, 46). Made a triumphant return to Britain as Stella in *September Tide* (48). Starred in the film of *The Glass Menagerie*.

LAWSON, WILFRED (1900–66). British actor, one of the very finest of his generation, though his career was destroyed by drink. After a tough provincial grounding he made his name in the 30s as a Shavian, also as John Brown in *Gallows Glorious* (33), as James I in *The King's Pirate* (33) when it seemed to Trewin that the King was acting the part, and, perhaps finest of all, his powerful, haunting Walter Ormund in Priestley's *I Have Been Here Before* (37). His postwar parts, which still had moments of greatness, included the Captain in *The Father* (53), Korrianke in *The Devil's General* (53), the Cell Warder in *The Prisoner* (54). His Sidney Redlitch in *Bell, Book and Candle* was hilarious on some nights. Final performances, films and TV apart, included H. C. Curry in *The Rainmaker* (56), Sailor Sawnay in *Live Like Pigs* (58) and Sailor Mahan in *Cock-a-Doodle-Dandy* (59) both at the Royal Court, Luka in *The Lower Depths* (62), The Button-Moulder at the Old Vic (62).

LEE, BERNARD (1908–). British actor whose strong personality has been seen to advantage in many West End roles, including, most notably, A.B. Turner in *Seagulls over Sorrento* (50) and Dan Hilliard in *The Desperate Hours* (55). The 'M' of the Bond films.

LEECH, RICHARD (1922–). British actor whose parts have included Humphrey in *The Lady's Not For Burning* (49), Crestwell in *Relative Values* (51), Henry VIII in *A Man for All Seasons* (60) and Charles Dilke in *The Right Honourable Gentleman* (65).

LEGGATT, ALISON. British actress whose many West End appearances have included a number of parts in *Tonight at 8.30* (36), Lavinia in *The Cocktail Party* (50) and Mrs. Guzzard in *The Confidential Clerk* (Edinburgh and London 53). Played Mrs. Elliott in *Epitaph for George Dillon* (Royal Court and New York, 58), Mabel Groomkirby in *One Way Pendulum* (59), three parts in the triple-bill, *Lunch Hour* (61) and, among other Royal Court appearances, Lady Pliant in *The Double Dealer* (69).

LEHMANN, BEATRIX (1903–). British actress. An early success of this powerful actress was as Emily Brontë in *Wild Decembers* (33). Other notable performances have been as Stella in *Eden End* (36), Lavinia in *Mourning Becomes Electra* (37), in which she looked like 'a cistern full of coiled snakes' (Trewin), Abbie in *Desire under the Elms* (40). Later parts have included Ines in *Vicious Circle*, Portia, Isabella, the Nurse and Viola at Stratford (47), Mrs. Alving, the Mother in *Blood Wedding* and Mme. St. Pé in *The Waltz of the Toreadors* (56). The Vic's Lady Macbeth

(58) and a centenarian in *The Aspern Papers* (59). Recent parts have included Mrs. Spoker in *A Cuckoo in the Nest* (64), Maria Kabanova in *The Storm* at the National (66) and Aase in *Peer Gynt* at Chichester (69). Parts at Stratford (73) are to include the *Nurse*.

LEIGH, VIVIEN (1913–1967). British actress whose beauty was universally admired, but whose considerable acting talents were hotly debated, especially in Shakespeare (see p. 116). Will probably be best remembered for a superlative trio of performances in the 40s—Jennifer Dubedat in *The Doctor's Dilemma* (42), Sabina in *The Skin of our Teeth* (45) and Blanche du Bois in *A Streetcar Named Desire* (49). No account of her career can leave out her Scarlett O'Hara in the film *Gone With The Wind*.

LEIGHTON, MARGARET (1922–). British actress renowned for her portrayal of neurotic parts and a major star who is greatly talented, alluring and stylish (also see p. 116). Her non-classical parts have included Sheila in *An Inspector Calls* (46), Tracy Lord in *The Philadelphia Story* (49), Celia in *The Cocktail Party* (50), Lucasta in *The Confidential Clerk* (53) and the two roles, Mrs. Shankland and Miss Railton-Bell in *Separate Tables* (London, 54; New York, 56), Elaine Lee in *The Wrong Side of the Park* (60), Ellida in *The Lady*

From the Sea (61) and Hannah Jelkes in *The Night of the Iguana* (61), which won her a 'Tony' award as the best actress of the year. Since then, amongst other plays she has starred in *Cactus Flower* and *The Little Foxes* in New York and *Reunion in Vienna* at Chichester and in London (71).

LEONTOVITCH, EUGENIE (1900 –). Russian-born American actress and director whose parts have included Grusinskaia in *Grand Hotel* (30), the Archduchess in *Tovarich* (London, 35) and the Dowager Empress in *Anastasia* (54) which won her a 'Tony' award. Mother Courage (Chicago, 64).

LISTER, MOIRA (1923–). South African-born actress whose career has included many modern and classical leading roles. Juliet, Desdemona, Olivia, etc. at Stratford (45), also Margaret in *Much Ado* and Regan there (55). Commercial parts have included Diana in *French Without Tears* (49), the Princess in *Love of Four Colonels* (51), Monica in *Birthday Honours* (53), Nell Nash in *The Gazebo*, Dorothy in *Any Wednesday* (65). Played Lesbia in *Getting Married* (67). A popular TV comedienne.

LIVESEY, ROGER (1906–). British actor, son of Sam Livesey. Possessor of great charm and a rich distinctive voice, his West End successes have included

Hsieh-Ping-Kuei in *Lady Precious Stream* (34), Frank in *Storm in a Teacup* (London, 36: New York, 37), Lt.-General Banbury in *The Banbury Nose* (44), Hoederer in *Crime Passionel* (48). His Old Vic parts have included Petruchio (39) and a Falstaff (50) in *The Merry Wives* which almost lifted the part to Henry IV levels.

His wife is the delightful actress URSULA JEANS (1906–) who has often acted opposite him in classical and commercial plays (see p. 112), and his brother is JACK LIVESEY (1901–) now an American, and a popular star of plays and musicals down the years.

LOCKWOOD, MARGARET (1916 –). British actress and the most popular female film star of British cinema in the late 40s, later a very popular TV star. Her stage successes have included a down-to-earth Peter Pan (49, 50, 57), Clarissa in *Spider's Web* (54), Sally in *Signpost to Murder* (62) and Mrs. Cleverley in *An Ideal Husband* (65). Her daughter, JULIA LOCKWOOD, now a star in her own right, has been one of the supreme Peter Pans.

LÖHR, MARIE (1890–). British actress. The career of this Australian-born actress has ranged from touring with the Kendals (02) to Lady Mortlake in *The World of Paul Slickey* (59). Played Mrs. Darling for five seasons and an astonishing

number of aristocrats. One of her finest performances was as Margery Battle in Maugham's *The Breadwinner* (30). Played Mrs. Whitefield in *Man and Superman* (65).

LORAINE, ROBERT (1876–1935). British romantic actor who began with Tree and Alexander, then, as Hesketh Pearson has said, went 'Shaw mad', directing *Man and Superman* in New York and playing John Tanner, adding Don Juan at the Royal Court (07) and, later, Bluntschli. After war service with the RFC, returned to make a huge success in the title part of *Cyrano de Bergerac* (19) which he later revived (27). Other romantic parts included the dual roles in *The Prisoner of Zenda*; but Loraine could subdue his romantic panache in his Tanner, also for Adolph in *The Father* (27).

LORD, PAULINE (1890–1950). American actress who triumphed as Anna in *Anna Christie* (21). Other great successes were her Amy in *They Knew What they Wanted* (25) and Zenobia in *Ethan Frome* (36).

LUNT, ALFRED (1892–). American actor and LYNN FONTANNE (1887–), English-born American actress. A husband-and-wife partnership whose technique has been the delight and despair of professionals and the joy of audiences from the time of their marriage in 1922. Most of their finest work has been in comedy, notably Behrman, Coward and Sherwood, sometimes in lesser material, but serious plays have included— for the Theater Guild—*The Brothers Karamazov, Ned Mc-Cobb's Daughter, Marco's Millions* between 1925–29, and, later, *There Shall Be No Night* (New York, 40: London, 43) and Dürrenmatt's *The Visit* (New York, 58; London, 60). Fontanne left London for the States in 1916, but has often returned. Brooks Atkinson considered her the finest of all Elizas. Lunt has been a distinguished director, and, in a period when Broadway was dominated by remarkable actresses, the only outright male star.

LYEL, VIOLA (1900–72). British actress whose many comedy parts in the West End and in the classics included her famous Miss Gossage (Call me Sausage) in *The Happiest Days of Your Life* (48).

MCANALLY, RAY (1926–). Irish actor. With the Abbey (47–63) where his parts included Christy in *The Playboy*, etc. George in *Who's Afraid of Virginia Woolf?* (London, 64). Lopakhin in *The Cherry Orchard* at Chichester (66). For the Royal Shakespeare Co., Quentin in *After the Fall* and Lawyer in *Tiny Alice* (70).

MCDOWELL, RODDY (1928–). British actor who, after acting

with Lassie, etc., has played many parts on Broadway, including Daventry in *Escapade* (53), Tarquin in *The Fighting Cock* (60), etc., also Ariel and Octavius at Stratford, Conn. Mordred in *Camelot* (60).

MACGOWRAN, JACK (1918–73). Irish actor, notable for his work in O'Casey, Beckett, etc., including Clovin *End-Game* (Aldwych, 64) and Lucky in *Godot* (Royal Court, 64).

MACGRATH, LEUEEN (1914–). British actress. In the West End from 1933, her parts have included the title role in *Young Mrs. Barrington* (45), Eileen Percy in *Edward, My Son* (London, 47; New York, 48), Sara in *The Potting Shed* (New York, 57), Peony Povis in *Farewell, Farewell Eugene* (New York, 60) and Lady Nelson in *A Bequest to the Nation* (70).

MACNAUGHTAN, ALAN (1920–). British actor. His career has included Scythrop Glowry in *Nightmare Abbey* (52), Max in *Dial 'M' for Murder* (52), leads in *Tonight at 8.30* (70–71 at Hampstead and the Fortune) and a Sir Oliver in *The School for Scandal* for the National (72), which could not have been bettered, followed by a fine Walter Burns in *The Front Page*.

MAGEE, PATRICK. Irish actor. Hamm in *Endgame* (Paris, 63; London, 64). For the Royal Shakespeare Co., as well as

Hamm, has played McCann in *Afore Night Come*, de Sade in *Marat-Sade* (London and New York, 65), winning a 'Tony' award, Harry in *Staircase*, etc. Since then, parts have included Inspector Hawkins in *Dutch Uncle* (69) and Mark in *The Battle of Shrivings* (70).

MARCH, FREDERIC (1897–). American actor famous on stage and screen. Mr. Antrobus in *The Skin of our Teeth* (42) and the first James Tyrone in *Long Day's Journey into Night* (56), which won him the New York Critics award for the year's finest performance. His wife FLORENCE ELDRIDGE (1901–) has often acted with him, and in *Long Day's Journey* played Mary Tyrone and was awarded the equivalent female accolade.

MASSEY, RAYMOND (1896–). Canadian actor (also see p. 119). Highlights of his fine non-classical career have included Harry Van in *Idiot's Delight* (London, 38), Abraham Lincoln in *Abe Lincoln in Illinois* (New York, 40) and Mr. Zuss in *J.B.* (58). Has appeared in many films. ANNA MASSEY (1937–) and DANIEL MASSEY (1933–) are his talented children, by his second wife, ADRIENNE ALLEN (1907–), the first Sybil in *Private Lives* (30). Anna Massey was the first *Reluctant Debutante* (London, 55; New York, 56). Since her Annie Sullivan in *The Miracle Worker* (61) has played a wide range of parts.

MATTHAU, WALTER (1920–). American actor. Before becoming a major film actor in the 60s, appeared in many Broadway successes including Michael Freeman in *Will Success Spoil Rock Hunter?* (55), Benjamin Beaurevers in *A Shot in the Dark* (61), which won him a 'Tony' award, and Oscar Madison in *The Odd Couple* (65), which won him another 'Tony' and the New York critics award. A fine comedian of range.

MATTHEWS, A. E. (1869–1960). British light comedian renowned for audience appeal and ad-libbing, usually to great effect— whatever some of his colleagues may have reasonably felt, to say nothing of his authors. In the 80s, was playing in *In The Ranks*, *Held by the Enemy*, etc., also in Pinero farces. His most famous modern part was the Earl of Lister in *The Chiltern Hundreds* (47), *Yes M'Lord* on Broadway, and in its sequel, *The Manor of Northstead* (54). Wrote an autobiography, *Matty*, and appeared in many films.

MEREDITH, BURGESS (1908–). American actor. His first great success was Red Barry in *Little Ol' Boy* (33). Mio in Maxwell Anderson's *Winterset* (35), the part being written for him. After the war, became a director. Conceived and staged *Ulysses in Nighttown* (New York, 58: London and Paris, 59). Staged *Thurber's Carnival* (60), which he also conceived. Parts since the war have included Pa in *The Remarkable Mr. Pennypacker* (53) and Eric in O'Neill's *Hughie* (London, 63). Directed *Blues for Mr. Charlie* (New York, 64; London, 65). Has appeared in many films.

MERRALL, MARY. British actress whose West End career stretches from the chorus in *My Mimosa Maid* (08) to many leading parts since the war, including a brilliant performance as the embittered Tilly Cuff in *The Foolish Gentlewoman* (49). The title-role in *Ellen* at Hampstead Theatre Club (71).

MICHAEL, RALPH (1907–). British actor whose parts have included Philip Brooke-Jervaux in *Love Goes to Press* (London, 46; New York, 47), Max in *The Seventh Veil* (51), Christian Melrose in *Saint's Day* (51), the Father in *Six Characters in Search of an Author* (54) and Lafeu, Bassianus in *Titus* and Banquo at Stratford (55). Since then his parts in modern and classical plays have included Theodore in *Guilty Party* (63) and Serebryakov in *Uncle Vanya* (Royal Court, 70).

MILLER, JOAN (1910–). Canadian actress, wife of Peter Cotes (see p. 35), who has given a number of memorably powerful and emotional performances, including Miss Julie (49), Karen in *The Children's Hour* (51), Julia in *A Pin to see the Peepshow* (London, 52; New York, 53),

etc. Her classical parts have included Candida and, at Stratford (57), Constance and Portia. Among recent parts have been Lucy Amorest in *The Old Ladies* (69).

MILLS, JOHN (1908–). British actor and a major film star for many years. After working in musicals in the 30s, and playing Puck, etc., for the Vic (39), his parts included George in *Of Mice and Men* (39), Lew in *Men in Shadow* (45) and Stephen in *Duet for Two Hands* (45), both by his wife, MARY HAYLEY BELL. Later parts have included Bertie in *Top of the Ladder* (50) Freddie in *Figure of Fun* (51), Lord Fancourt Babberley in *Charley's Aunt* (54) and the title-role in *Ross* on Broadway (61). D'Orsay in *Veterans* at the Royal Court (72). His daughters are the actresses JULIET MILLS and HAYLEY MILLS.

MOLLISON, CLIFFORD (1897–). British actor who has played in many West End plays, farces and musicals, including a long run as Nicki in *Balalaika* (36).

MORE, KENNETH (1914–). British actor famous for his comedy technique and equally successful in serious roles. Natural talent, infectious charm, 'feeding' at the Windmill and a grounding in pre-war Rep, some of it rugged, have contributed to this success. Made his name with his superb Freddie Page in *The Deep Blue Sea* (52) and the film *Genevieve*

(53). Recent parts have included the leads in *The Secretary Bird* (69) and *Getting On* (71). Known to countless millions of viewers throughout the world for his young Jolyon in *The Forsyte Saga*.

MORLEY, ROBERT (1908–). British actor of dominating presence, possibly the ultimate personality actor of our time. For all his fame in comedy roles, he will probably be best remembered—films apart—as George IV in Norman Ginsbury's *The First Gentleman* (45) and as Arnold Holt in *Edward, My Son* by himself and Noel Langley (47). Recently enjoyed yet another long run in Alan Ayckbourn's *How the Other Half Loves*. His son, SHERIDAN MORLEY, edits Hutchinson's excellent Theatre annuals and has written a biography of Coward.

MORRIS, MARY (1895–1970). American actress. Abbie in *Desire Under the Elms* (24). With the Civic Repertory, the Guild and the Group Theater. Victoria Van Bret in *Double Door* (33). A strong actress, she played Judith in *Granite* (36) and Mrs. Smith in *Suspect* (London, 37). Later roles included Volumnia and Tamora in *Titus Andronicus*.

MORRIS, MARY (1915–). British actress who has given many striking performances. Her parts have included Kathy in *Wuthering Heights* (43), Abigail in *Duet for Two Hands* (45), Peter Pan

(46), Elizabeth in *The Young Elizabeth* (52), the Step-Daughter in *Six Characters in Search of an Author* (54) and Lavinia in *Mourning Becomes Electra* (55).

MORTON, CLIVE (1904–). British actor who has played many major supporting parts in the West End and leads including George Kettle in *Mr. Kettle and Mrs. Moon* (55). Stratford (64), where his parts included Talbot in *The Wars of the Roses*. His wife, FRANCES ROWE (1913–) played Ann Whitefield in a record-breaking run of *Man and Superman* on Broadway (47) and, amongst other parts, played Alex in *Who Goes There?* (51) which won her a Clarence Derwent award.

MOUNT, PEGGY (1916–). British actress for whose sensational leap to stardom in *Sailor, Beware!* (55) see p. 225. Other parts have included the Nurse in *Romeo* at the Old Vic (60), Mrs. Spicer in *Mother's Boy* (64), Dame Daphne Winkworth in *Oh, Clarence!* (68) and Clara Soppitt in *When We Are Married* (70).

MONRO, NAN (1905–). South African-born British actress who has played many major supporting parts in the West End and leads in South Africa. Julia in *The Cocktail Party* (Chichester and London, 68).

MURPHY, ROSEMARY (1927–). American actress whose parts have included Claire in *A Delicate Balance* (66) which won her a New York Critics award.

NARES, OWEN (1888–1943). Very popular British matinée idol, so much so that his considerable ability was often overlooked. Two of his famous parts were Robert in *Robert's Wife* (37) and Max de Winter in *Rebecca* (40).

NATWICK, MILDRED (1908–). American actress whose parts on Broadway have included Madame Arcati in *Blithe Spirit* (42) and Mrs. Banks in *Barefoot in the Park* (New York, 63; London, 65). Mrs Gibbs in *Our Town* (69).

NAZIMOVA, ALLA (1879–1945). American actress. This Russian-born stage and screen star was for many the finest actress to appear in New York between the wars. Her most famous performance, none the worse for being accented, were in Ibsen, Chekhov and O'Neill, Mme. Ranevskaya being one of her greatest roles, and her performance as the Clytemnestra figure, Christine, with Alice Brady as Lavinia, in *Mourning Becomes Electra* (31) is now a theatre legend. John Mason Brown wrote of Nazimova's 'insidious and electric malevolence' in the part, 'brilliant with an incandescent fire'.

NELSON, BARRY. American actor whose parts have included Don in *The Moon is Blue* (51), Will in *No Time for Sergeants* (London, 56), Bob in *Mary, Mary* (61) and Richard in *Everything in the Garden* (67).

NESBITT, CATHLEEN (1889–). British actress whose career has been divided between Britain and America and the commercial and classical stage. Perdita for Granville Barker (12), Mabel in *Quinneys* (Liverpool and New York, 15). The first, beautiful Yasmin in *Hassan* (23). Later parts included Gertrude in an Old Vic tour of the Continent and Egypt (39), Mathilde in *The Shop at Sly Corner* (45), Julia in *The Cocktail Party* (New York, 50), Maude in *Sabrina Fair* (New York, 53; London, 54), Mrs. Higgins in *My Fair Lady* (56), The Grand Duchess in *The Sleeping Prince* (56), both in New York, also Julia in *Romulus* (62), The Dowager in *The Claimant* (London, 64).

NEWMAN, PAUL (1925–). American actor and film superstar whose Broadway parts included Alan in *Picnic* (53), Glenn in *The Desperate Hours* (55) and Chance Wayne in *Sweet Bird of Youth* (59). Emil in *Baby Want a Kiss* (64). Married to the very fine actress, JOANNE WOODWARD.

NIMMO, DEREK (1932–). British actor and comedian whose West End parts have included Hubert Shannon in *How Say You?* (59),

Private Willie Maltravers in *The Amorous Prawn* (59), Michael in *The Irregular Verb to Love* (61), Toop in *See How They Run* (64) and Nicholas Wainwright in *Charlie Girl* (65). A very popular TV star.

NOLAN, LLOYD (1902–). American actor and film star whose best known stage role has been Queeg in *The Caine Mutiny Court Martial* (New York, 54; London, 56) which won him the Donaldson and New York Drama Critics awards. He directed the play in London. An earlier success was Biff Grimes in *One Sunday Afternoon* (33).

NOVELLO, IVOR (1893–1951). British composer, dramatist and actor, and the ultimate matinée idol of his time. For his musicals see p. 216. His incredible profile, and his light-hearted shows in which he starred, together with his extreme popularity, gave him little chance to display acting ability—ability he showed in his own *The Rat* (24), *The Happy Hypocrite* (36) and *Henry V* (38), which, without setting Drury Lane on fire, was admired.

NUGENT, ELLIOTT (1899–). American actor, dramatist and director, two of whose biggest successes have been as Tommy Turner in *The Male Animal* (40), which he wrote with Thurber, and Bill Page in *The Voice of the Turtle* (43).

OLIVIER, LAURENCE (1907–).

British actor and Director of the National Theatre. From 1928 when he left Birmingham Rep to 1937, when he first went to the Old Vic, he was a handsome young West End leading man in commercial plays (*Romeo* in 35 apart). Notoriously, he turned down Stanhope in *Journey's End* after playing it for the Stage Society on a Sunday night (28), to play the lead in *Beau Geste*, a monumental flop. His best known non-classical parts in this period were Victor in *Private Lives* (30) and Bothwell in *Queen of Scots* (34). In his actor-managerial period at the St. James he played the Duke in Fry's *Venus Observed* and later played the Grand Duke in Rattigan's *The Sleeping Prince* (53), delightful lightweight interludes in an incomparable career. The title role in Anouilh's *Becket* in New York (60), later playing Henry II. Also see p. 124.

PAGE, GERALDINE (1924–). American actress of notable range and strength. Her roles have included Alma in *Summer and Smoke* (52), her touching Lizzie in *The Rainmaker* (New York, 54; London, 56), and her searing Alexandra del Lago in *Sweet Bird of Youth* (59), which won her the New York Drama Critics award. Her Nina in a revival of *Strange Interlude* (63) was notably powerful. Olga, later Masha, in *The Three Sisters* (64). Recent parts have included Baroness Lemberg in *White Lies*, Clea in *Black*

Comedy (67) and Angela Palmer in *Angela* (69).

PALMER, LILLI (1914–). Austrian actress whose career has mainly been in America and Britain. Amanda in *No Time for Comedy* (41), Shaw's Cleopatra (New York, 49), Gillian in *Bell, Book and Candle* (New York, 50; London, 54), Perpetua in *Venus Observed* (52) and Beauty in *The Love of Four Colonels* (53) both in New York. In the three Noel Coward plays, *Suite in Three Keys* (London, 66).

PARFITT, JUDY. British actress whose parts have included the title-role in *The Widowing of Mrs. Holroyd* (68) Annie in *The Hotel in Amsterdam* (68), Gertrude (69) and the Duchess of Malfi (71). A very fine actress.

PATRICK, NIGEL (1913–). British actor and director whose comedy technique is admired by actors and audiences alike. His many parts have included Dudley in *George and Margaret* (37), John Hampden in *Escape* (53) and Biddeford Poole in *The Pleasure of His Company* (60), which he directed. The Hon. Vere in *The Schoolmistress* (64). Garry Essendene in *Present Laughter* (65), which he directed. Starred in *Reunion in Vienna* at Chichester and London (71). Has appeared in many films.

PEARSON, RICHARD (1918–). British actor. Parts have included Stanley in *The Birthday Party* (58), Charles Sidley in *The Public Eye* (62), The Cardinal in *Tiny Alice* for the Royal Shakespeare Co. (70) and William Cecil in *Vivat! Vivat Regina!* (Chichester and London, 70), also many major TV roles.

PEEL, EILEEN. British actress. Regularly in the West End since the early 30s, her parts have included Lavinia in *The Cocktail Party* (New York and London, 50), Mrs. Carghall in *The Elder Statesman* (58) and Louise Harrington in *Five Finger Exercise* (59). Maude Headleigh in *The Claimant* (64).

PHILLIPS, LESLIE (1924–). British actor. Though best known for his many films parts, this good light comedian has appeared in a number of plays: Lord Fancourt Babberley in *Charley's Aunt* (50). Tom in *For Better, For Worse* (52), Lupin in *The Diary of a Nobody* (54), Robert in *Boeing-Boeing* (63), etc., and, at the time of writing (73), as '*The Man Most Likely To. . . .*'

PLEASANCE, DONALD (1921–). British actor whose striking performances in the 50s included Gunner in *Misalliance* (56). His hypnotic tramp, Davies, in *The Caretaker* (60) made his name, since when his parts have included the title-role in *Poor Bitos* (London and New York, 64), his brilliant Arthur Goodman in *The Man in the*

Glass Booth (London, 67; New York, 68) and two more Pinter roles, Law in *The Basement* and Disson in *The Tea Party* (70). His daughter is ANGELA PLEASANCE, a Mermaid St. Joan (70), etc.

PORTMAN, ERIC (1903–69). British actor who after notable work at the Vic, became a West End player, a film star, then one of the most moving and powerful actors in the commercial theatre of his day. His most notable parts were Crocker-Harris in *The Browning Version* (48), the Governor in *His Excellency* and Mr. Martin and Major Pollock in *Separate Tables* (London, 54; New York, 56).

RAINS, CLAUDE (1889–1967). British actor and a major character star in films from the early 30s. Visited the States with Granville Barker (14) as general manager and as Spintho in *Androcles*. His Klestakoff in *The Government Inspector* (20) was a big success, after which he played a wide range of parts, including Shavian leads, before returning to America (26) and becoming a leading actor for the Theater Guild. In films from 1933–50, after which his stage roles included a magnificent Rubashov in *Darkness at Noon* (51) and Sir Claude in *The Confidential Clerk* (54).

RAWLINGS, MARGARET (1906–). British actresses whose successes have included Katherine O'Shea in *Parnell* (New York, 35; London, 36), Lily in *Black Limelight* (37) and Karen in *The Flashing Stream* (London, 38; New York, 39); also Shavian and classical roles including Zabina in *Tamburlaine the Great* at the Old Vic (51), Ella in *John Gabriel Borkman* (63) and Lady Macbeth at Ludlow (65). Mrs. Bridgenorth in *Getting Married* (67).

RAYMOND, CYRIL. British actor famous for his performances in solid supporting roles: Dr. Sparling in *Home at Seven* (50) and Robert Lancaster in *Waters of the Moon* (51), etc. His wife is actress GILLIAN LIND.

REDGRAVE, MICHAEL (1908–). British actor whose career, and that of his family, can be found on p. 130. His commercial successes range from Charleston in *Thunder Rock* (40) and the title-role in *Uncle Harry* (44) to Frank Elgin in *Winter Journey* (known in the States as *The Country Girl*) (52), Hector in *A Tiger at the Gates* (London and New York, 55), HJ in his own adaptation of *The Aspern Papers* (59), Jack Dean in *The Tiger and the Horse* (60). Knighted (59).

REDMAN, JOYCE (1918–). British actress (also see p. 131). This Irish-born actress, once a perfect Wendy and Alice, has had many commercial successes, including Anne Boleyn in *Anne of a Thousand Days* (New York, 48), the title-role in *Colombe* (51), Irene in *Affairs of State* (52) and Hedda in *The Irregular Verb to Love* (61). 3 parts in *Plaza Suit* (69).

REDMOND, LIAM (1913–). Irish actor and director. With the Abbey for 50 plays in the 30s. His parts in London have included Christopher Mahon in *The Playboy of the Western World* (48), Burke in *The Anatomist* (48) and Cullen in *The Doctor's Dilemma* (63). His Canon McCooey in *The Wayward Saint* in New York (55) gained him a George Jean Nathan award. Recent parts have included Harry in *The Loves of Cass Maguire* (67) and McLeavy in *Loot* (68), both in New York.

REED, FLORENCE (1893–1967). American actress. Her career began in 1901 and embraced many-long forgotten plays, but also Lady Macbeth, Christine in *Mourning Becomes Electra* (32), the Fortune Teller in *The Skin of Our Teeth* (42 and 55) and Amy in *The Family Reunion* (58). In *The Yellow Ticket* (14) lowered the curtain on a drunken John Barrymore and continued with his understudy.

REEVES, KYNASTON (1893–1972). British actor whose air of distinction was only heightened by his magnificent profile. A fine actor who worked with Greet and Benson and played commercial leads. Usually a knight at least.

REID, BERYL (1920–). British actress and comedienne. As well as appearing in revues, and in films and on TV, played Sister George in *The Killing of Sister George* (London, 65; New York, 66), winning a 'Tony' for her performance on Broadway. Madame Arcati (Guildford and London, 70).

RELPH, GEORGE (1888–1960). British actor with a rich corncrake voice, who after years of steady work on both sides of the Atlantic, including Horatio to Barrymore's Hamlet (London, 25) was a distinguished member of the Old Vic company at the New (44–9), playing Clarence, Gloucester in *Lear*, Subtle, Sir Oliver, etc. Then gave a series of delightful performances including Herbert Reedbeck in *Venus Observed* (50) and the grandfather in *The Entertainer* (57).

REYNOLDS, DOROTHY (1913–). British actress and co-author of *Salad Days*. Classical leads at Bristol and Nottingham. Miss Mackay in *The Prime of Miss Jean Brodie* (66), Sophie, Baroness Bemberg in *White Lies* and Miss Furnival in *Black Comedy* (68). Matron in *Forty Years On* (68).

RICHARDSON, RALPH (1902–). British actor (see p. 132 for his classical career). His non-classical parts have included Collie in *For Services Rendered* (32), the title-role in *Sheppey* (33), Charles Appleby in *Eden End* (35), Dr. Clitterhouse in *The*

Amazing Dr. Clitterhouse (36) and a famous performance as Robert Johnson in *Johnson over Jordan* (39). Post war successes have included his cold Dr. Sloper in *The Heiress* (49), David Preston in *Home at Seven* (50), Dr. Farley in *A Day by the Sea* (53) General St. Pé in *The Waltz of the Toreadors* (New York, 57), Cherry in *The Flowering Cherry* (57) and Victor Rhodes in *The Complaisant Lover* (59). This extraordinary player of the ordinary man has crowned his career with two major performances: Jack in David Storey's *Home* (see page 64) and Wyatt Gillman in Osborne's *West of Suez* (71). A fascinating dominating actor; a brilliant comedian who can also be deeply moving. Some find his mannerisms too intrusive, which is their loss. At the time of writing (73) is playing the General in *Lloyd George Knew my Father*. His wife is the fine actress MERIEL FORBES (1913–) who has often played opposite him, including Mlle. de Sainte Euverte in *The Waltz of the Toreadors*.

RITCHARD, CYRIL (1898–). British actor, dancer and director. This Australian-born ex-chorus boy was a very popular star of musicals and revues between the wars, often opposite his wife MADGE ELLIOTT (1898–1959). He played Algy in *The Importance* (42), Danilo in *The Merry Widow* (43), an hilarious Lord Foppington (London, 48;

New York, 50), Hubert Manning in *Ann Veronica* (49) and played in Coward and revue in Australia. In the 50s this extremely versatile man-of-the-theatre was directing opera at the Met., playing Hook and Darling in the musical *Peter Pan* (New York, 54) and playing Biddeford Poole in *The Pleasure of his Company* (New York, 57: Australia, 60). His parts in the 60s included Colonel Tallboys in *Too True to Be Good* (63), Felix in *The Irregular Verb to Love* (63) which he also directed and Sir in *The Roar of the Greasepaint—The Smell of the Crowd* (65). Bottom, Oberon and Pyramus (!) in the *Dream*, which he also directed, at Stratford, Conn. (67).

RIX, BRIAN. See p. 229.

ROBARDS, JASON (1922–). American actor of power and authority whose roles have included Hickey in *The Iceman Cometh* (56) and (the first) Jamie in *The Long Day's Journey into Night* (56) which earned him the New York Critics Most Promising Actor award. His Manley Halliday in *The Disenchanted* (58) and Julian Berniers in *Toys in the Attic* (60) both won awards from the same critics for the Best Male performances. Later performances have included Quentin in Arthur Miller's *After the Fall* (64). At the time of writing (72) giving 'a performance for the theatrical memory book' (T. E. Kalem) in a revival of *The Country Girl*.

ROBINSON, JOHN (1908–). British actor whose many West End appearances have included Dennis in *The Living Room* (53) and Sir Howard Hallam in *Captain Brassbound's Conversion* (71).

ROBSON, FLORA (1902–). British actress renowned for her work in classical (see p. 133) and modern plays alike. In the latter, where her emotional acting soon made her a major West End star, some of her finest performances have been as Olwen in *Dangerous Corner* (32), Eva in *For Services Rendered* (32), Alicia in *Black Chiffon* (London, 49; New York, 50) and Janet in *The House by The Lake* (56). Her Tina in *The Aspern Papers* (59) won her an *Evening Standard* award. Recent parts have included the Mother in *Ring Round the Moon* (68) and Agatha Payne in *The Old Ladies* (69). D.B.E. (60).

ROSSITER, LEONARD (1926–). British actor whose parts have included Fred Midway in *Semi-Detached* (New York, 63) and Arturo Ui (Edinburgh, 68; London, 69), a brilliant, riveting, inventive and much acclaimed performance which won him Critics' and Variety Club awards.

RUTHERFORD, MARGARET (1892–1972). British (to the backbone) actress renowned for her eccentric character performances, not-

ably her definitive Madame Arcati in *Blithe Spirit* (41) and her Headmistress in *The Happiest Days of Your Life* (48). Played Miss Prism in London (39) and Lady Bracknell in New York (47) and Dublin (57). One of the matchless cast of *Ring Round the Moon* (50). Played the occasional sinister role: Mrs. Danvers in *Rebecca* (40). Her films made her adored in North America and elsewhere, as well as Britain. D.B.E. (67). Her husband is the actor, STRINGER DAVIS.

RYAN, ROBERT (1913–). American actor who, many fine film performances apart, has appeared on Broadway and in Britain. Joe Doyle in *Clash by Night* (41), Coriolanus (54). Becket in *Murder in the Cathedral* and Antony at Stratford, Conn. (59, 60). The title-role in *Mr. President* (63). Othello and James Tyrone in *Long Day's Journey* at Nottingham (67), playing Tyrone again in New York (71). Walter Burns in *The Front Page* (69).

SALLIS, PETER (1921–). British actor whose many West End appearances have included Roat in *Wait until Dark* (66), a villain who literally and regularly had audiences screaming at one memorable moment.

SANDS, DIANA (1934–). American actress whose parts have included Beneatha Younger in *A Raisin in the Sun* (59), Juanita in *Blues for Mr. Charlie* (64), Doris W. in *The Owl and the Pussy Cat* (New York, 64; London, 66). Classical parts include Juliet, Phaedra and Shaw's Cleopatra (which is classical in this book).

SCHIDKRAUT, JOSEPH (1896–1964). Viennese actor who became an American matinée idol —a splendidly swaggering one in *Liliom* (23). Later, his parts included Leonid Andreyevitch in *The Cherry Orchard* (44) and Mr. Frank in *The Diary of Anne Frank* (55). Appeared in many films.

SCOFIELD, PAUL (1922–). British actor. Apart from his many classical performances (see p. 135), this great actor has superbly played many West End parts, including the Twins in *Ring Round the Moon* (50), Prince Albert in *Time Remembered* (54), the whiskey priest in *The Power and the Glory* (56), which won him an *Evening Standard* award, and the lead in the musical *Expresso Bongo* (58). Clive Root in *The Complaisant Lover* (59) and his famous Sir Thomas More in *A Man for All Seasons* (London, 60; New York, 61). Laurie in *The Hotel in Amsterdam* (68).

SCOTT, GEORGE C. (1927–). American actor who, before becoming a major film actor, made his name in New York, in classical parts—Richard III, Antony, Shylock, etc.—and modern plays, including Lt.-Col. Chipman in *The Andersonville Trial* (59), the title-role in *General Seeger* (62) which he directed, Benjamin Hubbard in *The Little Foxes* (67) and three parts in *Plaza Suite* (68).

SCOTT, MARGARETTA (1912–). British actress who made a striking success, aged 18, as Lady Jasper in *A Murder Has Been Arranged* (30). Other fine performances have included Elsa in *Alien Corn* (39), Sister Margaret in *The Hasty Heart* (45) and Katherine Parr in *The Young Elizabeth* (53). Classical parts have included Juliet (Regent's Park, 34) and Mrs. Marwood in *The Way of the World* (56).

SEYLER, ATHENE (1889–). British actress, especially well known for her work in commercial and classical comedies. With Stephen Haggard she wrote *The Craft of Comedy* (44). Her enormous list of commercial successes includes Miss Moffat in *The Corn is Green* (39), Dame Beatrice in *Breath of Spring* (58) and Martha in *Arsenic and Old Lace* (66). Her many classical parts have included Mrs. Malaprop (56).

SHINER, RONALD (1903–66). British actor. After being a Mountie, went on the stage in 1928. Best remembered, films apart, for two brassy, superb comedy performances, Porter in *Worm's Eye View* (45), which he also directed, and Badger in

West End and Broadway 187

Seagulls Over Sorrento (50). He later played Joseph in *My Three Angels* (55) and Bertie in *The Lovebirds* (57).

SIDNEY, SYLVIA (1910–). American actress who since her memorable Rosalie in *The Gods of the Lightning* (28) has played a huge range of classical and modern parts in many American theatres.

SIM, ALISTAIR (1900–). Edinburgh-born British actor, famous for his work in Bridie down the years, his mock-heroic Hook and his rolling eyes and quizzical tones to match. Has regularly directed since the war and given many eye-catching performances in films. Apart from his fame as a Bridie actor, including his Dr. Angelus and Dr. Knox, one of his greatest successes has been as Pinero's Magistrate (Chichester and London, 69). The Marquis of Candover in *The Jockey Club Stakes* (70). Currently (73) starring in *A Private Matter*.

SINCLAIR, HUGH (1903–62). British actor and a popular West End leading man and film actor for many years. A good light comedian and romantic actor. Last appeared in London in *Guilty Party* (61). First appeared on Broadway with *Charlot's Revue of 1924*. One of his most famous parts was Sebastian in *Escape Me Never* (33), opposite Bergner.

SINDEN, DONALD (1923–). British actor (also see p. 136). After his successful film star period, has divided his time between major performances with the Royal Shakespeare Co. and commercial hits: Robert in *There's A Girl in my Soup* (66) and Gilbert in *Not now, Darling* (68). A fine Hook (60).

SKINNER, CORNELIA OTIS (1901 –). American actress, daughter of the actor-manager Otis Skinner, also author (*Our Hearts were Young and Gay*, etc.) and dramatist: co-author of *The Pleasure of his Company*, 58, in which she played Katherine. Apart from her appearances in plays, has given many solo performances of character sketches since the 20s in America and Britain.

SLEZAK, WALTER (1902–). Viennese-born son of the tenor, Leo Slezak. Many leading parts on Broadway have included Harry Mischka in *I Married an Angel* (38), Joseph in *My Three Angels* (53), Panisse in *Fanny* (54), which won him a 'Tony' award, the Prince Regent in *The First Gentleman* (57) and Elliott Nash in *The Gazebo* (58). Has appeared in many films.

SMITH, MAGGIE. British actress who before and after her National Theatre successes (p. 137) has established herself as a star of revue and West End plays, including *New Faces '56 Revue* (New York), *Share My Lettuce*

(57), Daisy in *Rhinoceros* (60) and Lucile in *The Rehearsal* (61). Her Doreen and Belinda in *The Private Eye and the Public Ear* (62) won her an *Evening Standard* award and her Mary in *Mary, Mary* (63) a Variety Club award. With her husband ROBERT STEPHENS (see p. 138) appeared in *Design for Living* (71) and *Private Lives* (72).

SPINETTI, VICTOR (1933–). British actor whose many performances for Joan Littlewood included his Drill Sergeant in *Oh, What a Lovely War!* which won a 'Tony' in New York (64). Felix in *The Odd Couple* (66). Also a director.

SQUIRE, RONALD (1886–1958). British actor whose stylish performances matched du Maurier's underplaying at its very best. Both were in Lonsdale's *The Last of Mr. Cheyney* (25) and Squire was in his *On Approval* as the Duke of Bristol (33). Title-role in *The Breadwinner* (30). Kenneth More is one of those who has publicly expressed his debt to him.

STANLEY, KIM (1925–). American actress and notable product of the Actors' Studio. Her roles include Millie in *Picnic* (53), which gained her a New York Critics award, Cherie in *Bus Stop* and, in London, Margaret in *Cat on a Hot Tin Roof* (58). Her 'impressive personal intensity' (Taubman) was seen at its finest as Masha in

The Three Sisters (64) in New York. The London production was ill-fated.

STAPLETON, MAUREEN (1925–). Leading American actress whose roles have included Serafina in *The Rose Tattoo* (51), an award-winning performance of 'earthy vitality' (Taubman), Masha in *The Seagull* (54), Lady Torrance in *Orpheus Descending* (57), Ida in *The Cold and the Warm* (58), Carrie in *Toys in The Attic* (60), Amanda Wingfield in *The Glass Menagerie* (65), her Serafina again (66), three parts in *Plaza Suite* (68) and Georgie in *The Country Girl* in 1972.

STEWART, FRED (1906–). American actor and director, associated with the Theater Guild, Group Theater, the Mercury Theater, the Actors' Studio, etc. His many New York parts have included The Cardinal in *The Deputy* (64).

STEWART, SOPHIE (1908–). British actress who has played many Barrie and Bridie parts and was the Old Vic's Rose Trelawny (38). The Mother in *Life with Father* (47). As befits a Scot, has acted extensively in Canada, Australia and America. Her husband is ELLIS IRVING (1902–) the Australian actor who has played leading classical and modern parts in Britain, America and Australia.

STOCK, NIGEL (1919–). British actor whose performances have included Tony Lumpkin and Beliayev in *A Month in the Country* for the Old Vic (49, 50) also A.B. Sims in *Seagulls over Sorrento* (50). Lieut. Maryk in *The Caine Mutiny Court Martial* (57), Werner in *Altona* (61) and Detective-Sgt. Brown in *How are you, Johnnie?* (63). His many TV roles included Dr. Watson.

STOTT, JUDITH (1929–). British actress whose West End parts have included Laurel in *The Chalk Garden* (56), Jessica in *The Pleasure of his Company* (59) Lily in *Toys in The Attic* (60), etc. Married to the brilliant comedian, DAVE ALLEN.

TANDY, JESSICA (1909–). Anglo-American actress whose rich and varied career has included classical work (p. 139) and many commercial parts, including Manuella in *Children in Uniform* (32), Kay in *Time and the Conways* (38), and, in New York, the original Blanche in *A Streetcar Named Desire* (47), a brilliant performance which won her major awards. Louise in *Five Finger Exercise* (60). Recent parts have included Dr. Mathilde in *The Physicists* (64). Marjorie in *Home* (71). These last three parts were on Broadway: she has been an American citizen since 1954.

TAYLOR, LAURETTE (1884–1946). American actress of ability and charm. Her two very famous parts were Peg in *Peg O' My Heart*, written by her husband,

John Hartley Manners (12) and —unforgettably—the Mother in *The Glass Menagerie* (45). John Mason Brown called it a deathless performance.

TAYLOR, VALERIE (1902–). British actress whose career has ranged from Birmingham Rep via West End juveniles and leads between the wars, to the Old Vic's Lady Bracknell in Moscow (60) and Edith in Osborne's *Time Present* (68).

TEMPEST, MARIE (1864–1942). British singer turned actress, who had what Agate called 'a small, exquisite talent', though he claimed she lacked pathos. The title-role in *The First Mrs. Fraser* (29), etc. Her most famous part, written for her by the author, was Judith Bliss in Coward's *Hay Fever* (25). D.B.E. (37).

THORNDIKE, SYBIL (1882–). British actress whose happy, monumental career is mainly noted on p. 140. Her many commercial triumphs have ranged from Judith in *Granite* (26), through Miss Moffat in *The Corn is Green* (38), Isabel in *The Linden Tree* (47), Aunt Anna in *Treasure Hunt* (49), Mrs. Whyte in *Waters of the Moon* (51), Laura Anson in *A Day by the Sea* (53), etc., to Abby Brewster in *Arsenic and Old Lace* (66). D.B.E. (31). Both her husband, Lewis Casson, and brother, Russell Thorndike, may be found in Chapter 2.

TITHERADGE, MADGE (1887–1961). Australian-born British actress. After working with Waller, she became a star as Peggy Admaston in *A Butterfly on the Wheel* (11). Later successes included Dommi Enfilden in *The Garden of Allah* (20), Monna in *Bluebeard's Eighth Wife* (22). Julie Cavendish in *Theatre Royal* (34) and the title-role in *Mademoiselle* (36). Her classical parts included Nora in *A Doll's House* and Beatrice and Desdemona.

TOMLINSON, DAVID (1917–). British actor and fine light comedian, whose talent for playing silly asses in plays and films has sometimes obscured—except for pros—his technique and inventiveness. Examples have been Henry in *The Little Hut* (50), Clive in *All for Mary* (54) and Robert in *Boeing-Boeing* (62).

TREVOR, AUSTIN (1897–). British actor. His long West End career has included the Parson in *Escape* (London, 26; New York, 27), Sir Ralph Bloomfield-Bonington in *The Doctor's Dilemma* (42) and Byron Winkler in *Affairs of State* (52).

USTINOV, PETER. See p. 65.

VANBRUGH, IRENE (1872–1949). British actress, the original Rose Trelawny (98). A bigger triumph, her Sophy in *The Gay Lord Quex* followed (99) and another early success was her Nina in *His House in Order* (06). Later successes included Olivia in *Mr. Pim Passes By* (20), the title-role in *Viceroy Sarah* (35) in which she succeeded Edith Evans, and Catherine of Braganza in *In Good King Charles's Golden Days* (Malvern, 39; London, 40). Noted for her charm and comedy skill. D.B.E. (41). Her sister was VIOLET VANBRUGH (1867–1942) and her brother, SIR KENNETH BARNES, the first Principal of RADA.

VAN FLEET, JO. American actress whose major performances have included Eliza Grant in *Look Homeward, Angel* (58), which won her a New York Critics award. Amanda Wingfield in *The Glass Menagerie* (65).

VOSPER, FRANK (1899–1937). British actor and dramatist. In his short career he gave many memorable performances, including Claudius in Barry Jackson's modern dress *Hamlet* (25), Henry VIII in *The Rose without a Thorn* (32), Old Schindler in *Musical Chairs* (32), a 'sleekly watchful' Dulcimer (Trewin) in *The Green Bay Tree* (33) and the murderer in his superb adaptation (of an Agatha Christie short story), *Love from a Stranger* (36). Also wrote *People Like Us* (29), a moving play about the Thompson-Bywaters case. Vosper was drowned at sea.

WALLACH, ELI (1915–). American actor whose parts have

included Alvarro in *The Rose Tattoo* (51), Kilroy in *Camino Real* (53) and Julien in *Colombe* (51). A very successful debut in London (54; New York, 55) as Sakini in *The Teahouse of the August Moon*. Recent parts have included Berenger in *Rhinoceros* (61) and Charles in *Staircase* (68).

WASHBOURNE, MONA (1903–). British actress whose successes have included Alice in *Billy Liar* (60) and Kathleen in *Home* (London and New York, 70).

WAYNE, DAVID (1914–). American actor whose Broadway successes have included his splendid Sakini in *The Teahouse of the August Moon* (53). Recent parts include Grandpère Bonnard in *The Happy Time* (68). Has made many films.

WAYNE, NAUNTON (1901–70). British actor. This popular commedian, who began in Variety, became a straight actor in 1937. Parts included Mortimer in *Arsenic and Old Lace* (42), Sir William in *The Bride and the Bachelor* (56) and the Earl of Lister in *The Reluctant Peer* (64) also Beecham in the same play. His partnership with BASIL RADFORD (1897–1952) in plays, including *Clutterbuck* (46), and films was a joy. Radford's parts included Hubert in *Night Must Fall* (35) and Charlie in *She Follows me About* (42).

WEBB, ALAN (1906–). British actor whose admirable leading and supporting performances have included parts in *Tonight at 8.30* (London and New York, 36), Roger in *George and Margaret* (37), Arthur Winslow in *The Winslow Boy* (New York, 47), Sir Timothy in *A Penny for a Song* (51), Polonius (51), William Collyer in *The Deep Blue Sea* (New York, 52), Eggerson in *The Confidential Clerk* (53), Sir Toby and Marcus Andronicus at Stratford (55). For the Royal Shakespeare Co. played Ernst Ernesti in *The Physicists* (62) and Gloucester in *Lear*. Pope Pius XII in *The Representative* (New York, 63). Bent in *The Chinese Prime Minister* (New York, 64; London, 65). Recent parts include Tom Garrison in *I Never Sang for My Father* (New York, 68).

WILLIAMS, EMLYN (1905–). British actor and dramatist, whose appearances in three other chapters should not obscure his role as a popular West End actor, notably as Morgan Evans in his *The Corn is Green* (38), Ambrose Ellis in his *The Wind of Heaven* (45), Sir Robert in *The Winslow Boy* (46), Will Tranting in his *Accolade* (50), the Author in *Shadow of Heroes* (58) and, in New York, More in *A Man for all Seasons* (62) and Pope Pius in *The Representative* (64); also his famous Dickens readings in many parts of the world and Dylan Thomas readings in London. The Headmaster in *Forty Years On* (69).

WILLIAMS, HUGH (1904–69). British actor, one of the last and finest examples of the Du Maurier school. Blessed with an attractive voice and looks, his parts included Neville in *While Parents Sleep* (32), Darcy in *Pride and Prejudice* (36) and the leads in his own and his wife's plays (see p. 68). His admired Trigorin in *The Seagull* (56) maddened some of those who felt that he had wasted his considerable talents on lighter matters. The definitive Steerforth in the film of *David Copperfield*.

WILLIAMS, JOHN (1903–). British actor whose long career began in the West End, but since the war, has been entirely American. Parts have included Inspector Hubbard in *Dial 'M' for Murder* (52), later filmed, Belmann in *The Dark is Light Enough* (55), General Allenby in *Ross* (61) and David Bliss in *Hay Fever* (70).

WILLIAMS, KENNETH (1926–). British actor, and a favourite comedian on stage and screen. The Dauphin in *St. Joan* (54–5), since when his parts have included Montgomery in *The Buccaneer* (55), Green in *Share My Lettuce* (57), Julian in *The Public Eye* (62), Truscott in *Loot* at Cambridge (65) and Drinkwater in *Captain Brassbound's Conversion* (71). Has appeared in pantomime, also in revue: *Pieces of Eight* (59) and *One Over The Eight* (61). Currently (73) starring in *My Fat Friend*.

WILLIAMSON, NICOL (1938–). British actor. After Flute and Malvolio at the Royal Court, played Albert Meakin in *Nil Carborundum* (62), Leantio in *Women Beware Women* (62), etc. Sebastian Dangerfield in *The Ginger Man* (63), followed by his most famous role, Bill Maitland in *Inadmissable Evidence* (London, 64–5: New York, 65), played with 'a sour eloquence and rancid fury' (Michael Billington). Later parts have included Peter Wykeham in *A Cuckoo in the Nest* (64), Vladimir in *Waiting for Godot* (65), Alexei in *Diary of a Madman*, Hamlet (London and New York, 69), which won him an *Evening Standard* award, and three parts in *Plaza Suite* (New York, 69). A most exciting and very gifted actor.

WINTERS, SHELLEY (1922–). American actress whose Broadway roles have included Celia in *A Hatful of Rain* (55), Maxine in *The Night of the Iguana* (62) and three parts in *Under the Weather* (67). A major film actress.

WINWOOD, ESTELLE (1883–). British actress who, after starting with Hare in the 90s, then becoming an original member of Liverpool Rep, has, since 1916, appeared in a colossal number of Broadway plays, including leads in Coward, Wilde, etc. Paid a rare visit to London as Alicia de St. Ephlam in *Gigi* (56).

WISEMAN, JOSEPH (1918–). Canadian actor whose Broadway parts have included Charlie in *Detective Story* (49), Eddie in *Golden Boy* (51), the Inquisitor in *The Lark* (55), etc. Becket in *Murder in the Cathedral* at Stratford, Conn. (66). The title-role in *In The Matter of J. Robert Oppenheimer* (New York, 69).

WITHERS, GOOGIE (1917–). British actress, whose most memorable performance in London has been her superb Georgie in *Winter Journey* (52). Other parts have included Alice Foster in *They Came to a City* (45), Hester in *The Deep Blue Sea* (52). Gertrude and a witty Beatrice at Stratford (57) and Mary in *The Complaisant Lover* (New York, 61). Has acted extensively in Australia and appeared in many films. Her husband is the actor and director, JOHN MCCALLUM (1914–), whose London appearances have included Hook (57) and Lord Dungavel in *Roar Like a Dove* (57). A major figure in Australian theatre management (from 58) after joining J. C. Williamson's Theatres and, later, becoming joint Managing Director. Made many films.

WOLHEIM, LOUIS (1880–1931). American actor, and the original Captain Flagg in *What Price Glory?* (24) opposite WILLIAM BOYD (1890–1935) as the equally famous Sergeant Quirt. *Not* the 'Hopalong Cassidy' Boyd.

WONTNER, ARTHUR (1875–1960). British actor whose handsome profile spanned work with Calvert, Mrs. Waller, Tree, etc., the title-role in *Raffles* (96), Ben Hur (12), Charles II in *Our Nell* (24), Cardinal Richelieu in *The Three Musketeers* (30) and classical parts including Buckingham in *Henry VIII* and Malvolio.

YOUNG, ROLAND (1887–1953). British-born actor who became a Broadway and film star. Parts included Neil McRae in *Beggar on Horseback* (24) and Uriah Heep in *the* film of David Copperfield.

THE MUSICAL

Some Notable Shows

ROSE MARIE   1924

This enjoyable musical is a prime example of the tuneful, sentimental, romantic hokum which Rudolf (*Rose Marie, The Vagabond King*) Friml and Sigmund (*The Desert Song, The Student Prince, The New Moon*) Romberg gave the world in general and amateur operatic companies in particular. Setting *Rose Marie* in the Canadian Rockies and using the Mounties as heroes was Oscar Hammerstein's idea. The story centres on the singer, Rose La Flamme, a Saskatchewan hotel singer beloved by trappers and Mounties alike, who is loved by wealthy Ed Hanley, but adores Jim Kenyon. Wanda, an Indian girl, who loves Ed, kills Black Eagle and fixes the blame on Jim. Rose Marie offers herself to Ed to save Jim, but Sergeant Malone of the Mounties solves the crime and Rose Marie and Jim are saved. Well-known numbers in the score include 'Indian Love Call' and 'Rose Marie'.

First produced at the Imperial, New York, September 2, 1924.

Book and lyrics	Otto Harbach and Oscar Hammerstein II
Music	Rudolf Friml and Herbert Stothart
Director	Paul Dickey
Choreographer	David Bennett
Leading players	Mary Ellis as Rose Marie and Dennis King as Jim Kenyon

The Broadway production ran for 557 performances and the show reached Drury Lane in 1925 with Edith Day as Rose Marie. It was the first spectacular American musical to dominate Drury Lane, a domination that lasted ten years until the reign of Ivor Novello began. The most famous film of the show, starring Jeanette McDonald and Nelson Eddy, had a very different plot grafted on to it.

SHOW BOAT   1927

This musical, with its incomparable score by Jerome Kern, marked a big breakthrough in the history of this form of entertainment, because of its fusion of music and drama and its believable, three-dimensional characters, as they certainly seemed in 1927. It was the first truly musical play. Even its opening made Broadway history, with its gang of Negro dock workers instead of the usual chorus line. The story happens on a Mississippi show boat, the *Cotton Blossom*, and also ashore, with the love affair of Magnolia, daughter of Cap'n Andy and the dashing gambler, Gaylord Ravenal, as the main plot, and a strong sub-plot featuring Julie, a Negress, and Steve who is white. A Negro, Joe, sings 'Ol' Man River'. Other numbers include 'Only Make Believe', 'Bill', 'Can't Help Lovin' Dat Man' and 'Why Do I Love You?'

First produced in New York at the Ziegfeld, December 27, 1927.

Books and lyrics	Oscar Hammerstein II
Music	Jerome Kern
Production	Florenz Ziegfeld
Choreographer	Sammy Lee

Cast included Norma Terris as Magnolia, Howard Marsh as Gaylord and Helen Morgan as Julie.

Show Boat has been frequently revived and has been filmed three times. It reached Drury Lane in 1928 with Edith Day as Magnolia, Marie Burke as a hauntingly good Julie, Cedric Hardwicke as Cap'n Andy and Paul Robeson as the definitive Joe. At the time of writing, it is back in London in a worthy production by Wendy Toye (worthy being a compliment, not faint praise), which has had the critics babbling ecstatically and the public queuing in the Strand outside the Adelphi Theatre.

BITTER SWEET   1929

The story of the British musical since the 1920s contains few 'significant' landmarks, but plenty of incidental pleasures, notably those given by Noël Coward and Ivor Novello. Recent revivals have mostly been staged too—shall we say?—economically to give a doubting younger generation a fair taste of their quality. *Bitter Sweet* is a romantic and charming piece which uses a long flashback to transport the leading character, Lady Shayne (Sarah) back to her youth in the 1870s when, just before she should have married, she eloped to Austria with a musician, with tragic results. The show's most famous number is 'I'll see you again' and its hero made history by being killed off (in a duel) before the last act.

First produced in London at His Majesty's July 18, 1929.

Book, music, lyrics and direction	Noël Coward
Sets and costumes	Gladys Calthrop and Ernst Stern
Choreography	Tilly Losch

Cast included Peggy Wood as Sarah, George Metaxas as Carl, Ivy St. Helier as Manon.

The show ran for 697 performances. It opened in New York at the Ziegfeld, November 5, 1929, and ran for 151 performances. It was filmed in 1933 with Anna Neagle and Ferdinand Gravet. Collectors' note: Miss Neagle had been in the chorus of *Rose Marie*.

OF THEE I SING   1931

Leaving aside George Gershwin's near operatic masterpiece, *Porgy and Bess*, *Of Thee I Sing*, for which his brother Ira wrote the lyrics, is his finest musical, and one which helped the form to grow up. It is a satire on American politics and Presidential campaigns. Wintergreen wins an election on a love ticket, but instead of marrying Diana Devereaux, the winner of a special beauty contest, falls for his secretary, a simple girl called Mary. He is saved from impeachment when his wife becomes pregnant and his Vice-President, one Throttlebottom, saves the day by marrying Diana.

Much satire is got from the impossible position in which all Vice-Presidents find themselves. Poor little Throttlebottom cannot even get a public library ticket unless he can find two references, and can only enter the White House on a conducted tour. The numbers include 'Wintergreen for President', 'Of Thee I Sing', 'Love is Sweeping the Country', 'Tammany', 'The Sidewalks of New York' and 'Hail, Hail, the Gang's All Here'.

First produced in New York at the Music Box, December 26, 1931.

Book	Morrie Ryskind and George S. Kaufman
Lyrics	Ira Gershwin
Music	George Gershwin
Director	George S. Kaufman
Choreography	George Hale

Cast included William Glaxton as Wintergreen, Victor Moore as Throttlebottom and Lois Moran as Mary.

The show made history by being the first musical to win a Pulitzer Prize. It ran for 441 performances on Broadway, but was considered too American, presumably, for London audiences, which was London's loss.

PAL JOEY   1940

This Rodgers and Hart musical ran longer at its revival in 1952 than when it first appeared—542 performances compared with 374. It marked another major step forward in the form. The composer later noted that the show 'wore long pants' and stated that it forced the entire musical comedy theatre to wear long pants for the first time. The main characters are a hard-boiled heel who is master of ceremonies in a night club, a rich married woman who gets 'Bewitched, Bothered and Bewildered' by him, and a girl called Linda. The atmosphere is sleazy, the mood cynical. Apart from its most famous number, already mentioned, two others stand out, 'In Our Little Den of Iniquity' and 'Take him'. This was the show that made Gene Kelly a star.

First produced in New York at the Ethel Barrymore, December 25, 1940.

Book	John O'Hara, from his own short stories.
Lyrics	Lorenz Hart
Music	Richard Rodgers
Director	George Abbott
Choreography	Robert Alton

Cast included Gene Kelly as Joey, Vivienne Segal as Vera, Leila Ernst as Linda, and June Havoc and Van Johnson.

Not until its revival was the show's worth fully realized. It broke all records for a revival of a musical and was hailed as a masterpiece. It was also filmed with Frank Sinatra in the lead. Londoners were clearly not ready for an American anti-hero in a musical when it was staged at the Princes in 1954.

OKLAHOMA! 1943

Though *Show Boat* (27) and *On Your Toes* (36), with its Balanchine ballet, 'Slaughter on Tenth Avenue', had prepared the way for it, *Oklahoma!*—which was not full on its opening night!—was a milestone musical that blended music, a strong story and dancing into a magical whole. Set in the Southwest at the turn of the century, its story of the shy cowboy Curly and his up-and-down romance with Laurey, plus the adventures of Ado (Cain't say no) Annie, her Will, the appalling Jud, the singing and the dancing have been enjoyed by countless millions in theatres and cinemas. Numbers include 'Oh, What a Beautiful Mornin'', 'The Surrey with the Fringe on Top', 'People will Say We're in Love', 'The Farmer and the Cowboy' and the title song.

First produced by the Theater Guild in New York at the St. James', March 31, 1943.

Music	Richard Rodgers
Book and Lyrics	Oscar Hammerstein II, from the play by Lynn Rigg, *Green Grow the Lilacs*
Director	Rouben Mamoulian
Choreography	Agnes de Mille

Cast included Alfred Drake as Curly, Joan Roberts as Laurey, Celeste Holm as Ado Annie, Howard da Silva as Jud and Lee Dixon and Joseph Buloff.

Oklahoma! ran 2,248 performances. It reached Drury Lane in 1947 where, after a first night that has become a theatre legend, it ran for 1,543 performances. Many tours and amateur performances later, plus a film, it remains not necessarily the finest Rodgers and Hammerstein show—*Carousel* has a better score and *South Pacific* is their masterpiece—but a glorious entertainment and a landmark among landmarks.

ANNIE GET YOUR GUN 1946

This musical, with its wealth of good tunes, which in sheer number has perhaps been equalled but never surpassed, is

Irving Berlin's finest achievement. Yet, strangely, it should have been written by Jerome Kern if he had lived, and Berlin had to be talked into doing it. He was worried about adapting himself to an integrated musical.

The story is not too distantly based on the real Annie Oakley. Annie is the backwoods gal who is a crack shot. She falls in love with, and finally marries, a rival crack shot, Frank Butler, after hearing that 'You Can't Get a Man with a Gun'. The background is Buffalo Bill's Wild West Show, with plenty of Indians thrown in for good measure, including Sitting Bull, who gave the historical Annie her nickname, 'Little Sure Shot'. Berlin and the authors of the book gave Ethel Merman her finest role. Numbers include 'Doin' What Comes Natur'lly', 'I've Got the Sun in the Morning', 'They Say It's Wonderful', 'Anything You Can Do' and 'There's No Business like Show Business'.

First produced in New York at the Imperial, May 16, 1946.

Book	Herbert and Dorothy Fields
Music and Lyrics	Irving Berlin
Settings and Costumes	Jo Mielziner
Choreography	Helen Tamiris

Cast included Ethel Merman as Annie and Ray Middleton as Frank. In the film the two were Betty Hutton and Howard Keel, in London (47), Dolores Gray and Bill Johnson.

KISS ME, KATE   1948

This was the finest achievement of Cole Porter's career and is considered by many to be the most stylish and witty of all American musicals. The book, by Bella and Sam Spewak, cleverly entwines Shakespeare's *The Taming of the Shrew* with a modern road company who are presenting the play. Its leading players, though divorced, are still more than somewhat interested in each other. The score includes 'So in Love', 'I Hate Men', 'Too Darn Hot', 'Always True to You, Darling, in My Fashion' and 'Brush Up Your Shakespeare'.

First produced in New York at the New Century, December 30, 1948.

Music and Lyrics	Cole Porter
Book	Sam and Bella Spewak
Director	John C. Wilson
Choreographer	Hanya Holm

Cast included Alfred Drake as Fred and Patricia Morison as Lilli.

The show ran for 1,077 performances on Broadway and has triumphed in many countries, especially in Germany and Austria. Opera companies, including Sadler's Wells Opera, have taken it into their repertoires with varying (artistic) success. At the Vienna Volksoper it proved the biggest hit for more than half a century. It reached London on March 8, 1951, playing 500 performances at the Coliseum. It was filmed in 1951 with Howard Keel, Kathryn Grayson and Ann Miller in the leads.

MY FAIR LADY   1956

Frederick Loewe's and Alan Jay Lerner's shows include *Brigadoon*, *Paint Your Wagon* and *Camelot*, but their passport to theatrical immortality is *My Fair Lady*. This fairly faithful adaptation of Bernard Shaw's *Pygmalion*, the story of the Covent Garden flower girl who is turned into a lady by the phonetics professor, was blessed with an original cast and production team who could have turned a merely average musical into a hit. But *My Fair Lady* is so superbly served by its music and book that some of its quality would probably survive the worst a number ten touring company, or the most dismal amateur operatic group, could do to it.

It deserves its place in this short list not because it broke new ground—in some ways it was a throwback to the days of operetta—but because it simply cannot be left out. The ballyhoo that attended its birth was such that only a very great show could have broken down the resistance of those who distrust overselling. It was a very great show. Among its best numbers are 'Wouldn't it be Luvverly', 'With a Little Bit of Luck', 'The Rain in Spain' and 'Get me to the Church on Time'.

First produced in New York at the Mark Hellinger, March 15, 1956.

Book and Lyrics	Alan Jay Lerner, adapting from Shaw's *Pygmalion*
Music	Frederick Loewe
Designer	Cecil Beaton
Director	Moss Hart
Choreographer	Hanya Holm

Cast included Rex Harrison as Higgins, Julie Andrews as Eliza, Robert Coote as Pickering and Stanley Holloway as Doolittle.

The show reached London's Drury Lane on April 30, 1958, with the same principals, all of whom were magnificent and two—Harrison and Holloway—definitive. The film Eliza (1964) was the delectable Audrey Hepburn, chosen, be it noted, before Julie Andrews herself became a superstar.

WEST SIDE STORY   1957

This reworking of *Romeo and Juliet* is as much a landmark in the history of the musical as *Show Boat*, *Oklahoma!* and *Pal Joey*. The scene is New York, with the brawling Montagues transformed into a gang of native New Yorkers and the equally brawling Capulets transformed into newly-arrived Puerto Ricans. Romeo becomes Tony, and Maria, the Puerto Rican, is Juliet.

If this ultra-powerful, shattering and moving musical fails to stand the test of time, it will not affect its twin achievements: the bringing of a grim, modern social problem into a musical for the first time, and the use of dance to carry the story more convincingly and fully than ever before. Jerome Robbins's contribution—idea, staging and choreography—was the major one, though Bernstein's score, almost as masterly as his *Candide*, was another major factor in the work's body-blow success. But the entire show had an integration rare even in the finest Broadway musicals. Numbers included 'Something's Coming', 'Maria', 'Tonight', 'America', 'I Feel Pretty' and 'Gee, Officer Krupke!'

First produced in New York at the Winter Garden, September 26, 1957.

Book	Arthur Laurents, from an idea by Jerome Robbins
Music	Leonard Bernstein
Lyrics	Stephen Sondheim
Director and choreographer	Jerome Robbins
Designer	Oliver Smith

Cast included Carol Lawrence as Maria, Chita Rivera as Anita and Larry Kert as Tony.

The show ran for 732 performances. It opened in London at Her Majesty's December 12, 1958, and ran for 1,040 performances, with Marlys Watters as Maria, Chita Rivera as Anita, Don McKay as Tony and George Chakiris as Riff. Though it was fighting talk to suggest that anything in the London production was less than perfection, looking back only the dancing was perfect. Yet the total conception of acting, singing and dancing on a tragic theme made reservations superfluous. It was—and remains—unique.

OLIVER 1960

Lionel Bart's free adaptation of Dickens's *Oliver Twist* holds the London record for a long running musical, with 2,618 performances. Unlike most post-war British musicals it is rich in genuine tunes, and only the tone deaf could fail to hear that it is far and away Bart's best score. He created a near flawless musical, very close to a folk opera.

First produced in London at the New, June 30, 1960.

Books, lyrics and music	Lionel Bart
Director	Peter Coe
Designer	Sean Kenny

Cast included Keith Hampshire as Oliver, Ron Moody as Fagin, Georgia Brown as Nancy, Danny Sewell as Bill Sikes, Martin Horsey as the Artful Dodger and Paul Whitsun-Jones as Mr. Bumble.

Oliver successfully crossed the Atlantic, a very rare feat for a British musical, and ran 774 performances at the Imperial, New York. It was filmed by Carol Reed and harvested a crop of Oscars.

MUSICALS: A WHO'S WHO

ABBOTT, GEORGE (1887–). American theatre man of many talents, who has written and directed a number of musicals, including *On Your Toes* (36) (with Rodgers and Hart), an integrated show which anticipated *Oklahoma!* in its use of dance, also *The Boys from Syracuse* (38), inspired by *The Comedy of Errors*, *Where's Charley?* (46), *The Pyjama Game* (54), *Damn Yankees* (55) and *Fiorello* (59), co-author with Jerome Weidman. Also see p. 27.

ADLER, RICHARD (1921–). American composer, lyric writer and director whose successes include *The Pyjama Game* (54) and *Damn Yankees* (55) with JERRY ROSS.

ALDA, ROBERT (1914–). American actor and the original— and superb—Sky Masterson in *Guys and Dolls* (50). His son is ALAN ALDA (1936–),

ANDREWS, JULIE (1935–). British actress and singer who made a sensational debut aged 12 at the London Hippodrome in the revue *Starlight Roof*, singing operatic arias. After a number of pantomime and radio performances, played Polly in *The Boy Friend* in New York (54). Created Eliza in *My Fair Lady* in New York (56) and London (58). Guinevere in *Camelot* in New York (60). Since then mainly in films, including the star role in *The Sound of Music*.

ASTAIRE, FRED (1899–). American dancer and actor. With his sister Adele until her retirement after *The Band Wagon* (31), the most popular and stylish dance team since the Castles. They are best remembered for their partnership in Gershwin's *Lady, Be Good!* (24) and *Funny Face* (27). Before becoming a Hollywood superstar, Fred was 'nimble grace incarnate' (Taubman) in *The Gay Divorce* (32).

BADDELEY, HERMIONE (1906–). British actress and a very popular revue star from the 20s to the 40s, since when she has acted in London and New York, including *The Killing of Sister George* (London, 66).

BART, LIONEL (1930–). British composer and lyric writer whose shows include lyrics for *Lock Up Your Daughters* (59), music and lyrics for *Fings Ain't Wot They Used T'Be* (59), and—his finest achievement so far—music, book and lyrics for *Oliver* (60), see above. Other shows include

Blitz (62), *Maggie May* (64) and *Twang* (65).

BERLIN, IRVING (1888–). American whose musicals include *Face the Music* (32), *As Thousands Cheer* (33), *This is the Army* (42), *Annie Get Your Gun* (46), see above, and *Call Me Madam* (50). Like Annie, this last starred Ethel Merman on Broadway. It contained a song, 'They Like Ike', which did Eisenhower's chances of getting the Presidency no harm. His last Broadway show was *Mr. President* (63). One of the supreme masters of the musical.

BERNSTEIN, LEONARD (1918–). American composer and conductor, whose musicals include *On the Town* (44), *Wonderful Town* (53), *Candide* (56), his finest score, at once a superb parody of opera and operetta and scintillatingly tuneful in its own right, and *West Side Story* (57), see above.

BLAINE, VIVIAN (1923–). American actress and the splendid Miss Adelaide in *Guys and Dolls* (New York, 50; London, 53).

BLITZSTEIN, MARC (1905–64). American composer and librettist whose *The Cradle Will Rock* (37) was hailed as 'the most versatile triumph of the politically insurgent theatre' (Brooks Atkinson). Like his second operatic musical, *No for an Answer* (41), it ran into trouble

with Authority. He later adapted *The Threepenny Opera* (54) which ran for 2,250 performances, and adapted—as *Regina* —*The Little Foxes* (49), a fine failure.

BOCK, JERRY (1928–). American composer. With LARRY HOLOFCENER as lyricist, wrote the songs for *Fiorello* (59), *Tenderloin* (60) and *The Apple Tree* (66). With SHELDON HARNICK (lyrics) and JOSEPH STEIN (book), created the longest running of all Broadway musicals (also a colossal hit in London), *Fiddler on the Roof* (62), a fine and original show, inspired by the Jewish stories of Sholom Aleichem. With Harnick and SHERMAN YELDEN, wrote *The Rothschilds* (70).

BOLGER, RAY (1904–). American actor, dancer and comedian. His most famous role was Phil Dolan III in *On Your Toes* (36), the Vaudeville hoofer who aspires to ballet. The highspot was his dance with Tamara Geva in *Slaughter on Tenth Avenue*, choreographed by Balanchine. Sapiens in *By Jupiter* (42) and Charley Wykeham in *Where's Charley?* (48), which won him major awards. Phineas Sharp in *Come Summer* (69).

BOLTON, GUY (1884–). British dramatist, author of the books of very many shows, collaborating with P. G. Wodehouse and others in many of them. Two which were revived in the 60s were *Lady Be Good* (24) with Fred Thompson, and *Anything Goes* (34) with Wodehouse.

BROWN, GEORGIA (1933–). British actress and singer whose parts have included Nancy in *Oliver* (London, 60; New York, 62).

BRYAN, DORA (1924–). British actress, very popular in plays, revue, musicals, also films and TV. Appeared in the *Lyric* and *Globe Revues* (51, 52). Lily Bell in *The Water Gypsies* (55). Lorelei in *Gentlemen Prefer Blondes* (62). Nurse Sweetie in *Too True to be Good* (Edinburgh and London, 65). The title-role in *Hello, Dolly* (66). Dol Common in *The Alchemist* (Chichester, 70).

BUCHANAN, JACK (1890–1957). British actor, and Britain's leading song-and-dance man between the wars. His most famous patner was ELSIE RANDOLPH (1904–), who appeared with him in cheerful shows like *Stand Up and Sing* (31) and *This'll Make You Whistle* (36). First appeared in New York with two other newcomers, Beatrice Lillie and Gertrude Lawrence, in *Charlot's Revue of 1924*. From 1944, played straight parts and showed himself a first rate light comedian. His film career began in 1925.

BURKE, MARIE (1894–). British actress and singer. The memorable Julie of *Show Boat* in the West End (28), and leading lady in many musical shows including *Waltzes from Vienna* (*The Great Waltz*) in London and New York. The actress PATRICIA BURKE (1917–) is her daughter.

BURNS, DAVID (1902–71). American actor whose parts included Mayor Skinn in *The Music Man* (57), Senex in *A Funny Thing Happened on the Way to the Forum* (62) and Horace Vandergelder in *Hello, Dolly* (64).

BYNG, DOUGLAS (1893–). British entertainer in revue, cabaret, pantomime, musicals and plays, renowned for his splendidly outrageous songs.

CHAMPION, GOWER (1921–). American choreographer and, more recently, director. Has also appeared in films, including *Show Boat*, with his actress dancer wife, MARGE CHAMPION. The brilliant director and choreographer of *Bye, Bye Birdie* (60), *Hello Dolly!* (64) and *The Happy Time* (68). Directed *I Do! I Do!* (New York, 66; London, 68).

CHANNING, CAROL (1921–). American actress and singer who became an overnight star as Lorelei in *Gentlemen Prefer Blondes* (49). Her radiant and boisterous Dolly was the first and best in *Hello Dolly!* (64). Appeared in revue at Drury Lane (70): *Carol Channing with Her Ten Stout-Hearted Men*.

COHAN, GEORGE M. (1879–1942). American actor, song-writer and showman. Regarded by many as the father of American musical comedy. Most of the great years of the career of this ultimate song-and-dance man lie before this book's time-span. His style was out of date in the 20s, and in the 30s he—triumphantly—became a straight actor.

COMDEN, BETTY (1919–   ) and ADOLPH GREEN (1915–   ). American book and lyric writers. Their shows have included *On The Town* (44) and *Wonderful Town* (53) both with Bernstein's music, also Styne's *Bells are Ringing* (56) and the lyrics (with book by Garson Kanin) of his *Do, Re Mi* (60). Their lyrics for the musical *Peter Pan* (54) can be saluted by even an Old Guard Barriean. A recent success was their book for *Applause* (70).

COURTNEIDGE, CICELY. See HULBERT, JACK.

COWARD, NOËL (1899–1973) makes another appearance in this book, for his musicals and revues, which include *On With The Dance* (25), part author and composer, also *This Year of Grace* (28), author and composer, *Bitter Sweet* (29), featured earlier, *Operette* (38), author, composer and director, the revue, *Sigh No More* (45), ditto, and *Pacific 1860* (46), author and director. Most of these superbly professional shows have given enormous pleasure, though not even the finest, *Bitter Sweet,* may have the lasting quality of his best plays. The best of his lyrics, however, are already part of the national heritage.

DE MILLE, AGNES. American dancer and choreographer, whose choreography for *Oklahoma!* (43), see above, advanced the musicals as a form. Later successes (ballets apart) have included *Carousel* (45) and *Kwamina* (61) which won her a 'Tony'.

DE SYLVA, BROWN AND HENDERSON. American song-writing team who produced three zestful musicals in the 20s: *Good News* (27), *Hold Everything* (28) and *Follow Through* (29). In 1930 came *Flying High*. Their hits include 'The Best Things in Life are Free', 'You're the Cream in my Coffee', 'Button Up your Overcoat' and 'You are my Lucky Star'.

DESMOND, FLORENCE (1905–   ). British star of revue, cabaret, musicals and variety, from the mid 20s. Vera Charles in *Auntie Mame* (58).

DICKSON, DOROTHY (1896–   ). American dancer and beauty who became a West End star, especially of musicals, including two of Novello's: *Careless Rapture* (36) and *Crest of the Wave* (37). Peter Pan (25–6). Her first straight part was as Cora in *The Ringer* (26). From 1944, appeared only in plays.

DOUGLASS, STEPHEN (1921–). American actor and singer whose parts have included Billy Bigelow in *Carousel* (New York, 47; London, 50), File in *110 in the Shade* (New York, 63; London, 67, when he played Bill Starbuck), etc.

DRAKE, ALFRED (1914–). American actor, singer and director, and the original Curly in *Oklahoma!* (43). Other leads in musicals have included Hajj in *Kismet* (New York, 53: London, 55). As befits the original Fred Graham in *Kiss Me, Kate* (48), he is also a Shakespearean, including a fine Iago at Stratford, Conn. (64). A magnificent all-rounder.

EDWARDS, SHERMAN (1919–). The begetter, composer and lyricist of *1776* (New York, 69; London, 70).

ELLIS, MARY (1900–). American actress and singer, and the original Rose Marie in New York (24). Played opposite Ivor Novello in *Glamorous Night* at Drury Lane (35) and again in *The Dancing Years* (39). A fine and powerful straight actress.

ELLIS, VIVIAN (1904–). British composer and lyric writer who worked for Charlot and Cochran in the 20s and has written music of considerable charm, including the score of *Bless the Bride* (47), the lyrics and music of *And So To Bed* (51) and the score of *The Water Gypsies* (55), etc.

FIELDS, HERBERT AND DOROTHY. American brother and sister who provided the books for several successes, including *Let's Face It* (41), *Up in Central Park* (45) and *Annie Get Your Gun* (46). She collaborated with Cy Coleman in *Sweet Charity* (65).

FRIML, RUDOLF (1881–1972). Czech-born American composer of operettas and musicals, including two likely to run for ever, *Rose Marie* (24), see above, and *The Vagabond King* (25).

GAXTON, WILLIAM. American star of musicals. Parts included the Yankee in *A Connecticut Yankee* (27) and Wintergreen in *Of Thee I Sing* (31).

GERSHWIN, GEORGE (1898–1937). American composer and a supreme writer of popular songs. With his brother IRA GERSHWIN (1896–) as lyricist, wrote a series of Broadway hits, including *Lady, Be Good* (24), *Funny Face* (27), *Strike Up The Band* (30), *Of Thee I Sing* (31), see above, and the Negro folk opera, *Porgy and Bess* (35).

GILBERT, OLIVE. British singer, associated with Ivor Novello's greatest successes. Sister Margatetta in *The Sound of Music* (61).

GINGOLD, HERMIONE (1897–). British actress and a supreme revue artist, helping win the war in *Sweet and Low* (43), *Sweeter and Lower* (44) and the peace in *Sweetest and Lowest* (46). Since the 50s, has appeared regularly on Broadway in plays and revue, and in films. A voice and personality like a glamorous serpent.

GRAVES, PETER (1911–). British actor and singer, especially associated with parts in Ivor Novello shows, and has also appeared in many plays. His wife, VANESSA LEE (1920–) has often appeared with him. She was Novello's leading lady in *King's Rhapsody* (49).

GRAY, DOLORES (1924–). American actress and singer and London's adored Annie in *Annie Get Your Gun* (47). Her Cornelia in *Carnival in Flanders* (53) won her a 'Tony' award. Frenchy in *Destry Rides Again* (59), etc.

GRENFELL, JOYCE (1910–). British actress, writer and entertainer. Though she has appeared in revue—*Sigh No More* (45), *Tuppence Coloured* (47) and *Penny Plain* (51), etc., she is best known for her one-woman shows, which she has given in many parts of the world. Also a very popular film actress and radio and TV entertainer.

HAMMERSTEIN, OSCAR II (1895–1961). American dramatist and the most successful lyric writer of his day. Grandson of the impresario, Oscar Hammerstein I, his first Broadway show was *Always You* (20) and his most significant, *Show Boat* (27) and *Oklahoma!* (43), both featured earlier in this chapter, and both

of which radiated his belief in American folk opera. Collaborated with (amongst others), Youmans, Friml, Kern and, most importantly, Richard Rodgers. His partnership with the last from *Oklahoma!* to *The Sound of Music* (59), ranks as the most popular since Gilbert and Sullivan. It produced at least one masterpiece, *South Pacific* (49).

HANSON, JOHN (1922–). British singer-actor-manager, best known for touring in Friml, Romberg, etc., plus successful forays to London.

HART, LORENZ (1895–1943). American lyric writer, widely regarded as the wittiest and most skilful of the inter-war years. His range also encompassed deep emotion, not always a trademark of lyricists in musicals. His collaboration with Richard Rodgers resulted in a brilliant series of shows, including *On Your Toes* (36), *Babes in Arms* (37), *The Boys from Syracuse* (38) and *Pal Joey* (40), whose very successful revival in 1952 (see above) he did not live to see.

HART, MOSS (1904–61). American playwright and director (also see p. 43) whose musicals included *Face the Music* (32), book *Lady in the Dark* (41), book and director, *My Fair Lady* (56), director, see above, and *Camelot* (60), director.

HENSON, LESLIE (1891–1957). British comedian and actor-manager. A 'superb droll' (Agate), whose hits included *Sally* (21), *Kid Boots* (26), *Funny Face* (28) and *It's a Boy* (30). Associated with Tom Walls in presenting the Aldwych Farces. A supreme artist of the ridiculous, his post-war shows, which did not allow him to exploit his own personality, were not such successes for him. They included *Harvey* (50) and the Pepys musical, *And So To Bed* (51).

HERBERT, A. P. (1890–1971). British writer, poet, wit and politician, and author of comedies and librettist of operettas. His shows included *Tantivy Towers* (29), *Helen!* (32), after Offenbach, *Derby Day* (32), *Bless the Bride* (47), *Tough at the Top* (49) and *The Water Gypsies* (55).

HICKMAN, CHARLES (1905–). British actor who has directed many musicals, revues, including *Sweet and Low* (43), and plays.

HOLLOWAY, STANLEY (1890–). British actor and singer. One of the Co-Optimist in the early 20s, and an entertainer for many years, his greatest success came with his Alfred Doolittle in *My Fair Lady* (New York, 56: London, 58). Has appeared in many films.

HOWES, BOBBY (1895–72). British actor and a major star of musicals, revue and pantomime between the wars. His boyish charm (an inevitable phrase

about him) made him an ideal Buttons. A 'stray cherub', according to Trewin, one of his happiest partnerships was with the massive, light-footed Vera Pearce. Starred with his daughter, SALLY ANN HOWES (1930–), in *Paint Your Wagon* (53). She later succeeded Julie Andrews as Eliza in *My Fair Lady* on Broadway (58).

HULBERT, JACK (1892–) and COURTNEIDGE, CICELY (1893–). Much loved English husband and wife stars of musicals and revues. Jack Hulbert has also directed many shows. Successes included *Clowns in Clover* (27) and *Under Your Hat* (38). Recently, mainly in plays. Novello wrote *Gay's the Word* (51) for Miss Courtneidge, who was made a D.B.E. (72).

KAUFMAN, GEORGE S. (1889–). American dramatist and director (see p. 46). Collaborating with Morrie Ryskind, his first major book for a musical was *Strike Up the Band* (27), a satire on war. *Of Thee I Sing* (31), also with Morrie Ryskind, and a major Gershwin musical, is featured above. *Let 'em Eat Cake* (33) was a not-so-successful sequel. With Moss Hart, wrote the book for *I'd Rather be Right* (37) a topical Rodgers and Hart musical about Roosevelt. With Leueen MacGarth and Abe Burrows, helped adapt *Ninotchka* into *Silk Stockings* (55). This remarkable man-of-the-theatre also brilliantly staged musicals, including *Of Thee I Sing*, *Let 'em Eat Cake* and, most excitingly, *Guys and Dolls* (50).

KEELER, RUBY (1909–). American actress and dancer. This star of the 20s and later of films, reappeared on Broadway as Sue Smith in *No, No, Nanette* (71) to great acclaim.

KERN, JEROME (1885–1945). American composer. His successes included *Sally* (20), *Sunny* (25) and his one classic, *Show Boat* (see above). Perhaps *Sally* was the most fabulous of his earlier shows, produced by Ziegfeld, starring Marilyn Miller, and containing the beautiful ballad, 'Look for the Silver Lining'. 'Smoke Gets in Your Eyes' was first heard in *Roberta* (33) and 'All the Things You Are' in a (39) failure, *Very Warm for May*. Sadly for the theatre, Kern concentrated on music for the films from then onwards.

KERT, LARRY (1930–). American actor and singer and the very fine Tony of *West Side Story* (57). Robert in *Company* (70).

KIDD, MICHAEL (1919–). American choreographer and director. His dances for *Guys and Dolls* (50) were widely praised. Later shows have included *The Rothschilds* (70) which he also directed.

KING, DENNIS (1897–1971). British-born singer and actor, star of American musicals, and the original Francis Villon in *The Vagabond King* on Broadway (25). His final appearance was in *A Patriot for Me* also in New York. His extraordinary career embraced Jim Kenyon in *Rose Marie* (London, 24) and in New York such diverse roles as Richard of Bordeaux, Vershinin, Higgins, Gaylord Ravenal, General Burgoyne and Jason in *Medea*. A Broadway superstar, little known in his own country by the younger generation of playgoers, and that rare thing, a first-rate actor-singer.

KIRKWOOD, PAT (1921–). British star of pantomime, revue and musicals. Her husband is the actor, composer and lyric writer, HUBERT GREGG (1916–).

LAHR, BERT (1895–1967). American actor and comedian and star of many musicals. Began in Vaudeville, becoming a musical comedy star in *Hold Everything* (28). An endearing rumbunctous comedian whose famous performance in *Du Barry was a Lady* (39) moved Richard Watts Jr. to write of his playing with the sort of 'spluttering violence and leering impudence that makes him one of the best comedians in the world'. One of the Tramps —the other was E. G. Marshall —in the New York *Waiting for Godot* (56). His son and biographer (*Notes on a Cowardly Lion*) is the critic JOHN LAHR, author of *Acting out America* etc.

LANE, LUPINO (1892–1959).

British Cockney comedian. For many years a star of revue and pantomime who appeared on both sides of the Atlantic. Small and neat he was known as Nipper and was a true clown. His most famous show, *Me and My Girl* (37) by Gay, Rose and Furber included 'The Lambeth Walk', which became a national institution.

LAURENTS, ARTHUR (1920–). American dramatist (see p. 48) who wrote the book of *West Side Story* (57) and *Gypsy* (59).

LAWRENCE, GERTRUDE (1898–1952). British actress (see p. 171) and a star of revue and musicals on both sides of the Atlantic. Even the un-star-conscious George Jean Nathan sang her praises. Began as a cabaret artist. Her first great success was in André Charlot's *London Calling* (23), written by Noël Coward, who also wrote *Bitter Sweet* with her in mind, though in the event, the music was too heavy for her voice. Two of her greatest hits were as Kay in Gershwin's *Oh, Kay* (New York, 26: London, 27) and as Anna in *The King and I* (51), the adaptation of which from the play *Anna and the King of Siam* she suggested to Rodgers and Hammerstein. She died during the run of the play. The over-worked phrase, 'a living legend' was uniquely true in the case of this star of stars. See *Gertrude Lawrence as Mrs. 'A'* by her husband, the manager, Richard Aldrich.

LAYE, EVELYN (1900–). British actress and singer, now best known as a very popular actress, but once the reigning queen of British musical comedy, even Agate saluting her singing, acting and beauty, which lasts to this day. Currently (73) starring in *No Sex Please—We're British*. Her most famous roles were the Merry Widow, Madame Pompadour and the title role in *Helen!* (32). Her husband was the actor FRANK LAWTON (1904–69).

LERNER, ALAN JAY (1918–). American lyricist and writer of musical books, whose partnership with Frederick Loewe began in the 40s and has produced, among other shows, *Brigadoon* (47), *Paint Your Wagon* (51), *My Fair Lady* (56, see above) and *Camelot* (61). With Burton Lane as composer, he wrote *On a Clear Day You Can See Forever* (65). *My Fair Lady*, far and away their best show, saw Lerner rising to lyrics which G.B.S. might well have applauded.

LILLIE, BEATRICE (1898–). Canadian actress and comedienne. Made her name in the Charlot revues of the 20s. 'Dashing from one *tour de force* to another', noted Agate (39) of her sketches in Harold French's *All Clear*, and her career achieved a new peak with a one-woman show, *An Evening of Beatrice Lillie* (54). This joyous comic, mistress of the grotesque and low comedy and of hair-trigger timing, has also appeared in straight roles, including *Aunt Mame* (58) in New York and London. Her Madame Arcati in *High Spirits* (64), a musical version of Coward's *Blithe Spirit*, created such a sensation on its first night in New York that she was forced to quell the audience by treating it to a series of hilarious, travestied moments from the ballet.

LLOYD-WEBBER, ANDREW and TIM RICE. British composer and librettist of the hit rock opera, *Jesus Christ Superstar*.

LOESSER, FRANK (1910–69). American composer and lyric writer. His first hit was *Where's Charley?* (48) adapted from *Charley's Aunt* by George Abbott. *Guys and Dolls* (50) was a triumph for him as composer and lyricist, with number after number worthy of Damon Runyon whose stories had inspired the show. His *The Most Happy Fella* (56) from Sidney Howard's *They Knew What They Wanted* was a not entirely successful blend of musical and opera, 'his' being the correct word, for as well as the lyrics and music, he adapted the play. However, for some it was an outright triumph. *How to Succeed in Business without Really Trying* (61) was a successful return to more traditional musical comedy, with Loesser as composer and lyricist.

LOEWE, FREDERICK (1904–). Austrian-born American composer, best known for his partnership with Alan Jay Lerner. This ex-concert pianist, gold prospector and cowboy became a composer of popular songs and shows in the 30s. His meeting with Lerner in 1942 changed his luck. Like Lerner, he excelled himself with his score for *My Fair Lady* (56). If his usual scores do not reach such heights, or those of greater composers, happy the country which has such fine musicians at the top of the second rank.

LOGAN, JOSHUA (1908–). American director and dramatist. His musical credits include *Annie Get Your Gun* (director: 46), *South Pacific* (part-author and director: 50), *Fanny* (part-author and director: 53). Also see p. 49.

MACDERMOT, GALT (composer): GEROME RAGNI and JAMES RADO, (Book and Lyrics): TIM O'HORGAN (director): JULIE ARENAL, (Dance): ROBIN WAGNER (Design): the team responsible for the Tribal Love-Rock hit on both sides of the Atlantic, *Hair* (69). The first show in Britain to benefit by the abolition of theatre censorship, and hugely enjoyable into the bargain. MacDermot composed the score for the musical *Two Gentlemen of Verona* (71).

MAMOULIAN, ROUBEN (1898–). Russian-born American director of plays (see p. 51), films, operas and musicals. Staged *Porgy and*

Bess (27), *Oklahoma!* (43) and *Carousel* (45).

MANKOWITZ, WOLF (1924–). British novelist and dramatist (see p. 51). His musicals include *Expresso Bongo* (58), *Make Me an Offer* (59) and *Pickwick* (63).

MARTIN, MARY (1913–). American actress and singer who became a star as Dolly Winsor in *Leave it to Me* (38) when she sang 'My Heart Belongs to Daddy', removing ermine wraps and singing in a baby voice. After a spell in films, she appeared at Drury Lane in Coward's *Pacific 1860* (46), toured as Annie in *Annie Get Your Gun* (47–8) and then became a theatrical immortal as Ensign Nellie Forbush in *South Pacific* (New York, 49; London, 51). While being 'as corny as Kansas in August' or washing that man right out of her hair, her personality, 'heart' and warm, tangy voice epitomized the Mid-Western girl of everyone's dreams. Later starred in *The Sound of Music* (59) with maximum success in a part that was not a patch on Ensign Nellie, just as the show was leagues less good than *South Pacific*. Dolly in *Hello Dolly* (New York and London, 65). Agnes in *I Do! I Do!* (68).

MARTIN, MILLICENT (1934–). British actress and singer whose success dates from her Cora in *The Crooked Mile* (59).

MASCHWITZ, ERIC (1901–69). British dramatist and composer. Author of a number of romantic shows including *Balalaika* (36), *Carissima* (48), *Belinda Fair* (49) and *Zip Goes a Million* (51). Worked for many years in radio and on TV, also wrote film scenarios.

MATTHEWS, JESSIE (1907–). British actress and dancer. By 1926 she was revealing 'talent of a singularly high order' in *The Charlot Show of 1926* to James Agate, graduating to being called 'that rogue in porcelain' by him in *One Dam Thing After Another* (27). After *Sally Who?* (33) deserted the stage for films for a number of years. Has been mainly a straight actress since, including radio's second and last Mrs. Dale. In the years between the wars she was a major star.

MELVILLE, ALAN (1910–). Lyric writer and dramatist. In the high noon of Intimate Revue during and just after the war, he wrote sketches and lyrics for some of the most successful of them, including three of the most famous, *Sweet and Low* (43), *Sweeter and Lower* (44) and *Sweetest and Lowest* (46); La Gingold appeared in all of them. He wrote the entire book of *Sweetest and Lowest*. His plays include an amusing comedy about a theatrical married couple, *Simon and Laura* (54). A witty writer and talker whose work is best enjoyed in the theatre before a live audience.

MERMAN, ETHEL (1909–). American actress and singer, trumpet-toned, breezy and a star of the first magnitude. After starting in Vaudeville, she shot to stardom in Cole Porter's *Anything Goes* (34), reaching National Institution level with her Annie Oakley in *Annie Get Your Gun* (46) and *Call Me Madam* (50). Her Rose, the ruthless mother in *Gypsy* (59) added to her laurels. Dolly in *Hello, Dolly!* (70).

MIELZINER, JO (1901–). American designer. Among the many musicals that he has designed are *Of Thee I Sing* (31), *The Boys from Syracuse* (38), *Pal Joey* (40), *Annie Get Your Gun* (46), *South Pacific* (49), *The King and I* (51), *The Most Happy Fella* (56), *Gypsy* (59) and *1776* (69). For this superlative designer's work in the straight theatre see p. 52.

MILLER, MARILYN (1896–1936). American actress, singer and dancer. Began in Vaudeville. Spotted by Lee Shubert (13) in London, she started annually in *The Passing Show* in New York. This delectable artist became a great star in *Sally* (20) in which she sang 'Look for the Silver Lining'. Played Peter Pan (24). In *Sunny* (25), she sang Kern's 'Who'. Her later successes included *As Thousands Cheer* (33).

MOODY, RON (1924–). British actor who made his name in revue, then as Fagin in *Oliver* (60). Played Grimaldi in his own show, *Joey* (62).

MOORE, VICTOR (1876–1962). American actor and comedian, some of whose greatest successes were in musicals, most notably as Stanley McGee in *Oh, Kay!* (26) opposite Gertrude Lawrence, Alexander Throttlebottom in *Of Thee I Sing* (31) and the Rev. Dr. Moon in *Anything Goes* (34).

MORISON, PATRICIA (1915–). American actress and singer, and the original, definitive Lilli Vanessi in *Kiss Me Kate* (New York, 48; London, 51). Anna in *The King and I* (54).

MOSTEL, ZERO (1915–). American actor and entertainer who, after years in show business, shot to fame, first in *A Funny Thing Happened on the Way to the Forum* (62), playing Pseudolus and Prologue, then with a classic performance as Tevye in *Fiddler on the Roof* (64).

MYERS, PETER (1923–). British author whose many revues include *For Amusement Only* (56).

NEAGLE, ANNA (1904–). British actress who graduated from the chorus—*Rose Marie* (26), etc.— to become a hugely popular film star. A Regent's Park Rosalind, her West End hits have included *The Glorious Days* (53) and Lady Hadwell in *Charlie Girl* (65). D.B.E. (70).

NESBITT, ROBERT (1906–). British dramatist and director, especially of musicals, revues, etc., from the early 30s and (since 56) a deviser and director of major pantomimes.

NEWAY, PATRICIA (1919–). American singer and actress, a star of operas and musicals. Her best-known parts have been as Magda Sorel in *The Consul* (New York, 50; London, 51), a supremely fine performance, and the Mother Abbess in *The Sound of Music*.

NEWLEY, ANTHONY (1931–). British actor and co-author and composer (with LESLIE BRICUSSE) of *Stop the World—I Want to Get Off* (London, 61; New York, 62), also *The Roar of the Grease Paint—the Smell of the Crowd* (Nottingham, 64; New York, 65), and *The Good Old Bad Old Days* (72), far and away their best show to date.

NOVELLO, IVOR (1893–1951). British actor, dramatist and composer whose musical romances dominated Drury Lane from *Glamorous Night* (35) to *King's Rhapsody* (49). *Gay's the Word* (51) was an energetic vehicle for Cicely Courtneidge, and less typical. His sugar-sweet works, beautifully presented, were hugely popular, like their creator who performed in them. Modern revivals, less well-staged, have not helped their reputation. Two other shows which must be mentioned are *The Dancing*

Years (39) and *Perchance to Dream* (45). Also see p. 180.

OLDHAM, DEREK (1892–1968). British actor and singer who followed years with the D'Oyly Carte with leading roles in musicals. His roles included Jim Kenyon in *Rose Marie* (25) and François Villon in *The Vagabond King* (27), etc. Returned to Gilbert and Sullivan from time to time. A very popular performer.

ORBACH, JERRY (1935–). American actor who won a 'Tony' for his Chuck Baxter in *Promises, Promises* (68).

PINZA, EZIO (1892–1957). Italian singer and actor who, after a career as the finest operatic bass of his day and a magnificent singing-actor, became a Broadway star as De Beque in *South Pacific* (49). Later starred in *Fanny* (54).

PRINCE, HAROLD (1928–). American producer and director, especially of musicals. Beginning with his production of *The Pyjama Game* (54), his extraordinary list of credits includes *Damn Yankees* (55), *West Side Story* (57), *A Funny Thing Happened on the Way to the Forum* (63), *Fiddler on the Roof* (64) and *Company* (70). Has also directed a number of plays and been associated with films of his shows, including *West Side Story*.

PORTER, COLE (1892–1964). American song-writer and composer of musicals for which he wrote his own lyrics. A trained musician, his shows include *Gay Divorce* (32), *Anything Goes* (34), *Du Barry was a Lady* (39) with Ethel Merman and Bert Lahr, *Panama Hattie* (40) and, his masterpiece, *Kiss Me, Kate* (48), featured earlier. The final two shows of this witty, exceptionally gifted composer, who wrote 'Begin the Beguine' and 'Night and Day', were *Can-Can* (53) and *Silk Stockings* (55), a musical version of *Ninotchka*.

RIVERA, CHITA (1933–). American actress and singer and the electric Anita of *West Side Story* (New York, 57; London, 58) also Rose in *Bye, Bye, Birdie* (New York, 60; London, 61).

ROBBINS, JEROME (1918–). American choreographer and director. Deviser as well as choreographer of *On The Town* (44), also *West Side Story* (featured earlier), which he also directed (57) and which revolutionized the musical. Other shows he has directed and choreographed have included *The Pyjama Game* (54), *The Bells are Ringing* (56) and *Gypsy* (59). Choreographed *Call Me Madam* (50) and *The King and I* (51) and other shows, and has directed a number of plays. Was responsible for staging and choreographing the colossal success, *Fiddler on the Roof* (64).

ROBEY, GEORGE (1869–1954). British comedian. A great music hall artist who was billed as 'the Prime Minister of Mirth', he later turned to revue with the decline of the halls, notably *The Bing Boys Are Here* (16) with its famous duet, 'If You Were the Only Girl in the World'. Played Menelaus in *Helen* (32), a part which involved so much toning down of his vigorous style that Agate was moved to describe it as a 'miracle of accommodation' like a 'trombone player obliging with a pianissimo'. Played Falstaff successfully (35), also—a collector's item—Sancho Panzo in the film, *Don Quixote*, starring Chalipin. Knighted (54).

RODGERS, RICHARD (1902–). American composer of some of the most successful shows and popular songs ever written. His two great partnerships, first with Lorenz Hart (20–43) then with Oscar Hammerstein Jr. (43–61) produced two shows, both dealt with earlier in this chapter, which changed the course of the musical's history: *Pal Joey* (40) and *Oklahoma!* (43). Though always a consummate master melodist, Rodgers adapted his style to his two great colleagues, his melodies for Hart being often sharp, witty and sophisticated, while for Hammerstein more sentiment crept in and the two successfully aspired to folk-opera.

Notable shows with Hart included *On Your Toes* (36) and

The Boys From Syracuse (38), the former containing the famous Balanchine ballet, 'Slaughter on Tenth Avenue'. His finest scores for Hammerstein were *Carousel* (45) and *South Pacific* (49), though *The King and I* (51) shows only a slight decline in standards. *Flower Drum Song* (58) saw a sharper decline. And, with all respect to the stupendous popularity of the piece, *The Sound of Music* (59) is musically far below the composer's best work. His *No Strings* (62), for which he also wrote the lyrics, was a success, though not a great one and *Do I Hear a Waltz?* (65), based on *The Time of the Cuckoo*, was a failure. *Avanti* (68). *Two by Two* (70). An immortal.

ROGERS, ANNE (1933–). British actress and singer. Polly Browne in *The Boy Friend* (54). Eliza Doolittle in *My Fair Lady* in Chicago, Los Angeles and in London (59). Agnes Hobson in *I Do! I Do!* (68).

ROMBERG, SIGMUND (1887–1951). Hungarian-born American composer whose musicals, firmly rooted in European traditions, are as popular as ever with amateurs and, occasionally, professionals, as are those of his musical twin, Friml's. His most famous shows are *Maytime* (17), *Blossom Time* (21), alas poor Schubert!, *The Student Prince* (24), *The Desert Song* (26) and *The New Moon* (28). Only a

musical snob could deny his melodic gift.

ROME, HAROLD (1908–). American composer and lyricist. Made his name as a Left Wing writer for his contributions to *Pins and Needles* (37). Later shows have included *Call Me Mister* (46), a topical revue about the problems of ex-soldiers, *Wish You were Here* (52), *Fanny* (54), *Destry Rides Again* (59) and *I Can Get it for You Wholesale* (62), which saw Barbra Streisand's Broadway debut.

ROUTLEDGE, PATRICIA (1929–). British actress and singer. Has appeared in London in musicals, plays and revue including the title-role in *Little Mary Sunshine* (62) and Berinthia in the musical, *Virtue in Danger* (63). Her Alice Challice in *Darling of the Day* (New York, 68) won her a 'Tony' award. At Chichester (69) her parts included Lady Fidget in *The Country Wife* and Agatha Posket in *The Magistrate*. Currently shining in *Cowardy Custard* (73).

RUSSELL, ROSALIND (1912–). American actress, particularly famous for her films, but also a stage actress and major star of two musicals, *Wonderful Town* (53) and *Mame* (56), in both of which she gave whirlwind performances.

SEAL, ELIZABETH (1933–). British actress and dancer, notably as Gladys in *The Pyjama*

Game (55), Lola in *Damn Yankees* (57) and in the title-role of *Irma La Douce* (London, 58; New York, 60), which won her a 'Tony' award. Has also appeared in plays.

SECOMBE, HARRY (1921–). This greatly loved singer and entertainer has starred in two musicals: *Pickwick* (London, 63; New York, 65), D'Artagnan in *The Four Musketeers* (67).

SLADE, JULIAN (1930–). British composer and dramatist who, with Dorothy Reynolds, wrote the tuneful, unpretentious musical, *Salad Days* (54) which ran for 2,283 performances, and several other 'anodyne whimsies' (John Russell Taylor), including *Free as Air* (57). *Salad Days* began at the Bristol Old Vic, which saw the opening of *Trelawny* (72), a success for which he provided the music and lyrics.

SONDHEIM, STEPHEN (1930–). American composer and lyricist. Lyrics for *West Side Story* (57), *Gypsy* (59). Music and lyrics for *A Funny Thing Happened on the Way to the Forum* (62). Later shows have included *Do I Hear a Waltz?* (65) with Rodgers, *Company* (70), lyrics and music, and *Follies* (71), lyrics and music. This last is a lush, loving throwback to the Ziegfeld style, while *Company* is a scintillating, searing (by musicals' standards) look at marriage, New York style.

STONE, PADDY (1925–). Canadian choreographer and director of musicals and revues, including *Pieces of Eight* (59) and *Maggie May* (64), direction only, in London.

STREISAND, BARBRA (1942–). American actress and singer who first made her mark as Miss Marmelstein in *I Can Get it for you Wholesale* (62), then became a star with her Fanny Brice in *Funny Girl* (New York, 64; London, 66). Next came film stardom.

STRITCH, ELAINE (1926–). American actress and singer. Her parts have included Regina in *The Little Foxes* (47), Mimi Paragon in *Sail Away* (New York, 61; London, 62), Martha in *Who's Afraid of Virginia Woolf?* (63), Ruth in *Wonderful Town* (67) and Joanne in *Company* (New York, 70; London, 72). Currently starring in London in *Small Craft Warnings* (73).

STROUSE, CHARLES (1928–). American composer whose scores include *Bye, Bye, Birdie* (60) and *Applause* (70).

STYNE, JULE (1905–). American composer and producer whose scores include *The Bells are Ringing* (56), *Funny Girl* (64) and *Hallelujah, Baby* (67) which won him a 'Tony'.

SWANN, DONALD (1923–). British composer. After contributing to revues, joined with

MICHAEL FLANDERS (1922–) to give their very popular two-man entertainment, *At The Drop of a Hat* in London (56–) and on tour, also in America and Canada. *At The Drop of Another Hat* (London, 63; New York, 66).

TOYE, WENDY (1917–). British director, choreographer and dancer. Has directed many musicals, operas, operettas, etc., also some plays. Her major successes include *Robert and Elizabeth* (direction and choreography, 64), *Show Boat* (ditto, 71) and her masterpiece, *Orpheus in the Underworld* (60 onwards) for the Wells.

VERDON, GWEN (1925–). American actress, singer and dancer who attracts awards as soon as she steps on to a stage. After making a striking impression as Claudine in *Can-Can* (53), became a star as Lola in *Damn Yankees* (55), since when she has played Anna Christie in *New Girl in Town* (57), Essie in *Redhead* (59) and the title role in *Sweet Charity* (66).

WALSTON, RAY (1917–). American actor whose parts have included Luther Billis in *South Pacific* (London, 51) and Applegate (The Devil) in *Damn Yankees* (55) which won him a 'Tony' award.

WELCHMAN, HARRY (1886–1966). British star of musicals between the wars: Pierre Birabeau in *The Desert Song*, François Villon in *The Vagabond King*, Karl in *The Student Prince*, Robert Misson in *The New Moon*, etc. Also played Long John Silver (46/47) and Lord Mortlake in *The World of Paul Slickey* (59).

WILLSON, MEREDITH (1902–). American composer and lyric writer. For his smash hit, *The Music Man* (57), also wrote the book. Neither *The Unsinkable Molly Brown* (60) nor *Here's Love* (63) were so successful.

WILSON, SANDY (1924–). British composer and dramatist who, after writing songs for revues, including *Slings and Arrows* (48), wrote *The Boy Friend* (53), a delicious pastiche of the 20s which ran for 2,048 performances in London and 483 on Broadway. Many consider his finest work to be *Valmouth* (58), inspired by Firbank's novel.

WODEHOUSE, P. G. (1881–). Master British comic novelist who was once a fine Broadway lyric writer. Was one of a famous triumvirate: Jerome Kern (no less!), Guy Bolton (books) and himself, their first hit being *Oh, Boy!* (19). Collaborated with Gershwin in *Oh, Kay* (26) which made a star of Gertrude Lawrence. His most famous song is 'Bill', originally written for Kern's *Oh, Lady! Lady!* (18), but transplanted to *Show Boat*.

WOOD, PEGGY (1892–). American actress and singer. Played in many Broadway shows until coming to London to star so memorably in *Bitter Sweet* (29). Another Coward role was Rozanne Gray in *Operette* (38). Gradually, her career in Broadway musicals gave way to straight acting, including Ruth in *Blithe Spirit* (41) and Amanda Wingfield in *The Glass Menagerie* (Chicago, 64).

YOUMANS, VINCENT (1898–1946). American composer of musicals, including *No, No Nanette* (25) whose tunes include 'Tea for Two' and 'I Want to be Happy'. A colossal success all over the world when it first appeared, and a smash hit on Broadway when revived in 1971.

ZIEGFELD, FLORENZ. See p. 266.

ZORINA, VERA (1917–). German-born American actress, dancer and director. Vera Baranova in *On Your Toes* (London, 37). Angel in *I Married an Angel* (New York, 38). Formerly a distinguished ballet dancer, she has directed operas in the 60s, appeared in films and played Ariel in *The Tempest* (45).

ZWAR, CHARLES (1914–). British composer associated particularly with revues including *Gate Revues, Sweetest and Lowest* (44) and *A La Carte* (48), and parts of *The Globe Revue* (52), *Airs on a Shoestring* (53), etc.

FARCE

Some Farces

ROOKERY NOOK   1926

This is perhaps the most famous of the Aldwych farces, and, though it would be risky to claim that it is the funniest of the fabulous output of Ben Travers, or the best of them, it is certainly one of the top three and a classic of its kind. It concerns the terrible dilemma of the unfortunate, and recently married, Gerald Popkiss when he arrives at Rookery Nook, Chumpton-on-Sea, Somerset, ahead of his wife, only to have a lovely damsel-in-distress named Rhoda fling herself on his mercy. His single ally is his friend Clive, and amongst his enemies are his acid, suspicious sister-in-law, Gertrude, the daily help, Mrs. Leverett, and a Prussian called Putz. All is mercifully resolved—just. Travers's situations and beautifully timed dialogue are both joyous and expert, and, if there will probably never be a Gerald to equal the original, that prince of farceurs and king of 'business', Ralph Lynn, the play is so brilliant that even a merely adequate cast can do it some justice.

First produced at the Aldwych, June 30, 1926.

Author   Ben Travers

Cast included Ralph Lynn as Gerald, Tom Walls as Clive, Robertson Hare as Harold Twine, Ethel Coleridge as Gertrude Twine, Mary Brough as Mrs. Leverett and Winifred Shotter as Rhoda.

YOU CAN'T TAKE IT WITH YOU   1936

This amiable portrait of a chaotic middle-class family, with Grandpa not troubled by the ambition to make money, the 'it' of the title, with Mother writing plays because a typewriter was delivered years before by mistake, with ballet practice in the living room and a Russian Grand Duchess in the kitchen, won a Pulitzer Prize. It has been called 'an affectionate hymn couched in farcical terms' to middle class values by Taubman, who has also called it a loosely constructed farce, whereas Brooks Atkinson has called it a comedy. To Britons brought up in the discipline of the Aldwych farces it is a farcical comedy and none the worse for that. As so often happens with transatlantic exports in either direction, the play—set in a 'madhouse with all the comforts of home'—failed in London, but not in the Reps. The Reps were right.

First produced in London at the Booth Theatre, December 14, 1936

Authors	Moss Hart and George S. Kaufman
Producer	Sam H. Harris

Cast included Henry Travers, Josephine Hull, Frank Wilcox, Paula Trueman, Ruth Attaway, Frank Conlan, Margot Stevenson and Jess Barker.

ARSENIC AND OLD LACE   1941

Whether it is a farcical comedy, farce, black comedy, or, as John Ganner called it, 'the most entertaining comedy-melodrama of the American stage', *Arsenic and Old Lace* is one of the few plays genuinely to deserve the appellation 'mirthquake'. Its heroines, the two old dears who relieve lonely old men of their lives with the utmost charm, are only slightly less dotty than their nephew who thinks he is Theodore Roosevelt. Another nephew, Mortimer, is a dramatic critic driven even further up the wall by his family than by the plays he sees. Yet another nephew, Jonathan, is a black sheep who looks like (and was originally played by) Boris Karloff—and there are other good roles as well. Howard Lindsay and Russel Crouse, who presented the play, also helped it to success by gentle guidance of their author, and, together with Mr. Kesselring, emerged as public benefactors, not least to Londoners, who were much cheered by the play in the war years.

First produced in New York at the Fulton, January 10, 1941.

Author	Joseph Kesselring

Cast included Josephine Hull, Jean Adair, John Alexander, Allyn Joslyn, Boris Karloff and Edgar Stehli.

The play ran for 1,444 performances. It opened in London at the Strand on December 23, 1942, and ran for 1,332 performances. The two old ladies were Lilian Braithwaite and Mary Jerrold, and Naughton Wayne played Mortimer. It has been twice revived in London.

RELUCTANT HEROES   1950

This play was the first of Brian Rix's Whitehall farces, certainly one of the best, and, arguably, the funniest of the lot, at least for its first two acts. A generation that has not done National Service cannot perhaps respond to it quite so ecstatically as the millions who have, but its barrack-room humour is likely to survive. A most daunting experience for a Rep actor in the 50s was to glimpse the published edition of the play, with the laughs the London company regularly got marked with asterisks. But the author, Colin Morris, was so skilled that any competent cast could get most of them. The play's slender plot concerns the early hours and days of National Service for a group of ill-assorted musketeers, including a definitive gormless (the first Rix essay in the genre in London), a public schoolboy, and a London lad. The play ran for 1,610 performances.

First produced in London at the Whitehall, September 12, 1950.

Author	Colin Morris
Director	Frank Dermody
Designer	Joan Tiffin

Cast included Brian Rix, Dermot Walsh, Wally Patch, Larry Noble and the author.

SAILOR BEWARE!   1955

Philip King has had a string of successes, two of which are likely to live. They are *See How They Run* (44), a flawless farce full of clergymen, real and false, and renowned for its situations and steady stream of very funny lines, and *Sailor Beware!*, written with Falkland L. Cary. Given a competent cast and a trombone-toned heavy who can play Emma Hornett, one of drama's supreme dragonesses, the audience is in clover. The authors call their play a comedy, but it happily has so many trimmings of farce that it can be included here as a farcical-comedy. Its story tells of how Albert Tufnell A.B., after a few hours of his mother-in-law-to-be, jilts his bride at the last moment. As Emma is part walking volcano, part shrew and the most explosive character in drama since Hotspur, but without his charm, you can hardly blame him. The play is stiff with good parts, most notably Emma's husband Henry who draws comfort from his ferrets, and Aunt Edie, who was once jilted herself, and rushes in and out of the action like a demented but affectionate hen.

First produced in London at the Strand, February 16, 1955.

Authors	Philip King and Falkland L. Cary
Director	Melville Gillam
Designer	Michael Eve

Cast included Peggy Mount as Emma, Cyril Smith as Henry and Ann Wilton as Edie.

This was the play that made an overnight star of the unknown —except to a number of Rep audiences—Peggy Mount, who had Kenneth Tynan using phrases like Earth Mother about her and J. C. Trewin calling her a flame-thrower. The play ran 1,231 performances and there were later two popular, though less distinguished, sequels to it.

STOP IT, WHOEVER YOU ARE   1961

This very funny farce, which is also part comedy and part fantasy, showed that the theatre had gained a major comic talent in Henry Livings. Its hero, the first of his little men in trouble with Authority, is Perkin Warbeck, a factory lavatory attendant. Troubles afflict him in battalions, including misadventures when the top brass bring a Distinguished Visitor to relieve himself, but he gets his own back on his wife and his landlord before dying of shock and returning (vocally) at a seance.

The play is in the tradition of North country working-class comedy, but with real social satire as a bonus, and a wealth of well-drawn characters, including Captain Bootle, Perkin's employer, Oglethorpe the landlord, Perkin's unloving wife, and the randy young Marilyn who adds unexpected colour to poor, down-trodden Perkin's life.

First produced in London at the Arts Theatre, February 15, 1961

Author	Henry Livings
Director	Vida Hope
Designer	Brian Currah

Cast included Wilfred Brambell as Perkin, Rosamund Green-wood as his wife, Brian Oulton as Bootle, Arthur Lowe as Oglethorpe, John Rutland as Harbuckle and Sydonie Platt as Marilyn.

LOOT 1966

Joe Orton's works are often dubbed black comedies, but black farce would seem to be the right description of this play, whose author admitted to being influenced by Strindberg and Travers, a heady mixture. Unlike Travers, Orton does not succeed—or try to succeed?—in differentiating the characters in *Loot*, who all talk alike. But what talk! He was a superb writer of dialogue and, assuming the spectator can take black farce in his stride, the rewards in *Loot* are considerable, for it is hilariously funny.

The play ends with the words, 'we must keep up appearances', which is one of the essences of farce: decency is there to be outraged. Another essential ingredient, 'possible people in impossible situations', is not, perhaps observed as the characters, manipulated by the puppet master, are too similar to be very plausible. They are all splendidly corrupt. The starting-point of the play is a young crook hiding the loot of the title in his mother's coffin. At the end, father is framed to the satisfaction of everybody else, including the most bent and nasty policeman imaginable. The characters are mostly Catholic, though the play is not anti-religious: the Catholic way of life helps the author set his macabre satire in motion.

First produced in London at the Jeannetta Cochrane Theatre by the London Traverse Company, September 29, 1966, and later transferred to the Criterion.

Author	Joe Orton
Director	Charles Marowitz
Designer	Tony Carruthers

Cast included Gerry Duggan, Sheila Ballantine, Kenneth Cranham, Simon Ward, Michael Bates and David Redmond.

FARCE: A WHO'S WHO

BROUGH, MARY (1863–1934). British actress, and the now legendary heavy lady of the Aldwych farces. The Margaret Dumont of British farce, but more explosive.

CHAPMAN, JOHN (1927–). British dramatist and actor. His farces and comedies include *Dry Rot* (54), *Simple Spymen* (60), *Now now, Darling!* (68) with Ray Cooney, *Oh, Clarence!* (68) and *Move over, Mrs. Markham* (71) also with Ray Cooney.

COONEY, RAY (1932–). British dramatist, actor and director. Apart from his collaborations with John Chapman (above), has written *One for the Pot* (61) with Tony Hilton, *Chase me, Comrade* (61), collaborated with Hugh and Margaret Williams on the book of *Charlie Girl* (65), etc., and has directed farces and comedies.

DRAYTON, ALFRED (1881–1949). Heavy, hairless British straight actor turned farceur. His partnership with Robertson Hare in *Aren't Men Beasts?* (36), *Banana Ridge* (38) and other farces was a battle of dissonant baldies that made for good box office returns and theatrical joy.

HARE, ROBERTSON (1891–). Beloved British farceur and comedian, whose timing, deeply fruity tones and bald pate have been cheering audiences up for decades, especially in plays by Travers and Sylvaine. In *Cuckoo in the Nest* (25), he was a minor character, but soon turned the duo of Walls and Lynn into a trio. Later, as recorded above, his partnership with Drayton added to the gaiety of the nation. No-one has ever lost his trousers with such flair.

FRANKLYN, LEO (1897–). British musical comedy actor turned farceur, who, since *Dry Rot* (54), has been a pillar of the Rix farces, good enough to satisfy even those who believe that the art died with the Aldwych school. His son is the actor, WILLIAM FRANKLYN.

LIVINGS, HENRY (1929–). The career of this British dramatist is sketched in Chapter 1. His very entertaining plays, part true farce, part comedy, part fantasy, are represented above by *Stop it, Whoever You Are* (61).

LYNN, RALPH. The supreme British farceur of the last half century, whose 'business' in Aldwych and other farces is still spoken of with awe by actors and remembered with joy by audiences. A genius.

ORTON, JOE (1933–67). British dramatist and writer of black comedies and farces, notably *Entertaining Mr. Sloane* (65) and *Loot* (66), which is featured above. Also see p. 56.

RIX, BRIAN (1924–). British actor-manager, whose Whitehall Farces, now transferred else-where, have carried on in a broader, less classic, but usually hilarious way the tradition of the Aldwych farces. An ex-Wolfit player, he began as a manager with his own Rep in Ilkley. His Whitehall career began with *Reluctant Heroes* (50), featured in the first section of this chapter, and later filmed. After his famous 'gormless' part, Godfrey, in this, he added other similar roles, like Fred Phipps in *Dry Rot*, to his repertoire, also 'straighter' farce parts. With a flair for guessing public taste and great business skill, includ-ing use of TV, he has prospered. His writers have included Colin Morris, John Chapman, Ray Cooney, Antony Marriott and Michael Pertwee, and his casts, apart from those mentioned in this chapter, have included Alfred Marks, Dennis Ramsden, Moray Watson, Derek Farr,

Muriel Pavlow, and his wife, Elspet Gray.

SYLVAINE, VERNON (1897–1957). British actor turned writer of farces, including *Aren't Men Beasts?* (36), *Madame Louise* (45) and *Will Any Gentleman?* (50). Apart from his skilful dialogue and good situations, his most notable achievement was to provide vehicles for Robertson Hare in his robust prime.

TRAVERS, BEN (1889–). Rightly revered British writer of farces, including his hat-trick of clas-sics, *A Cuckoo in the West* (25), *Rookery Nook* (26) featured above, and *Thark* (27), all for the Aldwych. His most famous later play was *Banana Ridge* (38), with Hare and Drayton. Essen-tial reading for farce lovers is his autobiography, *Vale of Laughter* (57).

WALLS, TOM (1883–1949). British farceur, comedian, producer and Derby winner (32). With Leslie Henson, put on *Tons of Money* at the Shaftesbury (22), which was such a success that it led to the taking over of the Aldwych for *It Pays to Advertise* (24), then the immortal Travers works, the Aldwych farces. Walls played the line of racy, amorous, bold-as-brass parts. His timing was im-peccable.

MELODRAMA AND MURDER

Some Chillers

THE CAT AND THE CANARY 1922

In his book, *On Seeing Things*, John Mason Brown laments the lack of successors to the melodramas of the twenties, culminating for him in a literate chiller called *Rope's End*, which is—blissful thought!—'a model of the macabre'. Inevitably, films have taken over the genre, being able to do such things more convincingly. The most famous of these grand old pieces, and the only one still occasionally staged, is *The Cat and the Canary*, a splendid example of the species, complete with a monster, a maniac at large, a body falling out of a secret panel, a Voodoo Mammy, and some laughs. Set at midnight in a lonely manor house where, twenty years after the death of an elderly eccentric, his will is to be read to the six surviving relatives, it is the real thing!

First produced in New York at the National, February 7, 1922.

Author   John Willard

Cast included Florence Eldridge as Annabelle, Henry Hull as Paul Jones, and Willard as Harry.

The play ran 349 performances and opened the same year in London at the Shaftesbury. It has been filmed three times, including a famous comedy-thriller version starring Bob Hope and Paulette Goddard.

THE RINGER 1926

Edgar Wallace's first stage success was greatly helped by the theatrical flair of Gerald du Maurier and his play-doctoring ability. Wallace's biographer, Margaret Lane, states that *On The Spot* is his best play, but others prefer *The Ringer*, pointing out that much of *On the Spot*'s success was due to the bravura performance of Charles Laughton as the organ-playing master criminal, Tony Perelli. And *The Ringer* is the one which is still occasionally revived, which is more than can be said for other

British melodramas of its period. It would be wrong therefore to say more than that the story has everyone trying to find the identity of a brilliant criminal, who turns out to be someone apparently on the side of the law. In the original, Gordon Harker played the first of his definitive Edgar Wallace-Cockney comedy roles, and a strong cast helped give the play 410 performances, which was a long run in the twenties.

First produced in London at Wyndham's, May 1, 1926

Author	Edgar Wallace
Director:	Gerald du Maurier

Cast included Leslie Banks, Nigel Bruce, Gordon Harker, Franklin Dyall, Leslie Faber and Dorothy Dickson.

TEN MINUTE ALIBI   1933

This very clever thriller, in which the audience knows who has done the murder and the only problem is whether or not he will get away with it, originally ran for 878 performances in London, where it has been twice revivied. Two suspicious detectives try to break down the hero's alibi, he having rid the earth of a splendidly 1930s smoothie of a villain (a vile seducer, half South American; what else?), who has a habit of taking ladies to Paris and, when he has tired of them, shipping them off to his half-native country and, one assumes, a life of shame. The hero's alibi all depends on the clock and what he has done to it after he has dreamt (on stage) of a perfect murder. Despite a few period moments and sentiments, it could be revived today with success, for it is as ingenious as *Dial 'M' for Murder*, and, like it, demands and deserves first-rate acting.

First produced in London at the Embassy, February 8, 1933.

Author	Anthony Armstrong
Director	Sinclair Hill

Cast included Anthony Ireland as Philip Sevilla, Robert Douglas as Colin Derwent, villain and hero respectively, and Celia Johnson as Betty Findon, the heroine (later played at the Haymarket by Maisie Darrell).

NIGHT MUST FALL   1935

Emlyn Williams, a master of the chiller, has never surpassed this play, which is one of the finest of its kind ever written. Powerful, atmospheric, and with a very strong story line, its ultimate strength lies in the quality of its characterization. The scene is a bungalow in a forest, and the principal characters are Danny, the charming, vicious young perpetrator of a particularly nasty murder, and Olivia, the lonely, repressed woman who is attracted to him despite herself, and who is the companion of the bungalow's rather repulsive owner, Mrs. Bramson. All the smaller characters are well drawn and grateful ones for the cast, and there is plenty of humour amid the undercurrent of unease and lurking horror. It is not the playwright's fault that the most famous thing about the play is the notorious hatbox and its unglimpsed, but guessed at, contents.

First produced in London at the Duchess, May 31, 1935.

Author   Emlyn Williams
Director   Miles Malleson

Cast included Emlyn Williams as Danny, Angela Baddeley as Olivia, May Witty as Mrs. Bramson, and Basil Radford, Kathleen Harrison and Betty Jardine.

The play ran for 435 performances, and Emlyn Williams later took it to New York, where it opened at the Barrymore Theater in September 1936, again with Angela Baddeley.

DIAL 'M' FOR MURDER   1952

This very clever thriller by Frederick Knott was originally written for television. A fading tennis star, Tony Wendice, devises what seems a foolproof plan to kill his unfaithful wife by forcibly hiring an old school acquaintance turned confidence trickster to do it for him. When she manages to kill her assailant instead, Wendice pins the crime on her. Audiences need their wits about them when the notably well-drawn detective explains all at the end, but few modern thrillers have matched the play's ingenuity. The scene between Wendice and Captain Lesgate, the would-be assassin, is written with flair and depth most unusual in such plays.

First produced in London at the Westminster, June 19, 1952.

Author	Frederick Knott
Director	John Fernald
Designer	Paul Mayo

Cast included Emrys Jones, Jane Baxter, Alan MacNaughtan, Andrew Cruikshank and Olaf Pooley.

The play ran for 425 performances in a theatre renowned at that time for its short runs, and ran even longer at the Plymouth, New York, for 551 performances from October 29, 1952. The American cast was Maurice Evans, Gusti Huber, Richard Derr, John Williams and Anthony Dawson. The play was brilliantly filmed by Alfred Hitchcock with a cast that included Ray Milland, Grace Kelly, Robert Cummings and—in the parts they played in New York—John Williams as the Inspector and Anthony Dawson as Lesgate.

WITNESS FOR THE PROSECUTION   1953

This play is generally regarded as Agatha Christie's best thriller. It is a fine court-room drama and concerns the desperate and clever efforts of a wife to save her husband from the gallows, with a treble twist at the end for good measure. Patricia Jessel, after a mainly classical career, played the wife in London and New York, where she gained four important awards for her performance.

First produced in London at the Winter Garden, October 28, 1953.

Author	Agatha Christie
Director	Wallace Douglas
Designer	Michael Weight

Cast included Patricia Jessel as Romaine, Derek Blomfield as Leonard Vole, David Horne as Sir Wilfred Robarts, and Milton Rosmer, D. A. Clarke-Smith and Percy Marmont.

The play ran 458 performances at the Winter Garden, a notorious death trap for every sort of show as a rule. It opened in New York at the Henry Miller on December 16, 1954, and ran for 644 performances. It was filmed in 1958, with Billy Wilder as director and a cast that included Marlene Dietrich, Charles Laughton and Tyrone Power.

SLEUTH   1970

Anthony Shaffer's conjuring trick of a play has been hailed as the best thriller for many years and, at the time of writing, is enjoying long runs on both sides of the Atlantic. A minority apparently object that the author's sleight-of-hand has gone too far, though it is hard to see the logic of this complaint in a thriller, of all things. Its plot cannot fairly even be hinted at in print beyond saying that it concerns a detective story writer (whose hero is one of the gentleman-amateur school) who decides to cope with his wife's lover in a most unusual and very theatrical way. The writing is funny, witty, stylish and highly effective, and the play is at once a satire on the average thriller and the genuine article. It offers two exceptionally rewarding roles—especially by thriller standards—for the leading players.

First produced in London at the St. Martin's, February 12, 1970.

Author	Anthony Shaffer
Director	Clifford Williams
Designer	Carl Toms

The cast included Anthony Quayle and Keith Baxter.

The play opened in New York at the Music Box Theater, November 7, 1970, again with Anthony Quayle and Keith Baxter. It has been filmed, starring Laurence Olivier and Michael Caine.

A WHO'S WHO OF MELODRAMA AND MURDER

ARMSTRONG, ANTHONY (1897–). British dramatist and author of the enormously successful *Ten Minute Alibi* (33), see above, and a number of other thrillers and also comedies.

CHRISTIE, AGATHA (1891–). British crime writer and dramatist, many of whose plays have enjoyed long runs, most notably a minor work, *The Mousetrap*, which opened in 1952 and is likely to run for ever. Her early plays were dramatizations of her novels by others, including the irresistible *Ten Little Niggers* (43)—*Ten Little Indians*, in America—which even many actors adore, who normally resent the strain of playing one-dimensional parts in thrillers where everything is subservient to the plot. Her finest play is *Witness for the Prosecution* (see above), while *The Spider's Web* (54) is a much better than average example of that despised genre, the comedy thriller. *Love From a Stranger* (36), dramatized by Frank Vosper from one of her best short stories, is a chilling piece which has gripped on stage and screen, and which has one of the most frightening moments of any thriller, a *coup de théâtre* that is too good to reveal to those who do not know it.

HAMILTON, PATRICK (1904–62). British dramatist with three masterly, macabre and well-constructed plays to his credit, *Rope* (29), inspired by the Leopold and Loeb case, *Gaslight* (38), a choice specimen of latter-day Victoriana, and *The Governess* (45). Also wrote *The Duke in Darkness* (42), a stark, strange psychological play.

KNOTT, FREDERICK. British dramatist and author of *Dial 'M' for Murder* (see above). His *Wait for the Dark* (66), another successful thriller, with a blind girl (originally Honor Blackman) as heroine, had a moment towards the end which regularly produced screams from its audiences, a phenomenon rarely heard in the West End in modern times.

PERCY, EDWARD (1891–1968), British dramatist and, with REGINALD DENHAM (1894–), co-author of a number of thrillers, including *Suspect* (37), whose heroine is part Lizzie Borden and part Madeleine Smith. The play, as is often the case in thrillers, is set in Cornwall, an additional reason for that county to gain its independence. If dramatists are to be believed, no part of the United Kingdom has such a collection of grisly deeds performed by grisly people. The two collaborated again in *Ladies in Retirement* (39). Percy also wrote *The Shop at Sly Corner* (41). Reginald Denham has directed many plays in London and New York.

SHAFFER, ANTHONY (1926–). British dramatist, twin brother of Peter Shaffer. His *Sleuth* (70) described earlier, is the finest thriller to appear for many years.

WALLACE, EDGAR (1875–1932). British novelist, playwright and journalist. His first successful theatre thriller, *The Ringer* (26), described earlier, is still performed from time to time. *On the Spot* (30) was a superb vehicle for Charles Laughton. Another favourite was *The Case of the Frightened Lady* (31).

WILLIAMS, EMLYN (1905–). British dramatist, actor, director and author (see chapters 1, 2 and 3). Has written several notable thrillers, including *A Murder Has Been Arranged* (30), *Night Must Fall* (35), described earlier, and *Someone Waiting* (53).

SOME THEATRE ORGANIZATIONS

OF YESTERDAY AND TODAY

ACTOR'S STUDIO. Very influential New York 'training-ground' for actors founded (48) by Lee Strasberg (see p. 64). Many of America's finest actors have been taught by this high priest of the Method, a serious but controversial approach to acting (see p. 278). In the sixties, the Studio began producing on Broadway. A revival of O'Neill's *Strange Interlude* (63) was a great success, but, unfortunately for the Studio's very real reputation, a most unsatisfying *Three Sisters* was exported to London.

AMERICAN PLACE THEATER. Started as a workshop for new writers by Rev. Sidney Lanier, it expanded (64) to present two parts of Robert Lowell's *The Old Glory*, directed by Jonathan Miller, in a church sanctuary on West 46th Street, New York. *Benito Cereno*, the second part, proved truly tragic. Artistic Director, WYNN HANDMAN (1922–).

AMERICAN NATIONAL THEATER AND ACADEMY (A.N.T.A.). Begun (35) by an Act of Congress to encourage the theatre in the U.S.A. From 1945, it became a significant voice for the American theatre at home and abroad and helped theatre training and experimental theatre schemes. Its Experimental Theater enjoyed three exciting seasons, whose productions included *Galileo* with Laughton and Robinson Jeffers' *Tower Beyond Tragedy*, with Judith Anderson. More recent successes were *Our Town* in the A.N.T.A. Theater (69) with Henry Fonda, Mildred Natwick, Ed Begley, Elizabeth Hartman and Harvey Evans, produced by the Plumstead Playhouse, and *Harvey* with James Stewart and Helen Hayes, produced by the Phoenix Theater, described later in this chapter.

AMERICAN SHAKESPEARE FESTIVAL. Held at Stratford, Conn. since 1955. A triumph for Lawrence Langner of Theater

Guild fame, whose efforts had been mainly responsible for launching the festival. For all the criticisms of the actual theatre, the use or non-use of stars, and the lack of a distinctive style down the years, there have been fine productions and performances, most notably Carnovsky's Lear(s) and Shylock, and productions have been regularly sent on tour, including a *Dream* with Bert Lahr as Bottom. Thousands of school children visit the festival each year. A particularly notable year was 1957, with Katharine Hepburn and Alfred Drake as Beatrice and Benedick, Carnovsky and Hepburn as Shylock and Portia, and Earle Hyman and Alfred Drake as Othello and Iago. A turning-point in the Festival's fortunes was John Houseman's period of Artistic Directorship (56–9). In 1972, *Major Barbara*, directed by Edwin Sherwin, was a great success, with Jane Alexander and Lee Richardson.

ARTS COUNCIL. Originally founded as C.E.M.A. (Council for the Encouragement of Music and the Arts) in 1940 to bring plays and concerts to evacuation areas. Run originally by the Pilgrim Trust and the Treasury, the latter taking over in 1942. Became The Arts Council of Great Britain at the end of the war and has been responsible ever since for allotting all available funds that can be extracted from the Treasury to the various arts.

Continually under fire for its division of spoils that are small in comparison with allocations of money for the arts in many European countries, it remains of crucial importance. Without it, all that is best in the British theatre, to say nothing of all opera and ballet in this country, would vanish overnight. Hampered by latent philistinism in Britain, despite the official support of both major parties, and therefore given adequate, though never more than adequate, funds, it is doomed to be publicly abused—as opposed to justly criticized and argued about—as long as it exists. Most worthwhile Reps now receive grants from the Council, which also organizes training schemes and backs new plays and revivals against loss. See *The Theatre Today*, published by the Arts Council (70).

ARTS FOUNDATION. After resolutely refusing aid to the arts, and with millionaire patrons running low, the U.S. Government and an even more hesitant Congress, accepted the idea of financial help (64, 65). A National Arts Council, led by Roger Stevens, became the equivalent of the Arts Council of Britain, early beneficiaries being the Phoenix A.P.A. Theater, as well as experimental groups. An historic turning-point even if the monies available were not large.

BRITISH COUNCIL. Founded in 1934, since 1937, it has sponsored overseas tours by great national companies, leading Reps. and individuals. Its Drama Department also distributes plays overseas, etc.

BRITISH DRAMA LEAGUE. Founded in 1919 by Geoffrey Whitworth, this most useful organization, with its considerable professional and vast amateur membership, runs training courses, drama festivals, an excellent library and theatre information service and play-writing competitions, and promotes a 'right relation between drama and the life of the community'. Scotland's similar organization is the Scottish Community Drama Association. Also see p. 273.

BRITISH THEATRE MUSEUM ASSOCIATION. It publicizes the need to create a National Theatre Museum. Its headquarters at Leighton House, Kensington, has many fine exhibits, which, at the time of writing (73), looks like finding a home at Somerset House, along with other great theatre collections, always assuming enough space is made available. Collections which could benefit also might include the Enthoven Collections at the Victoria and Albert, and the private collection of Raymond Mander and Joe Mitchenson. So a National Theatre Museum seems a possibility (?)

CHICHESTER FESTIVAL. The Festival Theatre was the idea of Leslie Evershed-Martin, and the first season in 1962 was under the direction of Laurence Olivier. There is an open arena-type stage, with the audience sitting on three sides of it. The next summer, Olivier's actors were virtually the National Theatre Company, which opened at the Old Vic that Autumn. By the time John Clements took over in 1966 a very wide range of plays had been performed, the authors ranging from Ford and Fletcher to Arden and Shaffer.

Since then the season has been extended to $4\frac{1}{2}$ months and

CTTP–Q

has become more popular than ever except with the more austere critics and theatregoers (mainly the former) who resent a repertoire of 'sound' plays, ancient and modern, the merely good (as opposed to National) standard of productions and the Director's avowed policy of a festival of acting. Even the audience is sometimes sneered at by these miserable Malvolios of higher drama.

Meanwhile, the 1972 season has ended—having given Gay, Shaw, Shakespeare and Fry. Few would pretend that Art is at so high a level as in the National days which first saw Olivier's *Othello*, an incomparable *Uncle Vanya*, Dexter's production of Shaffer's *The Royal Hunt of the Sun*, etc., but that was the National and perennial and highly subsidized company. More was expected and more achieved. In 1974, Keith Michell will take over from John Clements.

CIVIC REPERTORY THEATER. The creation of Eva Le Gallienne, the actress (see p. 116), as glamorous a figure as Lilian Baylis was homely, yet sharing the same dedication to the cause of drama for the people. It lasted from 1926–32 and presented over 1,500 performances from Shakespeare and Chekhov to Dumas and *Alice in Wonderland*, performing in what Taubman described as a 'huge, decrepit barn of a house on West 14th Street'. Salaries were low, though not quite Baylisian. In the fifties, the intrepid Miss Le Gallienne tried again, this time with her National Repertory Theater in conjunction with Margaret Webster and Cheryl Crawford. Despite a fine company and repertoire this company was killed mainly by the Unions (who insisted on full complements of stage hands even when a small cast Ibsen play was being given), and by the public's suspicion of plays in repertoire.

EQUITY. The actor's trade union. American Actors' Equity was set up in 1913 and was forced to call a strike (19) to get producers to treat its members fairly. British Actors' Equity was set up in 1929. Because of the very nature of an actor's life and employment, both these bodies have had a difficult and very worthwhile history.

ENGLISH STAGE COMPANY. The ultimate strength of a nation's theatre being its playwrights, this company, formed by George

Devine and others in 1956 to discover and promote new talent, is probably, on results, the most significant theatre organization in Britain. Established writers and new directors, designers and actors have also been encouraged, but Devine's vision of a Writers' Theatre has been retained. Another crucial belief of his was the 'right to fail'.

The first season, with Tony Richardson as assistant director, saw plays by established writers (Angus Wilson, Nigel Dennis, Arthur Miller and Ronald Duncan), also the 'breakthrough' play, Osborne's *Look Back in Anger*. Since then, among the playwrights who made their name at the Royal Court Theatre have been Arnold Wesker, N. F. Simpson, John Arden, Ann Jellicoe, David Storey, Charles Wood and Edward Bond. Many foreign plays and some classical revivals have also been staged, and D. H. Lawrence has been established posthumously as a viable playwright (in productions by Peter Gill).

William Gaskill took over when Devine died (66) and, until 1972 Lindsay Anderson and Anthony Page were co-directors. Productions Without Decor have been a feature of the theatre's work and in 1969 the Theatre Upstairs opened to discover new, mainly experimental writers.

At first, plays were given in repertoire, but transfers to the West End, public puzzlement (though opera and ballet publics survive) and the financial loss to authors, brought about a switch to repertory: runs of a month or so. Many plays have transferred, including most of Osborne's, and many great names, including Olivier, Ashcroft, Gielgud, Richardson, Guinness and Harrison have worked for the Company, along with an extraordinary number of the best younger actors and actresses who made their names working for it. At the time of writing (72) Oscar Lewenstein, who was one of the founders of the E.S.C., has become Artistic Director.

FEDERAL THEATER PROJECT. A scheme begun in 1935, indirectly inspired by the New Deal in America, which, until abolished by political pressure in 1939, produced more than 1,000 plays, amateur and professional, experimental and traditional, opera, ballet and puppet shows, etc., and gave work to some 12,000. Among its most important ventures was *The Living Newspaper*, a series of productions about topical matters, started by Elmer Rice, and several shows produced by Orson

Welles and John Houseman, notably *Doctor Faustus*, an all-black *Macbeth*, and the fiery anti-capitalist opera, *The Cradle will Rock*, by Marc Blitzstein. *It Can't Happen Here* (36), a tract against local fascism, was premièred in no less than 21 cities at once. This was written by Sinclair Lewis and J. C. Moffett. There were also—inevitably—many failures. The whole amazing scheme was run by Mrs. Hallie Flanagan. She and others were accused of being under Communist influence, and so was the organization, though actually the vast majority were New-Dealers. The accusations stuck and the project folded. Also see Mercury Theater (below).

GROUP THEATER. Founded by Harold Clurman (see p. 34) in 1931, after he left the Theater Guild (see below). It enjoyed a heady, glorious decade, which has been documented in Clurman's book, *The Fervent Years*. The directors were the founder and Lee Strasberg and Cheryl Crawford, and the company included Stella and Luther Adler, Morris Carnovsky, Franchot Tone, Mary Morris, J. Edward Bromberg, Elia Kazan, John Garfield and Clifford Odets.

With its left wing ideals and—until the group started to lose members to more lucrative activities—its corporate strength, the Group's greatest achievement was to produce the work of playwrights of the calibre of Odets, Robert Ardrey, Saroyan, Sidney Kingsley and Irwin Shaw. The impact of Odets' *Waiting for Lefty* (35) is discussed at length on page 17.

After the break-up of the Group, Lee Strasberg went on to found the Actor's Studio, dealt with above and under Method (p. 278).

INTERNATIONAL THEATRE INSTITUTE. An organization which acts as a clearing-house for theatrical information and facilities and for the exchange of professional theatre personnel. There are over 50 member countries. A very influential body.

LINCOLN CENTER FOR THE PERFORMING ARTS. This arts complex in New York, dating from the sixties and now the main home of the city's opera, ballet and music, along with arts' schools, also houses the Lincoln Center Repertory Theater. This last was the idea of Robert Whitehead before the Center existed. With Kazan as co-director, he started in a temporary theatre with Miller's *After the Fall* (64). But after difficulties with their Board, Whitehead and Kazan were superseded (65), since which time the Theater has never quite lived up to expectations and, indeed, is not a true repertory.

Herbert Blau and Jules Irving of the San Francisco Actor's Workshop took over and ran the new theatre, named the Vivian Beaumont after its patroness. It was designed by Eero Saarinen and Jo Mielziner. Two poor seasons followed and Blau resigned (67). Meanwhile a new experimental theatre was added, and, since then, despite what seems from this side of the Atlantic steady and rough handling from the critics, things have gone better. Notable occasions have been *Galileo* (with Quayle) and Lorca's *Yerma*, both directed by John Hirsch, and there were fine productions of Kipphardt's *In the Matter of J. Robert Oppenheimer* and Saroyan's *The Time of Your Life* (69). An all-American season followed, whose highspot, according to Clive Barnes, was a revival of *Camino Real*. The repertoire in 1971 included *The Playboy of the Western World* and Miller's version of Ibsen's *An Enemy of the People*. 1972 saw a fine revival of *The Crucible*, directed by John Barry. Sadly, it saw the resignation of Jules Irving because of financial squabbles. However, Joseph Papp, the distinguished Director of the New York Shakespeare Festival (see below) is to take over.

MALVERN FESTIVAL. Founded by Barry Jackson (who else?) in 1929 as a major Shaw festival which also presented rare classics and modern plays by Bridie, Priestley, etc. It saw seven Shaw premières. After the war it was revived for several seasons.

MERCURY THEATER. After working for the Federal Theater Project (see above) Orson Welles and John Houseman started their own theatre on Broadway, opening (37) with an anti-Fascist modern dress *Julius Caesar*, Caesar resembling Mussolini, Brutus an ineffectual liberal (British directors caught up with this idea years later). There followed a scintillating *The Shoemaker's Holiday*, *Heartbreak House* and *Danton's Death*—and closure. This glorious, rocket-like venture remains an inspiring highlight in American theatre history. Casts included Welles himself (Brutus, Shotover, St. Just), Joseph Cotten, George Coulouris, Vincent Price, Frederic Tozere, etc.

MERMAID THEATRE. The creation of Sir Bernard Miles (see p. 120), who first built an Elizabethan-inspired theatre in his back garden (51), where Kirsten Flagstad sang in *Dido and Aeneas* for a glass of stout per performance. Then, after a successful season of *Dido* and Shakespeare at the Royal Exchange (53), he built the present Mermaid at Puddle Dock. The opening performance (60) was a musical, *Lock Up Your Daughters*, from Fielding's *Rape Upon Rape*, since when Miles has ranged from Miracle plays to Milligan and from Greek drama to *Treasure Island*. The policy is now short runs of 4½ weeks or so, though big successes may be extended: *Cowardy Custard* (72–3).

The Mermaid, with its good eating, exhibitions, concerts, etc., is one of the only theatres in Britain which it is a pleasure to visit for itself, a true social centre. From an audience point of view it is pleasantly simple and functional. The first theatre built within the City of London in 300 years, its productions vary in standard, but the amazing Sir Bernard has kept his promise to give 'a bird's-eye view of World Theatre in ten years' with dividends.

NATIONAL THEATRE. First mooted by Effingham Wilson in 1848 and hopefully planned by William Archer and Granville Barker in 1903. A foundation stone was laid on London's South Bank by the Queen Mother in 1951, and, finally, in 1963, the National Theatre opened with *Hamlet*—at the Old Vic (for whose history see below). The theatre, designed by Denys Lasdun, is expected (at the time of writing) to open in early 1974.

The first and only Director was rightly and inevitably Laurence Olivier, whose original Associate Directors were John Dexter (now back with the Company) and William Gaskill. The other Associate Directors in 1972 were Michael Blakemore, Frank Dunlop (director of the Young Vic: see separate entry) and Paul Scofield. Guest directors have included Brook (Seneca's *Oedipus*), Zeffirelli (*Much Ado*), Jacques Charon (*A Flea in Her Ear*), Guthrie, Byam Shaw and many others, along with a galaxy of designers. Many memorable performances, among them Olivier's Othello, are noted in Chapter 2.

Except for a poor patch in 1971, when a season at the New

was mixed artistically and poor financially, and was only saved by a tremendous *Long Day's Journey into Night*, the Company's achievement has been remarkable. If the early seasons were the peak, it was because of a very strong group of players and some matchless productions, among them William Gaskill's *The Recruiting Officer* and Olivier's *Vanya*. Too many of those early players, including Robert Stephens (also an Associate Director), Maggie Smith, Frank Finlay, Colin Blakely and Derek Jacobi, have left, but the season in progress (72–3) is notable, especially Stoppard's *Jumpers*, Miller's production of *The School for Scandal* and Blakemore's of *The Front Page*. Peter Hall has been announced to succeed Olivier almost as logical a choice as when Olivier himself was appointed. Miller, Pinter and John Schlesinger will assist.

NATIONAL YOUTH THEATRE. The creation of Michael Croft who, when a master at Alleyn's School, directed some remarkable Shakespearean productions. When he left (56), a group of boys asked him to continue producing, and from this stemmed the N.Y.T., which has given annual performances in London (since 59) and has also toured Europe.

Members of the N.Y.T. who have become professional actors include Simon Ward, Derek Jacobi, John Stride, Martin Jarvis, Hywell Bennett and Helen Mirren, though only a small percentage go on the stage. The theatre's chronicler, ex-member Simon Masters, calls it not a drama school but 'simply an ensemble experience in practical theatre' (*The National Youth Theatre*, 69).

Apart from its Shakespearean productions, which made its name early on even with the most acid critics, the N.Y.T. has produced modern plays, the most famous being *Zigger-Zagger*, commissioned from Peter Terson (see chapter 1) by Michael Croft. The *Daily Mail* supported the enterprise for many years, Ralph Richardson is its President, and now it has its own centre, the new Shaw Theatre in the Euston Road.

NEW YORK SHAKESPEARE FESTIVAL. A free annual festival started and run (from 54) by Joseph Papp (see p. 126). The Festival was transferred from a church, then a cinema, next the East River Amphitheater, finally to Central Park (56) where a special theatre, the Delacorte, was opened (62). Two years later, a

portable stage enabled a second company to perform in parks
and playgrounds. Mr. Papp has directed many plays himself,
and produced many more.

Winter performances in schools throughout the State are
sponsored by the Board of Education, and vigorous produc-
tions of most of the plays have been given in Central Park.
The Festival presented rock musicals in its indoor Public
Theater (69–70). A fine musical version of *The Two Gentlemen
of Verona* was given in Central Park (71) free, which soon be-
came an (unfree) Broadway hit. Music by Galt MacDermot of
Hair fame; adaptor, John Guare; director, Mel Shapiro.
Joseph Papp is 'a man of fierce determination' (Taubman).
One can imagine, admiringly.

OLD VIC. For many years the most renowned theatre in the
English-speaking world. Since 1963, the main home of the National Theatre, of which the building should remain part when
the new National Theatre is completed on the South Bank.
The Old Vic dates back to 1818, when it was the Coburg
Theatre, later the Victoria Theatre. In 1880, Emma Cons turned
it into a respectable temperance Music Hall. A decisive change
came in 1914 when her niece, Lilian Baylis (see p. 83), took over
and was soon presenting opera and Shakespeare at popular
prices. Her directors in the early days included Matheson Lang,
Ben Greet, Russell Thorndike, Robert Atkins from 1921–5, a
crucial period which established the theatre's fame, Andrew
Leigh, also Harcourt Williams from 1929–33, the next giant
step forward. There followed Tyrone Guthrie's long association with the theatre (two seasons under Henry Cass apart).

Meanwhile, in 1931, Lilian Baylis had re-opened a new
Sadler's Wells Theatre, which soon became the home of her
Opera Company and the young Sadler's Wells Ballet, while the
drama, after a short span at the Wells, remained wholly at the
Vic. Baylis died in 1937, with her theatre firmly established and
world famous, but not subsidized. Her most vital years had
been in the twenties, when, at a time when the West End was
given over almost entirely to frivolity and safe commercial
successes, she kept the drama alive, and enabled the idea of
classical acting, great and good, to survive in London.

The Old Vic was bombed in 1940. The Company used the
New as its London base for the rest of the war and until 1950,

while also touring extensively. The legendary seasons of 1944–8 were run by a triumvirate, Olivier, Richardson and John Burrell. The final season at the New, a very happy one, had Hugh Hunt as Director. Since then the directors have been Guthrie, Michael Benthall, Douglas Seale and, finally, Michael Elliott, with a period (59–61) when there was no overall director. Except for a time in the fifties when Benthall was directing the whole Shakespeare canon over several seasons, the policy was to include non-Shakespearean classics, and European ones as well.

Far too many fine players appeared at the Old Vic to list. The interested should consult the following books: *Four Years at the Old Vic* by Harcourt Williams (35); *Old Vic Saga* by Harcourt Williams (49); *Old Vic Drama* by Audrey Williamson (Part I, 48: Part 2, 57); *Lilian Baylis* by Sybil and Russell Thorndike (38). Also biographies and autobiographies of Guthrie, Gielgud, etc., and general surveys like *Shakespeare on the English Stage 1900–64* by J. C. Trewin (64). The story of Sadler's Wells is told in the book of that name by Dennis Arundell (65) and by Edward Dent in *A Theatre for Everyone* (45), which also covers the Old Vic.

OLD VIC THEATRE CENTRE. Set up in 1946 with Michel Saint-Denis in overall control, Glen Byam Shaw in charge of the Old Vic Theatre School, and George Devine of the Young Vic, a touring company playing to students and children. There was also an experimental wing. In 1951, the three resigned owing to a dispute with the Old Vic's Administrator, Llewellyn Rees. The school lasted another year. It had trained, amongst others, Joan Plowright, Patrick Wymark, Alan Dobie, Keith Michell and Derek Godfrey. It was the most serious and important drama school ever run in Britain, and if its total lack of interest in the commercial theatre's needs was not, in everyone's opinion, realistic or fair on some of the students, its closure was a bitter blow, as was the Centre's aboliton the year before.

OPEN AIR THEATRE, REGENT'S PARK. Started by Sydney Carroll (33), since when a mainly Shakespearean repertoire has been given annually despite the machinations of the British climate. Owing to the nature of the theatre, productions down the years have been straightforward, and none the worse for that, with a tent available when the worst occurs. Robert Akins (see p. 80) directed all plays (33–43), acting in them as well, and was again in charge from 1946–60. Since his day, the very able, dauntless Director has been David Conville. The 1972 season opened with *The Tempest*, directed by Richard Digby Day, and with Michael Denison leading a strong cast, a most suitable choice of play after the worst May in living memory. Weather permitting, it is a delightful spot, as hundreds of thousands of spectators and a great many actors and actresses have found down the years.

PHOENIX THEATER. Founded by T. Edward Hambleton (1911–) and Norris Houghton (see p. 108) off Broadway (53), its first season ranged from Sidney Howard's *Madame, Will You Walk* to *Coriolanus*, staged by John Houseman, and *The Seagull*, directed by Houghton, with a cast that included Montgomery Clift, Kevin McCarthy, Judith Evelyn and Maureen Stapleton.

It continued in the same vein, its standards varying, its financial position hazardous, but its ideals high. Became the Phoenix-A.P.A. (64), when it combined with Ellis Rabb's notable touring repertory company, a meeting of two idealists in Hambleton and Rabb. The Lyceum Theater on Broadway was taken over. The A.P.A. (Association of Producing Artists) separated from the Phoenix in 1969, but Hambleton proceeded to a great success with a revival of *Harvey* (70) with James Stewart and Helen Hayes. Meanwhile the A.P.A.'s revival of *Private Lives* enjoyed a Broadway success with Tammy Grimes and Brian Bedford.

PITLOCHRY FESTIVAL has, since the fifties, given an annual summer repertoire of varied, well staged plays in its own theatre in the Highlands.

ROYAL SHAKESPEARE COMPANY, formerly the SHAKESPEARE MEMORIAL THEATRE COMPANY. The Shakespeare Memorial Theatre was opened in 1879, having been founded by Charles Flower, whose family have been associated with the Theatre ever since. Benson and his Bensonians performed there nearly every year from 1886–1919, after which W. Bridges Adams was Director (19–34). The old theatre was burnt in 1926, today's building being opened in 1932.

The seasons between the wars suffered from a chasm between the actors and audience, critical attacks, and low salaries which kept away the most famous actors, but its summer-long seasons attracted growing audiences, and actors of the calibre of Randle Ayrton (a magnificent Lear), Baliol Holloway and Wolfit. The very able Bridges-Adam was succeeded by the 'gently academic' (Trewin) Ben Iden Payne (35–42), and, less happily, Milton Rosmer (43), then Robert Atkins (44–5), all of whose careers are listed in the Classical chapter.

In 1946 came a turning-point when Sir Barry Jackson of Birmingham Rep fame took over (46–8), bringing with him a number of directors including the young Peter Brook, and the young Paul Scofield. The ever-youthful Sir Barry was ousted, apparently on the grounds of age, and a decade of great achievement, now underrated by the ignorant, began. The Artistic Directors were Antony Quayle (49–52), Quayle and Glen Byam Shaw (52–6) and Byam Shaw (57–9), and casts included Evans, Ashcroft, Tearle, Gielgud, Olivier, Richardson, Helpmann, Andrews, Redgrave, Wynyard, Tutin, etc. Directors included Glen Byam Shaw, Quayle, Guthrie, Hall, Brook, etc. Historic productions and performances included the Brook-Olivier *Titus Andronicus* (55), Olivier's Macbeth and Coriolanus, the only (and wonderfully) completely successful *Antony and Cleopatra* of modern times (Redgrave, Ashcroft, Byam Shaw, 53), and Guthrie's *All's Well that Ends Well* (59). The Theatre was now world-famous and attracting huge audiences, and touring as far afield as Russia and Australia.

In 1960, Peter Hall, aged 29, took over. The disadvantage of the previous regime had been that, for all the glory of individual productions, companies dispersed annually, so a true ensemble could only be maintained intermittently. Hall transformed this situation and, with Brook and Michel Saint-Denis as the other member of the triumvirate, and able newcomers like John Barton and Clifford Williams, created the longed-for ensemble and a company style. The flowering came with *The Wars of the Roses* (63 and 64) which built up into a sequence of seven of the historical plays from *Richard II* to *Richard III*.

Meanwhile, the Aldwych had been taken over in 1960 as a London base for the Company, which was now able to perform seasons of modern plays by Pinter, Mercer, Albee, etc., as well as giving some of its Shakespearean productions in London. The Aldwych is, however, a stopgap for the Company until it moves into a new home at the Barbican Arts Centre in 1977–8.

The R.S.C., now probably the most famous British theatre company in the world, has a core of artists on long term contracts, who can take on outside work from time to time. The Company officially disowns the word 'star', despite the fact that its leaders are as aware as everyone else that certain parts need stars (in the best sense), and despite its roster being, in fact, riddled with stars (Ashcroft, Dench, Rogers, Sinden, etc.), including some who have become stars with the company, like Elizabeth Spriggs. For certain productions 'names' are brought in from outside, stars like Richard Johnson (playing both Antonys in 72), Michael Hordern, and Dorothy Tutin and actors of the calibre of Barry Foster and Anthony Bate, etc.

Since 1968, Trevor Nunn has been Artistic Director, the other Associate directors being Barton, Brook, Hall, Hands, David Jones, Clifford Williams. The Associate designers are Bury, Farrah, Morley and O'Brien. Most of the names mentioned in this entry have their own entries in the Classical chapter. At the time of writing, a fine season of the Roman plays has ended, directed by Trevor Nunn, assisted by his colleagues. The old Stratford tradition of less than perfect first nights is still in evidence to confound theatre historians of the future, for, after a radical alteration of both stage and auditorium, the first night of *Coriolanus* was written off by many as a mere display of the very versatile stage's party tricks; whereas this author, seeing the production some weeks later, found it a magnificent interpretation of the play, an equally magnificent demonstration of ensemble and Ian Hogg's Coriolanus, so criticized on the first night, if by no means ideally cast, effective enough physically and vocally.

The Company's Theatregoround group plays at Stratford and in London and in theatres, colleges and schools and centres all over Britain, and experimental seasons are also given at The Place in London, including the searing production of *Miss Julie* by Robin Phillips (71) with Helen Mirren, Donal McCann and Heather Channing.

No visitor to Stratford who has any feeling at all for the

theatre's past, immediate and distant, should fail to visit the Theatre's Picture Gallery, which also has other theatrical treasures.

STRATFORD, ONTARIO, SHAKESPEAREAN FESTIVAL. The festival was the idea of Tom Patterson, a young journalist, who convinced the worthies of Stratford that an annual season was possible and was sent to England to consult Tyrone Guthrie. This was in 1952. The next year the first festival took place on an exciting open stage in a large tent. It consisted of *Richard III* (with Guinness) and *All's Well*, both directed by Guthrie and designed by Tanya Moiseiwitsch, and with Anglo-Canadian casts which down the years have become mainly Canadian. The fine permanent building opened in 1957. The present Director is Jean Gascon (see p. 99).

That first season is now a theatre legend and not just a Canadian one. And the theatre itself has influenced many others, notably Chichester. Canadian actors rapidly developed into Shakespeareans, most notably Christopher Plummer and, later, John Colicos, William Hutt and Douglas Rain. Michael Langham and Douglas Seale have been among the British directors and Peter Hall directed *As You Like It* (59). Douglas Campbell was a British regular for many years, and Paul Scofield, Irene Worth, Jason Robards Jr. and Julie Harris have been among the non-Canadian actors. The first Canadian director was George McCowan with *Henry VIII* (61). The Company has played on Broadway and at Edinburgh, and a typically interesting idea was a *Henry V* with French-Canadians playing the French, the Henry being Plummer. For a full account of the origin and the first season of this most important of North American Shakespearean companies see *Renown at Stratford* by Guthrie and others.

THEATER GUILD. This American theatre company was founded (18–19) to present fine plays which were assumed not commercial. It has been, as Brooks Atkinson has said 'the most enlightened and influential theater organization' that New York has ever enjoyed. Its original directors were Lawrence Langner, Lee Simonson, Helen Westley, Philip Moeller, Justus Sheffield and Rollo Peters, later joined by Theresa Helburn and Maurice Wertheim. Langner was the main organizer of this remarkable group, which in its early days gave mainly foreign plays because of lack of local talent. These included the world premières of *Heartbreak House*, *Back to Methusalah* and *Saint Joan*.

The Guild opened its own Guild Theater in 1925 with *Caesar and Cleopatra* and the Lunts later played *Arms and the Man* there and *The Taming of the Shrew*, and appeared in *A Month in the Country*. American plays were soon being presented by the Guild: *The Hairy Ape* (22), *The Adding Machine* (23), *They Knew What They Wanted* (24), and the 1927–8 season included *Marco's Millions* and *Strange Interlude*, with the Guild then having 30,000 subscribers. These were its golden years, but temperament was now beginning to break up the group, and board meetings without an ultimate authority were apparently becoming more than somewhat heated. With new serious producers on the scene, as well as the talkies, the situation was worsened by the loss of the playwrights Rice, Howard, Behrman, Sherwood and Anderson, who set up their own group, and players like Clurman and Strasberg who left to found the Group Theater, though with the help of the Guild.

Yet the thirties saw great nights including *Ah, Wilderness!*, *Mourning Becomes Electra*, *Porgy and Bess* and *Mary of Scotland* produced by the Guild, and in 1940 *There Shall be no Night*. *Oklahoma!* came in 1943. It produced Inge's first Broadway play, *Come Back, Little Sheba* (50). It gradually became first conservative (though retaining high standards) then merely another commercial management. Its historic importance remains, however.

THEATRE WORKSHOP. Founded in Manchester by JOAN LITTLEWOOD, who later took over the Theatre Royal, Stratford East (53), after touring the North with classical and semi-topical plays (by Ewan MacColl). This brilliant director, the most dynamic force in the British theatre in the late fifties and early sixties, who made the Theatre Royal London's Off-Broadway, presented a series of stunning productions which showed the influence of Brecht, music-hall, social commitment, song and dance. They were welded together to display her own view of popular theatre, often with the text not considered sacred. She contributed greatly, however, to her authors' successes.

But her assaults on the classics were less convincing. Since the mid-sixties, her returns to Stratford have been sadly rare.

Her Company's most famous productions were Behan's *The Quare Fellow* (56) and *The Hostage* (58), Delaney's *A Taste of Honey* (58), Frank Norman's *Fings Ain't Wot They Used T'Be* (59) and her masterpiece, *Oh What A Lovely War* (63), see p. 24. All these were transferred to the West End, which inevitably helped destroy her group, a true co-operative, expected to improvise and contribute to the whole at all times. Recent productions have included *Mrs. Wilson's Diary* (67). Her casts included James Booth, Barbara Windsor, Avis Bunnage, Frances Cuka, Murray Melvyn, Victor Spinetti, Maxwell Shaw, etc. John Bury (see p. 88) first made his name with the company. Miss Littlewood's career since her regular Theatre Workshop days, has ranged from Europe to Africa. She first directed on Broadway in 1960, repeating *The Hostage*. Fun Palaces and entertainment for children are among her other splendid interests.

YOUNG VIC. There have been two Young Vics, the first of which was the touring company, run by Devine, which played to students and children, casts including Keith Michell, Derek Godfrey, etc. The Company had a European as well as a British reputation, and the fact that the majority of critics gave it no mention in their pieces at the opening of the new Young Vic does that majority no credit. Begun in 1946, it foundered from lack of money (51).

The new Company sprang directly from the National Theatre, some of whose actors play for it. Its Director is Frank Dunlop of the National. It has its own small theatre near the Old Vic, which opened in September 1970 with *Scapino*, from Molière's *Les Fourberies de Scapin*. The auditorium holds 456 people, the prices are cheap, the audiences mainly young. Which is a good place to end this chapter.

BRITISH REP

Some Key Figures and Facts

ARMSTRONG, WILLIAM (1882–1952). British actor who was Director of Liverpool Repertory Theatre from 1923–44. Few Rep Directors were more successful and influential. Every type of play was produced and many of his actors, including Rex Harrison, Michael Redgrave, Diana Wynyard and Hugh Williams, became famous. After Liverpool, he went to Birmingham Rep. The theatre, the Liverpool Playhouse, dates as a Rep from 1911 and its first director was Basil Dean. Now (72) under Anthony Tuckey, it has been a three-weekly Rep for many years. Liverpool's other Rep is the Everyman, started (64) by Peter James and Terry Hands. Its work is part educational and part experimental.

AYLIFF, H. K. (1872–1949). South African actor turned director. The most notable of Barry Jackson's directors at Birmingham between the wars, especially of Shaw's plays. Directed regularly at Malvern.

BELGRADE THEATRE, COVENTRY. The first post-war theatre to be built (58) and, as such, a landmark in Rep history. Now run by a very experienced Rep figure, Warren Jenkins, among its most significant achievements was the first staging of Wesker's Trilogy, including *Roots* (58–60).

BIRMINGHAM. See JACKSON and SALBERG.

BRISTOL OLD VIC. The 18th-century Theatre Royal in King Street was taken over in 1942 by C.E.M.A. (now the Arts Council) and developed into the Bristol branch of the London Old Vic. For its history up to 1956, see *The Bristol Old Vic* by Audrey Williamson and Charles Landstone. It is a remarkable success story, not least its School which opened in 1946. Its casts down the years have been too talented to begin to list here, and its directors have included Hugh Hunt, Denis Carey and (since 61) Val May. The repertoire has always been wider than the London Old Vic's could be, Shakespeare sharing the bill with modern masterpieces and pleasant trifles like *Salad Days*, which started its long career at the theatre. The musical *Trelawny* is its latest lyric achievement.

The Bristol Little Theatre, which from the thirties to the early sixties was excellently run by Ronald Russell and Peggy Ann Wood as first a weekly, then a fortnightly Rep, is now part of the Bristol Old Vic. The Theatre Royal has been artistically modernized, a New Vic is under way, and Bristol's theatrical future seems assured.

COUNCIL OF REPERTORY THEATRES (C.O.R.T.). A non-profit-making association of professional repertory managements, founded in 1944 and aiming to 'keep alive all that is best in theatre in the regions throughout the repertory movement'. It survived the bleak period in the fifties when the advent of TV on a vast scale closed many good, bad and indifferent Reps, and it is now rewarded with seeing many of its members enjoying at least adequate subsidies and a veritable explosion—lately—of new theatre buildings.

COUNSELL, JOHN (1905–). British director and manager. Since 1933 has been Director and Manager of Windsor Rep (The Theatre Royal). Few Reps have been so consistently successful and well-run, and—because of good management, decent salaries, and nearness to London—been able to attract so many good players. Counsell's wife is the actress MARY KERRIDGE (1914–). Windsor was for many years a fortnightly Rep, but is now three-weekly.

GLASGOW CITIZENS' THEATRE. Founded in 1942 by James Bridie, it has been, despite storms and many Directors, Scotland's most significant theatre since it opened. At present run by Giles Havergal.

HANSON, HARRY (1895–1972). British actor turned manager, for many years king of the twice-nightly reps, a now extinct breed. His first company was at Hastings (32) and by 1945 he was running ten. His nearest rival was Frank Fortescue, whose companies were mainly in the North.

HORNIMAN, MISS A. E. F. (1860–1937). A rich Englishwoman who became one of the founders of the Repertory Movement, notably in Dublin and Manchester. She re-opened the Abbey Theatre, Dublin, as the Repertory Theatre of Ireland (03), then (08) established Britain's first Rep at the Gaiety, Manchester. Though forced to close (21) she had put on 200 plays, half of them new, including *Hindle Wakes* by Stanley Houghton (12) and *Hobson's Choice*, Harold Brighouse's famous play (16), which was an early choice in the National Theatre's repertoire. Her brave venture was a key factor in the spread of Rep throughout Britain. Much of her success at Manchester was due to her brilliant director, Ben Iden Payne (see p. 126).

JACKSON, BARRY (1878–1961). British manager, and founder and Director of Birmingham Rep, spending his own fortune in the process. Under his direction it became—and has remained —the leading Rep in the country. Among its premières there were Drinkwater's *Abraham Lincoln* (19) and Shaw's *Back to Methuselah* (23). Seasons were given in London; operas were staged in the early days, including *The Immortal Hour*, and his players included Olivier, Richardson, Hardwicke, Margaret Leighton, Scofield, Edith Evans, Albert Finney, etc., etc. Peter Brook first made his name at Birmingham. Jackson ran the Malvern Festival from 1928–37 and was Director of the Shakespeare Memorial Theatre, 1945–8. One of the modern theatre's most influential figures. Knighted (25).

Just a decade after his death, a new Rep opened, Director, Peter Dews (see p. 37). After being a monthly Rep for years, it now, under Michael Simpson, performs a repertoire.

LIVERPOOL. See ARMSTRONG.

MANCHESTER. The Library Theatre (47–) is a three-weekly Rep., Director, David Scase. Its standards have been high for years, and it is now linked with the Forum, Wythenshawe, with which the company alternates, giving runs of six weeks. Manchester's other companies are the Stables, and the 69 Theatre Company, whose very fine *Journey's End* had a long run in London (72).

NOTTINGHAM REP. The old Playhouse had a tiny stage and

seated under 500. Val May was one of its distinguished directors. In 1963 a new Playhouse opened, seating 756, and a famous spell under John Neville began, lasting six years, which ended in a traditional Rep Board *v.* Director controversy. Stuart Burge has been director ever since.

OXFORD PLAYHOUSE (The Meadow Players) has been run with distinction by Frank Hauser (see p. 106) since 1956, the theatre being taken over by the University in 1960. Casts are new for each production, and a number of new plays and revivals have transferred to London down the years. The theatre dates back to the legendary days of J. B. Fagan (23–5), who once, in an 8-week season, gave Shaw (twice), Wilde, Goldini, Congreve, St. John Hankin, Maeterlinck, Yeats and Sophocles. This was an older Playhouse, and Fagan's casts included Robson, Gielgud, Byam Shaw, Morley and Guthrie. Pamela Brown (Hedda, Juliet, Sadie Thompson, etc.) was a famous leading lady of the forties.

REP has been transformed in the last decade by adequate Arts Council grants, new theatres, and the number of theatres, even in smallish centres, which, because of financial help, have been able to go over to runs of three weeks or more. In even the shortest account of Rep, some names and theatres, apart from those given separate entries, stand out. With apologies (as an old Rep hand) to those left out, these include the Royal Lyceum (shades of Wilson Barrett and his long struggle) and the Traverse, Edinburgh; Guildford's Yvonne Arnaud, run since its opening (65) by Laurier Lister; the Queen's, Hornchurch; the Thorndike, Leatherhead, opened in 1970, and a vindication of many years' work by Hazel Vincent Wallace; Colchester, now with a new theatre, to replace the old one opened in 1937 by that Rep stalwart, Robert Digby; Derby, Folkestone, Ipswich, Nairobi (Donovan Maule and his family), Northampton, Perth, Farnham, Richmond, York, and the rest. May they flourish.

For further reading, consult John Elsom's *Theatre Outside London* (Macmillan, 71), a brilliant survey of the present and immediate past, but with little information about the pre-sixties period. For instance, John Hale's incomparable reign at Lincoln (then a weekly) in the fifties is omitted from the relevant section, and a slighting reference to seaside Reps at once brings back memories of, say, Barry O'Brien's companies at Bournemouth and Shanklin in the fifties, with casts that included Vivien Merchant, Harold Pinter, Sheila Hancock, Anthony Bate, etc.

A book on the history of Reps of every standard down the years is urgently needed while there are still hundreds of survivors of that best and worst of times in their theatrical careers. Lawyers should be at hand, though, for descriptions of certain companies could, if names were named, result in villainous libel damages.

SALBERG, DEREK (1922–). British manager, notably of the Alexandra Theatre, Birmingham, for many years now a fortnightly Rep, renowned for high standards, mainly in commercial plays (owing to the Birmingham Rep's repertoire). It was also renowned for high salaries at a time when the average Rep, usually of necessity, sometimes by design, was handing out pigmy pay packets. The Alexandra is also a touring theatre outside its Rep seasons. It saw the first performance of Olivier's *Othello*.

SHEFFIELD REP. Now a repertoire theatre under Colin George in the new Crucible and Studio, it has long been one of the finest Reps in the country. Started by Herbert Prentice in the twenties.

WHATMORE, A. R. (1899–1960). British actor and director, who founded Hull Rep in 1923, produced many plays at the Embassy, and, in the forties, made Dundee Rep one of the finest in Britain. Now a three-weekly company.

SOME IMPRESARIOS AND MANAGERS

ALBERY, Sir BRONSON (1881–1971). British theatre manager, for many years in sole charge of three key London theatres, Wyndham's, the New and the Criterion. Between the wars, when popular taste was not high, he crucially helped to raise it and influence important careers—Sybil Thorndike in *St. Joan* (24) and the Gielgud–Olivier–Ashcroft–Evans *Romeo and Juliet* of 1935, for example. He helped bring Tyrone Guthrie into prominence, and it was his New Theatre that housed the most exciting of all Old Vic seasons (44–48). Shared the management with his half-brother, Howard Wyndham, until the latter died in 1947. Many theatrical institutions, including the Old Vic and Sadler's Wells, used his genius for administration. His son Donald succeeded him in 1962. The New Theatre is now the Albery in his honour.

BEAUMONT, HUGH (1908–73). British manager and for many years Managing Director of H. M. Tennent Ltd., whose list of productions since the late H. M. Tennent founded the firm in 1936 can only be done justice to by several columns in *Who's Who in the Theatre*. As well as the cream of the commercial plays and shows, especially in the forties and fifties, Tennents have put on many notable classical revivals, including the unforgotten Gielgud season at the Haymarket in 44-5—*Hamlet, Love for Love, The Circle, A Midsummer Night's Dream* and *The Duchess of Malfi.*

CHARLOT, ANDRÉ (1882–1956). French-born British impresario who became joint manager of the Alhambra in London (12). One of the first to stage revues (15–35), he produced thirty-six of them in the West End. His *London Calling* (23) marked Noël Coward's debut as a revue writer and the following year, his *Revue of 1924* introduced Gertrude Lawrence, Jack Buchanan and Beatrice Lillie to Broadway, a triple debut without parallel. Ventures into comedies, farces and radio prospered which his trip to California and films in 1937 did not. Even the most 'hard-faced creditors' succumbed to his 'beguiling personality' wrote Eric Maschwitz later in the *Dictionary of National Biography*.

COCHRAN, CHARLES (1873–1951). Ex-actor and agent who represented, amongst others, Houdini, after which he became the greatest British impresario of his day. An early triumph was Reinhardt's famous production of *The Miracle* (11), but it was as a presenter of musicals that he excelled. From 1918–31, he presented revues at the London Pavilion, including Coward's *This Year of Grace*; also his *Bitter Sweet* and *Cavalcade* elsewhere. He imported a rodeo to the 1924 Wembley Exhibition, helped make boxing boom, and found time to write three books of entertaining memoirs. To top it all, he had immense charm. Knighted (48).

COHEN, ALEXANDER (1920–). American producer, and a leading figure on Broadway since the fifties and the West End since the sixties.

DALRYMPLE, JEAN (1910–). American producer, at home and in many parts of the world, of all the performing arts, especially drama and musicals. Was made General Director of the City Center Light Opera Company and City Center Drama Company in 1953, and by the sixties had reached impresario status.

DAUBENY, PETER (1921–). British impresario and manager who, since 1951, has allowed London to see most of the greatest theatre companies of the world in his World Theatre Seasons and on other occasions. Has also presented many ballet companies. Particularly notable have been visits by the Berliner Ensemble and the Moscow Arts Theatre. The debt owed by serious theatregoers to this brilliant, theatre-mad organizer is colossal. From 1957–61 his assistant was MICHAEL WHITE (1936–), now a leading manager himself, presenting *Soldiers*, *Sleuth*, etc.

HUROK, SOL (1888–). American impresario who presents plays, preferably whole companies (Comédie-Francaise, etc.), though is best known for his musical and ballet offerings. Has had the supreme accolade, a film of his life, *Tonight We Sing*.

IMPRESARIOS present shows, spectacles, opera, ballet, concerts, etc., but mere producers of plays can become one by thinking and living big.

MERRICK, DAVID. American producer and manager, and brilliant publicist. Since *Fanny* (54) has presented many plays on Broadway, ranging from the lightest pieces to Osborne, Weiss, *Oh What A Lovely War!*, etc. His style entitles him to impresario status.

PRINCE, HAROLD. See p. 216.

PRODUCERS, until recently known as managers in Britain, are defined in the final chapter. Space precludes giving any but those featured in this chapter and elsewhere their due, yet, to name only a few current British producer/managers, the health of the commercial theatre is very much in the hands of men like Peter Bridge, Michael Codron, John Gale, Toby Rowland, Peter Saunders, etc., while Oscar Lewenstein's elevation to Artistic Director of the English Stage Co., is a reward for years of important theatre work.

SHEREK, HENRY (1900–67). British impresario, and producer of everything from revue and a Royal Tournament to all T. S. Eliot's post-war plays. An expansive personality. Would-be impresarios should consult his *Not in Front of the Children*.

SHUBERT, LEE, SAM and JACOB. American producers and theatre managers who, until the fifties (Sam died in 05), wielded enormous power on Broadway. Businessmen first and very foremost, whose interest in Art was strictly limited, they nevertheless kept theatres open when they could have made fortunes out of the sites. Produced over 500 works in half a century.

STEVENS, ROGER L. (1910–   ). American producer who, since 1949, has presented an enormous number of plays on Broadway, including many British imports. Is on most key theatre boards.

VEDRENNE, JOHN (1867–1930). British businessman whose association with Harley Granville Barker (see p. 82) made theatrical and, especially, Shavian history, first at the Royal Court (04–7), then at the Savoy (12).

WANAMAKER, SAM (1919–). American actor, director and producer, busily engaged in bringing Shakespeare back to Bankside, first in a temporary playhouse, then in a reconstruction of an Elizabethan theatre. This colossal undertaking, the Globe Theatre project's well under way (72) after the first session in the temporary theatre, and with other schemes also under way, will deservedly make him renowned as a public benefactor and major impresario. His varied career has included work on Broadway in the late forties, playing Bernie in *Winter Journey* in London (52), and directing it; presenting *The Shrike* and *The Big Knife* in London, the first with Hylton, and playing in both; directing a brilliant *Threepenny Opera* (56), directing and playing in *The Rainmaker* and *A Hatful of Rain*; running the New Shakespeare Theatre, Liverpool, and presenting major plays; also playing Iago at Stratford (59) directing Tippett's *King Priam* (62), playing Macbeth in Chicago (64), directing and acting in films, etc. This wide range of experience, plus boundless energy and dedication, is now directed at his magnificent scheme.

ZIEGFELD, FLORENZ (1867–1932). American impresario whose slogan was 'Glorifying the American Girl' and whose famous Follies ran from 1907 through twenty-four editions. He labelled them 'An American Institution', which they were. Marion Davies, Irene Dunne and Paulette Goddard were among his Girls, and he helped major talents like W. C. Fields and Eddie Cantor. Also staged musicals, including *Show Boat* (27) and straight plays. The list of players who appeared for him, and creative personalities who worked for him, is colossal. For all his lavishness in and out of the theatre, his judgement and flair were legendary and supreme.

SOME HISTORIANS AND LONG-RUNNING CRITICS

AGATE, JAMES (1877–1947). The leading British theatre critic between the wars and until his death, his main platform being the *Sunday Times* from 1923 onwards. His twin strengths were his ability to assess acting and his immense readability; on new plays he was less secure. His nine gusto-laden *Ego* auto-biographies are mines of theatre gossip and lore.

ATKINSON, J. BROOKS (1894–). A leading American critic for many years. Dramatic critic of the *New York Times* from 1926–41 and again from 1946–60 after war service. On his retirement, received a unique honour: the Mansfield Theater was renamed the Brooks Atkinson. Author of the splendid and comprehensive *Broadway* (71).

BARKER, FELIX. British theatre critic of the *Evening News* since 1957 and author of *The Oliviers* (53), a book which overcame the real difficulties of writing a contemporary theatre biography.

BARNES, CLIVE (1927–). British ballet critic, who also writes on music, opera and the theatre, originally for the *Daily Express*, etc. Appointed Dance critic of the *New York Times* (65), he became its theatre critic (67) as well, and, because of the drastic reduction in New York's papers, the prestige of *The Times*, and a belief in critics by Americans which is not so prevalent in Britain, he found himself the most powerful sage in American theatre history. As Broadway economics now, more than ever, demand an instant hit or instant closure, only a man of sterling confidence in himself could endure such responsibility. The innate good nature of Americans has ensured that not all theatre folk regard him as the least welcome British import since the Redcoats. Perhaps they realize that someone who does not like the theatre might get the job in his place.

BENTLEY, ERIC (1916–   ). British-born American writer critic and director, and authority on Brecht. His books include *Bernard Shaw* (47) and *The Playwright as Thinker* (*The Modern Theatre* in Britain), etc.

BROWN, IVOR (1891–   ). British theatre critic and author, critic of *The Observer* from 1928–54. Has written a number of books on Shakespeare and his times, and published valuable records of his criticisms. His *Shakespeare* (49) is deservedly one of the most popular books on the subject ever written.

BROWN, JOHN MASON (1900–69). American theatre critic. Posts included critic of the *New York Evening Post*, later *New York Post* from 1929–41, and for the *Saturday Review of Literature* in several capacities from 1944. His *Dramatis Personae*, much of it taken from his earlier writings, is delightful and informative.

BRUSTEIN, ROBERT (1927–   ). American actor, director, critic, etc., Professor of Drama at Yale (65–   ). Author of several challenging books, including *Seasons of Discontent*, *The Third Theatre* and *Revolution as Theatre*. Currently guest critic of *The Observer* (73).

BRYDEN, RONALD (1927–   ). British dramatic critic. On the *Observer* from 1964–1971, when he was appointed Play Adviser to the Royal Shakespeare Co., confounding, presumably, only those in the Profession who see no good in any critic.

COOKMAN, A. V. (1894–196). British critic, assistant to Charles Morgan on *The Times*, 1928–39, after which he was senior critic until 1963, when he was succeeded by IRVING WARDLE (1929–   ). *The Times* critics are serious writers of (mercifully) wide tastes.

DARLINGTON, W. A. (1890–   ). British theatre critic and author. Critic of *The Daily Telegraph*, 1920–68. A kindly critic, whose best work has been reserved for his informative weekly article on things theatrical. His *The Actor and his Audience* (49) is an excellent analysis of great acting and—a factor rarely dealt with in any depth—the contribution of the audience. Other books include *Laurence Olivier* (68). Wrote the very successful extravaganza, *Alf's Button* (19). Succeeded by JOHN BARBER. His famous colleague, the Theatre Correspondent GEORGE BISHOP, has been succeeded by RONALD HASTINGS.

DISHER, MAURICE WILLSON (1893–1969). British theatre critic and author, his most valuable work being on the circus and the music-hall. His *Clowns and Pantomimes* (25) is a classic.

FINDLATER, RICHARD (1921–). British critic and author. His books include *The Unholy Trade* (52), a laser-like look at the theatre in the fifties, *Grimaldi, Banned*, about the Censor, and studies of actors, including Redgrave and Emlyn Williams, also *Six Great Actors*.

FREEDLEY, GEORGE (1904–67). American theatre critic and author. Was for many years Curator of the important Theater Collection of the New York Public Library. Wrote *The Lunts* (57).

GASCOIGNE, BAMBER (1935–). British theatre critic and author. Critic of *The Observer* (63–4). Author of *Twentieth Century Drama* (62) and *World Theatre* (66), a paradise for students of theatre design and illustration.

HAMMOND, PERCY (1873–1936). American theatre critic of the *Chicago-Tribune* and, later, *New York Tribune*. A theatre lover who had a line in deadly wit, as with: 'I have knocked everything but the knees of the chorus girls, and Nature has anticipated me there.' Such candour did not endear him to producers and their casts.

HARTNOLL, PHYLLIS. British author. Editor of *The Oxford Companion to the Theatre* and author of *A Concise History of the Theatre*.

HOBSON, HAROLD (1904–). British theatre critic. Succeeded Agate on *The Sunday Times* (47). Unpredictable, brilliant and downright capricious in equal proportions, he was Pinter's first and remains his supreme champion, once even comparing one of his plays with *Antony and Cleopatra* to the latter's disadvantage. His stimulating teasing technique provokes regular, often exasperated, controversy.

HOPE-WALLACE, PHILIP (1911–). British theatre and opera critic of *The Guardian* from 1946–71. Now concerned mainly with opera and ballet, MICHAEL BILLINGTON having ably succeeded him as theatre critic. Hope-Wallace's refusal to climb on any fashionable bandwagon has been as notable as his detachment (which has maddened some) and readability. The detachment has always evaporated in the presence of greatness, theatrical or operatic.

ISAACS, EDITH (1878–1956). American critic and editor of the finest of theatre magazines, *Theatre Arts*, now defunct, from 1919–45.

JOHNS, ERIC (1907–). Editor of *The Stage* (52–72) and responsible for hauling it from pleasant mediocrity to its present position as an informative, critical and very useful trade paper. PETER HEPPLE has now succeeded him. Its splendid opposite number in America is *Variety*, founded in 1905 by Sime Silverman.

KERR, WALTER (1913–). American dramatic critic and director. Critic of the *New York Herald Tribune* (51–) and a number of books on the theatre, including *Pieces of Eight*, *Tragedy and Comedy* and *How Not To Write A Play*. Sunday Drama Critic of the *New York Times*. His wife, JEAN KERR (1923–) is the author of the hit comedy, *Mary, Mary* (61) and other plays.

MACQUEEN-POPE, W. (1888–1960). Theatre historian and press representative, whose pleasant, chatty, rather romantic books on theatres (Drury Lane, Haymarket, etc.) and players (*Ladies First, Ivor*, etc.) endeared him to a wide public.

NATHAN, GEORGE JEAN (1882–1958). American dramatic critic and author. A notable, thoughtful and witty critic who could be both waspish and positively deadly about plays and players in *The New Yorker* and elsewhere. Fortunately, many of his reviews are preserved in book form, including *The Critic and the Drama, The World in False Face* and *Art of the Night. The Intimate Notebooks of George Jean Nathan* has portraits of O'Neill and others in it.

PEARSON, HESKETH (1887–1964). Minor British actor turned major popular biographer. His theatre biographies include studies of Gilbert and Sullivan, Bernard Shaw and, best of all, and certainly most entertaining, Beerbohm Tree, with whom he worked.

ROBERTS, PETER. Editor of *Plays and Players* from 1962–72, maintaining an excellent balance in its coverage of the serious and lighter theatre. The magazine's policy of including a new play every month is cheering. The editor is now PETER BUCK-LEY.

SHULMAN, MILTON (1913–   ). Canadian-born British critic of the *Evening Standard* (since 53). Has mellowed down the years, except in his TV criticism.

TAUBMAN, HOWARD (1907–   ). Former music and drama critic of the *New York Times*, whose book, *The Making of the American Theater* (65) is one of the most valuable and complete single volume histories of its kind.

TAYLOR, JOHN RUSSELL (1935–   ). British film critic and also author of *Anger and After, The Rise and Fall of the Well Made Play, The Penguin Dictionary of the Theatre* and other books.

TREWIN, J. C. (1908–   ). Arguably the most valuable British theatre historian of the last half-century, whose books range from biographies of Macready and Benson, and short studies of modern players, to histories of the Birmingham Rep, and the 20s and 30s, as well as general histories, especially of Shakespearean productions. One of his latest studies is of Peter Brook. Has held a number of critical posts, including, currently, the *Illustrated London News* and the *Birmingham Post* (55–   ) and has edited *Plays of the Year* since 1948.

TYNAN, KENNETH (1927–   ). Now Literary Editor of the National Theatre, but best remembered, even by those who rarely agreed with him, as the leading post-war dramatic critic. With *The Observer*, 1954–58 and 1960–63. At his best he could—and can—reach Shavian standards; at his brilliant worst his wit was wounding and unworthy. Began as an actor and director, but his precociously good *He That Plays The King* (50) showed his true destiny. His study of the National Theatre's and Laurence Olivier's Othello makes one regret he has deserted his vocation for the greener pastures of dramaturgy, as do volumes of his collected reviews.

WATTS, RICHARD (1898–). A leading American critic for many years, since 1946 on the *New York Post*. With the *Herald-Tribune* (24–36).

WILLIAMSON, AUDREY (1913–). British critic and writer of a number of theatrical histories, most notably *Old Vic Drama* and *Old Vic Drama II*.

WOOLLCOTT, ALEXANDER (1887–1943). A leading American critic, wit and personality, and the inspirer of the character Sheridan Whiteside in Kaufman and Hart's *The Man Who Came to Dinner*, a part he actually played on tour. This large, sentimental, often acid-tongued figure was a better judge of players than of plays. The 20s were his great period as a critic, after which he broadcast, wrote, lectured and shone, as he had earlier, in any company.

WORSLEY, T. C. (1907–). British theatre critic of the *New Statesman* (48–52) and the *Financial Times* (52–65), since when he has been the latter's TV critic. A serious critic, much admired by theatre people, some of his reviews can be found in *The Fugitive Art* (52).

SOME THEATRICAL TERMS

ABSURD, THEATRE OF THE. The purposelessness and absurdity of Man's existence has been explored down the centuries, but only in the 1950s (following Camus's *The Myth of Sisyphus*, 42) did a number of playwrights produce work which could be conveniently grouped into a school of the Absurd. These include Beckett, Ionesco, Genet, Pinter, N. F. Simpson, Albee, etc. Methods have varied—which makes the term useful rather than completely accurate—but the basic style is anti-realistic. As John Russell Taylor has succinctly put it: 'The ideas are allowed to shape the form as well as the content.' The movement has steadily faded partly because of the sheer difficulty of keeping such plays going any length of time. Beckett, whose *Waiting for Godot* (see p. 20) is the supreme example of the Absurd, has become continually more concise. However, the influence of the Absurd has been widespread. Even Shakespeare has been affected via Jan Kott's *Shakespeare Our Contemporary* which influenced Brook's Beckettian *Lear* (62).

ACTOR MANAGER. No one has ever summed up the old-time Actor Manager, good or bad, better than Ronald Jeans— 'One to whom the part is greater than the whole.' They faded in glory with Wolfit, and at their worst (well, at almost their worst) they were no more of a menace to Art than a brilliant director gone berserk. A new breed of actor managers appeared from the 30s onwards, admirable examples being Gielgud, Olivier at the St. James's and Clements at the Saville, etc.

ALIENATION. See BRECHTIAN.

ALL BOX OFFICE RECORDS BROKEN. A management ploy to conceal the fact that they've put the prices up recently.

AMATEURS are absolutely essential to the well-being of the theatre as a whole. Companies range from famous ones, like the Questors, Unity and the O.U.D.S., to the modest village and school groups, from dedicated and talented ensembles to egotistical set-ups, uninterested in the theatre as a whole. What matters is that the movement in Britain, America and elsewhere *exists*. The British movement has the British Drama League (see p. 241) to guide it, and its own periodical, *Amateur Stage*.

AUNT EDNA. Terence Rattigan's typical playgoer, now over 2,000 years old. She is quoted in his *Collected Plays* Vol. 2 (Hamish Hamilton): 'I always say you can rely on Sophocles'; but Euripides, though intriguing, shocked her. She is the eternal average audience—and must not be confused with Mrs. Whitehouse—she (Aunt Edna) was a mistress of the King in Restoration times. Without her patronage and word of mouth praise, no author, dead or alive, is going to succeed in a long run, even if he is subsidized up to the hilt. But if he is first-rate, Aunt Edna, says Rattigan, will never reject him . . . Of course, she may be a little late in getting there (author's comment).

BRECHTIAN. Though ultimately only half a dozen or so of his plays and operas may survive, the influence of Bertolt Brecht (1898–1956), the German dramatist, director and theorist, on the theatre of the last two decades has been immense. British playwrights who have been so influenced have included Arden, Osborne (*The Entertainer*), Whiting (*The Devils*), Bolt (*A Man for All Seasons*), Shaffer (*The Royal Hunt of the Sun*), etc. The visit of Brecht's Berliner Emsemble to London (56) created a decisive impression. It was in the 50s, in fact, that his stature was fully realized, by dramatist, actors and many playgoers.

Brecht's main influence has been as a theorist. As opposed to the Method (see below) school of thought, he did not expect an actor to live his part but, while understanding it fully, to be outside it enough to make a comment on the character. This in turn would result in the audience judging the character critically. This 'Alienation' was not so much a rigid discipline as a guide for working. Alienation, and Brecht's subject-matter, made for a theatre of debate, and the debate, especially in his early plays, stressed communism as the obvious goal. Yet his finest work, from the mid-30s to mid-40s, went far beyond any party line. His *Mother Courage* (41), the 'epitome of the haggling profiteer', as the author of the Theatre section of *Pears Cyclopaedia* has called her, is an indomitable and sympathetic figure. His other—very influential—major works include *Galileo, The Caucasian Chalk Circle* and *The Good Woman of Setznan*. The popular *Threepenny Opera* and *Mahagonny* depend very much on Kurt Weill's music for their success. Brecht advocated the Epic Theatre to appeal less to the spectator's feelings than to his reason, which is a different meaning of 'epic' from the more usual one with its Homeric, Wagnerian echoes. It means in Brechtian terms a clear episodic presentation of incidents unconfined by ordinary theatrical construction, sometimes using a storyteller and sometimes songs. Regardless of politics, Brecht, more than anyone else, freed the modern British theatre from the confines of even the best well-made play. The American theatre had freed itself earlier.

CENSORSHIP is dead in Britain (the law of the land apart) thus enabling the Lord Chamberlain to devote himself (since 68) to other duties. For those too young to know his curious habits, Richard Findlater's *Banned* is recommended.

CHILDREN'S THEATRE. Finding well-written plays for children, as opposed to more adult ones that they can enjoy, has always been a problem, a handful of immortals apart (*Pan, Toad of Toad Hall*). Among those trying with some success to remedy this situation is the playwright, NICHOLAS STUART GRAY (*Beauty and the Beast, The Princess and the Swineherd, Gawain and the Green Knight,* etc.). There were at least half a dozen plays and musical plays for children in the London area, Christmas 1971–72, including David Wood's *The Plotters of Cabbage Patch Corner*, a sign of increasing interest in the form. The pioneer managers and directors in this field since the war have been CARYL JENNER, whose Unicorn Theatre at the Arts in London is the culmination of many years in children's drama, and BRIAN WAY of the Theatre Centre. Apart from these two leaders—Miss Jenner died early in 1973—there have always been small companies visiting schools, etc., throughout the time-span of this book. As opposed to this worthwhile but rugged life, more and more Reps are—on occasions—encouraging schoolchildren to visit their theatres.

CLARENCE DERWENT. This award, named for the Anglo-American actor and producer (*d.* 59) goes annually to the best supporting actor and actress in London and in New York. 'Tony' Awards, named for Antoinette Perry, go annually to the best American actor, director, etc.

CLUB THEATRES were particularly important when the Lord Chamberlain (see above) reigned. No list, however short, can leave out the Arts Theatre (founded 27), the Repertory Players (21), now, alas, defunct, the Everyman, the Mercury, and the Gate, this last founded by Peter Godfrey (25), whose 1930–31 season included the banned *Desire Under the Elms* with Portman and Robson. The story of these and others is told in Norman Marshall's essential *The Other Theatre* (47).

After the Second World War, during which the Arts had flourished under Alec Clunes, notable achievements in the Club field included Peter Cotes's tenure of the New Boltons, where his productions included *The Children's Hour* and *A Pin to See the Peepshow*, both banned plays. He had earlier made his name at the New Lindsey where a much-enjoyed visit by Queen Mary to *Pick-Up Girl* made a laughingstock of the Censor. The most influential of all club theatres, the Royal Court, is discussed on p. 242.

Though few Club Theatres of the early days survive, there are now many Lunchtime Theatres in London basements, pubs, etc. The thriving theatre restaurant at the King's Head, Islington, where evening and lunchtime performances are given, is a sign of things to come.

CRUELTY, THEATRE OF. Antonin Artaud (1896–1948) believed that an audience's repressions, its sexual, violent and disorderly instincts, could be exorcised by a theatre in which words are merely incantatory and emotional and part of a total theatre of frenzy, music, mime, dance, ritual—and cruelty. However, just as no savage tribe is purged of latent cruelty by primitive dancing there is no evidence that 'civilized' audiences will be in any way purged of repressions, cruelty, etc., by a performance embracing Artaud's ideas. Fortunately, the theatrical results are often superb, especially when a disciple of Artaud like Brook is in charge. Weiss's *Marat-Sade*, as directed by Brook and performed by the Royal Shakespeare Co., was a superb example of the genre.

DESIGN. The good designer must be prepared to create anything from a drawing-room to a symbolic end of the world. Only a handful, like the Royal Shakespeare Co.'s brilliant design team of Bury, Farrah, Morley and O'Brien, can experiment regularly with new methods and materials, and many designers become typecast for the same reason. The fathers of modern anti-realistic design were the Swiss, Adolph Appia (1862–1925) and Gordon Craig (1872–1966), the son of Ellen Terry. Craig's main work lies before the span of this book, culminating in his *On the Art of the Theatre* (11), but the French were to be more influenced by him than the British. A number of designers are featured individually in this book but the selection has inevitably been narrow. Only discerning provincial theatregoers know what fine talents have never reached London; only actors and directors know just how versatile and hardworking a Rep designer has always had to be.

DIRECTOR. Until recently, in Britain, but not in America, he was called the Producer (see below). Responsible for staging and interpreting the play, and, in certain cases, for altering it in rehearsals with or without the author's permission. Now the most powerful figure in the modern theatre. At his best, he is a theatrical Toscanini or Klemperer, the inspired servant and interpreter of the dramatist. At his worst—and the same director can be the best of men and the worst of men—he can be as insensitively arrogant as the worst old actor manager. Except for those directors who are also actors or ex-actors, one cannot assume that the actor will be understood by his director. Which does not automatically affect the final result. In today's ensemble theatre, the director is king, and he has been increasing in power during the span of this book. Fortunately, he often deserves his power.

DRAMA SCHOOLS can be started by anyone, and often are. However, it is safer to try for RADA, the Central, LAMDA, or a handful of others.

FACT, THEATRE OF. Normally fiction, with the dramatist, if questioned as to his statements, mentioning unseen documents in banks, or excusing his characterizations by saying they are to be regarded satirically. The genre's practitioners, aspiring to some more 'significant' than historical dramas, flaw their work by selective bias, as is inevitable. The most famous plays of Fact have been Hochhuth's *The Representative* (*The Deputy* in New York) and *Soldiers*, and Weiss's *The Investigation*. Sadly, *Soldiers*, the finest of the genre, never recovered from the author's refusal to reveal the sources of his sensational allegation that Churchill connived at his ally Sikorski's death, offshoots of which have been keeping lawyers happy ever since. Thus, the play's main theme, the atrocity of large scale bombing, and a truly remarkable portrait of Churchill, were all but forgotten.

FARCE. Though often taken to mean knockabout comedy, the broader the better, to British (and French) audiences it is an austerely classical business at its best. Two definitions of this hard-to-define word are—'possible people in impossible situations' and 'tragedy turned upside down'. And Simon Trussler has commented that in farce a rigid code of social propriety is demanded in order that it may be outraged. See also the chapter on farce.

LIGHTING. Since the war and, especially, since the early 60s, the job of lighting a show has been increasingly given to an expert. Before, the director lit the play, as he still normally does in Rep, etc. Richard Pilbrow, Michael Northern, William Bundy and Charles Bristow are among those who have—with technical improvements—revolutionized this branch of theatre art, though, of course, the director still takes final responsibility for the lighting as part of his production.

METHOD. An adaptation of Stanislavsky's ideas about acting and also directing, developed and taught at the Actors' Studio in New York by Lee Strasberg and others. The fact that this very influential system has been endorsed by some very fine players (who would have been fine whatever their method) cannot disguise what for many is its fatal flaw, a lack of interest in technique, diction, etc., which would have startled

Stanislavsky. The Method is based on the building of a character as outlined in his *An Actor Prepares*, not his teachings on the all-important performance. The losing of an actor in a part to find the truth of a character may find that truth for an audience of one. Every actor naturally has his own method, some, starting with externals, a trick of walking, etc. Yet the Method has had remarkable successes in certain naturalistic plays and films. Its insistence on improvisation to explore character and exercises stems from Stanislavsky, and has been far more widely influential than the Method itself.

MUSICAL. For several decades now the blanket term for musical comedies, operettas, folk operas, etc., thus saving attempts at definitions which were never entirely satisfactory. In the chapter on musicals several shows are said to have advanced the genre, either by their subject-matter (*Pal Joey*) by by their use of integrated song, speech and dance (*West Side Story*), but it should be understood that musicals cannot get over thoughts and ideas as well as the finest plays. For instance, the splendid *Company*'s comments on marriage, New York style, can hardly run as deep as a similar play, though the play may be less enjoyable. What the musical can do, especially if the composer and lyricist are masters, is provide the theatre of entertainment with a most vivid and emotional experience, or sheer enjoyment, or both. However, with more un-musical shows than ever, with the wrong plays being turned into musicals, and with shows managing to get staged with one or no hit number in them, the outlook is bleak. Fortunately, experiments abound, and out of a plethora of shows, from rock musicals and quasi-religious musicals like the delightful *Godspell* to more traditional fare, hits of real worth will appear, even if the 30 or so glorious years of the American musical may never be repeated.

MUSIC HALL has been left out of this book for space reasons. Strangely, though the Halls were finally killed by television in the 50s, and the superb practitioners forced to depend on summer shows and pantomime (plus TV and radio), there has recently been a revival of Music Hall where it began in the mid-19th century—in the pubs. In America, the equivalent of Music Hall was Vaudeville, which was killed by the cinema, completely so by the talkies. It, too, had begun in the same way as Music Hall—in beer-halls.

OFF-BROADWAY. For many years theatre economics on Broadway have been such that scarcely anything has existed between a hit and a flop (unlike the West End where, until recently, a short run of a few months could be a moderate success). The situation gets worse, with fewer actual plays being staged. To counteract this, small theatre groups started appearing in theatres, cellars, halls, etc., in Greenwich Village and elsewhere from the 40s onwards, the actors and technicians—the latter get far more than their West End equivalents—being paid less than the Unions would allow on Broadway. A turning-point in the fortunes of Off-Broadway—it was always significant—was the 1950–51 season of the Circle in the Square, directed by José Quintero, which included a major success, Tennessee Williams's *Summer and Smoke* with Geraldine Page. During the decade its productions included Genet's *The Balcony* and the première of *Long Day's Journey into Night*.

Apart from Miss Page, other talents to emerge in the lively, experimental world of Off-Broadway have been Jason Robarts, Dustin Hoffman, George C. Scott, Colleen Dewhurst, etc., and most new American playwrights of note.

Even Off-Broadway has been affected by the economic malaise of New York's theatre as a whole (see John Lahr's chapter, *Mirror of the American Moment*, in *Theatre 71*, Hutchinson, edited by Sheridan Morley).

Historical note: some claim that the ancestors of Off-Broadway were the Provincetown Players (Cape Cod, 15: Greenwich Village, 16). The company was the first to stage O'Neill and introduce Strindberg to America. It closed in 1929.

PRODUCER. Until recently the British name for a play's director, though now 'director' is used on both sides of the Atlantic. In Britain, however, 'Production' or 'produced by' may still be used to indicate 'directed by' and the many theatre directors who work occasionally in opera suddenly become producers again.

The American producer is in charge of the management of the company, putting on a play, arranging finance, contracts, etc. In Britain this figure has been known as the Manager, though he, too, is often called a producer. However, 'The Management' still remains in use. Impresarios, who are basically producers on a large scale, have a chapter to themselves.

REPERTORY, Strictly, a Rep performs a series of plays in repertoire, as at the National Theatre, Royal Shakespeare Co., etc., and now some Reps. Yet in Britain the Repertory Movement, begun by Miss Horniman (in Dublin and Manchester) and others before the First World War, has performed plays for a week, a fortnight, three weeks, a month, sometimes even longer. See chapter on British Rep.

REVUE. A delightful, now almost dead entertainment combining song, dance and comic and satirical sketches. At the time of writing (73) *Cowardy Custard* at the Mermaid is a reminder of what everyone is missing. Intimate Revue, the same on a smaller scale, was particularly successful in the 40s and 50s in Britain, from the immortal *Sweet and Low* (43) and its successors with La Gingold, through the *Lyric* and *Globe Revue* of the early 50s, to *Beyond the Fringe*, which made stars of Messrs. Cook, Miller, Moore and Bennett. There have been two-man revues (Flanders and Swann) and One-Woman Revues (Joyce Grenfell and Ruth Draper). Most of the supreme stars— Gertrude Lawrence, Beatrice Lillie, Jack Buchanan, etc., and supreme impresarios like Ziegfeld and Charlot, are featured in this book.

Why Revue has died, even in its Intimate form, which attracted such diverse talents as Alan Melville and Harold Pinter, is a mystery. Presumably TV has swallowed up the genre which helped to make such stars as Dora Bryan and Ian Carmichael. Perhaps it was often too inbred, too West End theatrical. Yet a show like *Airs on a Shoestring* (53), devised by Laurier Lister, and starring amongst others the wickedly witty Max Adrian and Rose Hill, and with affectionately malicious send-ups of Benjamin Britten and the most popular singing duo of the day, was so scintillating that the absence of successors today is as mysterious as it is lamentable.

STAGE. For most of the time-span of this book, audiences expected—and got—a picture-frame stage with a proscenium arch, and with next to no forestage (as in most traditional

Anglo-American theatres). Even Shakespeare was fitted into the pattern, though from William Poel onwards this was disputed. In 1895, he produced *Twelfth Night* in a reconstruction of an Elizabethan theatre.

Though experiments were made between the wars on the Continent, it was not until the 50s that action was taken, most notably by Guthrie at Stratford, Ontario (53), to provide an arena stage with the audience on three sides of it, and close to the actors. In 1962, his Minneapolis theatre, named for him, continued this trend. The Mermaid opened in 1951 as an Elizabethan theatre in Bernard Miles's garden, and, later (59) at Puddle Dock, with an open stage and no proscenium arch. Chichester's Festival Theatre, inspired by Stratford, Ontario, dates from 1962.

A far more debatable concept than a stage thrusting out into the audience, is theatre-in-the-round, ably advocated by the late Stephen Joseph and others. Suitable enough for some plays, it will always frustrate those playgoers who feel it their right to see an actor's face and eyes at crucial moments.

Some modern theatres have adaptable stages, suitable for every style. The London Academy of Music and Drama's, designed by Michael Warre, was one of the first of these.

Playgoers who are emotionally geared to like a traditional and attractive theatre with a proscenium arch and a curtain are learning, with Coriolanus, that there is a world elsewhere, even if they see no benefit in being too near the players. It is a fair generalization that in older theatres most of the audience were and are too far away from them. A real difficulty is that West End and Broadway playhouses cannot easily embrace every sort of drama, though resourceful directors and designers can take, say, a transfer from Chichester to London in their stride (Othello, *The Royal Hunt of the Sun, Vivat! Vivat Regina!*, etc.).

STAGE MANAGER. In charge backstage during performances; the director's right hand man in rehearsals; in charge of understudy rehearsals; sometimes an understudy himself; often forced to act as company manager as well, i.e. he pays the cast and is the Management's representative in a company. On tour the stage manager must arrange the lighting in each new theatre and supervise the 'get-ins' on Mondays or, sometimes, Sundays; also the 'get-outs' on Saturday nights, though most companies have a touring Stage Carpenter who directly over-sees these tasks. The stage manager must also ensure that a play is kept up to standard after the director has left, or be-tween his (sometimes rare) visits. And he must establish good relations with permanent theatre staffs in and out of London. This superman was known as the stage director until the 50s in Britain, but the reversion to the earlier title of stage manager is now universal. His assistants are the deputy stage manager and one or more assistant stage managers.

STAR. One who cannot be hidden, be he great actor like Scofield or a lesser talent. Only mental eunuchs, theatrically speaking, object to stars who are also dedicated, talented actors, should a part call for a star performance. And certain Shakespearean parts, etc., must have a star actor, a truism sometimes denied by star directors and companies who rightly stress ensemble, but privately do their best to breed their own stars or import them. Unfortunately, the word, like others in this chapter, has emotional overtones, hence the vain bibble-babble of theatrical puritans against stars when they are really attacking the abuses of a vanished star system.

INDEX

I

FEATURED PLAYS, PRODUCTIONS, ETC.

PEOPLE

A Selective List